Voicing Subjects

SOUTH ASIA ACROSS THE DISCIPLINES

Edited by Muzaffar Alam, Robert Goldman, and Gauri Viswanathan

Dipesh Chakrabarty, Sheldon Pollock, and Sanjay Subrahmanyam, Founding Editors

Funded by a grant from the Andrew W. Mellon Foundation and jointly published by the University of California Press, the University of Chicago Press, and Columbia University Press

For a list of books in the series, see page 305.

Voicing Subjects

PUBLIC INTIMACY AND MEDIATION
IN KATHMANDU

Laura Kunreuther

South Asia Across the Disciplines

UNIVERSITY OF CALIFORNIA PRESS
BERKELEY LOS ANGELES LONDON

University of California Press, one of the most distinguished university presses in the United States, enriches lives around the world by advancing scholarship in the humanities, social sciences, and natural sciences. Its activities are supported by the UC Press Foundation and by philanthropic contributions from individuals and institutions. For more information, visit www.ucpress.edu.

University of California Press
Berkeley and Los Angeles, California

University of California Press, Ltd.
London, England

Library of Congress Cataloging-in-Publication Data

Kunreuther, Laura, 1969—.
    Voicing subjects : public intimacy and mediation in Kathmandu / Laura Kunreuther.
        pages cm.—(South Asia across the disciplines)
    Includes bibliographical references and index.
    ISBN 978-0-520-27068-8 (cloth : alk. paper)—ISBN 978-0-520-27070-1 (pbk. : alk. paper)—ISBN 978-0-520-95806-7 (e-book)
    1. Mass media—Nepal—Kathmandu   2. Communication—Political aspects—Nepal—Kathmandu.   I. Title.
    P92.N35K86   2014
    302.2095496—dc23

                                                    2013040220

Manufactured in the United States of America

23 22 21 20 19 18 17 16 15 14
10 9 8 7 6 5 4 3 2 1

In keeping with a commitment to support environmentally responsible and sustainable printing practices, UC Press has printed this book on Natures Natural, a fiber that contains 30% post-consumer waste and meets the minimum requirements of ANSI/NISO Z39.48–1992 (R 1997) (*Permanence of Paper*).

I dedicate this book to the memory of my mother, Sylvia Clifford Kunreuther, whose life was cut short far too soon but whose passion for life, listening, and people survives through these pages.

CONTENTS

ILLUSTRATIONS

ACKNOWLEDGMENTS

Despite the solitude, writing a book is truly a collective enterprise. Without the intellectual and emotional support of family, close friends, colleagues, students, research assistants, editors, and anonymous reviewers, most books—and I know *this* book—would not have come to fruition.

I am first and foremost grateful for all the help of people in Nepal, without whom this research would not have been possible. I benefited from conversations at the Martin Chauteri group and with other anthropologists at Tribhuvan University. I thank Nirmal Tuladhar for helping to sponsor the initial stages of research through CNAS. Pratyoush Onta has been an important interlocutor—both in his writing and in person—since we met in the early 1990s. I may not have returned to Nepal had it not been for the care and love I received from my first host family: my *didīs* (Ambika Karki, Tara Shrestha, and Kusum Shrestha), my *dāi* (Prem Shrestha), and especially my *āmā,* who died during my last stint of fieldwork in 2007. I am grateful for the enormous help I had with translation and transcriptions from Anil Bhatterai, Ganga Dangol, Laxmi Maharjan, Anita Sakya, and Prakash Thapa. Anita and Ganga were a part of this project from the start, and contributed to it in more ways than I can describe. I was fortunate to have found two excellent research assistants who became friends: Sanjeev Pokharel and Bhoju Raj Paudel both helped arrange interviews at different stages of the project, and I am especially grateful to them for our conversations interpreting the Nepali media and cultural events. I thank Bhoju for his work on transcription in the later stages of the manuscript. Kalyan Gautam's continued interest in this project was invaluable to me, and I will always remember the hospitality he and his wife, Sanjhana, extended to me. I thank all of my friends in Patan, particularly Gyanisoba Sakya—who became another *āmā* to me—for inviting me into her family and making me feel at home. Other friends made all of my visits to Nepal interesting and enjoyable: Steve Curtis, Carina Franz, Tatsuro Fujikura, Susan Hangen, Ann Hunkins, Lauren Leve, Mark Liechty, Anne Rademacher, Ashmina Ranjit, Sara Shneiderman, Mark Turin.

This book took its initial form as a dissertation at the University of Michigan during an especially exciting time. At Michigan, I truly learned the meaning of critical theory from Ann Stoler, who always encouraged me to push my analysis further and offered rigorous and supportive criticism in this project's initial stages. I am grateful to Val Daniel for the long and thoughtful conversations we had, and for teaching me a way of thinking about signs that informs much of my analysis of mediation. Bruce Mannheim introduced me to connections between language and cultural forms that have deeply shaped this book, and I thank him for the challenging analytic questions he always asks. Sumati Ramaswamy helped me see many historical linkages to other parts of South Asia. I might not have gone to Michigan if it hadn't have been for my visit with Laura Ahearn during her graduate research in Nepal, who showed me what fieldwork could be.

At Michigan and after, I was supported by an amazing group of colleagues and friends: Rachel Heiman, Pamila Gupta, Mandana Limbert, Charles Lord, Janet McIntosh, Ellen Moodie, Brian Mooney, Carole McGranahan, Esra Özyürek, Karen Strassler, Julie Subrin, Penelope Papailias. I benefited greatly from the "NYU writing group" during the initial stage of writing, and I thank Ben Chesluk, Henry Goldschmidt, Susan Hangen, Susan Lepselter, Amanda Weidman, and David Valentine for their critical readings.

I was fortunate to receive generous grants from Fulbright-Hays (Dissertation and Faculty research), SSRC (Pre-dissertation and Dissertation), the Mellon Foundation, and the Bard Research Funds that enabled me to travel to Nepal and pay for the research assistance I received at various stages of my research. I presented versions of this book at several forums that helped me dramatically transform the work from a dissertation into its current form. I am grateful for the invitation by Aaron Fox to participate in a panel on "Voice." Comments during this conference, particularly those offered by Michael Silverstein, helped me begin to see the outlines of the book's argument that appeared first in "Technologies of the Voice: FM Radio, Telephone, and the Nepali Diaspora in Kathmandu," *Cultural Anthropology* 21(3) (2006): 57–95. I would also like to thank Ilana Gershon for inviting me to participate in a panel on "Media Ideologies" that helped sharpen many of my points about media. This led to a special-issue volume of *Journal of Linguistic Anthropology* (2010), in which small portions of chapters 3 and 4 were published as "Transparent Media: Language and Media Ideologies of Voice in Nepal." A portion of chapter 4 appeared in "Voiced Writing and Public Intimacy on Kathmandu's FM Radio," *Studies in Nepali History and Society* 7(2) (2004): 57–95. A version of chapter 1 appeared as "Between Love and Property: Voice, Sentiment, and Subjectivity in the Reform of Daughter's Inheritance in Nepal," in *American Ethnologist* 36(3) (2009): 545–62. Comments from faculty participants of the "New Ethnography of Media" lecture series at Indiana University helped me reshape chapter 4, and I thank Jesse Shipley for inviting me to present a portion of this work at the *Hurford* Humanities Center Faculty Seminar on Changing Technologies of Entrepreneurship at Haverford College. Thank you to all the editors and participants of these forums. The Department of Anthropology at the University of Pennsylvania provided me a lovely place and community as a Visiting Scholar where I completed the last stages of this book.

At University of California Press, Reed Malcolm proved to be the most encouraging and dedicated editor an author could ever want and the editorial assistance of Stacy Eisenstark and Robert Demke was first-rate. Wendy Dherin sheperded this book through production. I thank Jan Williams for her work on the index. This book was made stronger through the careful readings of my reviewers: William Mazzarella, whose own work is an inspiration, and another anonymous reviewer. It also benefited from the incisive critiques of my reviewer at the press. All errors remaining are my own.

I am fortunate to have many generous colleagues at Bard College. My closest colleague, Yuka Suzuki, makes everyday a pleasure to be at work; her reading of many chapters of this work has helped me hone my arguments immensely. I am grateful to Mario Bick and Diana Brown for their continued support in and out of the department. Tom Keenan has been a generous mentor and dear friend at Bard, whose work on human rights and media deepened my understanding of both. I thank Greg Moynahan for his critical, historical eye and quick responses to my philosophical queries. Sanjib Baruah and Richard Davis have been excellent mentors, and their own work in South Asia has contributed to my thinking about Nepal. Rob Culp has been a devoted supporter and colleague, and I have often relied on the sage advice, humor, and friendship of Tabetha Ewing. I have also benefited from conversations with other anthropologists who have worked at Bard: Megan Callaghan, Omri Elisha, Abou Farman, Jeff Jurgens, Nadla Latif, Neni Pangouria, and

Jesse Shipley. Finally, I thank Michele Dominy for for bringing me to Bard and her support ever since.

At Bard, I am fortunate to have had some remarkable students who contributed to this book in various ways. I have learned so much about Nepali politics and cultural practices from extended conversations and work with my student and close friend Dhana Laxmi Hamal. Dhana's work on transcription in the late stages of the manuscript was critical. Cristeena Chitrakar introduced me to the history of Nepali photography and was instrumental in gathering and taking many of the photos in the book. Siddhartha Baral read the entire, finished manuscript, and I benefited enormously from his comments, suggestions, and translations, as well as the photos he took for the book. I also thank Saroj Dhakal for his assistance in earlier stages of the manuscript.

There are some close friends whose readings and critiques have made a deep impact on this book. I am grateful for the in-depth conversations I have enjoyed with Penelope Papailias over many years. I am also indebted to Karen Strassler and Mandana Limbert, who read every word of my manuscript many times over and remained willing to engage me on any question, big or small, at any time in the midst of their own productive lives. Daniel Karpowitz has generously shared his passions for ideas, and remained a devoted reader and editor, whose beautiful photographs appear on the cover and throughout the book. His enthusiasm for the project, support, and companionship throughout all stages of this project often kept me going.

My family stands behind me in many unspoken ways. I thank my brother, Joel Kunreuther, and my stepmother, Gail Loeb Kunreuther, and stepbrothers, Michael and David Loeb, for their care and patience. The generous support and passionate enthusiasm of my father, Howard Kunreuther, for his own research is always an inspiration. I could not ask for more generous and caring in-laws, Stephen and Joanne Karpowitz as well as Tania Karpowitz and Andrew Wingfield, whose stimulating conversations have pushed me to convey what is distinctive about an anthropological approach to everyday life. My two sons, Rafael and Sascha, continually remind me how exquisite are our daily ways of becoming subjects in this world.

AUTHOR'S NOTE ON TRANSLITERATION
AND PSEUDONYMS

In spelling Nepali words, I have relied on Turner's (1931) method of transcription with a few exceptions: (1) I have used the Nepali pronunciation as a guide for certain words that are used regularly throughout the text, such as *bikās* and *angsa*. (2) I have used the simple *s* for *s, ś,* and *ṣ* because unlike other South Asian languages, Nepali does not distinguish these sounds at a phonemic level. The only exception I made was for the word *darśan,* a widely shared South Asian concept (pronounced *darshan*) that is most frequently spelled this way in the literature. (3) I have left Nepali publications that are frequently cited in the manuscript in Romanized spelling.

Following accepted anthropological practice, I have used pseudonyms for many people represented in this book, with a few notable exceptions: (1) I have used real names when the person is a public figure who is widely known in Kathmandu, through either politics or mass media. (2) I have used real names when the person has specifically requested that I use their real name. In such cases, all other identifying information has been changed. (3) I have used real names when the person is pictured in a photograph and wants to be identified as such.

INTRODUCTION

Public Intimacy and Voicing
Subjects in Kathmandu

IN THE LATE MONSOON MONTH of September 1989, during my first visit
to Nepal, I was given a tour of Kathmandu by my Nepali friend Raj Gopal
on the back of his motorcycle. During our first meeting earlier that morning,
inside his office, he told me that Nepal was in a critical state. People were
angry with the king. Something was bound to happen *soon*. He did not know
what, but it was certain to be violent. People wanted to be able to speak more
freely, he told me, and for this they will fight. Raj Gopal, a young man in his
twenties, had been active in politics when he was a student some years back
and had spent nineteen days in prison after protesting, as he said, "for democracy." He bore a scar on his hand from those prison days, which he wore
proudly as proof of his activism. Since his activist days, Raj Gopal had settled
into work as a cartographer in the government environmental park and forest
conservation project.

In the afternoon, on his motorcycle, we careened around the city, past the
drenched, grey cement houses that lined most streets and the patches of a few
remaining fields made brilliant green by monsoon rains. Raj Gopal began to
show me some of the important spaces in the city. He pointed out the new
suburbs of Baneswar, where families and students from all over Nepal were
beginning to settle and build, a testament to Kathmandu's status as the
center of the nation. We passed the national stadium and then the large open
grassy space in the middle of the city—the Tundikhel. Raj Gopal told me this
field was not open to the public and used only to perform large royal functions or demonstrations by the army, which were all controlled by the king.
From afar, Raj Gopal pointed out Singh Durbar, "the lion palace." At the
beginning of the twentieth century the palace was home to the ostentatious
Rana rulers and was now the official home of government offices: the

FIGURE 1. Cityscape with *The Kathmandu Post* billboard celebrating the newspaper's readership: "Your Values, Your Voices." Photo: Daniel Karpowitz.

Parliament, National Assembly, Radio Nepal, and Nepal Television. We then went past the walled gates of the palace, on the only tree-lined street in Kathmandu, and I made an offhand remark about how I understood people's anger at the king, whose unabashed wealth was so clearly a sign of his contempt for the subjects over whom he ruled. To my surprise, Raj Gopal stopped the motorcycle, and looked at me fiercely. "Don't talk to me about such things *here*," he reprimanded. I looked up at the 1960s-style modernist palace, which was fully adorned with guards wearing Gurkha rifles slung over their shoulders, who stood with remarkable nonchalance unless they caught someone glancing in their direction. Without any more explanation, I understood that despite our fast speed, which no doubt kept us out of earshot, matters of politics, especially those that concerned the king, were to be discussed behind closed doors.

The movement that Raj Gopal alluded to in his office did in fact unfold over the course of my year there. At the time, I came to know the effects of the movement primarily through incidental events that perforated my daily life. My host family had to stand in long lines during the kerosene shortage in the fall of 1989, an effect of the Indian Trade Embargo that occurred earlier in the spring, which several claim provoked much ire against the government. In the early spring of 1990, we heard the sounds of protesters shouting slogans against the government during the multiple voluntary blackouts that left the streets in complete darkness and that were meant to signify the darkness of the kingdom. One day, around this same time, I rode my bike past the main post office and watched a bonfire of unopened letters burn outside the building. Civil servants in the post office had started and fed the fire, and this image of a conflagration of letters, consuming at once mountains of commercial, bureaucratic, and intimate discourse from across the country and around the world, persisted in my mind as a profound symbol of the crisis of government in contemporary Nepal. Later, during the three-day curfew from April 6 to 9, 1990, imposed by King Birendra, there was an eerie sense of constant surveillance as helicopters hovered above the city, attempting to locate any public protests. These moments signified the use and collapse of various systems of communication or forms of voicing—the protests, the burning letters, the king's own communication techniques that sought to crush those that spoke out against his orders.

Until the three-day curfew, King Birendra was publicly ostracized, statues of the royal family were desecrated, and lifelong civil servants began insulting the King. My landlord, a longtime civil servant, came into my apartment one day during the height of the crisis and said, "Our king is crazy," and promptly walked out, as if to say that such sacrilege did not warrant discussion or response. Simply uttering such words, particularly by a government worker, was an act of defiance and treason. What struck me most in the days after April 9, 1990, when King Birendra conceded to a multiparty system, were comments the landlord made to me, which I later heard many others also make: *"balla, balla bolna sakchaũ"* (finally, finally we can speak). This book seeks to unpack what these statements have come to mean in the years following this first People's Movement, or *jana āndolan* I, which reestablished a multiparty democracy.

Voicing Subjects is an inquiry into the figure of the voice and the set of discourses, practices, and technologies that give it meaning. To speak of a figure of the voice is to draw attention to the multiple and varied meanings of voice that traverse this ethnography. These meanings have proliferated in the years of conflict surrounding the establishment of democratic reforms in Nepal. In studying these meanings, I pay particular attention to speech that is explicitly about talk or voice, or "metalanguage." In this kind of speech, exemplified by my landlord's statements, the act of speaking comes to stand more generally for a new set of social relations, between citizen and state, between men and women, between youth and older generations, between emerging private media and their audiences. It reveals the significance of speaking to be at once deeply personal and practically political. In Nepali, the common word for "voice"—*āwāj*—refers to the meaningful sounds made by the human voice as well as to meaningless noise more generally (as in the phrase *kati thulo āwāj!* or "what a loud sound/noise!").[1] These associations with sound generally and with human voices specifically are both at play in the political and intimate voice discussed below.[2] During *jana āndolan I* and the second *jana āndolan* in 2006, in particular, invocations of voice *(āwāj)* and the raising of one's voice *(āwāj uṭhāune)* were often used to describe something entirely new about the emerging government. The figure of the voice was used to indicate the plurality of voices that are thought to exist in a well-functioning democracy.

In this discussion, I show the voice to be a sign of the personhood and individuality that are considered inherent in any human body, a particularly intimate cultural and historical convention of identification that marks personal specificity. It is considered to be as natural in its relationship to identity as the fingerprint or signature. The voices that populate this ethnography, invoked by people referring to their own voice or that of others, often seem to be animate things, possessing a living agency inseparable from the dense materiality of embodied existence: the soft, soothing voice of a radio host; the scratchy, harsh voice of a politician; the loud voice of a father; the silent voice of a daughter. People often express a sense that the medium of the human voice bears particular, powerful significance, speaking of it as if it is itself an uncanny common ground between an embodied personality and the detached, circulating medium of symbolic speech. In daily life, the voice appears as a physical medium of highly personal transmission, at once physical and symbolic, material and disembodied, present and on the move, associated often with the most significant utterance and yet deeply affective at levels beyond the meaning of the spoken word. Thus the voice, conceived of as a material sound uniquely generated within the human body, has a social life associated with its role as the primary medium of human utterance. In this life, it is an embodied mode of transmission, imbued with an irreducible authenticity, yet itself ubiquitously mediated through a range of always more pervasive technologies.

I also show how the voice serves as a figure of speech in daily discourse. In rhetorical speech, reference to "the voice"—finding it, having it, raising it—refers to something seemingly of the nature of a personal possession, a property of selfhood. This sense and use of a voice, the voice that can be had or lost, repressed or developed, is in fact a central figure circulating with ever-greater frequency and shifting significance in the daily speech and political discourse of contemporary Kathmandu. Throughout this book, the phrase "figure of the voice" refers to a nexus of metaphors associated with the voice as a sign of intimacy, consciousness, and presence, associated, above all, with those modes of selfhood central to democratic political agency. I distinguish, but treat in tandem, the rhetorical figure of the voice and the social life of those material sounds that are embodied and circulated in human speech. At all times, this ethnography attends to the relationship between contemporary subjectivity and emergent media technologies, exploring what it means in contemporary Kathmandu to say that one desires to find and raise one's voice.

POLITICAL AND INTIMATE VOICE IN KATHMANDU

Today Kathmandu is one of the fastest growing cities in South Asia, with more than one million people in the Kathmandu metropolis alone.[3] The city is bursting with the influx of migrant workers from villages, college and university students, Indian businessmen, Tibetan and Bhutanese refugees, foreign diplomats who drive white Land Rovers through Kathmandu streets, government officials from various parts of Nepal, and foreign tourists who visit the city en route to trek in the Himalayas or on their way to or back from India. Kathmandu is also home to a vast number of nongovernmental organizations (NGOs) and internationally funded NGOs (INGOs), especially since the 1980s. The total foreign aid money flowing into Nepal since 1956 has been an important part of the country's overall economy, and in 2011–12, Nepal received US $1.21 billion from donors across the world, which amounted to approximately 5.4 percent of Nepal's GDP (Government of Nepal 2013: 1).

In addition to foreign aid, there has been a steady rise in the remittance economy. Since the mid-1980s the Nepali state has entered into contracts with other states through foreign employment agencies—colloquially known as "manpower agencies"—that send Nepali laborers to foreign countries. By 2002, there were an estimated 696,965 people working abroad in countries other than India (Adhikari 2007: 9). The huge remittance economy generated by Nepalis overseas is as impressive as the foreign aid presence in

Kathmandu, and in 2003–04 it was estimated to be 66 billion rupees (approximately 1 billion dollars) and as much as 25 percent of the total gross domestic product (GDP) (Adhikari 2007: 13). In 2011–12, Nepal received the third highest proportion of remittances in relation to GDP among countries around the world, at 23.1 percent of the GDP.[4] These facts alone show the extent to which foreign money and ideas have become a vital part of the fabric of Nepali society, accompanied by a host of competing national and liberal ideologies. Urban residents of Kathmandu directly or indirectly interact daily with the world outside their borders.

This book discusses the Kathmandu Valley during the 1990s and early 2000s. In these anxious years, Nepalis lived through and participated in two national People's Movements (in 1990 and 2006), a decade-long Maoist civil war, an ongoing sequence of ethnic nationalist movements, and the final dissolution of the monarchy. The domestic economy was radically liberalized, and a significant portion of the youthful, adult population has sought its livelihood abroad, generating a large part of the remittance economy. A civil war has been fought and has ended, an interim republican constitution has been written, elections for the constitutent assembly finally took place in November 2013. This book illustrates the revolutionary spirit and the waves of frustration and despondency characteristic of this particular moment. In its analysis of emergent media and daily life in both its political and personal forms, it also traces longstanding social relations and cultural practices that continue to reshape people's lives.

Tensions between state censorship and the liberalizing of the public sphere, between imposed silence and public speaking, recurred at different moments during the fifteen years this book describes. On June 1, 2001, King Birendra, who ten years earlier had yielded to people's demands and allowed a multiparty democracy, was murdered, along with his entire immediate family, at a family dinner party in the Narayanhiti Palace. The official story accused Prince Dipendra of the murders, drawing attention to his conflict with his mother, Queen Aishwarya, over his choice of a wife. But most Nepalis do not believe this official story, and many feel we may never know what really happened. The next morning a violent stillness was imposed on the teeming voices, political perspectives, and public narratives that had come to define the life of Kathmandu in the decade since the *jana āndolan* of 1990. All state and private media refused to broadcast the news for a full twenty-four hours, and most Nepalis heard about the incident through either the BBC, other international media, or personal telephone calls (often from the diaspora), with rumors quickly spreading across the nation. As I discuss in the epilogue, the silence maintained by the media immediately exposed the complex relationship between voice, censorship, and mediation that recurs throughout discussions in this book.

Four years later, on the morning of February 1, 2005, another act of censorship occurred after King Gyanendra (crowned days after his brother's death in 2001) dismissed the Nepali parliament and seized sole control of the government. In a gesture as characteristic of the monarchy as it was shocking to this garrulous city, the king cut all lines of technological communication between the capital Valley and the rest of the country, and between the country and the rest of the world, including a Nepali diaspora that had become so peculiarly central to the daily life of the city in the preceding decade of liberalization. Z-Net Asia prefaced its report about the situation on February 3:[5] "The following report was brought out by courier from Kathmandu, where all communication with the outside world is cut off, except for select satellite telephones and internet connections mostly controlled by embassies. The general public had no access to communication with the outside world from 10 A.M. on 1 February 2005 until at least 7 P.M. on 2 February 2005. All domestic telephones are also shut off, both mobile and land lines. People are traveling from one place to another to communicate." As familiar electronic technologies of voice were seized and suppressed, daily life was suffused with an eerie nostalgia as much news traveled for a brief time by "courier," word of mouth, and face-to-face encounter.

King Gyanendra's coup in 2005, known commonly by the Nepali date Magh 19 *gate,* was an attack on technologies of voice. By technologies of voice, I refer here to a nexus of practices, discourses, and machines of everyday life that have emerged and proliferated in Nepal since the first liberalizing *jana āndolan* of 1990. It refers, literally, to technologies like the telephone and FM radio that digitize, radiate, or electronically circulate simulations of the human voice and, metaphorically, to practices of speech and conceptualizations about ways of speaking associated with Nepal's burgeoning liberal democracy. Even prior to this coup after the *jana āndolan,* as Michael Hutt (2006) has argued, the press had their own form of internal censorship in which journalists knew the "things that should not be said" (largely relating to the king and monarchy) and generally respected these implicit restrictions.

For many Nepalis, the royal coup conjured memories of an earlier royal coup enacted by King Gyanendra's father, Mahendra, following the first decade of democratic government in Nepal (1951–60). King Mahendra similarly curtailed all civil liberties, banned all existing political parties, and established the autocratic thirty-year royal Panchāyat regime (1960–90), with political power and authority vested solely in the monarchy.[6] The coup in 2005 also harked back to an earlier period of imposed isolation, when the oligarchy of Rana prime ministers (1857–1951) maintained exclusive control over virtually all technology, media, and foreign goods, and severely restricted the movement of all Nepalis and all foreigners, particularly within the Kathmandu Valley.

Nepal was never an officially colonized nation, but during the time of the British Raj in India, the Rana prime ministers maintained close relations with the British. By supplying the British with manpower for their army in India (the famed Gurkha soldiers) and conducting all foreign policy through the Raj, the Ranas ensured Nepal's sovereignty and maintained access to desired luxury goods and technology (Des Chene 1993). Rana rule itself might even be considered a form of internal colonization.[7] Their strategy of imposed isolation paved the way for Nepal to become celebrated throughout the world as a secluded Shangri-la, presumably unsullied by the forces of colonialism that reigned outside the country's borders.

Yet the context of a daily life, both political and personal, constituted by technology and media communication made the coup enacted by Gyanendra in 2005 crucially different from either Mahendra's coup or the earlier Rana era of ruthlessly enforced isolation. In the intervening generations, the daily experience of speech and voice, image and face, had been transformed. Nor was the coup was completely unexpected. King Gyanendra had been consolidating political power since 2003, when he appointed Surya Bahadur Thapa as prime minister without holding a general election. By 2004, Thapa resigned after growing pressure from the political parties. Days after this resignation, people publicly gathered in the streets wearing black cloths over their bodies—a standard sign of protest prior to 1990—and carrying flags with Nepali colors but erased of any royal insignia (see figure 2). Gyanendra's final seizure of power in 2005 rent a momentary breach in this new social fabric, and thus paradoxically threw into stark relief those very modes of mediation, public life, and personal intimacy that have come to characterize life in Kathmandu and its electronically mediated diaspora.

Having spent my time in Nepal in the years during and after the first People's Movement, I have observed the emergence of private media and its connections with a vast number of related liberal projects. Many persons, often quite self-consciously, considered their political and their intimate lives as part of the daily creation of a new Nepali *nāgarik samāj*, or "civil society." The coup

FIGURE 2. Student protest against King Gyanendra's inital takeover of political power from elected government, May 9, 2004. Photo: Gopal Chitrakar.

of 2005 was an assault on many of these democratic structures, particularly those concerned with public expression and the fabric of people's personal daily lives. Ultimately, King Gyanendra underestimated the extent to which technology had thoroughly infiltrated daily life in Kathmandu and beyond. This coup became the beginning impetus for a second People's Movement, which ended, three years later, with the dissolution of the monarchy entirely.

During these two decades, public life in Kathmandu was marked by at least two significant cultural phenomena. The first was the visible explosion of political expression evident in the proliferation of ethnic nationalist *(janajātī)* movements, new newspapers, and new media throughout the 1990s, and in the nationwide strikes *(bandaharu)* and reform movements. These were certainly not wholly new activities, but they acquired new forms since such public actions were no longer banned or as heavily censored as they had been during the Panchāyat government prior to 1990. Phrases like *mahilāko āwāj* (women's voice), *janajātīko āwāj* (voice of ethnic nationals), *bidhyarthīko āwāj* (student's voice), and *āwāj uṭhāune* (raising voice) were peppered throughout newspapers and public protests during the period after 1990, which suggested a proliferation of collective groups demanding to be heard by politicians and the state.

"Discovering the power of speech" and "raising voice" *(āwāj uṭhāune)* were key metaphors to describe activities that brought Nepalis onto the street in protest. The close association of *āwāj uṭhāune* with political representation and public discourse creates what I refer to as a "political voice."

To be sure, the concept of *āwāj uṭhāune* did not emerge whole cloth from democracy movements, nor is it associated exclusively with large-scale political movements. Rather, it characterizes forms of discourse in Nepal that seek to gain the attention of and persuade any authority in a position to effect change. For example, if a man beats his wife and others in the neighborhood or village protest against his actions, it is referred to as a form of *āwāj uṭhāune* on the wife's behalf. If a community wishes to maintain rights to a nearby forest that has been declared a forest preserve by the government, they would refer to the confrontation between the government and villages as a form of *āwāj uṭhāune*. *Āwāj uṭhāune*, like its English equivalent, refers not only to raising one's own voice, but also, to those who speak on behalf of others or who represent the collective interests of a particular group.

The second phenomenon was a notable proliferation in public expressions of personal feelings and intimate relations, particularly among youth. Entertainment programs and conversations on television, radio, or telephone pronounced the voice to be an ideal medium for conveying emotional proximity and presence and defined an "intimate voice." In this neoliberal economy of symbolic and material exchange, the FM radio emerged as a symbol of democratic "free speech," where listeners often referred to the power of voice. A range of FM programs sought to draw out the intimate lives of their listeners and describe this process as a form of personal assertion and defiance. One of the early FM radio hosts, who hosted a program called *Heart-to-Heart,* told me that getting people to talk about their romances or desires was a way of personally empowering them, allowing them to not be "only guided by society." By talking with the two radio hosts of this program about intimate matters and listening to others' problems, people will learn, in the words of another FM program, to "deal with problems on their own."[8] The voice and speaking are central to the process of learning to be a self-conscious individual with a complicated interior life. This idea of a conscious and problem-solving individual is bound up with the ideal person of neoliberal ideology: a subject who is self-sufficient and can make their own choices, such that one's "private" life becomes the main site of political transformation (Gershon 2011; Matza 2009).

In addition to collective and individual agency, the figure of the voice conjures a sense of immediacy and presence. The sense of presence that the voice seems to convey is often associated with material sound, the lilts, rhythm, and intonations of a person's speech. Ethnomusicologists and ethnographers of sound describe such voiced sound as "soundscapes," or the interlacing of expressive sounds that articulate links between social concepts and emotional feeling (Feld 1996; Feld and Brenneis 2004; Fox 2004; Helmreich 2007; Hirschkind 2006). In Kathmandu, listeners of FM radio make frequent references to the melodramatic or melodic tones of the radio hosts' voices, which make them feel as if they are really there with them. Similarly, politicians from the emerging *janajātī* movements suggest that the ideal political speech is one that moves listeners to tears, making them feel the presence of the political leaders through the sound of their voice.[9] This seeming directness of the voice evokes a presence that people assume provides greater closeness and that becomes an index of truth and emotional authenticity. "Political voice" and "intimate voice" are analytic categories that seek to distinguish two seemingly different understandings of voice. In actual practice, these invocations of voice intersect in the ethnographic phenomena described in this book, and more often than not they overlap. Both forms of public expression emphasize the provocative powers of the voice.

In *Voicing Subjects,* I argue that a political voice (associated with democratic participation, consciousness, and agency) and an intimate voice (associated with interior feeling, emotional directness, and authentic communication) are mutually constitutive, since both are important aspects of modern subjectivities emerging and present in contemporary Kathmandu. The contours of these subjectivities are shaped by broad material and ideological projects, such as international foreign aid, the enormous remittance economy, the proliferation of business, media, and other schemes of privatization, and political contests over the meaning and substance of a democratic government. Both the political voice and the intimate voice depend upon and are intermingled with a vast media complex—newspapers, television, documentary and commercial film, radio, phones, and cellphones—through which "the voice" is generated, circulated, and reproduced.

VOICE AND SUBJECTIVITY

Rather than maintain a focus on high-level political drama like the massacre at the palace, the February 1 coup, or the *jana āndolans* in 1990 and 2006, *Voicing Subjects* explores more everyday urban practices. Its ethnographic fields include a property reform movement, ritual practices of seeing and recognition, FM radio entertainment programs, and telephone and radio communication between Nepalis in Kathmandu and abroad. Throughout the book, I argue that contemporary ways of being a social person in Kathmandu are thoroughly entwined with a discourse about the voice *(swar, āwāj)* and "raising voice" *(āwāj uṭhāune)*. I center on a few key questions that explore the links between the voice and subjectivity:[10] What forms of agency have come to be associated with the figure of the voice, and how are these forms of agency linked to ideas about personhood and consciousness? To what extent can we understand the voice by tracing its different modalities, not just in the political realm but also in more intimate spheres as well? What are the processes of mediation—the forms, practices, and technologies— through which people come to see themselves as social beings (as men, women, activists, citizens, youth, middle class), and why does the "voice" figure so centrally in these processes?

My understanding of subjectivity builds upon the concept of interpellation put forth by Louis Althusser (1971). In his well-known essay "Ideology and Ideological State Apparatuses," Althusser shows the inextricable link between ideology and subject formation that works through practices of hailing. An individual becomes a subject, endowed with consciousness, desires, and specific values, through reiterated forms of address and conventions that delineate a social position. Through these forms, a person comes to recognize herself as a subject within a social world. In Althusser's account, this recognition is the work of state ideology. He gives the example (classic and oft-repeated) of a person who turns when a policeman yells, "Hey you there!" This person in that moment is constituted as a subject of state ideology.

I explore several moments of interpellation in this book, through everyday acts such as brothers calling their married sisters back to their natal home, ritualized acts of "seeing face" *(mukh herne),* and radio programs that create a community of unseen listeners through their call to participate. All of these interpellative moments bring a subject into being, constituting a woman or sister, a man or brother, a citizen, a subject of the king, a member of a public. I also expand Althusser's focus on subjects of state ideology and do not limit my view to subjects of the state alone.

The voice has an important place within the theory of interpellation. The voice of the policeman is an activating force, the creative power that turns persons into subjects of the state.[11] In explaining interpellation, Althusser indeed draws upon the divine act of naming as his model: the divine voice creates what it names and simultaneously subordinates this subject (Butler 1997: 31).[12] Social ideology, Althusser suggests, works in an analogous fashion. While building upon Althusser's insights about subject-making, Judith Butler draws attention to some of the problems with the role of voice in Althusser's theory of interpellation. People do not need to turn around in order to be constituted as a subject of social ideology, Butler points out, and the name that makes one who one is does not need to come from an utterance within earshot: it can come through other forms of state documentation (Butler 1997: 34).

Butler's arguments implicitly draw upon and resonate with Jacques Derrida's (1988) well-known thesis, in which he suggests that a common understanding about how writing works (that is, its ability to circulate without the presence of the author) rather than how speech works (that is, its dependence on context and present speaker) structure all forms of discourse. Social ideology and discourse need not be tied to the present moment, Butler notes, since many forms of state documentation—adoptive papers, the census, bureaucratic forms—also constitute a subject's being. Furthermore, the power behind a policeman's words comes not from himself,[13] but from the authority vested in him as an agent of the state; he is enabled to hail a person on the street through the "force of reiterated convention," which is tied to both his bodily performance and his words (Butler 1997: 33). The force of interpellation need not be so closely tied to the voice, argues Butler, "in order to become the instrument and mechanism of discourses whose efficacy is irreducible to their moment of enunciation" (32). Subjectivity derives from discourse and performance that always already exceeds the present and exists outside the individual, rather than being a product of an individual's internal will (Butler 1997; Foucault 1977, 1978; Mahmood 2005).

In her critique of Althusser, Butler does not consider the particular properties of the voice as a medium that creates the effect of presence or the effect of interpellation—nor does Althusser, for that matter. Despite its absence in their analyses, we do imagine the texture and harsh sound of the policeman's voice as male and loud, as he shouts, "Hey you!" The material sound of his voice is part of his authority as an agent of the state. As a result, in Butler's work the dichotomy between voice and the written word is simply reversed, favoring writing and performance instead of voice as the model through which subjectivity (and language) comes into being (hence Derrida's celebrated idea of iteration/citationality and Butler's idea of resignification).

While my general argument follows along the lines of these poststructural thinkers, I consider the voice as a medium that works in concert with writing, performance, and other media to constitute subjects. As Jonathan Sterne, one of the foremost scholars in sound studies has argued, we need to break away from these dichotomies altogether and simply redescribe voice and sound as being made possible through a network of social relations that occur between senses (visual and aural) (2003: 18). We need not assume, for example, that the figure of the voice simply conveys self-presence or the agency of the speaker. Rather, this presence is an *effect* based on ideologies of the voice and the voice as a specific kind of medium (Fox 2004; Weidman 2006).

Instead of juxtaposing voice and writing, in the chapters that follow I show the intersections of voice and writing, of the body and discourse, of presence and absence, of immediacy and mediation, of authentic and derivative forms. Ethnographic analysis of technologies of voice (radio and telephone), domestic and national rituals of seeing face, and political reform movements that are bound up with different notions of voice all ask us to rethink assumptions about writing and voice that underlie the theoretical formulation of interpellation.

SOUND OF THE VOICE

The work of ethnomusicologists and anthropologists of voice has been instructive in tracing the social significance of vocal sound. In an emerging and rich literature about the sound of the voice, several scholars have shown the link between the material voice and modern ideas of self (Bate 2009; Feld et al. 2004; Fox 2004; Hirschkind 2006; Inoue 2006; Sterne 2003; Taylor 2009; Weidman 2006). Many of these studies show the important role aural technologies (radio, cassettes, gramophone, stethoscopes) have played in fashioning modern subjectivity; in particular, the role of the voice as a medium plays in this fashioning. Bernard Bate's (2009) evocative ethnography of Tamil oratory practices, for example, discusses the use of a literary style and vocal techniques by new democrats in Tamil Nadu that distinguishes them from older politicians, creating a new and archaic mode of speech based on writing that is distinctly modern. While my focus is not on politicians, this book also explores the prominence of voiced writing as one preferred modern mode of voice, especially on FM radio.

The voice is such a powerful metaphor because of its capacity to embody specific qualities through tone and register (its iconic properties) and to convey particular subjectivities and identities, like class, gender, ethnicity, or regional origins (its indexical qualities) (Weidman 2006: 13). As Charles Hirschkind shows, pious Muslims are hailed by Islamic cassettes that play recordings of a *khatib*'s sermon. In the sermon, the *khatib* calls his audience to rhythmically repeat portions of his oratory and to respond when he begins a prayer or mentions the Prophet's name, producing a sonic environment that cultivates a modern and pious Muslim subjectivity (2006: 84–85). In her ethnography of classical Indian music, Amanda Weidman (2006) also demonstrates that modern ideologies of the voice are often coupled with and supported by the sonic and material aspects of voice. By taking seriously the materiality of voice—its sounds and how these sounds are linked to particular persons—we can enrich our understanding of how subjectivity and intimacy are constituted, not only through the hailing practices of interpellation, but through the hailing by a *particular sound of voice,* which is itself entirely social. "It is always," writes Steven Feld and his colleagues, "the body social that is enunciated in and through the voice" (Feld et al. 2004: 341).

Along similar lines, Jessica Taylor (2009) examines the interesting history of a material voice divorced from its referential value in speech by looking at the transition from silent to sound cinema. She traces the problems encountered during this transition, exemplified in the film *Singin' in the Rain,* and shows the ways in which the voice becomes what Miyako Inoue calls a "socially powerful truth" (Inoue 2002: 393; cited in Taylor 2009: 7). The film depicts two silent film stars (played by Gene Kelly and Jean Hagan) who attempt to make the transition to sound cinema, yet only the male actor's voice is deemed an acceptable match to the body of his character. As Taylor notes, the "assumption of a natural fit between body, voice, and self . . . shapes the intense focus on the act of hearing the stars" (2009: 7). The silent film actress's voice is dubbed by a more suitable female voice, and when her voiced double (the male character's girlfriend) is revealed in the end, the actress's film career is ruined. The assumed match between body and voice reveals a powerful language ideology, argues Taylor, in which "the authenticity . . . resides in the speaking subject, "the human voice" that can "open the secret chamber of the heart." ". . . To speak (and to hear the voice) is to be human" (Taylor 2009: 8).

These studies of the material properties of the voice and the cultural dimensions of sound provide invaluable insights about the relation of vocalized sound to politics and modern subjectivity that have influenced my own study of voice. The voice in modernity typically works an index of interiority, consciousness, agency, and self (Bauman and Briggs 2003; Weidman 2006). While drawing on these studies, *Voicing Subjects* approaches the figure of the voice from a different direction. First, instead of focusing on a defined performative moments (such as the cassette sermon, voiced song, musical performance, or film production), I look at several different contexts—some part of everyday habit and some clearly performed—in which the figure of the voice looms large, particularly in relation to emerging forms of public intimacy and democratic, liberal politics. Second, I explore the cultural construct of voice along with its material sound, namely, its association with agency, empowerment, and consciousness that informs political and affective subjectivities produced during the democratic reforms in Nepal.

This book is devoted to analyzing *why* the figure of the voice has become so prevalent in Kathmandu during the fifteen years of an emerging democratic public. What does it mean, I ask, that people come to recognize themselves through modes of address that are conceived of largely through the figure of the voice and yet are equally embroiled in written or mediated forms? How do the subjectivities constituted through interpellation come to appear self-evident, authentic, and unmediated? In what ways does the figure of the voice resonate with other common tropes of modernity, such as development, the importance of justice, authenticity, and truth? To do a cultural analysis of voice in Kathmandu requires analysis not only of the discursive invocations of voice, but also of the various technologies and practices through which the figure of the voice is associated and through which it is produced.

ETHNOGRAPHY OF MEDIATION

How does one do an ethnography in a metropolitan setting in a way that does not flatten out the variety of experiences and diversity of people one encounters on a daily basis? I chose to organize this study around a concept and a discourse—the figure of the voice—that proliferated from mid-1990s through the first decade of the 2000s, when I did research in Kathmandu. The everyday lives of all Kathmandu Nepalis, including those in seemingly isolated farming communities, are caught up in multiple social worlds during the course of a day (as no doubt is the case for most everyone): from the realm of the family to the world of Indian pop music and film, from local media that aim to create a local cosmopolitan sensibility to the national education and legal system, from state to international policies to family and friends living in the diaspora. The figure of the voice cuts across all of these fields and it traverses ethnic, caste, and class lines, even at it is interpreted and inflected slightly differently in each context. This meant that I traveled to different parts of the city that are not obviously connected: from NGO offices and legal advocacy centers to the offices of FM radio stations; from the homes of FM listeners around the Valley to the homes of families I had known from my initial visit to Nepal; from local teashops, where I would meet professionals or scan the local newspapers, to temple complexes or ritual sites, which I visited with some of my friends. As in most ethnographies, particularly those not limited by a specific social identity or rigidly demarcated space, there were no clear boundaries of when I was "doing research" and when I was not. When I went to buy vegetables for dinner one night, the merchant told me that she had heard me on the radio the night before (which was the only time I ever spoke on the radio), and I knew then how broadly the FM radio waves reached. I accompanied one of my close friends to a celebration of the annual national holiday for honoring one's mother, *āmāko mukh herne din* (day to see mother's face, Mother's Day), with little intention of this ritual becoming part of my study. But later, I realized that the discourse about the face and visual practices of seeing face during this holiday were closely linked to discourse about the voice.

This book follows the emerging literature on media and mediation that has reimagined what constitutes a suitable object for anthropological inquiry. Beginning in the mid-1990s, anthropological studies about media proliferated, primarily as attempts to understand the intensifying effects of "globalization" throughout the world. By 2002, there were two edited volumes published simultaneously on the subject of anthropology and media, both tracing the roots of media analysis in anthropology and pronouncing the significance of media to contemporary studies in anthropology (Askew and Wilk 2002; Ginsburg, Abu-Lughod, and Larkin 2002). Both volumes provide an important corrective to the Euro-American focus of media studies in the academy and to earlier anthropological conceits that proclaimed media to be superficial forms of cultural production. They also note that anthropological studies of media, like studies of media in other fields, have been dominated by studies of visual media. Most of the essays in these volumes, as well as monograph-length ethnographies of media, focus on the analysis of a single medium: television, video, radio, film, or photography (for example, Ginsburg 2002; Mankekar 1999; Pinney 1997; Rajagopal 2001; Spitulnik 2002; Strassler 2010). These detailed studies provide us with a rich analysis of the production and consumption of media programs in relation to specific social and cultural contexts. In this book I discuss the intersection between diverse media along with other cultural processes of mediation that occur through nonmedia forms.

Insights from ethnographic studies of media and technology have reshaped fundamental beliefs about good ethnography, particularly the methodology that privileges "face-to-face" encounters as an ideal source of ethnographic knowledge. As Jacques Derrida ([1967] 1976) has famously argued, the very idea of face-to-face interaction being a most primary form of communication is rooted in the dominant logocentric philosophies of language. Anthropology's own historical preference for face-to-face interactions as the key site of authentic and credible cultural information is similarly rooted in this logocentric understanding of the voice (Axel 2006).[14] "'Face-to-face' is an index of this time before [new technologies of communication]," writes Brian Axel, "which is also glossed in terms of 'physical proximity,' 'contexts' in 'real time and real space'" (2006: 368–69). Modern conceptions of the voice and aurality are similarly associated with immersion in the world, affect, and subjectivity and are often idealized as providing access to a "pure interiority" that is linked with subjective self-presence (Sterne 2003: 15). Voice and sound seem to hark back to a premodern (and pretechnological) moment of oral tradition and hearsay (Bull and Back 2003; Erlmann 2004; Ong 1982).[15] Because of these conceptions, Axel argues, many ethnographies view speech and voice as the source of authentic, unmediated communication (Axel 2006: 369). *Voicing Subjects* argues the opposite: the figure of the voice, as a cultural construct, has gained novel significance in this modern moment of democratic reforms, with the explosion of new media and technology.[16]

While Nepalis often shared these modern ideologies of voice, many Nepalis also described the "realness" of radio conversations in contrast to face-to-face conversations (no doubt many Americans would as well). Such comments serve to highlight the intensely mediated quality of face-to-face encounters. The presumed "realness" or directness of radio is linked to the indexical properties of the technology, which has a contiguous and direct relationship with that which it represents (that is, voices, music, and other surrounding sounds). Like all technologies of voice (radio, telephone, gramophone, voice recorder), radio records not only the symbolic, meaningful sounds of language but also intrusions of meaningless noise, such as the hissing of the machine. This dense materiality, such as the oft-cited clarity of FM radio broadcasts in contrast to the static broadcasts of the state's Radio Nepal (on AM radio waves), contributes to the social meanings of any particular medium and to the idea of voice itself. As Fredrick Kittler (1999) has suggested, the sense of immediacy, directness, and originality associated with the figure of the voice may in fact be an aftereffect of technological recording.

To do an ethnography of mediation is to question our commonplace ideas of direct, unmediated communication and its association with interior, authentic selves. To pursue this question we must take seriously the material and formal qualities that define any particular media.[17] In many of the ethnographic examples I discuss in this book, the figure of the voice is thoroughly entangled with the media in which the voice is projected—newspapers, radio programs, telephones, and rituals that do the work of conveying presence, like the voice. Often the work of technology seems to function as a neutral vehicle for carrying and distributing these "voices" directly and widely. Just like the figure of the voice, so too do social concepts like culture, society, and self appear to exist outside the mediated practices through which they come into being. The saturation of media in everyday life thus has the effect of producing an anterior space, which appears to be more direct and immediate—one that is often termed "culture" (Axel 2006). By implying and simultaneously erasing the work of technology and media, the voice is a sign of presence, a seemingly transparent medium for conveying one's true feelings and authentic political concerns, as well as social concepts ("culture," "nation," "society," "self") that seem to exist prior to their animation in different media.

A focus on the material and social aspects of technology disrupts the illusion that media are neutral vehicles for transmitting social and cultural ideas. Drawing attention to various forms of mediation is one way to reveal the work of modern power in shaping subjectivities. At the same time, as Brian Larkin argues, the material forms of media and technology are part of what make media unpredictable, contingent, and therefore not completely under the control of their designer's and sponsor's intentions (2008: 3). The quality of sound or noise coming from the radio box, the accidental interruptions that occur due to a momentary failure of technology, the placement and coordination of the radio, telephone, or television in relation to one another and other domestic objects, and the reach of radio waves outside the intended spaces of transmission all contribute to the unexpected effects of media.

Where this book departs from related studies of mass media is that I situate my analysis of mass media within a broader analysis of the figure of the voice,[18] and show the work of mediation in fields and practices outside mass media as well. This difference relates to a fundamental assumption about connections between "culture" and "media" that runs through the book. Many scholars in the anthropology of media inadvertently replicate the idea that "culture" and "media" are fundamentally different processes. With a focus on the "local" consumption or production of media such as TV, film, and video, many of these studies implicitly assume that culture stands outside the processes of mediation they seek to describe. Writing on indigenous media, for example, Faye Ginsburg states: "indigenous people are using screen media not to mask but to recuperate their own collective stories and histories . . . that have been erased in the national narratives of the dominant culture and are in danger of being forgotten within local worlds as well" (2002: 40). Ginsburg's important move to challenge dominant theories of mass media involves the analysis of local conceptual schema and political interests that shape indigenous people's encounters with new technology. In her analysis, Ginsburg describes how some of these local worlds are reconceptualized through media, but there is little sense that the very idea of "the local" is created anew through mediation that includes, but is not limited to, the use of mass media. Projects examining indigenous media are important interventions in anthropology, but my aim here is not to indigenize media by focusing only on such represented voices. *Voicing Subjects* instead expands the ethnographic study of media by integrating it with other cultural practices, which might be seen productively through the frame of mediation. In highlighting the mediating aspects of both culture and media, we can place these seemingly different social processes within the same field of analysis.

This book analyzes both "culture" and "media" as interpenetrating fields of mediation. "The problem is less the meeting of 'culture' and 'media,'" writes William Mazzarella, "and more the intersection of two or more systems of mediation" (2004: 353). *Voicing Subjects* shows the place of the voice in several intersecting systems of mediation that include technology and media (such as radio and telephone), as well as other social fields (such as the law and national reform movements, everyday face-to-face greetings, and family and national rituals). All of these practices, even those considered more direct, more "traditional," or more "authentic," might be better understood through the lens of mediation and the figure of the voice that inflect their practices. While the voice is often considered to embody all that is classically thought of as "culture," it has, like any medium, highly contextual social histories. The analytic appeal of the figure of voice lies in the resilience with which it defies a separation between "culture" and "media."

One conversation with an adolescent FM radio fan led to me to see the common though somewhat counterintuitive association made between media, voice, and directness or presence. We were sitting in the bedroom of my landlord's daughter, and she was listening to a popular FM call-in program. I asked her what made FM radio different from Radio Nepal or from talking with people face-to-face, and she replied immediately: "On FM, people say things straight or directly *(sidhā bhanchan)*. You can't talk that way to someone's face." Contrary to common assumptions about the directness of face-to-face interactions, these comments point to the highly mediated aspects of everyday conversation that cultural and linguistic anthropologists have held as a truism. Mediation occurs through cultural symbols, gestures, and social hierarchies that inflect every interaction. "Social life has a mediated character," writes Asif Agha, for example, "whenever persons are linked to each other through speech and other perceivable signs" (2011: 163). Media, and particularly the voiced medium of FM radio, often appear to offer a more direct form of communication, serving as apparently neutral transmitters that mask their role in shaping people's subjective knowledge about themselves. Rather than assume this "metaphysics of presence" (Derrida [1967] 1976), in which the body (voice and face) are sites of pure presence, *Voicing Subjects* demonstrates the mediated and historical processes through which agency, interiority, and presence emerge, and come to be associated with the figure of the voice.

My turn toward mediation comes initially from studies of language and semiotics that propose a method for avoiding the thorny issue of whether the sense of directness produced by the figure of the voice is real, prosthetic, or illusory. Though I only rely on some semiotic terminology in this book, my analysis of the figure of the voice is inspired by ethnographers and theorists who analyze "culture" through the mediation of signs.[19] Mikhail Bakhtin, for one, refers to "voice" and "voicing" to show that speech is both an effect of multiple social positions and a mediating form in itself. For Bakhtin (1981), the analysis of "voice" refers not simply to the words of a single individual, but more broadly to the articulation of a particular social position and worldview. All utterances are a composition of the multiple social perspectives or "voices" that battle for a place to speak. Discourse constitutes a social world, and one that is hardly harmonious or uniform. No word or utterance is ever completely "one's own," and all discourse is saturated with prior utterances and voices: "All words have the 'taste' of a profession, a genre, a tendency, a party, a particular work, a particular person, a generation, an age group, the day and hour" (Bakhtin 1981: 293). This fundamentally social perspective emphasizes that the voice is always directed toward a listener and an answer (even when one speaks alone).

The voice for Bakhtin is situated in *voiced practice* and genre composition, in the dialogues of novels, in everyday conversations and narratives that populate our world. Speakers quote, mimic the speech of others, and directly draw attention to the voice as a channel of communication in phatic statements like "do you hear me?" or "are you there?" (Bakhtin 1981; Jakobson 1987). These statements course through everyday speech in face-to-face conversations and conversations on the FM radio or telephone, and highlight the voice as a *medium* through which social meanings arise. Explicating Bakhtin's notion of voice, Dennis Tedlock and Bruce Mannheim note that "one of the things language does best is to enable its speakers, in the very moment they are present to one another, to breach that presence" (1995: 8). Subjectivity itself, they write, must be conceived of as "an embodied constellation of voices" (8). In discussing Nepal, Laura Ahearn (2001) has used such theories of language and social action to understand changing ideas of marriage and love, and her study has paved the way for this study of public intimacy and its mediation through the figure of the voice.

In the analysis of conversations, discourse, and people's narratives about themselves throughout this book, we encounter explicit references to "voice" as well as its implicit invocation. In linguistic anthropology circles, this kind of talk is referred to as "metapragmatics" or "language about language use" (Silverstein 1981). Metapragmatics turns our attention to the acting force of words. Speech is understood for what it does and for what people imagine that it does. Considered against the dominant idea of language as a system of tools for referencing the world, this idea of language is instead theorized as constituting the social world. Since language in this view is a form of social action, the richest and most revealing sort of language is discourse about the uses of language itself, the sort of heavy crème of discourse that reveals its particular constitutive effects at the metalevel.

The figure of the voice is the thing that defies a separation between "culture" and "media." On the one hand, the voice is quite clearly the medium that generates social meanings and social positions, or all that is classically thought of in anthropology as "culture." On the other hand, like any other medium, the voice has social properties and a specific, contextual social history. The voice is therefore a cultural medium at both the pragmatic and the metapragmatic level. A focus on voice, subjectivity, and mediation throughout this book has theoretical implications for refining our concept of culture as emerging from a variety of mediating practices.

. . .

To do an ethnography that centers on the figure of the voice is to confound the usual categories around which many ethnographies are organized in Nepal and elsewhere. This book takes on the provocative task of writing ethnographically without having identity as the primary or indeed the main issue guiding the analysis.[20] Under the conditions of democratization, the question of identity has become especially highly charged. As Lauren Leve (2011) notes, the prominence of identity categories in international law (that is, the protection of indigenous cultures and the recognition of sexual identities as well as distinct ethnic or gender identities) suggests a "global consensus" on what is most distinctly human.[21] In Nepal, since the first decade of the 2000s, particularly in the context of rewriting the Nepali constitution, politicians in Parliament have been debating the contentious issue of creating a federal system that would allow proportional representation along ethnic and caste lines. It is possible that in a few years Nepal will be divided into distinct federal states along these lines. These political concerns about representation and identity are reinforced and reflected in much of the academic scholarship on Nepal over the past fifteen years, which has tended to focus on ethnic, religious, and caste identities (for example, Cameron 1998; Gellner 1998; Gellner 2009; Hangen 2009; Lawoti 2005; Leve 2014; Shneiderman 2009).[22] Assertions of distinct cultural groups with specific needs are often the basis for the arguments needed for these groups to be recognized by a liberal democratic state.

The legacy of colonial scholarship on Nepali identity has also contributed to contemporary cultural and political categories as well as academic scholarship. The very few colonial officers and scholars who were allowed into Nepal defined Nepalis primarily in terms of ethnic tribes and races, distinct from the castes in India (Hodgson 1874). These same categories are now being reinvoked by *ādivāsi janajāti* (indigenous ethnic nationalist) movements throughout the nation, which use ideas of ethnic and racial origins to argue for more political representation in the democratic state (Hangen 2005). Deriving from colonial scholarship, much of the scholarly work in the Kathmandu Valley has tended to focus on the language and ethnic group of Newars, known from colonial times to be the original inhabitants of the Valley and its authentic bearers of culture (Gellner 1992; Leve 2014; Levy 1990; Lewis 1999; Rankin 2004; Slusser 1982).

While the Nepali state saw itself as a pure Hindu realm during colonial times (Burghart 1996), colonial officers and foreign scholars often envisioned the Kathmandu Valley as a pure and unchanged version of India, where ancient forms of Indian Buddhism flourished, unsullied by the forces of colonialism.[23] Newars were the group that most clearly exhibited this ancient form of Buddhism. As the French Sanskrit scholar and ethnologist Sylvain Lévi wrote at the turn of the century, Nepal—by which he meant the Kathmandu Valley—was a laboratory to observe "India in the making" (1905: 37).[24] Newars became the primary local informants for many of these British officers, who passed down their contacts over the years, so that the descendants of research assistants to colonial scholars have often become the assistants to contemporary scholars of Newar society. Yet even within Newar society, there are great divisions of caste and religion (though often the line between Buddhist and Hindu practices is blurry in many Newar practices), and it clear that Newars do not come from a single origin (Gellner 2009).

Many of the people I got to know well over the years in Kathmandu, whose lives and voices enter this ethnography, are Newar. Along with Brahmins and Chetris, Newars are dominant in public culture in Kathmandu. I learned some of the Newari language, but conversed with them primarily in Nepali. I do not, however, describe these Nepalis primarily from the perspective of their ethnicity or identity; instead, Newars are part of the broader urban culture of Kathmandu that includes many other ethnic groups. The idea of *not* writing about ethnic or caste identity at this time in Nepal may itself seem like a political statement. But an ethnography in the metropole of a rapidly urbanizing country, with field sites that include broadcast radio and a national legal reform movement, challenges the viability of framing this study exclusively through identity categories. By shifting our emphasis away from a single identity to the figure of the voice—in everyday conversation, media representations, and practices of recognition—we see the effects of voice not only on social identity, but also on the temporal and perceptual field through which people come to recognize themselves as social and political beings.

In the beginning of 2003, one of FM radio's most popular radio hosts, Kalyan Gautum, whom I discuss in chapter 4, published a book of story-letters that serve as the foundation of his program called *Mero Kathā, Mero Gīt* (My story, my song). In the preface to this book, Kalyan illustrates the close relationship between an intimate story and its public expression. Attempting to account for the popularity of his show among youth, he writes:

> If [youth] run out of money, they can go to their parents. If someone hits [them], [they] can go to their teacher. If someone steals [their] property, they can go to the police, to an administration, to a court of law. But if one's feelings have been shattered, where does one go? Where is the place to unburden one's wounds? Where is the court of law *(khoi adālat)?* Where is the place of justice *(khoi nyayapālikā)?* My *Mero Kathā, Mero Gīt* program is designed to be such a place of justice. (Gautum v.s. 2059: 10)

The idea that one's desires *ought* to be expressed is perhaps one of the key transformations in public life in Kathmandu after 1990. What desires one ought to publicize ranged from the political demands of underrepresented social groups to the intimate sentiments broadcast on programs like Kalyan's *Mero Kathā, Mero Gīt.* The figure of the voice has become a symbol and medium of these expressed desires, a sign of transformation, authenticity, and interior worlds. Kalyan advertises his program as a forum for individuals to voice their feelings of sadness, distress, and betrayal, a forum that he claims has not ever existed. And this is not just on Kalyan's program. A host of other FM programs, weekly magazines, newspapers, and television serials demonstrate this inextricable link between intimacy and publicity that has become ubiquitous in Kathmandu.

The examples of public intimacy I discuss here are modern forms of recognition and urban sociality that relate to personhood and voice.[25] By voicing their desires in public, strangers begin to relate to one another as intimates, creating what Michael Warner (2002) calls the stranger intimacy of modernity. Stranger intimacy is a prerequisite for Jürgen Habermas's model of the bourgeois public sphere. As Habermas argues, democratic politics and rational discourse depend upon this cultivated intimacy between strangers. While Habermas (1989) suggests that stranger intimacy in the public sphere was made possible by the forms of intimacy cultivated in the modern conjugal family through diaries and personal letters, he also contends that this cultivated intimacy of the family is transformed into the abstracted public sphere of democratic citizens, where rational debate can take place. When intimacy and affect become the *subject* and not the mode of interaction, Habermas suggests that a process of depoliticization is underway.

Stranger intimacy and a sense of belonging to a wider cultural and national sphere are clearly crucial to the emerging Kathmandu publics. But my discussion of public intimacy reveal forms of public expression that are not fully anticipated by the models that Habermas describes. During a key moment of democratic reform, the discussion of intimate matters—girlfriends and boyfriends, failed marriages, sexual desires and problems—was a fundamental part of public discourse in Nepal. This discourse was highly politicized, for it performatively reshaped social hierarchies and relations that were inscribed in how, to whom, and what one spoke about in public. Popular media and affective practices very often shape public sensibilities, and as Charles Hirschkind (2006) argues, sentiments deeply influence people's understanding of themselves and of political method. Habermas's model further presumes that the newly constituted publics that rely on stranger intimacy do not, in turn, reshape intimate, private lives (Özyürek 2006). In fact, as Esra Özyürek shows for Turkey and I show for Nepal, intimate lives are profoundly reshaped—in practice and in representation—by discussions of intimate affairs in a host of public forums and mass media.

The very idea of having an "intimate life" to share comes into being precisely through the public expression of sentiment and intimate affairs within a newly constituted, democratic public sphere.[26] As several people told me, in discussions about radio programs or simply about their own reflections on themselves today: "I never knew what I wanted or how to talk for myself. But now I do." This talk about oneself is both political and intimate, involving radical critiques of the state and the reformation of sentiments in public and domestic spaces. To distinguish my analysis from Habermas's celebration of the rational subject of the modern public sphere, I discuss the ubiquitous "affective publics" (chapter 4) emerging on FM radio, which produce intimate subjects that are integrally connected to political subjects of democracy.

Public intimacy hinges on a tension between the purported timeless universalism of an intimate and interior self and the cultural and historical contingencies that enable this discourse and form of personhood to emerge at this moment in Nepal's history. Public intimacy seems to provide a language for people to express their close relation to one another as *human beings.*[27] The humanism inherent in public intimacy creates a fiction of equality, where social hierarchies of caste, gender, ethnicity, race, and class are submerged in favor of relations that appear to recognize the mutual humanity of all people. In the ethnography that follows, these ideals of liberal humanism appear in different yet sometimes overlapping forms. Legal activists of the 1990s argued that a daughter's right to inherit property would create the possibility of authentic intimate relations between husband and wife; it would enable women to voice their desires in the home and be recognized as true *human beings.* Many FM hosts I talked with claimed that while their program addressed a particular group of Nepali listeners, the program discussed themes such as "love" that applied to everyone. "Love has always been going on, everywhere, with everyone," one of the FM managers told me.[28] "It's a phenomenon, everyone knows about it. So why hide it? If love is there love is there *ni.*[29] What's wrong with talking about it?" While the public expression of intimacy appears to be made possible through FM programming and other participatory media, the forms of attachment are imagined to be timeless and universal. I trace the emergence of this timeless discourse about intimacy and the necessity to express it by showing it to be contingent on new technologies of communication and emerging discourses of democracy, justice, and self that characterized public life in Kathmandu during the mid-1990s and early 2000s.

Like the universalism implicit in public intimacy, discourse about the voice—a force of consciousness and change—is often thought to be something every human being has, though not everyone has access to its expression. "Raising one's voice" *(āwāj uṭhāune)* becomes a liberal motto that suggests a universal consciousness and capability inherent in all human beings. This union of consciousness and voice implies the presence of an interior, self-reflective self, a quality that scholars of modernity have persuasively argued defines modern subjectivity (for example, Foucault 1978; Taylor 1989). In Nepal, this modern interiority of the self has been produced in the educated and literate class of Nepalis since the mid-twentieth century in novels and short stories.[30] There has simply been an expansion of its forms with the proliferation of new participatory mass media in the 1990s. Voice and public intimacy, I argue here, coconstruct these contemporary ideas of interiority.

Even though this quality of an interior self appears to be an a priori essence of a person, the seemingly timeless and universal "essence" emerges through historically specific practices of mediation—through public protest, law, national rituals, everyday greetings, and mass media such as radio, television, and film. Furthermore, in tension with the presumed universal and timeless expressions of romantic love, there are other expressions of public intimacy that do not rely on liberal notions of universal equality. Instead, they construct attachments and intimacies that support gender divisions in the family and asymmetries between king and subject, between brothers and sisters, and between higher and lower coworkers and politicians. By juxtaposing these different expressions of public intimacy, we encounter models of voice that differ from liberal notions of *āwāj uṭhāune*.

HISTORIES OF VOICE, HISTORIES OF PUBLICS IN KATHMANDU

Invoking "voice," directly or indirectly, Nepalis were often discussing a nexus of three related ideas: agency; interior consciousness; and directness, presence, or transparency. These ideas are fundamental in shaping people's perceptions of themselves and of the ideal ways of being and knowing in this particular moment in Kathmandu. Subtle shifts in the understanding of voice can be seen after 1990, in the increasing association of voice with the agency of the individual speaker. During the period of the King's Panchāyat government (1951–90), the state had imposed laws that banned not only political parties, but also meetings in public and the publication or broadcast of any material that spoke directly against the king. Panchāyat nationalism was founded on a monarchical version of Hinduism, ideas of *bikās* (development), and the Nepali language, all of which were actively promoted in state media and schools. While there were harsh censorship rules in place during this period, they were not always strictly observed. All newspapers not granted approval by the government were banned, but the government did very little to enforce this ban unless the paper publicly criticized the king (Raeper and Hoftun 1992: 15). Papers were shut down either by the government buying them or by seizing whole editions of the paper and putting journalists and editors in jail. In response to such measures, similar critiques would appear in a new newspaper with a different name a few weeks later. As Raeper and Martin point out, the press could publish material about the activities of political parties as long as they labeled the party as "banned" in parenthesis before the party's name (15). Though political parties were banned, there was very little intervention in their political activities at home, as long as they did not organize public events (Burghart 1996: 308).

The ethnographic historian of Nepal Richard Burghart, who devoted his life to writing about the Nepali state and the idiom of Hinduism and kingly power woven into its fabric, wrote one of his last essays about the relationship between voice and listening in the mid-1980s. Burghart's analysis of the 1980s suggests fascinating connections between interiority, voice, and agency, which shifted somewhat in the period of time I discuss in this book. His essay "The Conditions of Listening" aims to discover how under conditions of severe censorship, Nepali critics of the state could be heard by the king, who officially denounced the possibility of criticism.[31] Burghart recognizes the double lives people lived under a monarchy that officially acknowledged only the king as the sole speaker and listener of the nation. There is the life under the king, their lord and master, and there is the life they lead separate from the state:

> The lives do not necessarily meet, and in so far as they do not, one's personal life becomes a rich inner life. Things are left unsaid, kept inside one's mind, mentioned only to close friends. In the public arena there are no rival truths; rather there is simply truth surrounded by some ironic detachment. By double lives I do not refer to different roles ... but to desire and its constraint. It is the awareness of how one is constrained in a situation, so that one cannot express how one would like to be, that gets one's double life going. (Burghart 1996: 306)

The inner life of a person, or what is perceived to be one's authentic feeling, was not linked to what was said in public, but rather, to what was not said. In a moment when public speech against the government (that is, the king) was considered treason, irony, indirection, and insincere praise became a prevalent mode of expressing one's opinion, particularly if it differed from the official line (Burghart 1996: 306). Much of the public protest occurred through provocative silences that indicated the inability to be heard.[32]

The People's Movement in 1990 ushered in neoliberal economic and social changes that made possible a sudden proliferation in novel avenues for public speech. Public speech transformed from being primarily a screen behind which authentic desires were hidden to becoming a vehicle and sign of authenticity, truth, and interiority. As we will see in chapters 4 through 6, FM radio hosts began promoting their programs as a place to "say what you always wanted to say." *The Kathmandu Post,* one of the largest English-language newspapers, advertised itself as a place where "*Your* Values, *Your* Voices Always Stand Higher with Us." (See figure 1 at the beginning of the chapter. The photograph in the billboard depicts the annual Newar festival of *Machendranath,* when a chariot is pulled around the circumference of the city.) One student union involved in the protests in 2006 printed T-shirts that read, "Our Politics, Our Choice" or "My Voice Counts." (See cover photo.) Being able to state one's desires directly, whether political or personal, was accorded novel value and associated clearly with the figure of the voice.[33]

The inner life that Burghart suggests remained hidden, unspoken, or only shared with close friends in the 1980s became more regularly a subject of public expression, circulation, and even exhibition in the 1990s. The idea of the voice became much broader than simply being the idea of political critique or agency (as in the phrase, "having a voice"). Instead, voicing one's desires became a new way to imagine oneself, a way to contrast one's "older" and "newer" self, in short, a way to reconfigure subjectivity through modes of address and public expression made possible by modern technology and neoliberal politics associated in Nepal particularly with the world of development *(bikās).*

These changes brought forth a more active public sphere in Nepal, a space of discursive interaction, unattached to the state, through which people could presumably deliberate about common interests (Habermas 1989). In these deliberations, people were addressed in terms that made them rethink who they were as individuals and as collectivities. Public space was transformed through a range of mediated practices, including privatized television, FM radio, and a host of new dailies and weekly papers, as well as discussion groups around intellectual or political subjects that were organized around the city. The figure of the voice quickly came to stand for these emerging publics and the consciousness of these collective groups.

After 1990, citizen speakers—rather than the king—began to hear themselves speak. *Āwāj uṭhāune* now not only indicated political agency, but also implied the true, interior state of the speaker, relating directly to either a collective group or an individual's consciousness. It related specifically to the ability and desire to speak out in public, as well as to the growing public sphere. Enabled by the constitution of 1990, the number of newspapers rose from 459 registered newspapers in 1985 to 1536 in 2000;[34] and FM radio, which was established in 1996, transformed quickly from a single, semiprivate FM 100 broadcast exclusively for the Kathmandu Valley to over one hundred stations throughout the nation. In 1990, virtually no family I knew had a telephone; most would rely on corner shops for their calls. At that time, people would gather around a single neighborhood television to watch the weekly episode of the Hindu epic the *Mahābhārat* and would listen to Radio Nepal primarily for the news.

When I stayed in Nepal in 2007 and 2008, nearly every middle class family I knew had both a landline and mobile phones, often for each member of the family, and most Kathmandu families I visited had more than one television inside the house. Of course, such rapid transformations in domestic technology are evident in many places (including the United States), but in Nepal these transformations register the profound effects of particularly rapid neoliberal privatization and a stunning growth in the remittance economy, produced by Nepalis working abroad, that has marked the 1990s and early 2000s.[35] These economic and technological changes, which form the backdrop of this book, paved the way for the novel forms of mediation that took shape in the emerging publics of the 1990s and early 2000s.

This burst in private media is clearly connected to a significant rise in consumption by the middle class (Liechty 2003) and the prominence of media and technology in Kathmandu Nepalis' everyday lives. Many FM programs broadcast listeners' phone calls or narrative letters that refer explicitly to the consumption practices of FM radio—where one is listening and with whom one is listening. As Michael Warner argues, this self-reflexive circulation of mass media's own space of consumption is one of the primary ways in which a public reproduces itself (2002: 66). Clearly the voice is central to this process. Take the strategy pursued by the property reform activists in the 1990s that I discuss in chapter 2. They rode on public buses and loudly discussed the legal reform movement among themselves first and then with strangers, reflexively referring to themselves and their aims. In doing so, they created a public discourse about the reform bill and a public that emerged in discussion of this issue. When activists hear their discourse in the conversations of strangers and FM listeners and hosts hear their voices mediated through the radio box, they come to recognize themselves as if from a distance. This "close distance" (Mazzarella 2003) is central to all forms of mediation in this book, and central to the process through which subjects and their identities come into being.

The figure of the voice became key to discussions of *pāradarshitā* (transparency), a keyword frequently invoked to discuss a less corrupt and more participatory government, which was associated in much of the journalism after the *jana āndolan* in 1990 with transparent communication. Some of this language of transparency no doubt came from the establishment of Transparency International Nepal (TIN) after 1996. Among their most pressing activities, TIN lists the distribution of stories and information through "various media engagement," including newspapers, FM radio, the establishment of a TIN library, and publications (TIN 2000: 19–20). This transparency was made possible through the new media and technologies that became prevalent after 1990. In a section titled "Strengthening Mechanisms of Voice and Transparency" the media journalist Dev Raj Dahal writes, "In Nepal, computerised networking of local private offices, government ministries and departments is gradually introducing transparency in their activities and operations and creating a bridge between the state and society. This process is expected to build a culture of trust. In other words, technology has a key role to play in governance" (2002: 35). The political voice espouses such ideals of transparency alongside the notion that "voice" is thought to be the direct route to a particular groups' consciousness and desire.

Transparency loomed large as an ideal and structuring principle of democracies, particularly after the wave of emerging democracies and the unimpeded triumph of liberal political economies around the world that followed the collapse of the Berlin Wall, of which the *jana āndolan* of 1990 was part.[36] Ideas of liberal change during Gorbachev's *perestroika,* or restructuring of the state, were signified by the term *glasnost,* "voicing, or making something known" (Pesman 2000: 7). The implication is that through voicing there is an opening up and revealing of things that previously were kept hidden, secret, or secluded from public view, a process that is enabled by and depends upon media. Nepali political leaders at the time were inspired by these transitions in Eastern Europe. "With Gorbachev's announcement of perestroika and glasnost," said Ganesh Man Singh, one of the key political leaders in the *jana āndolan* in 1990, "something like this became possible even in Nepal" (quoted in Raeper and Hoftun 1992: 97). Similar to *glasnost,* the notion of being able to talk in public after *jana āndolan* I (1990), despite persisting forms of censorship and self-censorship, contrasted deeply with the censorship during Panchāyat government that proceeded it, and *āwāj uṭhāune* was one mode of signifying this change.

The ideology of transparency to describe a less corrupt, more participatory form of government and this ideology's association with liberalizing political regimes have parallels in many parts of the world (West and Sanders 2003). Quite often, it is used not only to signify good governance but also, more specifically, to mark a shift in political power or in modern political regimes. Interestingly, these political ideals are elsewhere often associated with a particular technological innovation or mediated expression that makes the ideals of transparency material and sometimes even visible.[37] In Nepal, dreams of transparency are often expressed through reference to the technology of radio, particularly FM radio, and the seemingly unmediated quality of the voice it conveys.

Over the past fifteen years, then, *āwāj uṭhāune* has come to signify speech, political or otherwise, that is especially associated with political and social changes brought on by the various democratic movements. In this sense, it resonates with the metaphor of voice used in Euro-American discourses to describe consciousness and empowerment, particularly among groups of people who have not been adequately represented in the politics of history. The link between voice and political agency is evident, for example, in a host of feminist writings, such as Carol Gilligan's well-known *In a Different Voice* (1982) or the feminist academic journal *Voices*. It also appears in the quest of the subaltern-studies historians of South Asia for a story (often through oral history) that remains outside the purview of the state and has therefore not yet been recorded in official history (Guha 1996).[38] This link can also be seen in the world of international development that affects Nepal directly in a World Bank (2002) report on poverty in South Asia titled *Voices of the Poor* that projected a direct connection between their findings and the organization's ability to "speak to/for the real world" of impoverished people. It is this collusion of agency and voice that Gyatri Spivak (1988) takes issue with in her controversial essay "Can the Subaltern Speak?"

While *āwāj uṭhāune* might be, at first glance, considered a local translation of the liberal global discourse of "voice," the term *āwāj* is a global discourse in its own right that resonates in many parts of the Global South. Often associated with radical politics in several regions of South Asia,[39] *āwāj* is a common name for left-leaning newspapers throughout South Asia as well as in Kenya, where there is a large South Asian population. Because of the term's global reach outside the hegemonic media sources produced in Europe and North America, exploring the global and local political significance of *āwāj* (as opposed to the English term "voice") is a way to "provincialize" Euro-American discourses of voice, in the same manner that Dipesh Chakrabarty (2000) proposes provincializing Europe in the reconstruction of Indian history. The act of provincializing Europe through the term *āwāj* is neatly captured in the global leftist political and civic movement organized by Avaaz. org, which advertises its name as "meaning 'voice' in several European, Middle Eastern and Asian languages" (www.avaaz.org). Ostensibly derived from the

Persian term *avaaz,* which also means "sound" or "song," most South Asian versions of the term similarly contain both a political and a sonic meaning, and these two meanings often overlap. The Awaaz Foundation of Mumbai, for example, is an environmental activist organization that devotes itself, among many other things, to solving the problem of "noise pollution." Among their targets are extremely loud political rallies and the crackly, often incomprehensible loudspeakers that travel around the city (and throughout South Asia) on electric rickshaws announcing political processions or religious festivals.

Both of these meanings of *āwāj* came together, for example, in many of the political protests during and after the *jana āndolan* in 1990. During the nineteen-day curfew in April 2006, for example, in addition to flooding the streets against the king's orders, people frequently would go to the top of their roofs and bang metal plates with spoons. The effect was an almost deafening noise that some explained as a method of humiliating King Gyanendra. It was as if to say to the king: "You say you will not hear or listen to us by declaring curfew, but we will, from within the confines of our houses, make sure that you literally *hear* the sound of our discontent." A similar tactic of beating drums, pots, and pans has been deployed by many different protesters, such as the group of *kamaiyā* (bonded laborers) who, in their protests in Kathmandu, sought to "wake up the conscience of the government officials" (Fujikura 2007: 343). In both of these instances, as well as many others, an effective form of *āwāj uṭhāune* was paradoxically without words. The *āwāj* of banging and beating loud instruments became a political tool for asserting discontent and making one's presence audibly heard.

The figure of the voice continued to recur with particular force in the years after 1990, each time invoked as if it were something new. During the *jana āndolan* II, which culminated in April 2006, articles appeared in newspapers with titles such as "Election of the Student Union and the Loktantrik (Democratic) Voice" (in *Kantipur* on February 22, 2006) and "Voice against the Monarchy" (in *The Kathmandu Post* on January 4, 2006). Kanak Mani Dixit, a prominent Kathmandu intellectual and the editor of *Himal South Asia,* wrote from his prison cell, where he was secluded for a brief time during the movement in April 2006: "A voiceless people discovered their powers of speech; they developed a confidence unprecedented in their history" (2006). In all of these invocations, the figure of the voice becomes a sign that stands for action, for change, and for the consciousness of the people whose "voice" is animated.

From the outset, *Voicing Subjects* complicates the common metaphor of voice used by Nepali activists and intellectuals, international aid workers, and Euro-American scholars. All of these different representations have tended, in distinctive ways, to fetishize the voice as providing direct access to consciousness and agency, particularly of marginalized peoples. The human rights organizations that proliferated during the 1990s, particularly those linked to the Maoist civil war (1996–2006), often treated the face and voice as seemingly transparent mediums conveying sentimental and political messages. Those working to recover the thousands of disappeared people during this war would circulate their photographs through the newspapers and other media, stating that finally the families' "voices have been heard." But this notion of direct access to a group or person's consciousness obscures the processes of mediation that take place in and through the voice. The notions of presence and directness associated with the voice are effects of an ideology of voice linked to many of the liberal and democratic reforms that characterize this moment.

VOICING SUBJECTS

The title of this book, *Voicing Subjects,* aims to highlight the work of voice in creating subjectivity and the subjects' practice of speaking or voicing. The term *subjects* is suggestive of two important and seemingly contradictory forms of personhood. On the one hand, "subject" refers to the way individuals come to see themselves as a particular kind of social actor (as in the grammatical subject), with a particular identity, through which others also recognize him or her. In this meaning, a person suddenly recognizes that they are a "woman" or a "Buddhist" and are expected to perform in a particular way to sustain that identity. On the other hand, the very idea of subjecthood is bound up with power, as in the power of a sovereign who rules over his or her "subjects." "There are two meanings of the word *subject*," writes Foucault, "subject to someone else by control and dependence, and tied to his own identity by a conscience or self-knowledge. Both meanings suggest a form of power which subjugates and makes subject to" (1982: 212). Saba Mahmood describes this paradox succinctly: "the very processes and conditions that secure a subject's subordination are also the means by which she becomes a self-conscious identity and agent" (2005: 17). *Voicing Subjects* explores this paradox by discussing the ways in which voice and other related forms of mediation are implicated in producing these different meanings of subjectivity.

During the fifteen years this book describes, both of these meanings of subjecthood were under drastic transformation. As I have described above, a range of novel subject positions, linked to ideas about possessing a conscious interior self and the desire to participate in public culture, emerged in the period following the *jana āndolan* in 1990 through the figure of the voice and novel forms of speech and media. It was also during this time that political rule was in crisis, from the establishment of a multiparty democracy in 1990, through the decade-long civil war with the Maoists (1996–2006), and finally to the dissolution of the 240-year-old monarchy in 2007–08. Shifts in the term for democracy responded to these changes. In 1990, the term for democracy was *prajātantra,* a term that includes the idea of a king's power over his subjects through the word *prajā,* or "subject (of a ruler)" (Turner 1931: 394). As the nature of the monarchy became increasingly unstable, from the time of the massacre at Narayanhiti palace through the second People's Movement in 2006, people began using the term *loktantra* (*lok* means "folk" or "people," rather than "subject") to describe a democracy without a king. In both of these meanings, the nature of political and intimate subjectivity was being reshaped, and these transformations were registered through the figure of the voice. Each chapter examines a different site in which this reshaping of political and intimate subjectivity took place from the mid-1990s through 2010.

In the mid-1990s, several legal reforms took place that challenged the constitution, which had been rewritten after the *jana āndolan* in 1990. The first of these constitutional challenges was the heated legal reform movement of the 1990s that sought to entitle daughters, like sons, to a share of their parents' ancestral property. Activists declared that the existing inheritance law, which gave a birthright to sons, was unconstitutional. In the first chapter, I discuss this legal reform movement by looking at two competing formations of voice mobilized through the activism and opposition to the proposed law. Giving daughters such property rights, activists argued, would empower women by giving them a voice in the family to resist oppression and a form of selfhood with which to engage in modern relations of romantic love. Opponents (including many women) argued that such a change would undermine the idealized love shared between brothers and sisters, particularly the practices of *bolāune* (to call, invite, or, literally, "to cause someone to speak") in which brothers call their married sisters home for family gatherings and holidays. At stake in this debate were two radically different structures of recognition and subjectivity: liberalized notions of voice that align identity, experience, and point of view (Keane 1999) and a nonliberal form of familial recognition produced by practices of *bolāune*.

This chapter presents challenges to a strictly liberal feminist reading of this property reform movement by drawing on Saba Mahmood's persuasive argument about nonliberal forms of subjectivity among pious women in Egypt. As Mahmood (2005) argues, liberal theories of subjectivity (including feminism) assume a modern subject to be a person whose agency is defined *against* rather than in support of a cultural norm. These normative assumptions preclude any deep analysis of nonliberal, modern subjectivities, as is produced through practices like *bolāune*. Implicitly, I argue, the debate centered on which mode of voicing, along with which attendant ideas of love, family recognition, and genealogy, should prevail.

To deepen our understandings of the forms of subjectivity and familial recognition produced in practices like *bolāune,* I turn to Nepali ritual and everyday practices of looking at faces *(mukh herne).* As I argue in chapter 2, the face and the voice share a "semiotic ideology" (Keane 2003) insofar as both work as indices of immediacy, presence, and social intimacy (often along familial and genealogical lines). *Mukh herne* greetings and rituals extend my discussion of family recognition by looking at the way the face, like the voice, becomes a mediating site for structuring intimate relations and spoken utterance. The term for face *(mukh)* is the same term for mouth, and ideas about whose face one should or should not encounter are bound up with ideas about who one can and cannot talk to. From national rituals of beholding the king's image and seeing one's mother's or father's face *(āmā/ buāko mukh herne din)* to the everyday intimate exchange of glances between people on the street, I explore these different forms of "tactile seeing" as expressions of intersubjectivity and merging between people. "Tactile seeing" challenges common philosophical understandings which often presume that seeing is opposed to aurality (Sterne 2003) and that visuality is about distancing, objectification, and drawing distinctions between individuals (hence, a quintessentially modern understanding) (Crary 1990; Jay 1993). In the discourse and practices of *mukh herne,* we see that visuality and aurality are thoroughly entangled with each other. In showing the face to be a complex medium of interaction, this chapter argues against the assumption that face-to-face interaction offers direct, unmediated contact between people. Instead, it must be situated alongside other forms of mediation, such as the radio or telephone.

In the next three chapters, I address the figure of the voice through analysis of two prominent technologies of voice—the FM radio and the telephone. Established in 1996, the highly interactive FM radio became a symbol of democratic free speech and offered the possibility of speaking out against the state (Dahal 2002; Onta 2003, 2006; Onta and Mainali 2002; Parajuli and Onta 2003). At the same time, listeners speak of its powerful appeal in terms of the direct emotions conveyed by the sound of the radio host's voice and the broadcast of listeners' intimate narratives (Kunreuther 2004). The novel FM radio invokes, then, both the political and the intimate mode of voice.

A cultural history of FM stations (chapter 3) shows the way in which FM programming cultivates a particular sensibility toward time as well as political and intimate subjectivities. This effect is achieved through a sense of directness and transparency associated with FM radio, at the level of both the technological form and the content of its programs. At the level of form, for example, the exclusively live broadcasting in its initial stages and the better quality of sound facilitated the illusion of presence and directness associated with FM radio speak, making it an ideal medium for forwarding the program of democracy. Many of the programs on FM radio encouraged a kind of talk associated with "being direct," particularly about intimate and personal matters, which is also formative of listener's subjectivity. Directness is clearly associated not only with what one says, but with how one says it: the voice as a medium is critical to achieving this sense of transparency and directness. Throughout this chapter, I discuss the extent to which the FM radio aided the *jana āndolan* in 2006, as well as to what extent it illustrates what Lauren Berlant (1997) describes as a colonization of the public by the private. While FM programs advertise themselves as places to "say what you always wanted to say," the genre of expression and acceptable content was initially limited by government licenses that banned explicit discussion of politics. Furthermore, the emphasis on personal expression reveals connections to neoliberal ideology in which work on the self is conceived of as a critical form of political expression. Yet to reduce FM radio only to its privatized, antipolitical effects, I argue, fails to recognize the ways in which FM personnel engaged in protests against several moments of censorship and the place FM programming created for people to interact and imagine themselves as actively involved in a wider public.

To fully understand the politics of public intimacy, I turn to an analysis of one popular program that draws upon the intimate and suffering lives of its listeners as the basis of its broadcast. *Mero Kathā, Mero Gīt* (My story, my song), on the one hand, constitutes ideas of interiority that are central to the figure of the voice and modern subjectivity and, on the other, demonstrates how public intimacy is supported by the distinctive sound of the radio host's voice. The program is based upon "life stories" sent by listeners about their failed love affairs that are read over the air by the host in a style that listeners feel make their stories seem more true or real. These voiced writings are interspersed with Nepali folk or pop songs that add another important quality of voiced sound to the texts. In this chapter, I trace the conflicting perspectives on the purpose of the show that often arise between the program's host, Kalyan Gautum, and his audience. I discuss Kalyan as the quintessential Kathmandu entrepreneur and neoliberal subject, who uses his listeners' stories as material through which he can cultivate his own self-image. His listeners are also interested in gaining recognition, but they are not seeking therapeutic advice to "work" on themselves. Instead, they seek recognition by both familiars and strangers in a moral community. Several genealogies intersect in shaping the genre of voiced writing and the program's overall form, including discourses of *dukha* (pain, suffering) in Nepali literature, narratives of popular Indian film, the genre of personal love letters (Ahearn 2001), the discourse of development, and the national imaginings of villages (Pigg 1992).

The final chapter discusses the vastly expanding Nepali diaspora and its significance within Kathmandu. The importance of the diaspora within the life of Kathmandu is an effect of the media that represent it within the publics of the city. I focus on how the diaspora is *heard* and *voiced* through the FM radio and the telephone. Unlike many studies of diaspora that define diaspora communities in terms of territory or a particular community abroad (for example, Schiller-Glick and Fouron 2001; Shukla 2003; van der Veer 1995), this chapter suggests that the temporality and affect produced through technology (telephone, internet, FM radio) constitute the category of Nepali diaspora in Kathmandu (Axel 2002; Kunreuther 2006). The focus is on a short-lived program called *Rumpum Connection,* which broadcast three-minute telephone calls between Kathmandu residents and their friends or families abroad. On this program the most intimate and most common conversations center on future or past telephone calls, letters, and emails. This excess of discourse about other technologies of connection I call "technological phatic" speech. Like other forms of phatic speech, such references to past or future communications simply reiterate the strange fact that people seem to "connect" through technology. Consideration of voice and the diaspora reveals transnational features of the Kathmandu publics made possible through technological mediation.

In the epilogue, I return to the subject of the royal massacre in June 2001 as an incident that refracts many of themes I have discussed throughout the book: the relationship between media, transparency, and voice; competing ideas of political subjectivity as the monarchy itself was in question; and the politics of public intimacy. Questions of censorship emerge anew here, but now in a context that has been already thoroughly saturated by a booming public sphere.

When I returned to Kathmandu for my last extended stint of fieldwork in 2007–08, I frequently rode on the same route I had traveled with Raj Gopal many years before. While the general outline of the built environment remained the same, there were palpable differences in the uses, appearance, and significance of the cityscape. The so-called suburbs of Baneshewar were filled in with so many more cement houses, private schools and colleges, and international NGOs that it was hard to imagine this area was ever considered the periphery to the center. The open space of the Tundikhel was no longer the site of royal functions or demonstrations of the royal army. It now was open to the general public to serve as a space for massive political gatherings, for performances of cultural programs, and even for mass yoga classes, as when the famous Indian yogi, Ram Dev Baba, came to town. Singha Durbar, or "the lion palace," that Raj Gopal told me was the home to many government offices still houses those same offices, but now includes the Parliament, which comprises several different political parties. In 2008, the tree-lined palace where Raj Gopal had scolded me for speaking too loudly about the king was on the verge of a radical transformation. Just months after I left, Nepal was officially declared a republic and the palace was almost immediately turned into a museum, opening its grounds and the building to the public on weekdays.

Evidence of the vast amounts of money that has flowed into the capitol city was also striking in contrast to my ride in 1989. Across from the palace, the neoclassical gardens of a former Rana ruler had been renovated by a German NGO and private donors. This "Garden of Dreams" became a park space that nostalgically recalls the Rana rule and in 2007 it was largely populated by foreigners and some Nepali students, who can enter for a fee. I now traveled largely by taxi instead of motorbike or bicycle, because of my own fear of the vastly increased traffic, and there was always music or a talk program from one of the FM stations blaring through the taxi's windows. Glossy billboards punctured the skyline, advertising one of the many media forms that has emerged since that time, Western Union, and other money transfer companies that testify to the enormous remittance economy in the Valley. In addition to mobile phones, many of my middle class friends were buying or saving money to buy a car. Within this somewhat changed city and soundscape, new and old forms of mediation intersect to shape urban residents political and intimate lives. By looking at formations of voice that are both historically and culturally contingent, we can see this dramatic period in Nepal's history as one where Nepalis come to understand themselves as voicing subjects within the limits and possibilities of a host of emerging publics.

ONE

Intimate Callings and Voices of Reform

LAW, PROPERTY, AND FAMILIAL LOVE

> We believe that feelings are immutable, but every sentiment, particularly the noblest and most disinterested, has a history.
>
> MICHEL FOUCAULT, *"Nietzsche, Genealogy, History"*

> A son's property is *angsa* (family property); a daughter's property is *māyā* (love).
>
> *Common Nepali saying*

ON A SPRING AFTERNOON IN 1998, I witnessed a small event in Nepal that was a common sight at the time. Several young women, dressed in saris and sandals, were standing at the central Palace Square of Patan (a city adjacent to Kathmandu). Behind them lay a white sheet draped across the palace stones and decorated with hundreds of signatures scribbled in thick magic marker that they later paraded around the city. This was one of the numerous demonstrations organized around the hotly debated legal movement that argued for a daughter's birthright to her parent's ancestral property or *angsa*.[1] *Angsa* literally means "share" or "portion," and it refers to the share of joint property of land or houses passed from grandfather to father to son. Until recently, all sons and their mother had equal inheritance rights to a share of *angsa* from the father's family. Daughters only received *angsa* through marriage or from their parents if they remained unmarried until age thirty-five. While the activists stood at the Palace Square and as they walked through the city, they yelled into a microphone at pedestrians who passed by on the street: "Women should have equal rights to property! Women of Nepal are also citizens! We deserve our equal rights! Sign here for freedom and equality! Raise your voices for women!"

In this chapter, I discuss the invocation of voice by contemporary activists of the property reform movement alongside a competing formation of voice,

FIGURE 3. Family tree tracing the lines of a father's genealogy (*vamsa*). The falling leaves are daughters; the branches are sons who inherit property (*angsa*). Photo: Daniel Karpowitz.

linked to intimacies of home, that emerged within debates about this reform. Divergent birthrights to *angsa* not only create material divisions of wealth between sons and daughter, I argue, but also produce gendered divisions of speech and action, which are particularly evident in this second formation of voice. To trace the different meanings of voice at play in this *angsa* reform movement is to trace the links between class and gender subjectivities, both of which are inseparable from property relations and different ideologies of intimacy. In my analysis, I pay close attention not only to the arguments of liberal reformers, but also to the words of people who opposed the introduction of a new right for daughters. It is here where we begin to see the links between voice, subjectivity, and *angsa* unfold.

The *angsa* campaign highlights several social issues that have characterized the period of democratic reforms after 1990. The reform movement was one of the early examples of an attempt to destabilize the center and the foundation of the state, albeit an attempt undertaken from *within* the state apparatus, the law.[2] It also resonates with other attempts to reimagine a New Nepal today, from those of the Maoists to those of the southern Madeshi separatists,[3] which are also contests about property relations. In these other attempts as well, people in Nepal are imagined as "raising their voices." While clearly a national issue, there are many Nepalis, such as *sukumbāsī* (squatter communities), *kamaiyā* (former bonded laborers), and many *dalit* (low-caste) families, who do not have property to inherit or to pass down. Their relationship to landed property involves complex interfamily relations within villages or in the urban center, which differ considerably from the middle- and lower-middle-class urbanities I discuss here.[4] While I do not address the specific ways in which this law affects such groups, it is worth noting that people without property still share certain key cultural concepts, such as *māitī* (married woman's natal home), that figured centrally in the debates about *angsa* reforms.

The debates this reform movement generated resemble the debates that raged around the Hindu Succession Act of 1956 in India, which similarly sought to give women an equal share to their parent's property (Agarwal 1994; Basu 1999, 2001; Majumdar 2009). Yet, the Nepali solution differed significantly from the Indian one several decades earlier. In India, "the Hindu law debates made it clear that property inhered in the family, identified by its male lineage" (Majumdar 2009: 237). The *angsa* reform movement in Nepal, by contrast, was felt at the time to be one of the more radical challenges to Hindu hegemony in that it posed genuine threats to the gender relations that were a foundation of Hindu national patrimony rooted in a Hindu state. It is no surprise, then, that the law granting full and equal rights to *angsa* for daughters from birth, before and after marriage, was passed in November 2006, after the interim constitution declared Nepal a secular state. Here I focus on the imagined possibilities and debates at the time about what *could happen* if this reform bill were passed, which tell us something important about deep cultural tensions around questions of class, gendered subjectivity, and voice during this period in Kathmandu.[5]

VOICES OF REFORM

Debate about this proposed property reform was a public affair. It was not secluded to bureaucratic offices nor confined to courtroom dramas. Rallies were organized. Banners of signatures in support of the reform were paraded around the city. Piles of newspaper articles and opinion pieces were written. TV serials were broadcast. Informal and staged conversations about the proposed bill could be heard on buses, in rickshaw rides, and in heated discussions on the street or in homes. The furious debates that erupted in response to the proposal for daughter's property rights forged deep clefts between religious purists and those arguing for novel democratic reforms, between conservative ideologues arguing against a shift in property relations deemed to be an "authentic and timeless Nepali tradition" and those embracing liberal paradigms who felt the existing *angsa* system hindered individual agency. All of these practices invoked the figure of the voice.

There are two distinct understandings of voice that emerged in the property reform movement. First, the notion of *āwāj uṭhāune* (raising voice) is associated with democratic participation and political consciousness, and implies a common parallel between voice and collective or individual agency. In relation to this particular reform, *āwāj uṭhāune* resembles feminist scholars' frequently invoked "voice," a metonym that stands for women's agency and desire for freedom. Within this terminology is the supposition that the voice directly channels subjectivity, and that a "subject with a voice" is a universal liberal subject who always, even in small, subversive ways, seeks freedom and autonomy from cultural, social, religious, and other traditional constraints (Mahmood 2005). Activists supporting the property law reforms frequently invoked this liberal form of voice, such that *āwāj uṭhāune* became a metaphor for "empowerment."

But those defending Nepali "tradition" appealed to a different discourse of voice. This second formation of voice emerges in the hailing practices of brothers, who call their married sisters back to the place of their birth. These practices support family intimacies and gender divisions within the family, and regulate who speaks and who replies. The two forms of voice invoked through the property law debate both suggest a close relation between voice and subjectivity, but they represent distinctions between liberal and nonliberal subjectivities in Nepal. In both cases, the figure of the voice and the politics of speaking (or being hailed) constitute different subject positions that are implicated in the debate about daughter's inheritance of *angsa*. By attending ethnographically to these different invocations of voice, rather than using them uncritically in our own scholarship, we avoid occluding the intimacies, affects, and subjectivities at stake in these legal reforms.

Activists and opponents alike viewed the *angsa* reform movement as a realization of democratic ideals and, therefore, as an effective form of *āwāj uṭhāune:* the movement worked both to engage a largely nonpolitical public sphere and to promote the first political challenges to the constitution in a multiparty democracy.[6] Activists had attempted to reform the law in two primary ways: by submitting several bills designed by NGOs and the Government's Ministry of Women to change the law, and by filing a Supreme Court case against the government. In their register associated with democratic speech, *āwāj uṭhāune* practices often seek to challenge the state at its deepest level. The lawyers involved in the campaign were proud to claim that this legal reform was the first constitutional challenge since the rewriting of the constitution in 1990. They used the new constitution's statement of equality to declare the existing *angsa* laws unconstitutional, providing precedent for future constitutional challenges. The way the campaign and controversy were staged also provided examples of different forms of voicing as political expression, from the public marches with signature banners, to the planned loud conversations on buses in which activists discussed the proposed bill with strangers and set the discourse about the reform in motion, to the ample media coverage.[7]

Finally and most poignantly, the phrase *āwāj uṭhāune* implies a connection between voice and agency that relates explicitly to the final aim of this campaign. Giving daughters equal rights to property, activists argued, would empower women by giving them a voice in the family to resist oppression; they would be able to act on their own and feel themselves to be members of their family and, more profoundly, citizens of the state. "*Angsa* is one's own property, right?" one of my friends shouted to her father, during a heated argument on the subject. "If a person has something of one's own, that person can *do* something." This ability to act is embedded within the material relations of *angsa,* and having property, like "having a voice," is deemed to be directly linked to women's agency in relation to the family and the state. Such an ability to act when given *angsa* is quite striking when we look at the biographies of the prominent women activists and lawyers involved in this campaign. Nearly all of them had received a portion of land or house from their family in the form of an *icchā patra. Icchā patra,* or "document of wish," functions much like a liberal will system; it is a legal category of inheritance law that enables a person to give away a portion of their personal property to anyone they wish. As Daniel Karpowitz (1998) shows, the significance of *icchā patra* grew when *niji ārjan* (individual or privately earned money) became a more clearly identifiable legal category in 1977. Significantly, the activists did not argue for *angsa* to be abolished and replaced with the category of *niji ārjan,* which could be willed away by an individual, as is the case in a liberal model of property law. Despite their seemingly liberal rhetoric of voice, the activists sought to retain an illiberal, Hindu form of inheritance that kept property within the family.

The alternative formation of voice invoked by those opposing the bill is tied to familial intimacies, particularly the intimate relations between brothers and sisters. When I talked to Nepalis living in Kathmandu about the bitter controversy surrounding this legal reform, most would try to explain what they thought I did not understand. The essential but implicit meanings of *angsa* needed to be spelled out to someone like myself, since I might be partial to the international groups supporting this reform.[8] Without hesitation, many would sum up their objections with the following pithy statement: "A son's property is *angsa,* and a daughter's property is love" *(Chorāko sampatī angsa, chorīko sampatī māyā ho).*

Māyā (family love)[9] is expressed most poignantly in the common practice of a brother calling his married sister back to the home of her birth. A son's inheritance and possession of *angsa,* most people told me, *requires* him to invite his married sisters home. Such visits are described using a common Nepali word, *bolāune. Bolāune* is often translated with the innocuous "inviting" or "addressing," but I prefer a more pointed English gloss that captures the social relations embedded in the word: "summoning," "calling," or "hailing."[10] Inheritance of *angsa* is, they suggest, intimately intertwined with a daughter's frequent visits home: indeed, this is where the power of *angsa* circulates. Though undocumented in the actual laws, women's frequent movement back and forth might be seen as an inscription of the written law in daily habits, marking a daughter's dislocation from her parents' home, while including her, temporarily, within a home she has left behind. Translated literally into English, *bolāune* means "to make someone else speak," and it generates a different form of recognition, speech, and agency than the activists' vision. Practices of *bolāune* are, then, constitutive of gendered subjectivities; they are the means by which people come to think of what makes a man into "a man" and a woman into "a woman."[11] The practice of *bolāune,* as everyday as it is, emerged so frequently in conversation about the reform because, I gradually learned, it reveals and defines the hierarchies of gender that the activists sought to change with the proposed new law.

PROPERTY, KINSHIP, AND "WOMEN'S VOICE": CHALLENGES TO FEMINIST INTERPRETATION

My analysis of these competing formations of voice uses crucial insights generated by anthropological studies of property and feminist analyses of kinship and family intimacy. While I draw upon many feminist theories of kinship and intimacy, from the outset this campaign poses important challenges to the standard feminist analysis that would interpret the activists as "empowering women" through the law and thereby representing a "women's voice." Such arguments do not offer a deeper understanding of the different subjectivities at stake in this campaign, and are rooted in a common feminist concern for women's agency. In the early 1990s, Saba Mahmood points out, this attention to women's agency among feminist theorists was often articulated through the rhetoric of "resistance" to structures of male dominance (2005: 10). Even among writers who problematized the notion of "resistance" as a simplistic understanding of power relations (Abu-Lughod 1990; Ahearn 2001; MacLeod 1992; Ortner 1995), feminist scholars typically remain committed to a liberal notion that all women (or all people for that matter) desire freedom from relations of subordination (culture, tradition, male dominance) (Mahmood 2005: 10–17).

Saba Mahmood's book on reimagining the feminist subject provides a model for understanding other modern subjectivities that do not fit the liberal model. As Mahmood argues, feminist analyses make certain "normative liberal assumptions about human nature" (2005: 5); feminism is, after all, a liberal discourse. These assumptions include that there is an innate desire for freedom, that all human beings assert autonomy when they can, and that human agency is exerted in acts that challenge the norms rather than uphold them (5). From Mahmood's perspective, these assumptions occlude any deep analysis of nonliberal subjectivity, such as the religious Islamic women in Egypt with whom she works who adhere to "feminine virtues" (modesty, humility, shyness) as a condition for their place in religious and political life. Religious Egyptian women, then, challenge many of the feminist assumptions about human nature. This chapter expands upon Mahmood's insights by thinking ethnographically about the various forms of voicing used in the property reform, and the different subjectivities they assume.

To begin, we must consider the question of what is property and what it does. Anthropological studies of property emphasize the social relations embedded in all property relations (Verdery and Humphrey 2004). Complicating the writings of John Locke, who saw property as a particular relation between citizen and state, anthropologists have questioned the assumed notion of personhood embedded in Euro-American concepts of private property.[12] In her study of the shift from collective farms to individual family farms in Transylvania, for example, Katherine Verdery argues that a focus on "rights" obscures a more significant change occurring in the *kinds of person* constituted by different forms of property: "Rights terminology creates only one kind of person, who has or does not have rights. Deemphasizing such language helps to reveal more clearly the different kinds of persons that property restitution creates: the efficient 'master of the land' on the one hand, and those ground down by accountability, risk, and debt on the other" (Verdery 2004: 16). In a similar vein, I argue here that the social relations and especially the intimate sentiments that inform specific subjectivities and ideas of personhood cannot be fully accounted for as a relationship between citizen and state (cf. Tamang 2000). Clearly, the national codification of property relations produces a legal subject and citizen, but relations of property are much broader than this. They also shape affective and moral subjects associated with practices of speech and recognition like *bolāune* and *āwāj uṭhāune*.

Despite the rhetoric of some lawyers, change in the inheritance law does not do away with sentiment in favor of a more rationalized legal structure. Feminist anthropologists have long underscored the centrality of sentiment in understanding broader political and economic agendas of the state and beyond.[13] Much of state knowledge and rule depends on what Ann Stoler refers to as a "calculus of sentiments and on interventions that would cultivate compassion, contempt and disdain" (2002: 93). The state laws of *angsa* support feelings of attachment between brother and sister, as well as husband and wife, and patterns of care and compassion among particular family members. While it may be obvious why opponents framed their arguments around issues of sentiment, it is important to recognize that many activists did as well. Rather than celebrate the love relationship between brother and sister, however, activists focused on the ideal bonds of romantic love between husband and wife. Sentiments of love, care, and compassion lie at the core of political debates about the *angsa* and they reveal what is at stake for both activists and their opponents alike. It is here that we see some of the pervasive and subtle means by which *angsa* exerts its most powerful cultural effects.

Debates about property are bound up with debates about changing relations of love. Nepal's first woman lawyer, Silu Singh, wrote the first polemic against the existing *angsa* system in 1975, in which she argued that reform in *angsa* would engender a more "genuine" love between husbands and wives. This more "genuine" love would flourish with a reform of the *angsa* laws, she wrote, and would be the kind of love presumably unaffected by differences in wealth (Singh n.d.b). Silu Singh imagines authentic love to be the love of an equal, companionate marriage, in which husbands and wives grow to think about themselves primarily in affectionate rather than instrumental terms. But this notion of "genuine love" is not divorced from material concerns, for according to Silu Singh it is the fact that women will come to the marriage with property that provides the conditions for "genuine love" to flourish.

Silu Singh's invocation of "genuine love" bears a striking resemblance to the connection between love and inheritance that Fredrick Engels made, almost a century earlier, in industrial Germany. Engels was arguing against the common perception that modern marriages were consensual, that is, based primarily on the love between two individuals rather than a contract between families. As Engels argued, the choice implied in love marriage or marriage by consent is never completely free, particularly when matters of inheritance are at stake. Even in countries that pride themselves on marriage by "free consent," property and children's inheritance nevertheless shape the choices children make. "Full freedom of marriage can therefore only be generally established when the abolition of capitalist production and of property relations created by it has removed all the accompanying economic considerations which still exert such a powerful influence on the choice of a marriage partner" ([1884] 1891: 144). In contrast to Silu Singh's confidence in liberal capitalism eradicating familial gender hierarchies, Engels argued that a true love marriage could only take place among the proletariat.[14] The notion of "genuine love" that Silu Singh espouses entails a particular intimate subject who is imagined to be unencumbered by social pressures, a person who can love without restraint and who has access to "their own voice," a freedom ostensibly made possible by capitalist accumulation and an equal inheritance of property.

The category of "genuine love" that activists like Silu Singh declared would result from a change in property law must be seen as a socially constituted form of affection closely tied to bourgeois material interests, the growth in capitalism, and liberal democratic ideals. And this is not all that surprising. As Rochona Majumdar (2009) has argued, the question of romantic love and companionate marriage has been at the center of marriage debates in India since the early part of the twentieth century, as the joint family persists as an ideal alongside the romantic couple. Rejecting the idea that arranged marriage is a sign of tradition, backwardness, or lack of consent in Indian marriages, Majumdar points out that this view is "a byproduct of the coupling of love marriage with progress, choice, agency, and modernity" in much literature about modern European marriage (2009: 7). Feminists scholars, anthropologists, and social historians have worked hard to show that gender relations acquire novel forms of inequality in modernity, and that romantic love or intimacy itself is not separate from material interests and social forces that create the conditions for individual choice (for example, Ahearn 2001; Berlant 1998; Illouz 1997; Jankowiak 1995; Povinelli 2002). The move from "instrumental" love to "consensual" love, ostensibly based on authentic, individual feeling, is itself an ideological effect of modernity that obscures the historical links between romantic love and the political economy of modernity.

The property law reform movement's advocacy of a more equal, companionate marriage invokes the same kind of intimate subject as that presumed and produced via the FM radio programs discussed in later chapters. At the same time, as I show throughout this book, ideas of romantic love exist alongside other forms of familial love (between parent and child, between brother and sister) that appear to challenge the ideals of parity implicit in companionate marriage. But to simply tag this form of love as "instrumental" is to confine it to a liberal model that does not fully recognize the richness of the matrix of social relations that emerge in practices like *bolāune*. These various modes of love and their attendant variations of intimacies are simultaneously (re)produced in the property laws and debates about *angsa* I discuss here and in rituals of "seeing face" that I discuss in the next chapter. As contested transformations of the intimate subject within a Nepali public sphere, they both appear as practices that reveal, alter, and call into being a voicing subject, the subject with a voice, or a subject called to speak.

The importance of sentiment and desire in many feminist analyses has also reshaped anthropological studies of kinship. While there was little concern for intimate domestic arrangements or emotions in mid-twentieth-century studies of kinship (Carston 2004),[15] early feminist anthropologists sought to revise theories of kinship by showing the broader political, economic, and social significance of family, domesticity, intimacy, and sentiment, areas of social life then deemed "feminine" and thereby considered "private" and peripheral to more central aspects of social life (Carston 2004; cf. Ortner 1974; Rosaldo 1980; Rubin 1975; Yanagisako and Collier 1987). Attention to gendered sentiments, as they relate to property, capital, and kinship, enables a more subtle understanding of people's desires and investment in the continuity of their family line. In Sylvia Yanagisako's (2002) work on family firms in Italy, for instance, she criticizes kinship studies for privileging law over sentiment, and turns her attention to the gendered sentiments and forms of patriarchical desire that shape capitalist families' vision of family continuity. Sentiments, for Yanagisako, "operate as a force of production and reproduction in family firms" (2002: 85). For theoretical as well as ethnographic reasons, Yanagisako separates the sphere of law and sentiment, claiming that while law provides important means to help families maintain security in changing political-legal contexts, law is not the basis of family continuity, contrary to early kinship studies (2002: 84). In the context of the Nepali legal reform, we see clearly that sentiments of love and care are crucial for maintaining the lines of family, but these sentiments are imagined to be integrally entwined with state law. In this case, then, for theoretical and ethnographic reasons law and sentiment must be seen as coproducing each other.

It is no coincidence, Laura Ahearn suggests, that serious scholarly consideration of sentiment and particularly romantic love across cultures occurred in the late 1990s, when there were more women, with more power, in the academy (Ahearn 2001: 270–71; cf. Jankowiak 1995; Rebhun 1999). Ahearn's own work on marriage, love, and kinship patterns in Nepal has paved the way for understanding the discourse of romantic love, the changing forms of intimacy, and the agency that underlie my exploration of public intimacy throughout this book. By critically examining the category of "love" in Nepal, Ahearn's work shifts the analysis of marriage and kinship from a discussion about a static social institution of sociocultural reproduction toward an emphasis on social change. Her focus on love-letter writing among Nepali villagers reveals the effects of many modern institutions—from education to development—on desire, intimacy, and representations of self. Ahearn looks at what she calls "indigenous theories of agency," or when people directly speak about causes of action or decision-making. She finds that the young Nepalis she spoke with tend to more often assume their own responsibility for practices like marriage and elopement, in contrast to decades earlier when villagers attributed the cause of their own marriages and elopements to witchcraft or fate. A study of the discourse of love and marriage in the contemporary moment, Ahearn suggests, reveals shifting ideologies of agency.

Liberal notions of agency suffuse practices and discourses of romantic love, with love marriage conceived as a paradigmatic "contract" presumably founded on individual choice. Love may in fact be considered the ground upon which autonomous judgment first emerges, which is later deployed in the space of civil society such as the legal reform discussed in this chapter and the FM radio discussed in later chapters. The love letters Ahearn discusses are forms of intimate recognition through which young Nepali villagers come to see themselves and become who they are by addressing another. This form of address recalls Habermas's discussion of the development of an "audience-oriented subjectivity" in modern Europe that initially took shape through the "private" exchange of letters within a conjugal family (1989: 46–51). In Habermas's argument, modern forms of domestic intimacy consider love to be a judgment of the individual, radically separated from any instrumental consideration. Intimate recognition, Elizabeth Povinelli (2002b) points out, became a way to refuse utilitarian domestic relations in modern Europe. "To assert a bond of love," writes Povinelli, "was to assert simultaneously a rejection of social utility" (2002b: 230). Such domestic relations, in turn, make possible aesthetic and political considerations in the public sphere, where, as I discuss in the chapters on FM radio, a similar form of intimate subject emerges that is always already oriented toward an audience, addressing another through the representation of self. Though the activists did not use the same kind of self-addressing narratives (aside from the signature campaigns), their notions of autonomous judgment implied in the discourse of *āwāj uṭhāune* may very well emerge from the discourse and practices of romantic love that they also profess.

While activists used ideas of romantic love to support their campaign, it is important to recognize that these modern forms of intimacy do not replace genealogical and familial attachments. Love provides the means of linking genealogy with emergent notions of national citizenship (Povinelli 2002b). The Nepali property reform movement aimed to keep a traditional form of Hindu patrimony and simultaneously transform the gender relations upon which this genealogy is based. As Nepali activists proposed, this legal change not only would change familial intimacies but also would realize a national citizenship based on individual equality, as prescribed by the constitution of 1990. "To be sure," writes Povinelli, "intimate love makes a family human, but love must still culminate in a family, a domestic or communal plot, a social group that adheres" (2002b: 234–35). Similarly, as Ahearn points out, individuals work hard to confirm the interests of their families even as they profess their own love for another that may oppose the family in their love letters.

What is striking here is that the activists do not imagine a new form of family (that is, nuclear family) or a legal doctrine founded upon ideals of individual choice. Instead, by including daughters as rightful heirs to property that traditionally marks a Hindu patriline, the activists reimagined the lines of Hindu genealogy. The Hindu Succession Act of 1956 in India ultimately failed (Basu 1999; Majumdar 2009) because it did not maintain the birthright within a joint family, creating "loopholes" in the form of wills ensuring that the male patriline remain intact (Basu 2001). Summarizing conflict in the Indian reform, Srimati Basu states, "Those who wanted to retain male privilege in joint family property were thus reassured that legal loopholes had been left to ensure that the status quo would not be unduly disturbed, and that wills could be written to disinherit women if so desired" (Parashar 1992: 128, cited in Basu 2001: 260). The more radical challenge the Nepali reform posed to the genealogy was revealed in the changing relations of love this new law would entail. The love between brothers and sisters—a love described as based upon daughters' unequal relation to their father's property and genealogy—comes under stress with this proposed shift, and emerges as a central feature of the Nepali legal debate.

These two forms of love took shape through two different formations of voice that I mentioned briefly above. "Raising voice" *(āwāj uṭhāune)* relates to the role of the state in cultivating individual will, choice, and desire, and practices of *bolāune* characterize a subjectivity defined through familial relationships, duty, and obedience, which was supported by state laws of *angsa*. Interestingly, in much of the activists' work on this reform the familial and the democratic forms of voice overlapped. On the one hand, they challenged both the state and the family patriarchal order upon which state law is based; on the other hand, in refusing a liberal will system, they confirmed existing family and state ideals of traditional Hindu property. It is important to state explicitly that part of the reasoning behind the activists' policy suggestions was their own anticipation that parents (that is, fathers) would not make choices based on equality, should they adopt a will system. By keeping ancestral property within the family through state law, activists reasoned, daughters would be granted more equality and "voice" within the family than if they completely liberalized the law with a will system. By maintaining a nonliberal system, in other words, they would enable liberal ideals of equality to be realized and would encourage a "woman's voice" to surface in the family and in public. Opponents—many of them women—rejected these claims and argued that such a change would eradicate the platform on which they were called to speak, through their brother's hailings.

By focusing on the figure of the voice in this property reform, we encounter broad questions about the relationship between speaking and subjectivity as they connect to gender and class. All of these relations take on new meanings as Nepal bears witness to dramatic reforms that seek to restructure the state, the public, and the idea of a personal and political voice. This emphasis on the voice and its mediation of intimacy articulates the broader stakes of this debate, which goes far beyond the question of "women's rights" and ultimately raises questions about the relationship between property and personhood, sentiment, law, and subjectivity.

ANGSA: A BRIEF HISTORY OF A SOCIAL AND LEGAL CATEGORY

Angsa produces specific material and affective relations between kin that, over the past forty years, became a national model that stood for the "Nepali family," despite the ethnic diversity of Nepal. For men, *angsa* has been a declaration of ownership and a material mark of their name.[16] For daughters, who usually leave their parent's home in marriage, *angsa* has been their father's family property from which they were excluded, unless they never marry. For married women, it has been the property their husband has or will inherit, to which they also have a legal claim as wives. *Angsa* has been a legal regulator of women's sexuality and a defining feature of masculinity: a mark of what all men possess at birth and what women only tentatively acquire when they marry. Precisely because of this birthright to parental property, sons are the keepers and active agents in a public display of family memory. It is because of *angsa,* many people said, that sons care for their parents in their old age (though this is a subject of much debate),[17] perform the death rituals for their parents when they die, and invite their sisters home.

Many anthropologists have discussed the significance of inalienable possessions like *angsa* as powerful because they are things that can never be lost and they transcend the permanence of death (Weiner 1992). Inalienable possessions, Paul Kockelman (2007) has argued, are "almost a necessary and sufficient condition for being fully and prototypically human" (2007: 351). Across a range of domains, from grammatical categories to discursive objects and life-cycle rituals, Kockelman shows that the category of inalienable possession is tied to things that are inherent in being a person. At the same time, they are also uniquely identified with particular persons in all stages of their life, as is the case with *angsa* and its association with brothers and sons.[18] While much more could be said about inalienables, these links between personhood and inalienable possessions that Kockelman identifies suggest the deeper stakes of the *angsa* reform movement. Put simply: to inherit *angsa* is to be a full human being in Nepal.

The roots of the *angsa* reform movement go back at least to 1964, when various customary inheritance practices were replaced by a uniform code of state law (Gilbert 1992; Hoefer 1979). Prior to this time, during the century-long Rana oligarchy (1846–1950), laws of inheritance were considered matters of custom, practiced differently among the diverse ethnic groups that populated the hills, the plains, and the Kathmandu Valley of Nepal. With the establishment of the Panchāyat government in 1960, the Mulukī Ain (state legal code) was significantly transformed. Caste *(jāt)* and ethnicity, the very cement of the prior Rana legal code, virtually disappeared from view.[19] In place of caste, the laws inscribed the individual, and the individual family member (Gilbert 1990). As Kate Gilbert writes on the laws of 1964: "All individuals are *free* to act in accordance with the national law, and are acting legally *so long as they comply with it,* regardless of the customs appropriate to their *kul* [kin group]" (1990: 7). Authority over rules of inheritance thus shifted from the power of the kin group to the power of the state, just as the legal identity of Nepalis shifted from an ethnic or caste identity to individual citizenship.[20] Changes in these and other laws were part of the creation of a national, citizen subject.

Changes to the laws of property were exemplary of a broader Panchāyat nationalist program built around Hinduism, the Nepali language, and the ideals of *bikās* (development). This was a moment when international development became a significant presence in the Nepali economy, and ideologies of *bikās* took root in school textbooks and histories (Fujikura 2001; Onta 1996a; Pigg 1992). The property laws of 1964 responded to these national aspirations. On the one hand, the Panchāyat government sought to modernize and therefore secularize the legal code, eliminating all punishments that discriminated according to caste (Gilbert 1990; Sangroula and Pathak 2002). At the same time, the new legal individual in the revised legal code also supported a state nationalism that promoted the idea that to be Nepali was to be Hindu.[21] The property laws of 1964, for example, substantiated a specifically Hindu patriarchy, based on patrilineal lines of descent and a strict regulation of women's sexuality.[22] This system of inheritance, which grants all sons a birthright to *angsa,* became a nationally mandated practice, potentially affecting even Nepalis who do not consider themselves to be Hindu. Even though these laws were only thirty years old, conservative opponents of the legal reform in the 1990s appealed to them as embodiments of "Nepali tradition and custom from time immemorial." Most modern states similarly stake their legitimacy upon claims to a specific and long-standing tradition. In the context of the debates around this reform, it is important to keep in mind that these practices and laws do have a history, and in this case, a national history that is not that old.

In the first incarnation of the new national inheritance laws, unmarried daughters only had rights to half of an inheritor's share of the *angsa* property, which they had to relinquish should they marry. In 1975, during the International Year of the Woman, Queen Aishwarya made sure that some changes were made to the constitution that reflected well on Nepal from the eyes of the international community. There were two amendments made to the law that gave unmarried women a right to property, after thirty-five, and enabled easier divorce with rights to *angsa* after fifteen years of marriage (Government of Nepal 1975: §13:10). The amendment of 1975 might be seen as a precursor to the recent change in the *angsa* laws.[23] Many of the same activists were involved in both attempts at legal reform, and it was after these changes that several women lawyers first suggested a change to daughters' inheritance rights.

These amendments, like the law of 1964, defined a state-sanctioned idea about the proper sphere of women's sexuality. A wife who slept with her husband and bore him children had rights to her husband's property should he die. But if this widow remarried, or was even seen with another man whom others find suspicious, she lost her rights to her former husband's property. Similarly, an unmarried woman who was over thirty-five (and presumably a virgin) had rights to her father's property, but should she marry after thirty-five she would lose these rights (Gilbert 1990: 28).[24] Activists working in the 1990s implicitly aimed to shift the significance of *angsa* away from being a sign of women's sanctioned sexual activity or virginal status to a provocative sign of her inclusion in the father's genealogy *(vangsa)*.

In 1977, there were certain subtle but important legal adjustments to the laws of *angsa* that responded to and encouraged critical economic changes occurring at the time. A bill was passed that enabled an easy, practical separation between brothers who, as members of a joint family, often shared both earnings and inherited property. The bill made it much easier for men to distinguish their personal acquisitions *(niji ārjan)*—money earned from one's own skills, gifted property, or salaried jobs—from the *angsa* property that they were required to share with their brothers (Karpowitz 1998). This was the first time the word *niji* (personal, individual) was used in the law code, reflecting its significance as a viable legal and social category. Privately earned money was obviously becoming an important form of wealth, particularly for men, as the professional class in Kathmandu grew.

Men who advocated for this slight change viewed it as "their law" and acknowledged the radical shift this amendment posed. One businessman explained the change to me in practical terms, "Men were earning but their brothers were claiming it. So they were getting fed up." Another middle-class lawyer told me: "In 2034 v.s. [1977], a new concept came." Chuckling, he added, "the capitalist system." Clearly, this change in the law had significant effects on the so-called traditional Nepali joint family that was constantly invoked during *angsa* movement in the 1990s. Strikingly, the reform of 1977 passed without a peep, with no public controversy. No doubt this silence has to do with the fact that it did not disturb the existing gender hegemonies inscribed in *angsa* laws.

The activism around this legal reform culminated in the final passing of the bill in 2006, just after the second People's Movement (*jana āndolan* II). Months after Nepal was declared a secular state following the *jana āndolan* II, several crucial amendments were made to the existing legal code. Most notably, married daughters no longer had to return property after their marriage (as was the case when King Gyanendra passed the daughter's birthright bill in 2002) and thus *angsa* was effectively granted to both married and unmarried daughters. But when I was in Nepal in the winter of 2008, very few people I talked with knew that all daughters now have birthrights to their parents' *angsa*. The reasons for this may have to do with the fact that the bill was passed in the midst of heated political debates about when the elections would be held for a constituent assembly. People's attention was occupied elsewhere. It may also be related to the fact that few women wanted to exercise this right, and it certainly was not culturally sanctioned to do so. The question of the effect of these legal changes on the actual practices of inheritance thus remains to be seen.

CLASS AND GENDER SUBJECTIVITY: MORAL ARGUMENTS AND CLASS DISTINCTION

How one relates to *angsa* in the contemporary moment is a mark of how one has adjusted to the demands of global modernity; it has become a key marker of class distinction in today's Kathmandu. Class and gender, like all social categories, are discursive and performed social constructs, that is, they emerge through specific styles of talk and practices that index class and gender (Bourdieu [1979] 1984; Liechty 2003). One of the key performances of class is in how one narrates one's relation to property. The property reform movement was a crucial site for examining such narrations because it got everyone talking about the proper and ideal relation to property. It got everyone talking about how property was essential in creating crucial distinctions between people with different access to the market and resources. It got everyone talking about the subtle and not so subtle differences between men and women. Though "class" was rarely a category explicitly invoked in discussions of the *angsa* reform bill, it was implicit in most of my conversations and most articles about the campaign. Instead of referring directly to the *madhyam barga* (middle class), people used other markers of class: the movement was really for and about "standard" people, some said, or professionals, or simply "the lawyers." Caught up in the foreign world of dollars and international campaigns, some complained, the middle-class Nepali activists had lost touch with the more essential meanings of *angsa* property.

There are several different (and sometimes conflicting) currents of the debate that all relate to the emerging transformations of the middle class. Indira Rana, Silu Singh, Shanta Thapaliya, and the other early activists began their work on the *angsa* reform for women in the mid-1970s, when there was a general shift in middle-class Kathmandu residents' relation to material possessions and to *angsa* specifically. As more and more people became engaged in salaried labor, *angsa* was no longer simply a means to live—a field on which to grow rice or a house in which to dwell. One's relation to *angsa* became a statement of *how* one lived. For male entrepreneurs seeking their fortune or education in Kathmandu, attachment to one's family land became a statement of sentiment, not of need. Thus the symbolic and affective significance of *angsa* remained the same, or may even have begun to swell, precisely in a moment when landed property was becoming less important for middle-class families to actually survive. The *angsa* reform bill was initiated by a group of lawyers who were part of this emerging professional class.[25] While they were certainly arguing for material and political benefits for daughters, they were also tapping into the changing semantics of *angsa* in contemporary times.

The various invocations and uses of *angsa* property quickly became signs of moral character and respectability *(ijjat)* that reflect differently on people in different class positions. *Angsa* is a vital part of what Mark Liechty calls the "*ijjat* economy," which is crucial to the construction of middle-classness (2003: 84). As I discuss in more detail in chapter 2, *ijjat* can be lost or gained by participating in certain practices, by associating with appropriate, "respectable" people, and by consuming particular things (ranging from the latest electronics to private school). As Liechty points out, *ijjat* "brings together old and new logics of prestige in competing often contradictory hierarchies of value.... Calculating middle class ijjat requires an intricate reckoning of caste background and orthodox religious practice as well as consumer prestige, in a host of registers from weddings to education to consumer status symbols" (83). To many professionals and entrepreneurs in the Kathmandu Valley, *angsa* was no longer considered the most valued form of property, except on a symbolic level to secure one's *ijjat*. Those who do depend on *angsa* were often regarded by middle-class urbanites as lazy and incapable of earning on their own. Dependence on *angsa* has become a way for middle-class professionals to distinguish themselves as *bikāsit* (developed) in contrast to those who are thought to remain *abikāsit* (underdeveloped) or lacking initiative in today's Kathmandu.

"Education is today's *angsa*," one of my close friend's father, Gyanu, told me. "It is through education that a child is given skills to earn." This comment was echoed by all kinds of people, including activists arguing for daughter's rights to *angsa*. Like many opposing and supporting the reform, Gyanu insisted on the equal access to education for all his daughters and his single son. The importance of education as a valid and desired right is even more evident when we look at the cases that emerged after an initial reform bill was passed in 2002, granting all daughters a birthright to *angsa*. The majority of the cases filed by daughters claimed they were not given the chance to go to school.[26] They wished to sell their portion of *angsa* in order to purchase an education for themselves. Gyanu's remarks highlight the important fact that the *angsa* reform movement emerged on the political scene at the moment when personal *(niji)* property, earned through education and skill, gained importance as a legal and social category, especially for the middle class.

Professional men I talked with would often assert the significance of *angsa* as property they had a right to claim, but were proud *not* to use or consume it. A youthful eighteen year old, Rajesh, who was preparing to study computer programming in the United States, told me he was disgusted by the entire system of *angsa*. He boasted that his family had not divided the property for six generations and that he had no intentions of ever separating his rightful portion: to do so would be admitting a dependence he did not want to claim. It was the reliance on this birthright, Rajesh suggested, that ultimately was "ruining" Nepal. "If I were to take *angsa*," Rajesh said to me, "I would feel lazy *(alchī lāgcha)* like those boys who hang out all day on the streets, around temple complexes, or in their rooms playing guitar and composing songs all day. I would simply want to play and travel around."[27] For Rajesh, a man's dependence on *angsa* is a sign of his *inability* to earn and adjust to the current demands of modernity. Many others like Rajesh enjoyed the idea of retaining *angsa,* but similarly abstain from transforming land into money and thereby consuming it.[28] They desire the luxury of being connected to tradition, without being tethered to its more restricting demands.

For men who do rely upon *angsa* as a potential source of income, *angsa* property is a crucial sign of their manhood. Laxman, an electric rickshaw driver from a relatively high-caste Newar family, spoke vehemently against his former wife's demand for her rightful portion of *angsa* largely because of the humiliation it caused him. For Laxman, *angsa* was a sign that he maintained some control in the house, even if in the broader urban setting he remained on the margins of wage labor, shuttling wealthier Nepalis, tourists, and students throughout the city. I asked Laxman to imagine what it would have been like if his wife came to the marriage with *angsa* from her parent's home. He laughed at the question: "I would not have been able to do anything." If women claimed a right to *angsa,* Laxman and many others feared, they would become arrogant, proud, or egotistical *(ghamaṇḍi huncha).*[29] Squirming a bit in his seat, Laxman imagined the effects: "It would be humiliating. 'I have *angsa,*' she would begin to say. *No man would be able to speak to her.*" Here, *angsa* is explicitly connected to who can address whom. For both Laxman and Rajesh, *angsa* also determines how one acts and speaks in other spheres of life.

These oblique references to class and masculinity that emerged through the *angsa* debate were often explicitly about women and their proper place. Indeed, the link between maintaining middle-class respectability and gender has a long history in the subcontinent, as in the rest of the world. In colonial India, the "woman question" became a central feature of middle-class nationalist rhetoric that aimed to reveal the distinctiveness of Indian culture by asserting the difference between Indian and European women (Chatterjee 1993). Middle-class respectability was and still is a moral virtue, built upon maintaining the respectability of middle-class women (Liechty 2003; Mankekar 1999). "Since respectability, sexual modesty, and family honor were predicated on the conduct of women," writes Mankekar, "women's behavior was monitored especially intently" (1999: 114). The *angsa* laws were one means by which this monitoring of women's behavior and speech took place.

Inscribed within the *angsa* laws are moral ideas about women's respectability, tied both to the regulation of her sexuality and to the proper way to pass down and receive inherited wealth. These ideas of respectability inform how and when a woman can speak on her own behalf. According to many I spoke with, a woman should never appear to demand any form of inheritance, particularly land. I recall a conversation with a well-heeled director of an NGO, Manika Thapa, who had received a portion of land equal to her brother's as a gift *(icchā patra)* from her father, and she made it clear that she did not ask for *angsa (māg garena)*. Many saw the demand for *angsa* rights by the activists as a sign of middle-class women's greed and arrogance, even though these very same people also declared that *angsa* was no longer important as a form of material wealth. Thus, the symbolic significance of *angsa,* with its tie to maintaining gendered divisions of speech and action, retains its value even though *angsa* is also devalued as a form of wealth by the middle class.

While Manika Thapa opposed the proposed bill, she was equally critical of the birthright sons maintained through the prior law. This system only leads to familial and political corruption, she maintained. Like many of her class Manika proposed that Nepal adopt a will system, which would lead to an alternative system of prestige and honor that could benefit the whole country. A person could donate their money to a charitable organization, she suggested, or provide money for a social trust and create an "establishment in one's own name." These proposals signify a more general shift in how people should align themselves, away from the family and genealogy, toward their public place within the history of the nation. *Angsa* works in tandem with other signs of nationhood, and thus a reform to the *angsa* law was often cited as detrimental to the nation of Nepal and its independent status (Des Chene 1997).

The proposal of the will system does not fundamentally disturb the hierarchies of gender upon which the *angsa* system is based. In the will system, parents remain the sole agents and authorities of the inheritance, but this does not necessarily ensure that they will deviate from the gender hierarchies inscribed in the prior law. Indeed, the experience in India, after the passing of the Hindu Succession Act of 1956, suggests they will not. Not pursuing a will system was the most radical aspect of the Nepali reform movement. Perhaps the fact that Nepal is such a small country within South Asia means that it can pursue a reform that would keep a traditional institution, while attempting to transform the gender relations upon which it was based.

JOURNEYS HOME: *MĀITĪ, GHAR,* AND GENDERED SUBJECTIVITY

To understand the hierarchies of gender produced through *angsa* practices, we must turn our attention to the Nepali ideas of home and kin that constitute a powerful core of a gendered subjectivity for women and men alike. In Nepali, the terms for home cannot be spoken without context. A married Nepali woman, for example, speaks of her *māitī,* her parents' and brothers' home, the home she left in marriage. When a woman invokes *māitī* she is also referring, implicitly, to her legal and material erasure from her parent's genealogy. However, in ideological and sentimental terms, *māitī* is the home where love overflows. On return visits, it is where a woman can momentarily be carefree, where she escapes the daily drudgery of work in her married home (Bennett 1983; Cameron 1998). The number of visits a married sister makes depends, of course, on how close or far she lives from her *māitī,* as well as whether her husband's family allows her to leave. What she possesses from her parents and her brothers is not the immortal mark of genealogy that *angsa* provides, but a more fragile relation of care, affection, and love that she expects once she leaves.

In contrast to *māitī,* another word for "home" is *ghar,* which expresses genealogy, law, and possession: it is, for both men and married women, the house to which they have legal rights and the family that goes down in history. When I asked my close friend, Gyanisoba, to show me a picture of her family, without specifying *ghar* or *māitī,* she held up a picture of her deceased mother-in-law and then tried to find a picture of her father-in-law so that my friend Ann, the photographer, could take another picture of them all together. Her family was her *ghar.* The significance of a married woman's natal home (her *māitī*) and her *ghar,* along with the practices that define each of these homes, differs between ethnic groups, castes, and specific families. Nevertheless, for all Nepali speakers, *māitī* and *ghar* are fundamental to their consciousness of past and present, their experience of home, and their sense of a gendered self. (See figure 4.)

Home for married Nepali women is idealized as a *place of movement,* a double life between *māitī* and *ghar.* These frequent travels inscribe a woman's precarious relation to her own past, even as there is a furtive pleasure in these movements. While the movement might be felt as a kind of "freedom," it also marks a daughter's dependence on her husband's family, who usually must agree to the visits beforehand, and on her *māitī* as the fail-safe place a woman

FIGURE 4. Gyanisoba Sakya holding a photograph of her deceased mother-in-law. Photo: Ann Hunkins.

can go if she needs an escape. Movement is important here, for no woman would want to stay at her *māitī* too long. To do so would be admitting a reliance on her parents and her brothers that few married women would choose to claim. In addition to its mingled feelings of shelter and escape, then, *māitī* can also be a place reflecting exclusion and rejection, a place where a married woman must flee if her marriage fails or if her husband's family sends her back for an extended visit. One of my unmarried woman friends expressed *māitī*'s double edge in a statement that captures both the nostalgia and the erasure embedded in the term. "Only women need to remember," she told me. "Men don't have to remember. They *live there.*"

It would be easy to dismiss the sentimental adulation of *māitī* as false consciousness that merely keeps women in their place. This is indeed the position of many Nepali activists. But to do so is to miss the material reality of these sentiments and its force in shaping ideas about self, which women know quite well. One group of lower-class women from a Newar butcher caste (a low caste), all agreed that "without *māyā* (family love), we have nothing." They worried that if *angsa* were given to daughters it would be absorbed by the husband's family, and they would ultimately have no control over it. "If we had to return to our *māitī*, there would be nothing there for us," one explained. Women know the male control over property as a reality, and thus they cling to the bonds of love expected from their *māitī* and the material security this home appears to provide. For these lower-class women, other institutions that offered similar support outside the family worked in ways that resembled *māitī*. In the mid-1990s, they became subjects of an NGO project that provided them with resources to begin a literacy program and a savings-and-loan credit system. After a long discourse about their attachments to *māitī*, one of the younger girls began to speak about the NGO in similar terms. "Compared to leaving our *māitī*," another said, "we fear that Lumanti (the NGO) will leave us." The link between material support and care implicit in the idea of *māitī* has taken new forms in the world of NGOs. Middle-class Nepalis who run such NGOs not only have become financial donors, but also have taken over role of caretaker and rememberer for many lower-class women, a role these women might have otherwise expected to receive from their *māitī*.

Māitī is always considered "lower" than *ghar*, and some Nepali kinship patterns reinforce this hierarchy.[30] As many anthropologists have pointed out, patriarchy is usually supported by patrilineal kinship patterns, of which there are several in Nepal. The common "matrilateral cross-cousin marriage" that many hill Nepalis prefer is one such pattern. In this system, as one Nepali friend explained to me, a man can marry a female cousin from his mother's *māitī*, but this same man's sister cannot marry a male cousin from her mother's *māitī*. "It all comes down to the *ijjat* of the grandfather," my friend explained, with some disdain. "A grandson can bring a daughter-in-law into the family from his mother's *māitī*, but there is no way that same grandfather would let his *own* granddaughter to be given to her mother's *māitī*." In anthropological parlance, asymmetries develop between those families who are "wife givers" and those who are "wife takers," though, as Laura Ahearn points out, unlike in many places in India, it is the "wife givers" who are ritually superior among some hill Nepali groups (2001: 82–83). Even within a single family, the distinction between "giving" and "receiving" women supports asymmetries between the *ghar* and *māitī*. It is the family of the *ghar* that goes down in history. Relatives of the *ghar* perform the death rituals for one another, and their names are recorded together in *vamsāvali* (genealogies) or family trees. For men, a *ghar* is the home in which they were raised and often the home where they presently live. This pattern is changing significantly, especially in Kathmandu, as many men with the means are eager to separate and build their own home away from their brothers. Even so, these same men often were critical of the proposed property reform bill.

One Patan family I knew portrayed the history of their *ghar* quite literally in a painted family tree, which they hung in the sitting room for everyone to see. Daughters in this painting were represented by the leaves; sons were the branches. Daughters are born and grow big with the branches, he explained, later they blow away or simply die and fall to the ground. Their hold on the branches is temporary. The leaves are signs of a healthy tree: if a tree is strong, these leaves blossom each season. Married daughters, like the leaves, are expected to return to their *māitī* regularly for seasonal holidays and family celebrations. Without its leaves, a tree appears barren and fails to display its full grandeur. A *ghar* similarly remains feeble without its daughters. In this family, there was one daughter of about fifty who never married, and who proudly pointed out her own name on the family tree (see figure 3 at the beginning of the chapter). No daughters-in-law appeared on this painted tree. When I asked why, the man laughed with some embarrassment and replied: "Ha, they are part of their husbands. They are with the sons on the tree." In their journeys to and from their *māitī*, women remain connected to their brothers' genealogy, and through these journeys their brothers' genealogy grows strong.

I suggested to Manish, a lawyer friend who actively worked on this reform, that perhaps one of the key problems people had with the proposed legal change was that it provoked unsettling questions about genealogy *(vangsa)* and the significance of *māitī*.[31] He scoffed at my suggestion. No, he told me, this reform was about equal rights. It was about being in a democratic society. It was about men and women coming to marriage with equal rights to their familial property. No, this really had nothing to do with *vangsa*, he insisted. Moments later, Manish began to tell me a story about his five-year-old daughter and his seven-year-old son. Manish had arrived home one day to find his daughter messing with some of the papers on his desk. He came shouting into the room, scolded his daughter, and immediately sent her outside. She turned around in tears and, in the way only a five-year-old can, she yelled back without restraint: "You are only scolding me because you are going to send me away. You wouldn't scold Nirmal because he's going to bring a wife here. You're going to send me to someone else, and Nirmal will get to stay right here. That's why you are sending me outside."

Clearly, I thought, the reform movement is about *vangsa* as well as equal rights and democracy. Manish wanted to emphasize the liberal nature of this reform. He wanted to look forward to a new kind of democratic reform and toward a future when his daughter would leave for marriage with a portion of his family's property. But as his story suggests, the reform is also about Manish's daughter being able to see herself, and her past, as part of his family's *vangsa*. The recent change in law, which gives daughters as well as sons a birthright to *angsa,* suggests that the very nature of *vangsa* is changing, something that even activists like Manish may sometimes have a hard time accepting. The connections drawn between *vangsa* and *angsa* (evident at the linguistic level) may be an effect of this reform. At the very least, Manish's story points to the intricate relation between the rule of law and the sentiments sustained by the law, which are cultivated and known at a very early age. These sentiments shape gendered and class subjectivity, giving both men and women a deep understanding of who they are, as well as how and when they may speak and act.

SENTIMENT AND VOICE: "KILLING THE LOVE"

One of the most widely circulating complaints against the legal reform bill, in the media and in nearly every interview I conducted, was that such a law would "kill the love" between a brother and sister *(dāju-bahiniko māyā marcha).* This trope of brother-sister love used in literature, film, and popular songs throughout the South Asian subcontinent expresses married women's desires and longings (Agarwal 1994; Bennett 1983; Raheja and Gold 1994; Tharu and Lalita 1993). Intimacy between brothers and sisters is not unique to South Asia. Annette Weiner describes brother-sister relationship in the Trobriand Islands as the "basic core of all kinship relationships" (1976: 208–10), and siblings' love for one another is expressed through exchanges of gifts and care. "Marriage, in providing additional resources to sister-brother siblings," writes Weiner, "further enhances the power of their intimacy and gives them resources from other groups" (16). In the Middle East as well, Suad Joseph (1994) argues, brother-sister love has been romanticized by scholars as one of "love" or explained in structural terms as a relationship of "power" that is critical for the reproduction of Arab patriarchy. In both Weiner's and Joseph's cases, while inequalities are clearly established between brothers and sisters, sisters are still considered to be genealogically tied to their natal home after marriage. Throughout South Asia by contrast, unless a woman remains unmarried, a sister who marries is decidedly not part of her brother's genealogy, and this fact looms large in popular and scholarly discussions of brother-sister love. It was salient in many of my conversations about the proposed property reform, even in many activists' perspective that a change in daughter's inheritance rights would lead to a less "instrumental" and more "genuine" intimacy between husbands and wives.

In her book *A Field of One's Own*, Bina Agarwal (1994) goes so far as to suggest that the emotional and material salience of brother-sister love, along with the wish to be called back to their parent's home by their brothers, is one of the reasons why so many South Asian women relinquish their rights to family property, even when the property is legally theirs to claim (Agarwal 1994; Basu 2001).[32] She begins her polemical book, which argues forcefully for women's rights to land, with a common folk song sung by Hindu women in north India that aptly portrays this nostalgia and sense of loss:

> To my brother belong your green fields
> O father, while I am banished afar.
> Always you said
> Your brother and you are the same
> O father. But today you betray me. . . .
> This year when the monsoon arrives, dear father,
> Send my brother to fetch me home (Agarwal 1994: i)[33]

Similar arguments transpired in Kathmandu.

"I don't like the idea of getting *angsa*," Gita, a twenty-year-old, unmarried woman, told me, as I sat with her and her friend, Anita, discussing the possible effects of this law.

"Why?" I asked.

"It would 'kill my brothers' love' *(māyā marrcha)* in the future.[34] Definitely they would forget, absolutely forget about me. After taking *angsa,* they would say, 'Now she also has a part.' Of course they'll forget. Tomorrow or the next day, if I got married, they would definitely not invite me back home. Definitely not."

Anita and Gita, who live on the edge of Patan in a community of Newar farmers and craftsmen, focused their rumination about this reform bill on the desires generated between brother and sister, like many in their class. To be clear: there are no doubt many occasions when married sisters visit their brothers without being officially "called," and in the case of Anita and Gita, urban Newars who both eventually married men who live close by, these visits will be frequent. But the ideological weight of these calls home for holidays, weddings, and family events holds remarkable sway over many young women's imagination. So it is not surprising that Gita's response to my question was rooted in the desires cultivated primarily through the nostaglic images of *māitī,* associated with brothers' summoning her back.

Anita tried to clarify her friend's words for me: "Look, boys are given houses. [Boys think,] 'We have been given this much. They [their sisters] have not been given anything. We thus should, from time to time, call *(bolāune)* them, and feed *(khuwāune)* them. We should *love* them.' There is that feeling now." Though rarely mentioned by legal reformers, *bolāune* was a central theme that invariably arose in conversations with those opposed to the reform, particularly women. *Bolāune* appear to be an innocuous, everyday practice that has little do with the broader political significance of *angsa.* It is used in many other contexts to simply refer to the act of calling out to someone on the street, to inviting a friend or relative to a party, a wedding, or one's house. In this particular context of a brother inviting his sister home, the word carries within it hierarchies of gender produced by *angsa* laws that the activists hoped to overturn with a new law. In analyzing this practice, we see more clearly the tensions between ideas of democratic speech and the political consciousness implicit in *āwāj uṭhāune* that the legal reformers relied upon in their pursuit of *angsa* reforms and the gendered pattern of speech and action between family members that *angsa* property generates.

Bolāune is the causative form of the verb *bolnu,* "to speak." When literally translated into English, *bolāune* means "to cause someone to speak." The act of calling out to someone constitutes that person as a speaking subject through the speech of another. This calling is also a request for a response. A brother anticipates his *own* recognition through the visits of his sister; they serve to make him what he is. On a fundamental level, then, *bolāune* is a practice of mutual, but asymmetrical, recognition between brothers and sisters, not only in relation to each other but for themselves as well.

On one level, the practice of *bolāune* clearly corresponds to what Louis Althusser (1971) calls "hailing," a mode of address that establishes a person's subjectivity and even their body through speech. Hailing, or, in Althusser's more technical terminology, interpellation, reveals the discursive nature of identity and subjectivity. As I noted in the introduction, the person who turns and recognizes himself as the subject of a policeman's call is thereby constituted as a subject of the state at the same time as this subject is injured or wounded by the call. A person comes to recognize herself not only as an individual but as a subject positioned within a social world through reiterated forms of address and conventions that delineate her social position. Judith Butler reflects on this aspect of Althusser's concept: "Interpellation is an address that regularly misses its mark, it requires the recognition of an authority at the same time that it confers identity through successfully compelling that recognition. Identity is a function of that circuit, but does not preexist it. The mark interpellation makes is not descriptive, but inaugurative. It seeks *to introduce a reality* rather than report an existing one; it accomplishes this introduction through a citation of existing convention" (1997: 33).

The process of interpellation continuously transforms individuals into subjects, even though individuals are always already subjects the moment they enter social life (which is, usually, prior to birth). But *bolāune* does not so much construct a single subject as constitute a social relationship and the subjects formed within it. The practice of *bolāune* compels the recognition of a sister by her brother, thereby creating their differences, their identities, and their subjectivities. It recognizes a sister's presence alongside her brothers as well as marks her absence and exclusion from the family's genealogical memory. In doing so, it re-members a married daughter into the house she has left.

As Anita continued to reflect on the potential effects of this legal reform, she suggested a striking connection between the right to inherit *angsa* and what it means to be a woman or a man.

"But if *angsa* were given to daughters," Anita imagined, "[brothers would think,] 'But we are all equal. Why should we give? We don't need to call them either. *Because they are also boys.* They are just like boys, so why give? Why call?' It will be like that."

According to Anita's comments, *angsa* seems to destabilize the lines between sex and gender. By acquiring a birthright to *angsa,* Anita says, girls will become boys. In a fundamental way, *angsa* and the conventional practices that accompany it mark the bodily, material, and symbolic differences between women and men in a state regime that favors this form of inheritance.

If *bolāune* is a way to interpellate a daughter temporarily into her parent's *vangsa,* the process can only work if daughters actually begin to act and speak about themselves in the same fashion. Interpellation rests on the notion that a "speech act brings the subject into being, and then . . . that very subject comes to speak, reiterating the discursive conditions of its own emergence" (Bell 1999: 165). This alternative formation of voice—the gendered patterns of speech and action established by *bolāune*—appears in Anita's and Gita's own reflections about the potential effects of the law. Neither Anita nor Gita provides their own reasons for rejecting the reform bill; instead, they invent and cite the words they imagine their brothers would speak. The "we" in Anita's quotation is not herself and Gita, but an imagined collective voice of their brothers. Both young women reflect on the consequences of this reform *through the words of their brothers*. They imagine what it would be like for them by imagining the speech and perspective of their brothers. "But we are all equal," Anita quotes her brother saying, "Why should we give? We don't need to call them either. Because they are also boys. They are just like boys, so why give?"

I soon began to recognize this as a patterned way in which people who opposed the law spoke about reform, especially though not only young women. Recall Laxman, who reflected on what might happen if his wife came to marriage with *angsa*. He responded with the words he imagined his wife saying: "'I have *angsa*,' she would begin to say. *No man would be able to speak to her.*" Here *angsa* is explicitly tied to who can address whom.

In another example, two sisters, whose brother had gone to Singapore to study dentistry, argued about the reaction their brother might have should the law be changed. The elder sister, Sarjana, began: "If our brother is alone, if everything was taken, poor *daī*! Later, also, he might also say, 'You already took it, why should I call you home?' He will—" Her younger sister, Ambika, interrupted: "But my brother would not say that." She repeated, looking over at me, "He would never say that." Ambika wanted to be clear that his love for them was not solely guided by his inheritance of their parent's property. Then, reflecting for a moment on what would transpire should the daughters receive a share of *angsa* property, Ambika burst out with a laugh: "We would even have to invite *daī* home! Right?! We would also have to do the calling!" This imagined and always humorous outcome of the proposed law was quite common.

While I sat with Anita and Gita as well, Gita thought up a similar scenario. "Perhaps," she said hesitatingly, with one hand covering her wide smile, "*we* would have to call them." Her voice rose as she thought this through: "We daughters would have to call our brothers *(hāmī chorīharule dāju-bhāilāi gharmā bolāune parcha holā)*, it seems, we would have to call them! Right? Then it would work. If sisters also summoned their brothers home, it would work, maybe. The love would work then, maybe."

Anita giggled at the thought. A strange idea, she mused, and yet she agreed that if the reform bill were passed, daughters would also be compelled to summon their brothers to their homes.[35] Possession of *angsa* at birth quite strikingly *incites* these callings (Keane 1997; Weiner 1992). As Webb Keane (1997) has pointed out in his book on ritual language in Indonesia, it is not language itself that grants recognition and personhood in a symbolic world, but rather the way language and material objects work together to create social connections and divisions. Keane focuses on ritual exchanges—of words and things—because these are formal moments when actors are particularly self-conscious about their actions. These are also moments when voice and agency can be separated, when the person speaking is not always considered the agent of their speech, for example, if they are speaking the words of an ancestor or the divine. None of these ritual encounters could function without the dual representation of words and material objects, Keane argues. "To be valid," writes Keane, "words must be spoken in tandem with material transactions.... The requirement that words and things be transacted together means that the authority of speech and the economic power conveyed through goods should each index each other" (1997: 22).

Keane's point might be extended to everyday forms of performative speech and practice like *bolāune*. Though not transacted at the same moment in time, it is clear in discussions about *bolāune* that the authority of speech and economic power (birthright to *angsa*) index each other. More than this even, the imagined effect of a changed law suggests that a birthright to *angsa* is the motor that drives a brother to call his sister home. What these young women are imagining is a new relation to speech and action established by the material property of *angsa* itself. A daughter's right to *angsa* would enable the young women to also do the calling or speaking while their brothers respond.

Annette Weiner (1992) has astutely shown that inalienable possessions, such as the ancestral property of *angsa*, effectively produce power and authority, and endow those who possess them with attributes that are socially desirable on many levels. It is not reciprocity that is the rule in the passing of these possessions; rather, what makes inalienable possessions powerful is that they are both given and kept, thus transcending the loss inherent in any kind of exchange. By inviting their sisters home, an act often described as an act of memory, brothers maintain their contact with their sister, and at the same time these comings and goings continuously reenact the sister's departure, her displacement from the family genealogy, her loss.

The frequent musings about what a brother might say should the law be passed or the contexts in which a sister might call her brother home that occurred when discussing this campaign suggest that we expand upon the assumptions of voice inherent in theories of interpellation. "Interpellation must be dissociated from the figure of the voice," writes Judith Butler, "the power of the speaking subject will always, to some degree, be derivative . . . it will not have its source in the speaking subject" (1997: 32–33). Like Keane, Butler demonstrates that the authority of speech is never autonomous or rooted exclusively in the speaking subject. Indeed, the power of the brother to call his sister home derives from the documents of state law, from his birthright to *angsa*.

That the source of the brother's authority lies outside of him does not mean, however, that his voice is not instrumental in his capacity to hail. The materiality of the voice—its sound and form—makes a difference in these hailing practices. It matters, for example, not just *who* but *how* a daughter is called home. As I noted in the introduction, the material qualities of the voice are implied in Althusser's example of the policeman; we hardly imagine a soft-spoken, gentle voice uttering the words, "Hey, you there!" Similarly, though people said it didn't matter whether their brother or his wife actually made the call (both are authorized by the law), it needs to be clear through the tone of voice, appropriateness of time, and context that this summoning is genuine. In contrast to these regular invitations, many Nepalis also explained that on the one holiday a year when a sister calls her brother home—the national holiday of *tihār*—it *must* be the sister's voice, and must be recognizable as such. That *tihār* is the one nationally celebrated occasion when sisters are *required* to invite their brother's to their *ghar* actually highlights how exceptional this practice is. Theories of interpellation can be deepened by considering the material qualities of voice that constitute a subject, an issue I explore in greater detail in chapter 4 and 5.

The recognition gained through these acts of *bolāune* is not only from the brother; it also includes a much wider social world. While walking down the street, women frequently greet their neighbors and friends with pride and self-possession, asserting that they are on their way to their *māitī*, that they had been called back. It is as if to assert the *ijjat* (honor, prestige) of being a married woman and also of being called back, re-membered, into one's parents' or brother's genealogical home. Perhaps more profoundly, these visits back and forth are an acceptable means for a married woman, who doesn't have an office, a school, or work that would allow her to appear alone in public, to walk down the street. Professional women, college students, and women working for NGOs do not experience the same sense of surveillance walking or being alone in public, and many would likely cringe at the suggestion that some Nepali women do think twice about being in public alone, even during daylight. But for those who live on the edge of middle-class life—people like Anita and Gita, who now send their children to private English-medium schools but who themselves do not have a "career" outside their family and home—simply strolling on the street is rarely something they do by themselves. When they do, most of the time friends, husbands, or a small child accompany them, giving them license to be publicly visible without any apparent agenda, or they are on their way to work in the family shop. Even "disempowered" subjectivities must be built upon feelings of empowerment *within* the domains of where patriarchy does the work of domination, such as the public space of streets.[36] *Māitī* and practices of *bolāune* provide a means of being public. Interestingly, the middle-class activists invested in *āwāj uthāune* are imagining a kind of public based on the ideals and subjects of democratic speech that threatens to do away with the known and acceptable public space that married women move through in their visits to and from their *māitī*. While this public is certainly changing with the growing number of young Nepali women pursuing education and careers, the fear that many women have of losing acceptable access to the public space of streets was a key aspect of the controversy over the proposed law in the mid-1990s.

A brother's call and a sister's visit are where the material power of *angsa* circulates and establishes their differences. These visits reenact the sister's departure and her loss. These visits are spoken of as the "love" that daughters receive from their *māitī*. "If daughters took that property," my former landlady, Laxmi, explained, "they would have no place to go. Staying all the time in that place [that is, their *ghar*] is upsetting to one's heart. There would be no chance to go here and there. That's what we call love *(māyā)*." This love requires the loss of a sister. Should daughters also have a legal right to their parent's *angsa,* it is unclear what will be lost. It is unclear what would happen to a brother's love for his sister and to his expected calls. By extension, it is unclear what would happen to the very idea and desires associated with *māitī*.

DESIRE TO MOURN

Most of the activists had little tolerance for the nostalgia that people and the media conjured up in their depictions of *māitī* and brother-sister love around this reform. Such sentimentality is merely rhetorical cant used to maintain the current Hindu and state hegemony, they claimed. When I asked Indira Rana, one of the early and key activists, what she thought about the common fear of losing love from one's *māitī*, she scoffed and simply stated: *"Māitī* no longer exists." "After a parent dies," she told me defiantly, "there is no *māitī*. Forget it. It's just not there anymore."

Indira Rana was one of the first lawyers to draft and sign the first and most radical reform proposal drawn up by the Ministry of Women in 1993, which posed the first direct constitutional challenge to the constitution of 1991. She became the first woman judge at the Supreme Court, and when I met her, she was serving as secretary of the Judicial Council at the Ministry of Justice. She was also known across the city for her provocative act of public mourning in which she performed the funeral rites for her mother (see also Thompson 1993).

When Indira shaved her head, donned the all-white, pure cotton cloth, and lit her mother's funeral pyre like a son, much of Kathmandu was aghast. Normally this act of mourning is carried out exclusively by the eldest son, or by the closest male relative. Floods of articles, sometimes written in derisive tones, appeared in several newspapers. This was the first time a Nepali woman had completed the prescribed Hindu mourning rituals, one newspaper decried.[37] In fact, I learned from many interviews that several women had performed the death rituals for their fathers, when there were no sons. But their actions (and no doubt countless others) were not public acts, performed by a public figure like Indira, and thus were not documented as such.[38] In her analysis of Indira's provocative act of mourning, Julia Thompson (1993) notes that there were multiple interpretations of this action, ranging from those that thought her motives were "socially-minded" to those that felt she was simply greedy in her wish to get a share of her parent's property. These interpretations, not surprisingly, echo the interpretations most widely circulated about the *angsa* reform several years later.

Indira explained that she had remained unmarried and had supported her mother for approximately twenty years after her father had died. Her one surviving brother lived in another house nearby with his wife and children. Because she had cared for her mother for so many years, Indira felt that she should perform the final service *(kriyā-kāj)* after her mother died. In her wish to mourn in public, Indira recalled, she confronted furious anger and resistance, from her brother and from many other neighbors and friends around her. Her voice rose as she remembered: "Even my priest tried to stop me. 'I am a lawyer,' I said to my priest. 'So you show me where in our religious text it says that women should not do the final religious ceremony. Actually it is not written. I have gone through my religion. I know my religion. I know that there is no point there. If you want to show me, show me. If you don't do it [the ceremony], get lost and I'll find another priest. You get lost—I don't want you.'"

Indira's challenge to the priest reveals a tension about who and what regulates, authorizes, and legitimates current practices of commemoration. On the one hand, activists like Indira Rana insist upon the authority of legal texts and the written word. This knowledge-based authority of texts runs counter to the birth-granted authority of a Brahmin priest (who is always a man). Indira's challenge to the priest relies on the authority of the religious text and the fact that, as a lawyer, she clearly has textual dexterity. Rather than assuming that religious texts are a different order of texts, closer to the hand of God and the Brahmin priest, Indira spoke of the religious texts in the same way she might speak of her law books. They were implicitly compared and seem to require the same interpretive skills. "I am a lawyer," Indira said, "Actually it is not written. I have gone through my religion. I know my religion."

The priest could not refuse. Indira performed all the rituals as her brother would have. She sat at the cremation grounds, draped in a white cloth with a shaven head, repeating words the Brahmin priest told her to repeat, performing whatever ritual actions he asked her to do. For thirteen days, Indira sat, as her brother would have, in mourning. On the fourth day, her brother finally paid a visit, but to this day, Indira said, he has not forgiven her. Strikingly, the authority of the Brahmin priest, a person who ostensibly has ontological priority in religious matters, shrank when Indira referred to her profession, her knowledge and skills at textual interpretation. Her lawyerly debate about religious texts held more sway over him than his inborn position of authority as a Brahmin priest.

There is an uncanny association between the mourning rituals sons perform for their parents and their duty as brothers to summon married sisters home. Several young men in Kathmandu, as in much of South Asia, spoke of their sister's marriage in similar terms: "When a sister marries, it is as if she has died." Even descriptions about the annual memorial feasts echo descriptions of hailing a sister home. When a brother calls his sister home, he must also feed her just as he feeds his living relatives in memory of his parents at the annual feast. In both cases, sons and brothers publicly recall people who are otherwise absent from the family. Their role as agent and speaker rests largely on their birthright and exclusive inheritance of *angsa*.

Angsa is commonly regarded as compensation for performing the funeral rituals, but it also solidifies a connection between the performer and the person who has just died. Embedded within the practices of public mourning are ideas about how the living person will be remembered in the future. It ensures that both parent and child (that is, the son) will be remembered together, well beyond their own temporary lives. If daughters were to receive *angsa,* they would provocatively disturb the structures of feeling—the patterns of care, love, and memory—sanctioned by the current law. The gender-bending Indira performed in this ritual was as much a political act as a way to personally commemorate her mother. "That is *why* the son is getting all the property," she told me. "That is *why* I went against my religion."[39] Most strikingly, this ability to publicly perform the Hindu death rituals would rearrange a daughter's relationship to her *māitī,* changing her from the subject who is remembered and addressed in practices like *bolāune* to the subject who speaks and mourns publicly alongside her brothers, and therefore is remembered with her parents. "I will get the property eventually," Indira told us, "but if *I* have this much trouble, imagine the other, more common, uneducated women."

Chirmei Dangol was one of these more common women. A Newar daughter from a family with no sons, Chirmei inherited *angsa* through a gift *(icchā patra)* from her parents, which was to be held until she herself gave birth to a son. Chirmei's inheritance of landed property has a history in her family, for she was in the third generation of marriages that bore no sons. Through special maneuvering, Chirmei's grandparents managed to keep their land and houses from the rest of their genealogical kin by passing it on to their daughters and sons-in-law legally through the *icchā patra* (document of wish). By placing the house in their sons-in-law's names, for example, Chirmei's maternal grandparents warded off the possibility that the grandfather's brother would easily claim this property as his rightful portion of *angsa.* In this way, the property that would have remained within the immediate family through a son's inheritance of *angsa* was still conserved by the family's gifts to their daughters and sons-in-law. Chirmei married Gyanu, whom I have already mentioned, and gave birth to only one son, while her sister gave birth to three. Chirmei thus relinquished most of her share of the family property and passed it on to her sister. When I asked Chirmei whom she would gift this house and property to, she quickly replied that it would simply become her son's *angsa.* Unless he failed to care for her, she said with a glimmer in her eye, in which case, she could and would willingly pass the property on to her four daughters.

Ganga, Chirmei's daughter and my close friend, often told me that her mother's life—not the NGO where she worked—convinced her of the importance of *angsa* for women. Chirmei was thrown out of her husband's house three times by Gyanu's mother, each time just after she gave birth to a baby girl. Allowing this abuse by his mother seemed uncharacteristic of Gyanu, whom I knew to be assertive and bold in his moral stance and who seemed to respect his wife deeply. When I asked Ganga why her father did not address the situation, she explained that her father could only speak out on his wife's behalf after he was earning money on his own. At the time he was in school, Ganga explained, and he was "eating off" of his parent's fields. "Much later, he got angry with his mother, a little. *After he got a job and started earning money,* after we got older, then he got angry at my grandmother."

After bearing a third daughter and having been sent to her *māitī* twice before, Chirmei began to "hear the voices of the gods." She began to dance in the streets and compulsively worship, nearly every hour, whenever and wherever the gods told her. Her fingers were permanently stained red from the vermilion powder she smeared on the images of every god. She sang prayers and did not eat. Chirmei told me that she could not hear anyone else, just the voices of the gods, who talked to her alone. She was hailed by the gods and only through this calling could she and did she act. As Chirmei perhaps anticipated before this transformation, she was again quickly sent by her husband's family back to her *māitī.* Chirmei's mother had already died by now, and her sister did not take her in. "Sisters don't *have* to invite," Ganga explained to me, as she told this story in her home. "They invite only if they want to. It's not their duty. A sister's brother *has* to invite. But my mother had no brothers."

The main problem for her mother, as Ganga saw it, was that there were no brothers and therefore no invitations and no *māitī.* This is precisely what many fear would occur should women acquire a legal right to *angsa.* Opponents of the reform insisted that the new law would ultimately lead to a sister being forgotten by her brothers. This fear was closely associated with a fear of losing the desires and love cultivated in and through a son's possession of *angsa* and in women's frequent visits to their *māitī.* Even if she did have brothers, who were culturally bound to invite, it is unclear whether or not they would invite such a sister in distress, or for how long they would care for her.[40] Wandering from house to house, sometimes singing, sometimes crying, Chirmei was finally brought by the neighbors to a *guru-mā,* a religious healer, up in the hills of the Valley. The healer took her in and cared for her for seven months. "She called me daughter," Chirmei told me, many years after this initial meeting. Ganga remembers visiting her mother as she gradually came back to her former self. No food cooked from unknown hands, no salt, no meat, the *guru-mā* prescribed. Since that time, Chirmei has visited the *guru-mā* at least three times a year and she has donated some land she inherited to the healing center. Until her own death, in 2000, she called this place her *māitī*.

THE PLACE OF FOREIGNERS: INDIA AND THE UNITED STATES

Critiques about the potential loss of *māitī* or the sentiments that *māitī* evokes were often framed in trenchant but perhaps predictable terms: namely, that the entire reform movement was initiated by foreign ideas and therefore posed a threat to authentic Nepaliness.[41] In Khagendra Sangroula's summary of the debates, he notes that many felt "the demand for equal property rights comes from NGO women in an attempt to consume dollars" (Sangroula 2053: 5). Indeed, much of the money used to support NGOs that work for women's property rights came from large international donors, such as the U.S. Agency for International Development (Tuladhar and Joshi 1997). While journalists and intellectuals tended to emphasize the influence of dollars and international donors, popular critique almost always placed the blame on India.[42] In India, many people told me, echoing widely circulating and far-fetched rumors, they "burn their women" if the woman's family does not supply enough of a dowry.[43] "It is only like that over there," one middle-aged Newar man told me proudly. "Only to wear their [India's] customs here, that is the reason the issue was brought up here in Nepal." India is thought of as a place of base materialism, an immoral realm where people mistreat their women. Framed as a product of Indian thought, the demand for a daughter's inheritance right is simultaneously understood in relation to the growing materialism in Nepal, which itself is thought to be due to Indian influence.

It is not unusual that such criticism against India stems from a controversy about women and their cultural and legal rights. As many social critics have shown in a vast number of contexts, women's actions, more than the actions of men, carry heavy symbolic weight for the society as a whole, particularly in discussions about the destruction of cultural or national values (Chatterjee 1993; Mosse 1985; Parker et al. 1992). Arguments about nationalism are called up for every issue of central political importance in Nepal (and elsewhere), and these are almost always entwined with arguments about gender and sexuality.[44] In Nepal, the arguments about women and Nepal's national identity have for a long time been related to its position in relation to India.

Previous challenges to the state met with similar responses against foreign influence, especially targeting India. The overthrow of the Rana regime in 1950, for example, was blamed on Indian rupees and ideas by the ousted Ranas and others who opposed the regime change (Gupta 1993; Sangroula 2053). These ideas were exaggerated by the presence of Indian troops in Nepal, when the new Nepal government sought the help of India just after the coup against the Ranas in 1950. Similar accusations were made during the *jana āndolan* of 1990 (Sangroula 2053). The proposed property law animated these same antiforeign accusations. As in most forms of nationalism, the biggest threat was seen as coming from those people who were the most similar and living in the closest geographic range.

Anti-Indian sentiment has a long history in Nepal and is a seed from which many forms of Nepali nationalism have blossomed, from the nineteenth century through the twentieth. The juxtaposition of Nepal as a pure nation and India as a depraved, materialistic, and overly sexualized nation was used to bolster the Court of Nepal during the initial stages of state formation in the late eighteenth century. This image equally bolsters the prestige *angsa* offers to men, along with the control over female sexuality that has flourished with it. Prithvi Narayan Shah, known as the father of Nepal and a hero of Panchāyat nationalism from the 1960s to the 1980s, spoke vehemently against Moghul and British India in his efforts to unify the newly conquered territory that became modern Nepal. In his *Dibya Upadesh* (Divine or Brilliant Teachings) of 1774, he wrote: "Muglan [India] is near.[45] In that place there are singers and dancers. In rooms lined with paintings they forget themselves in melodies woven on the drum and sitar. There is great pleasure in these melodies. But it drains your wealth. They also take away the secrets of your country and deceive the poor. . . . Let no one open the mountain trails for these classes of people" (Stiller 1968: 46).

The political method for creating boundaries around this new conquered territory was developed through strategies of internal control, especially in the realms of sexuality. The melodies and dances that Prithvi Narayan Shah evokes in his teachings immediately conjure images of the decadence of court life and the uncontrolled sexuality that reigned there.[46] As Richard Burghart writes, these initial stages of forming a Nepali nation-state were rooted in this juxtaposition between a disciplined, true Hindustan (Nepal) and a morally depraved realm of pleasure (India) that could not resist such powers as the Mughals or the East India Company (1996: 269).

Similar ideas were the fuel of nationalism nearly a century later in slightly different forms. Pratyoush Onta (1997) discusses the work of Bal Krishna Sama, a Rana educated in India at the beginning of the twentieth century, who returned to Nepal to become one of Nepal's most prominent literary figures. Discussing one of Sama's most celebrated nationalist plays, *Mukunda Indira,* Onta shows that the image of a pure Nepal emerges against the backdrop of the immoral life in Calcutta. The main character of the play, Mukunda, travels to Calcutta only to descend into a life of constant drinking and frequent visits with prostitutes. Meanwhile, his wife, Indira, waits patiently in Nepal, like a Penelope for her Odysseus, until a friend brings Mukunda back from Calcutta to test his wife's fidelity, a test that she clearly passes. "Sama's portrayal of Calcutta," writes Onta, "[shows it as] a site of the absence of morality against which to imagine a pure Nepali nation" (1997: 88). This imagination depends on the image of a pure, virtuous Indira, who appropriately waits in her husband's home, in her *ghar.* Should Indira have had a cultural and legal place in her parents' home, there is no telling where she might have awaited his return. Waiting in the *ghar* defines her, in part, as a loyal, virtuous woman, whose sexuality is under severe scrutiny by her husband's family. (Similar themes occur in the more widely circulated *Munā-Madan,* an epic poem by Devkota frequently compared with the FM program I discuss in chapter 4. In this program, listeners' stories of suffering often weave in stories of journeys to places outside Nepal's borders.) In Bal Krishna Sama's play, we see that the nationalism of the early twentieth century in Nepal is closely linked to the institution of the *ghar,* the place where women's sexuality is controlled. In the play, *ghar* is a metonym for the nation, and thus it rings with a sense of territorial possession as well as possession over Nepali women's sexuality. While it is unclear how early this connection was made, by the 1920s *ghar* was a central idea and space through which ideas of national patrimony and women's place within it took shape.

The association between the home and national territory is a common one in many parts of the world. Throughout the eighteenth and nineteenth century in Europe, maintaining a proper home became a potent site for imagining the boundaries of the nation and the political power and prosperity of early European colonialists (Chakrabarty 1992; Comaroff and Comaroff 1989; Grewal 1996). As Dipesh Chakrabarty (1997) has suggested, the home in mid-nineteenth-century Bengal was also a place where emerging and conflicting ideals of Indian nationalism took shape. For some, the home was considered a place of an unhappy present, which should be subordinated to the more pressing project: the creation of a public, civic sphere of independent citizens.[47] For others, as represented in Rabindranath Tagore's (1916) famous novel *The Home and the World,* the Bengali home was the sole realm where a pure, ancient, mythic, Hindu social community lived separate from a British-infested, civil society. Civil society was merely tolerated in this idea of the home, but it was not the place where national sentiments could adequately flourish. As Chakrabarty points out, both of these notions are inflected by the Victorian ideals of the time, even though these early nationalists positioned themselves, in different ways, against the British.

Many of these nationalist ideas were making their way to Nepal at this time and after. Despite the difficulty common Nepalis had traveling, Nepali elites, like Bal Krishna Sama, went to India to study, and many Indians made their way to Nepal. In the late nineteenth century, for example, the ideas of the Hindu social reformers from the Arya Samāj came to Nepal through the teachings of Madhav Raj Joshi, a Newar Brahman who had lived in India for some time (Sever 1993: 277–78). Though Joshi was eventually exiled because of the antagonism he evoked in several members of the conservative priestly castes, the spirit of reform continued with younger generations, who became active in promoting Nepali nationalism in the 1920s. Balkrishna Sama himself arrived in Calcutta at the dawn of serious Indian nationalist agitation in 1921 (Onta 1997). He was no doubt surrounded by the well-established discourses about the home as an Indian realm used to oppose to the British. But rather than operating against the British, Sama uses the *ghar* in his play *Mukunda Indira* to describe a pure realm that served to contrast with the debauched lifestyle thriving in colonial Calcutta. Colonial India became a place of foreign impurity, and the *ghar* became a place where pure Nepaliness thrived.

Today, the symbolic and economic significance of the *ghar* for maintaining territorial divisions between Nepal and India still holds sway in the popular imagination of Nepalis. Many opponents of the *angsa* reform bill suggested that Nepal runs the risk of losing its land to India should daughters have the right to inherit. Because so many Nepali girls marry Indians, especially in the south, they argue, much of this land would quickly be incorporated into Indian households. Such arguments, Mary Des Chene points out, rest on the assumption that women ultimately have no control of their own property (Des Chene 1997). They also implicitly suggest that maintaining the *ghar,* as an inherited possession of sons, is an important means to securing Nepal's national sovereignty as distinct from India. Despite these paranoid accusations against India, the movement for women's inheritance in Nepal was no doubt directly or indirectly influenced by similar reforms in India. Many of the early reformers, such as Indira Rana and Silu Singh, went to school in India during in the 1950s and 1960s, just after the passing of the Hindu Succession Act of 1956, which, I have already noted, provided some important benefits to daughters, yet ultimately failed to achieve its stated aims.[48] They returned to Nepal as young lawyers, eager to put some of their education to work in Nepal.

BETWEEN LOVE AND PROPERTY

In an essay arguing for a political concept of love, Michael Hardt writes that the phrase "'I wouldn't do that for love or money' means I wouldn't do that in exchange for anything" (2011: 676). Rather than focus on the opposition, Hardt argues that this phrase might be read to reveal the similar function and power of love and money in creating and maintaining social bonds. Turning to Marx, Hardt shows that for the theorist of capitalism, love is clearly related inversely to the rule of private property. By abolishing property altogether, as Marx argues for, a new form of love must be created, "and this new love must fill the social role that property does now: It must have the power, in other words, to generate social bonds and organize social relationships" (Hardt 2011: 680–681). In the reflections on the changes that Nepalis envisioned might occur through this reform, it is clear that changes in relations of property would entail changes in relations of love, for activists and opponents alike. It is equally clear that the power of property to create and maintain social relations is not conceived of in opposition to love; but rather, love and property are closely entangled with each other, and their relation can be better understood by considering the different formations of voice at stake in this debate.[49]

At the time of the debate over the property rights of daughters very few people, including the activists, thought the *angsa* reform bill would pass. Nevertheless, the proposal generated an impressive degree of furor, a proliferation of talk and texts. From an ethnographic perspective, the possibilities people imagined reveal contests over cultural meaning and registered social anxieties felt in the wake of political change. Such contests, and the realms of cultural significance they expose, often get buried in "personal" texts that never surface, or they disappear when the transformation is made from rhetorical proposal to codified law. The bill *did* pass into law after the interim constitution declared Nepal to be a secular state in 2006. The future of the material, practical, and discursive life of sibling relations remains to be seen, and no doubt, as in India, many women may relinquish this birthright.[50] The passionate debates over its imagined fate highlight aspects of the democratic moment after 1990 that have continued to evolve since. The movement for the inheritance of daughters was the first major constitutional challenge of the liberal era in contemporary Nepal. At its heart was a contest over emerging subjectivities that were repeatedly defined through the figure of the voice and related practices of address, hailing, and recognition. The figure of the voice, most notably by way of the omnipresent discourse of *āwāj uṭhāune,* continues to define and shape both intimate and political subjectivities in the movements that have followed.

As central as the figure of the voice was to the liberal property rights movement of the 1990s, it has become an even more prominent discursive agent in Nepali public life in the years since.[51] With the widespread victory of the Maoists in the 2008 elections, an end to the monarchy quickly followed, and in the years that followed a series of rapid changes in government revealed the uncertain status of liberal democratic forms. As successive political movements have worked to reshape even more radically the relationship between monarch and subject as well as citizen and subjectivity, the questions raised in this chapter about voice and subjectivity may have become, if anything, more useful in gaining a more nuanced understanding of what is at stake in the widely divergent approaches to political and intimate freedoms in contemporary Nepal. The private and public lives of the one who raises her voice are inevitably bound up with ideas about a new democratic state and what its champions call New Nepal.[52]

Indira Rana's desire to publicly commemorate her mother's death and Silu Singh's invocation of the "genuine love" between husbands and wives described above evince a liberal subjectivity that echoes with those subjects who perform *āwāj uṭhāune.* Notions of free will and individual agency suffuse ideas about romantic love (Ahearn 2001), or what Silu Singh calls "genuine" love. Like all sentiments, such romantic love depends upon the cultural practices and social discourses that bring it into existence. The affects associated with mourning and inheritance at issue here are part of a broader field of sentiments that emerge in practices like love-letter writing (Ahearn 2001), confessional programs on the FM radio, and phone exchanges between lovers who have never met, all of which I discuss in chapters 3 and 4. Each of these fields enacting "genuine love" appears to be unencumbered by familial pressures and societal constraints,[53] and constitutes an inner desire that is key to the emerging subjects of Nepal's liberal democracy.

The practice of *āwāj uṭhāune* assumes a similar subject, either a person or a collective body, which is itself often figured as an individual agent able to directly and publicly express desire and discontent and, most importantly, to make wishes heard by other citizens and the state.[54] The subject of *āwāj uṭhāune* is constituted by choice and desire, rather than the categories of duty and obedience that characterize the subject of *bolāune*. The practices of *bolāune,* in particular, show us the fundamentally social nature of subjectivity, constituted through discursive and hailing practices, that sheds light on a broader truth about human subjectivity that liberal notions of "autonomous love" occlude. Through interpellative practices like *bolāune,* men and women recognize each other and themselves as gendered beings, making them who they are in relation to one another. We have also seen that one's sense of agency is inscribed in these subjectivities, which differs according to class and gender position.

To understand the debate about *angsa* only in terms of citizenship, rights, and the state is to remain too narrowly within a liberal framework, in which the citizen is considered primarily, if not exclusively, an individual subject. As we have seen, even though the activists invoke a liberal notion of voice and equality between men and women, their policy changes are not based upon an individual, autonomous subject. Instead, by advocating to keep the traditional Hindu system of property, they acknowledge that parents/fathers probably will not make liberal choices based on equality within the family. In their aspiration for a liberal model of personhood, they recognize and contend with the fact that many people do not act or even desire this liberal model.

The broader contests over competing subjectivities that emerge in this campaign and similar campaigns around the world require that we think beyond simply a question of rights and individual legal subjects. The social and discursive nature of subjectivity is often obscured in activists' emphasis on "equal rights," and in analytic discussions about such movements that center on legal rights and citizenship. Instead, nonliberal subjectivities that the activists wish to challenge are contingent on everyday hailing practices, patterns of speech, and talk about who speaks and who should be called to speak. To challenge property relations meant to challenge existing practices of speech and to alter the meaning of the voice. To have rights to *angsa* is to assume the position of a speaker, who summons rather than is summoned, and who thereby acquires a place of public recognition.[55] This transformation, expressed in the language of rights, fundamentally disturbs what it means to be a man and a woman in contemporary Nepal, but it also obscures the radically social figures of voice and subjectivity upon which such changes are based.

In the following chapter, I deepen the discussion of interpellated subjects and practices like *bolāune* by exploring the way the practice and discourse of *mukh herne* (looking at or seeing a face) interpellates subjects into political and intimate fields. While the rituals and practices of *mukh herne* constitute a field quite different from that of family property law and its public transformation, they are equally bound up with the creation of intimacy, subjectivity, and the contemporary "public" subject. In both property law and national family rituals of "seeing face," intimacy—whether romantic, familial, or political—is mediated through the figure of the voice and an embodied sense of presence. We turn, then, to an exploration of the relationship between voice and face, as two parts of the body that are assumed to share similar properties of self-presence and intersubjectivity between people.

TWO

Seeing Face and Hearing Voice

TACTILE VISION AND SIGNS OF PRESENCE

A person has no internal sovereign territory, he is wholly and
always on the boundary; looking inside himself, he looks into
the eyes of another or with the eyes of another.

MIKHAIL BAKHTIN, *Problems of
Dostoevsky's Poetics*

IN THE COURSE OF FIELDWORK, small, passing comments will occasionally strike the ethnographer as unusual, unexpected, or not entirely compre-
hensible. More often than not, such offhand remarks—words that, while
striking or odd, seem to lie outside one's field of study—are noted, and if they
do not occur again they are gradually forgotten. Sometimes such words are
simply disregarded as individual idiosyncratic remarks that do not have much
bearing on broader cultural or social questions. But sometimes there are
turns of phrase, figures of speech, or unexpected metaphors that stay in the
back of one's mind and recur in the margins of one's notes, only to reassert
themselves as one encounters their frequent repetition in other contexts.

Such was the case for me while I was conversing with Reena, a young
Newari woman, whom I did not see very often but whom I had known
since she was a young English student of mine several years prior to this
meeting.[1] We were talking about the recent bill to give daughters a birthright to their parents' property, the *angsa* (ancestral property) reform bill
that I discussed in the previous chapter. On the day I visited with Reena in
her house in Patan, a daily Nepali newspaper carried an article bearing the
title "It's Not Just *Angsa* That Is Needed, *Vangsa* (genealogy) Is Also
Needed."[2] As I have already argued, *vangsa* was the rarely discussed subject
that turned out to lie at the center of the controversial attempt to change
the laws of family property. So I was interested in hearing people's reactions
to this uncommon juxtaposition of *angsa* and *vangsa* in the context of the
reform bill.

FIGURE 5. At the water's edge on the holiday of *Āmāko mukh herne din*: a ritual example of "seeing face." Photo: Gopal Chitrakar.

Before visiting Reena, I had talked about the article with a close friend of mine who was studying anthropology at Tribuhuvan University. He had looked at me coyly and asked if I knew what the journalist meant. Without waiting for my reply, he raised his fist high and said in English, "*Vangsa*—genealogy—means 'power.'"[3] I was curious if I would get a similar response from a young woman who had not been reading anthropology for the past two years. When I met Reena, I asked her what she thought of this article. Having not read it, she simply shrugged her shoulders. Then I asked her what *vangsa* meant. She stared at me blankly and did not reply. I tried again, this time asking how she would say *vangsa* in Newari. She responded with two words: *khwa suweu,* the Newari words for "look at face." In case I did not understand, Reena repeated in Nepali: "*Khwa suweu* means *mukh herne* in Nepali." *Mukh herne* is a common colloquial phrase often used when people have not seen each in a long time (that is, "I finally get to look at your face"; *Balla balla timro mukh herna pāio*) or when they are morally condemning a person and avoiding their company (that is, "I will never look at that person's face"; *Tyo māncheko mukh kahile pani hernechaina [herdina]*).[4] Reena continued to explain, using a mix of Nepali and Newari:

"If a person has the same habits *[bānī]* as their grandparents, then we say: they have looked at their grandparents' face *[khwa suweu]*. Then they are within their grandparents' *vangsa.*"

"So what is the difference between looking at face *[khwa suweu]* and *vangsa?*" I asked her.

"No difference. To look at face *is vangsa [khwa suweu vangsa ho].*"

I knew immediately that this was an unusual comparison. Perhaps it is best understood as an awkward attempt by a young woman to explain a rather abstract but well-known concept—*vangsa*—to an eagerly inquiring anthropologist. I never again heard this comparison made, and when I asked several people, both Newars and other non-Newar Nepalis, about the relation of "looking at face" and *vangsa,* I was greeted with a puzzled look. And yet, after the conversation with Reena, I began to recognize a number of ways in which the phrase *mukh herne* resonated with the concept of genealogy: the national holidays to honor one's mother and father are called *mukh herne* days; in many Hindu Nepali weddings there is an opportunity to look at the bride's face for both the groom and the bride's relatives *(bwariko mukh herne);* the Newar postmarriage ceremony, when the bride's family comes to see their daughter after she has just moved into her new married home, her *ghar,* is called the *mukh herne* ritual *(khwa suweu,* in Newari); visits made to welcome a newborn baby into a family are described as moments of "looking at baby's face" *(baccako mukh herne).* Most strikingly, in relation to the previous chapter, when brothers describe the desire and obligation to call their married sisters home, they often link the practice of summoning their sisters with *mukh herne.* "We must call *[bolāune]* our sisters home," one Nepali young man told me, "I always want to look at my *didī's* [older sister's] face *[Didīko mukh jahile pani herna man lācha].*" The voice and the face are linked as two parts of the body that restore a sister's presence within her natal home. All of these practices are different forms of familial recognition that confirm one's entry into or continued belonging in a particular *vangsa,* or "genealogy." They reaffirm the moral standing of the entire genealogy.

When I asked Nepalis directly what the phrase *mukh herne* meant, most people were outwardly perplexed. How can one explain such a commonplace phrase? *Mukh herne* simply was a sign of mutual recognition, one person replied. Many people explained *mukh herne* in the negative, explaining why they would take pains to avoid seeing the face of another. One woman, Shizu, noted that the negative form of the phrase was often used to avoid a person of questionable moral status. "Let's just say, there is a boy who is not so good *[narāmro kettā]*. To avoid also becoming not so good, people say, 'Hey, you shouldn't look at that one's face' *[Eh, tyesko mukh herna hundaina]*."

Shizu's statement expresses an anthropological truism: how a person is seen by others depends, in part, on whose company they share, on whose faces are seen together. But Shizu goes further than this, for she suggests that the act of seeing another's face is potentially a contagious moment; there is a risk of also becoming not good. Seeing face regulates a person's moral standing within the family, among intimates, and in the political field. The act of deliberately avoiding a person's face is a means of asserting moral censure. Translated into colloquial English, *Tyesko mukh herdina* (I don't look at that person's face) is the equivalent of saying, "I don't talk to that person anymore."[5]

The politics of seeing face, I soon learned, is intertwined with the politics of voice. The term for face used here *(mukh)* is also the term for mouth, such that the mouth and practices of the mouth—eating and talking—serve as metonyms for the face.[6] Moments of *mukh herne* unleash waves of unspoken feeling and discipline the social boundaries between family members, between the king and his subjects, between young and old politicians, between close friends.

In this chapter, I explore the shared "semiotic ideology" (Keane 2003) of the face and the voice. Webb Keane defines semiotic ideology as the "basic assumptions about what signs are and how they function in the world. It determines, for instance, what people will consider the role that intentions play in signification to be, what kinds of possible agents . . . exist to which acts of signification might be imputed, whether signs are arbitrary or necessarily linked to their objects, and so forth" (2003: 419). As Keane argues, words and things can share a semiotic ideology that determines their status as objects, subjects, or agents in culturally and historically specific ways. Here I suggest that the semiotic ideology that links the face and the voice is their similar function as indices of immediacy, presence, and the intimacy of social (and often genealogical) relations. The voice inherent in practices like *bolāune* and the face inherent in practices of *mukh herne* both imply the self-presence of actors to one another and often their hierarchical relation vis-à-vis each other. At a broad level, then, this shared semiotic ideology suggests similarities in the ways Nepalis interpret the visuality of face and the aurality of voice.

This chapter deepens our understanding of the voice in practices like *bolāune* by focusing on a similar form of intimate and genealogical recognition that occurs in the practices of *mukh herne*. Both *bolāune* and *mukh herne,* I argue, are processes of mediation through which genealogical and intimate subjects come into being, revealing overlaps between the ideology of the face and the voice. What it means to be and to feel oneself as a man, a woman, a wife, a husband, a son, a daughter, a mother, or a father does not exist prior to these practices; instead, such subjectivities depend upon and emerge from them. Both *bolāune* and *mukh herne* also present themselves as immediate and direct connections between two or more individuals, yet as I argue here and throughout the book, the sense of presence and immediacy is itself an effect of a mediating process. The face in *mukh herne* and the voice in *bolāune* are not external expressions or windows onto a prior given self; instead, they are the media through which that subject is produced in relation to others. As forms of mediation, they are all means by which "the self recognizes itself by returning to itself . . . [and] this constitutive mediation also produces a fiction of premediated existence" (Mazzarella 2004: 357). In other words, through the face and the voice a person recognizes whom he or she is in relation to others, while at the same time denying the process of mediation that constitutes this self in the first place.

Practices of *bolāune* and *mukh herne* explicitly rely upon and require another person as the means of subject formation. To look at a face one needs another person or an object: a mirror, a photograph, a film. The practices of *bolāune* and *mukh herne* therefore accord with Bakhtin's insight about intersubjectivity; namely, that "a person has no internal sovereign territory . . . looking inside himself, he looks *into the eyes of another* or *with the eyes of another*" (1984: 287). This view contrasts with liberal notions of the democratic public sphere, whereby selves are conceived of as autonomous, interior, and already-formed entities jostling with other autonomous and authentic selves for expression. This liberal, autonomous, and authentic selfhood Bakhtin and his compatriot Voloshinov continuously challenged throughout their writings: "both Voloshinov and Bakhtin insist on the essential role of otherness in shaping and defining the self" (Morson and Emerson 1990: 200). In practices like *bolāune* or *mukh herne,* we see a clear display of intersubjectivity—selves represented not as autonomous beings but as emerging in and through relations with others. And this display of intersubjectivity exposes the mediated quality of all social interaction, particularly in instances when mediation is denied.

All semiotic ideologies are subject to transformation. While the face and the voice are aligned in certain intimate and political relations, there are other situations in which the face and the voice are explicitly distinguished.

We can see transformations in this semiotic ideology when activists, especially after *jana āndolan* I and during the 1990s, call upon a liberal notion of voice that they clearly differentiate from the way the face has traditionally mediated political and familial relations. By calling upon a liberal notion of voice, they deploy another semiotic ideology that distinguishes the face and the voice. Like the voice of *bolāune,* the face of *mukh herne* and related visual practices invokes presence, mutual recognition, and familial intimacies, and often constitutes relations of social and political hierarchy. A democratic and liberal notion of voice, however, assumes parity between speakers and assumes that the voice is a direct expression of an already-formed interior self. Its ideology appears to undermine the intersubjective relations created by *mukh herne* and *bolāune.* In this chapter, I explore both the shared semiotic ideology of the face and voice, particularly in constituting intimate, genealogical relations, as well as an alternative ideology of voice that increasingly challenges this alignment between face and voice.

Once the face (like the voice) is thought of as a medium, we can begin to explore more complexly the "intermedium relationships" (Mazzarella 2004: 345) between the face and other mediating practices in which the face is implicated, such as photography, film, and ritual. These other media may extend or enhance the semiotic ideology of "seeing face," often to enhance its political and intimate effects. These different media intersect and work in tandem with one another, as in the rituals of *mukh herne* or the viewing of royal photographs that I describe below. Here I explore the intermedium relationship between face, voice, ritual, and technology as different and equally prevalent media for bringing subjectivity into being (Mazzarella 2004: 345). While film, photography, ritual, and the face may follow slightly different semiotic ideologies, all of these media partake in the formation of intimate and political subjectivity. Nepalis may not explicitly describe the face as a medium in the same way as they would a photograph, but they certainly will recognize the constitution of subjectivity and social identity that takes place through practices of looking at the face.

Mukh herne is a shorthand term for a range of visual encounters that are characterized by tactility and mutuality, moral and social inclusion, and a merging between those who exchange glances. By focusing on the phrase *mukh herne,* this chapter emphasizes the everyday and often secular form of these encounters. But there are obvious connections between intimate and familial visual greetings and other more overtly political or religious visual practices. Not every visual encounter is described as *mukh herne;* rather, the idiom describes affectionate relationships that are usually hierarchical and involve multiple social duties and obligations. *Mukh herne*—along with a range of other terms, such as *mukhā-mukh* (face-to-face), *dekhā-dekh* (see each other), and *darśan* (seeing and being seen by a higher being, which I discuss below)—also refers to the intimate exchange of glances between people or between a person and an image that can be devotional, political, or familial or can mark a powerful beginning of romance.

A final point of this chapter, then, is to show the continuity between the political and religious and the everyday, intimate forms of recognition that occur through the medium of the face. The chapter moves from everyday examples of *mukh herne* to the more clearly political and religious visual encounters, such as well-known Hindu devotional practices like *darśan* and the national holiday and ritual called *āmāko mukh herne din* (literally, day to look at mother's face). As a set of social, ritual, and discursive practices, *mukh herne,* like the voice, interpellates both intimate and political subjects, bringing them into being within the family, the nation, and the former Hindu kingdom.

SEEING FACE AND HEARING VOICE: EPISTEMOLOGIES OF PRESENCE

Parallels between the face and the voice are not entirely surprising. Most Euro-American philosophies of the body as well as popular modern thought, for example, invoke both the voice and the face to describe the immediacy of certain "face-to-face" social relations.[7] Poststructuralist scholars have critiqued assumptions about the voice and the face as self-present forms that exist outside of and prior to the advent of technology (for example, Axel 2006; Derrida [1967] 1976 ; Kittler 1990, 1999; Sterne 2003). Technology and media are thought to rupture once-holistic worlds, creating disembodied experiences and artificially isolating the senses. In the history of anthropology as well, face-to-face interactions are often celebrated as the most basic, fundamental form of social interaction, upon which all other mediated or technological relations are based. In this line of reasoning, the face, like the voice, becomes a sign of authenticity, of a person's interior consciousness and individuality, of presence and immediacy.

Although face and voice are often conflated as indices of presence in popular and philosophical thought, the act of seeing and the act of hearing are just as often opposed to each other. Jonathan Sterne refers to the common distinction made between vision and aurality as the "audiovisual litany" that recurs in many writings on the senses and with which he takes issue (2003: 15). According to this litany, vision removes us from the world, tends toward objectivity, primarily involves the intellect, and requires distance from its object of perception. Hearing, by contrast, is a sense presumed to be about interiors, subjectivity, affect, and immersion in the world (Ong 1982). Following this logic, vision is most frequently deemed to be the quintessentially modern sense, one that is alternately demonized by critics and celebrated by those who associate vision with reason and clear thinking. As Martin Jay (1994) argues, what distinguishes European modernity from other places and times was not so much the sudden rise of the visual in dominant culture as the prevalence of *critical analyses* of the hegemonic status of seeing in post-Cartesian thought.[8] Hearing, which extends to voice and face-to-face interactions, is likewise idealized as a nostalgic residue of premodern culture—often called "oral culture"—that exists most prominently in some places and among some people (that is, in postcolonial nations and among the laboring classes).[9]

Anthropologists have intervened in these universalist understandings of vision and hearing by showing that the semiotic ideologies associated with face and voice differ across cultural contexts (for example, Benson 2008; Fox 2004; Hirschkind 2006; Pinney 1997; Strassler 2009; Weidman 2006). In discussions of face, these differences are often related to culturally specific understandings of personhood, and show the face to be a sign often bound up with politics. In Indonesia, for example, several scholars have argued that the face is not conceived of as a direct expression of interiority, but rather as a mask (Florida 1995; Siegal 1986; Strassler 2009).[10] In his analysis of photographic portraiture in India, Christopher Pinney similarly shows that the face is not perceived as a window into the soul nor as an expression of internal moral character; rather, photos are perceived as depicting a sitter's *vyaktitva* (demeanor or personality), which is clearly distinguished from their *charitra,* "an essentially internal moral quality or character which was apparent only in deeds" (1997: 199). Dorinne Kondo's (1997) *About Face: Performing Race in Fashion and Theater* uses the face as a metaphor to forward the theoretical argument that all identities are enacted through performance. For Kondo, like the other scholars mentioned, the face is not a transparent window into a stable and essential interior self. The manipulation and changing nature of faces that are particularly obvious in theatrical performances and fashion ultimately support Kondo's contribution to theories of performativity. Instead of providing direct access to a unique individual's interiority, each of these examples shows the face to be a medium for establishing social personae and relationships.

So, too, does *mukh herne* inscribe a social relationship and make the presence of that relationship paramount. On the one hand, *mukh herne* reveals associations made by Nepalis between face, presence, immediacy, intimacy, and directness. Yet in spite of this ideology of presence, when we look ethnographically at practices of *mukh herne,* the face—like the voice—is a form that clearly mediates social relations in anything but direct ways. *Mukh herne* practices further complicate the assumption that seeing is a sense based primarily on objectification and distance between observer and observed. Instead, *mukh herne* implies a tactile connection between the viewer and the viewed. *Mukh herne* reveals an underlying semiotic ideology at work in Nepali conceptions of face and voice that emphasizes persons often defined through relations of asymmetry and authority. This semiotic ideology persists even as it is being challenged by liberal notions of voice (evident in phrases like *āwāj uṭhāune*) that place primacy on the individual or collective actor and his or her direct expression in contrast to prevailing authorities. The idea of contact-establishing relationships is still at work, for example, in practices like *mukh herne* and in some invocations of voice like *bolāune.* Different understandings of personhood coexist alongside one another, sometimes without trouble and sometimes in uneasy ways.

The idiom and the practices of *mukh herne* resonate with Emmanuel Levinas's (1969) discussion of the face as the foundation of intersubjectivity and the primary medium through which ethical action and responsibility begin. As Levinas (1969: 194–219) argues, seeing a face marks the beginning of a social and ethical world connected to language and voice: only in the act of facing one another do we actually learn to speak. Levinas describes the face as a transcendent category that signifies the absolute Otherness of God and, by extension, the experience of infinite alterity.[11] The face is that which resists full incorporation into another, and is thought to be without any mediation: "without the intermediary of any image or sign" (200). Therefore confrontation with another's face, for Levinas, constitutes a primary ethical relationship between humans that takes on the stature of an ethical relationship between human and divine. *Mukh herne* practices align with Levinas's theory because the act of looking at a face is always an ethical and a moral encounter.[12] But the presence implied in *mukh herne* is not the same presence implied in Levinas or other European philosophical discussions of face. Instead of encountering the essence of a person directly and without mediation, *mukh herne* makes immediately apparent the *presence of a social relationship* constituted by two individuals facing each other.

EVERYDAY VISUAL ENCOUNTERS:
FACE AND MORAL CENSURE

The ethical and moral aspects of *mukh herne* become clearer when we turn to ethnography: the everyday uses of the phrase that frequently evoke an ambivalent relation between intimacy and the regulatory power of the family and the nation. The inclusive, affectionate, tactile connection that the act of looking at a face produces between family members or citizens and their rulers also entails a set of moral prescriptions and obligations. When a family member transgresses moral or sexual boundaries, the most common response is to refuse to invite this person home *(bolāūdina)* or to refuse to look at their face, acts that practically amount to the same thing. Like *bolāune,* looking at a face is implicated in the *ijjat* (respect, prestige) economy (Liechty 2003: 83). "The ijjat economy is never only a *moral* economy or only a *material* economy," writes Liechty. "It is always both" (85, italics in original). The exchange of glances that occurs during *mukh herne* rituals is part of a larger set of exchanges—of gifts, services, products, and so on—that constitute a family unit and its *ijjat*. *Ijjat* is frequently glossed as social prestige, honor, respectability, and sometimes even "face,"[13] and as I discussed in the previous chapter, the concept remains central to maintaining social expectations and respect. To possess *ijjat* requires the acquisition of proper services, goods, education, jobs, and marriages, as well as the observation of proper rituals and sexual mores, all of which contribute to familial prestige. Though *ijjat* is essential to the construction of middle-class identity, as Liechty shows, it is much broader than a class concept. The material and moral dimensions of *ijjat* and its relation to face are also at work in practices that are not exclusively performances of class.

When a new bride enters her husband's family, for example, she is formally welcomed by members of her husband's family, who line up to look at her face. With her legs crossed, and clad in a thick brocade red and gold sari, the bride usually sits for several hours with her eyes downcast as people gaze upon her face. This is also the moment in which family members of the groom give the requisite gifts that welcome a bride in (from the groom's side). At one wedding I attended, a friend pointed out this ritual of *mukh herne* and told me, "Now, she [the bride] belongs to them." The downcast eyes and stoic features of a bride do not in any way indicate her unique individuality; rather, the act of seeing her face incorporates the bride into the husband's genealogy, with all the obligations, moral duties, and material exchanges that this new relationship entails. The first time a son-in-law visits his new wife's home he, too, goes through a *mukh herne* ritual to meet his wife's family. Among Newars, there is a separate *mukh herne* day (*khwa suweu*, in Newari), when relatives of the bride visit her in her new home, bearing gifts that symbolize the present and future support she will get from her *māitī,* her natal home. As at weddings, these rituals are photographed and videotaped, creating visual records of the practice that add a sense of importance and a sense of being seen. In watching herself be seen in this fashion—during the event and later in photos and videos—the bride also comes to see herself in her new positions: as a wife, a daughter-in-law, a sister-in-law, and a potential mother.

In some respects, the act of seeing face in *mukh herne* rituals resembles what Deleuze and Guattari refer to as faciality, in which the face becomes a generic sign that carries moral messages about a person's social character and abilities. In their discussion of faciality, the face serves as a medium through which similarities or differences between groups of people are established, "as when the aesthetics of the face play an important role in racial schemes, class structures, and other classificatory logics" (Deleuze and Guattari 1987: 185–93; cited in Benson 2008: 596). Peter Benson (2008) uses the concept of faciality to show how perception and power interact , shaping what people see when they look at other people's faces. Tracking the relation between Mexican laborers in a North Carolina tobacco plantation and their bosses, Benson gives the example of a laborer mimicking the face of his boss as he surveys his laborer. Such acts of mimicry reveal "the fact that the face bears traces of social processes and pressures, not the asocial singularity of an individual" (2008: 612). The stoic face of a Nepali bride similarly reveals the generic sign of becoming a wife and potential mother and entering a new genealogical line. The face in both cases is a fully social sign rather than a sign of a unique individual.

And yet, the concept of faciality presumes that faces are constantly being read, interpreted, and put through a social hermeneutics in ways that do not occur in most *mukh herne* rituals. People do not "read" the face of the bride, the baby, or a parent during such rituals to determine who they really are socially and personally. Instead, the face serves as a site of mediation, through which people actively engage and establish their genealogical and intimate connections, or actively sever such ties by refusing to see a person's face. There are certainly instances in which the face is "read," such as when Nepalis examine photographs of potential marriage partners. In the exchange of such photos, all members of the family—especially the mother—are called upon to determine whether this is a suitable match by interpreting their faces, body, and composure. "You can tell this one is a 'naughty one' *[badmās],*" one mother of a friend told me, showing me a picture sent by a suitor to her daughter. The photo depicted a young man who stood in front of a motorcycle, with long hair covering his eyes, a T-shirt, jeans, and a stoic, tough-guy expression. "Just looking at his face you know that! *[mukh herera thāhā hun-cha!].*" These are clear examples of faciality. But in ritualized and most everyday expressions of *mukh herne,* people are not engaging in a social reading of the face.

When put into its negative construction—one of the most common ways I heard the phrase uttered—"not looking at a face" *(mukh herdina)* marks the moral or sexual transgressions that threaten the respectability or *ijjat* of the family as a whole. The divorced man, Laxman, whose ex-wife's claim to *angsa* property I discussed in chapter 1, often spoke about his former wife by telling me he refused to look at her face. Once his wife began demanding her rightful portion of *angsa,* Laxman had to appear in court several times a month to fill out numerous bureaucratic papers. He sent his lawyer to do the task for him, he told me, in order to avoid meeting his wife face-to-face. "Why should I look at that one's face?" he asked me, rhetorically. "I don't want to look at her face, so I don't go." In refusing to exchange glances with his former wife, Laxman was expressing his moral condemnation of her and his desire not to engage in other material exchanges with her (which he felt the court was forcing upon him, against his will). To not see her face was a way to reject her claims to what Laxman viewed as his exclusive property. He explained that his children similarly avoided seeing their mother's face. "When she [the mother and ex-wife] used to come to the house, and when they saw their mother, they would run quickly inside. To not look at her face *[usko mukh nahernalāi].* My daughter says, 'I don't want to look at her face.' To others, my daughter says, 'My mother is not [here] *[merī āmā chaina].*'"

The words that Laxman attributes to his daughter, *merī āmā chaina,* are used to describe a person who has moved away or a person who has died.[14] Explicit assertions of not looking at a face indicate a broken relationship, a fall in reputation, exclusion, a form of social death. By not looking at his former wife's face, particularly in the context of this legal battle, Laxman was effectively proclaiming the fact that he no longer had any material or moral responsibility toward her, for she had tarnished the family's *ijjat* not only by leaving, but by making claims to *angsa*. In effect, not looking at her face was a declaration that she no longer existed in his social world.

A similar kind of social death befell a thirty-year-old high-caste Newar woman from Patan who eloped with a Newar man of the butcher caste. I had come to know Ambika's family after living for several months in Patan, but I did not meet Ambika until much later. Ambika was only sixteen when she decided to marry the boy she liked from school. To evoke her sense of isolation and her family's anger at ruining their *ijjat*, Ambika spoke repeatedly about their avoidance of her face:

> Up to one whole year, [they] didn't look at my face. Out of anger. After one year, my younger sister came.... Really, after three months of being here, I had a feeling like I wanted to go back to my own *ghar*.... It's not like I wanted to marry someone else, I just wanted to go back to my own house. But it wasn't possible to go.... It was as if I died. For one whole year they didn't look at my face. Then slowly, slowly—how can one leave one's own daughter? Later I went to look at [their] face[s]. My mother was about to beat me *[piṭne]* me. Of course. After nine months of carrying me in her womb, sixteen years of raising me, feeding me, educating me, then one day, without saying anything, the daughter just walks away from home—and even then, to another caste—the anger will of course rise up. That's the reason for her anger. I just sat there silently. She was about to hit me and my grandmother stopped her, [and said,] "Whatever's happened, happened. What's done is done. What's the point of beating [her], you can't kill her now. She's already gone."

To not look at her face marked Ambika's fall in reputation, the loss of her family's *ijjat,* and her exclusion from the family that Ambika explicitly compared to death. More than sixteen years later, Ambika does return to see her parents. But she does so in the dark, after her grandfather has gone to sleep, and through the back alleyways so as not to be seen on the main street. Again, she explained that she did not want others to look at her face. "What, am I going to walk on the street in the open, so arrogantly?" she asked me, rhetorically. To do so, Ambika implied, would be failing to display that she still recognized her prior transgressions. Her surreptitious walk through the alleyways was a way to preserve her family's *ijjat,* by not letting the neighbors see her family welcome her home.

Ījjat is about conducting and negotiating oneself in public, and women, perhaps more than men, feel the burden of the *ījjat* economy, for they carry more of the weight in upholding a family's *ījjat*. As I discussed in chapter 1, the inheritance of *angsa* property mediates and monitors a woman's sexuality and a family's *ījjat*. Even so, young men also expressed their sense of visual surveillance by family members, though to a lesser extent. Many young men described to me the pressure from their friends and peers of upholding the appearance of modern masculinity, which meant having a girlfriend, a peer group of friends, and not being bound to the family—a form of pressure that worked outside the bounds and often in conflict with the familial *ījjat* economy. They often feared the effects of encountering a relative who would disapprove. Some, like Dilip, a young man in his late twenties who had studied in Delhi for several years, felt this form of surveillance to be unwarranted or incomprehensible. Dilip recounted meeting one of his elder relatives on New Road, one of the major shopping streets, while he was walking with his girlfriend.

"I can't understand it sometimes, here in Kathmandu. One day I was walking with my girlfriend down New Road, and one of my father's relatives came along. I wanted to introduce him *[paricaya garāuna]*. But then, almost as soon as he saw me, he ran into the gully!"

"Why do you think?" I asked him.

"To not look at (my) face! *[Mukh nahernalāi!]*"

Dashing into a small alleyway, the older relative stepped out of the range of Dilip's vision, interrupted their contact, and silently but directly conveyed his judgment of Dilip by not encountering him face-to-face. To look at Dilip directly would be to sanction his actions, a way of conveying "you are part of my moral and social world." Avoiding such an encounter pronounces judgment on Dilip and his actions, or at the very least obviates the elder relative's responsibility to make such judgments directly. In such social encounters, not looking at a face is a way of denying a set of familial ties and obligations that remain invisible and unspoken until transgressions are made.

TACTILE SEEING

In the above ethnographic examples, the discourse about *mukh herne* implies a mutuality and tactile connection between those who exchange glances. Like a host of other South Asian visual practices, *mukh herne* might be described as a form of what Michael Taussig, drawing on Walter Benjamin's work, calls "tactile seeing," whereby "seeing something or hearing something is to be in contact with that something" (Taussig 1994: 206).[15] Tactile seeing breaks down the audiovisual litany that Sterne critiques and the opposition between seeing and hearing that it implies. Instead, tactile seeing reveals striking parallels in the visual and the aural, the face and the voice. By emphasizing the tactile and physical connection that some visual practices establish between people, seeing can no longer be conceived of as exclusively a distancing sense as it is in many critiques of modern visuality. "Tactile seeing" may be hard to discern, given the dominance of other modes of seeing. But in visual practices like *mukh herne*, the sensory qualities of vision are explicit and central to everyday forms of recognition.

The tactile seeing entailed in practices of *mukh herne* are particularly obvious in the closely related and much discussed Hindu devotional practice of *darśan*, a viewing or audience with a more powerful being, such as a god, a holy person, or an elder (Chakrabarty 2000; Davis 1997; Eck 1981; Jain 2007; Pinney 2002, 2004; Rajagopal 2001). Generally, *mukh herne* is a more broadly used and secular form of visuality that can occur between equals or differently positioned people, whereas *darśan*, a Hindu devotional practice, always indicates asymmetries between the parties exchanging glances. *Darśan* gains its authority from the religious context, but it is also used in everyday contexts in ways that often overlap with *mukh herne*. Arvind Rajagopal's description of *darśan*, as discussed among viewers of the popular *Ramayana* TV serial in India, nicely captures its tactile qualities: "*[Darśan]* connotes a more physical sense of space than its English language equivalent; the deity gives *darshan*, and the devotee takes *darshan*; one is "touched" by *darshan*, and seeks it as a form of contact with the deity. The relationship it establishes is tactile as much as it is visual, rendering the televisual image into a material presence, at least for the duration of the dharmic serial" (2001: 93).

Most scholarly discussions of *darśan* focus on its primary religious significance in creating what Richard Davis (1997: 32–33) terms an "aesthetics of presence," whereby the divine is literally embodied by its iconic image. Here I show that the practice encompasses a wide range of encounters with a higher being, from the sacred to the everyday: doing *pujā* at a temple; an audience with the king or high political leader; the viewing of photographs of dead relatives; greetings on the phone or in person between a child and their parent(s) or elder relatives, between a lower and higher politician, or between two colleagues of different status in the workplace. In all cases, like *mukh herne,* seeing is a form of sensory connection between two parties that exchange glances, who mutually constitute their relationship through their gaze.

Christopher Pinney (2004) characterizes the tactile qualities of *darśan*-related practices as a "corpothetic" (sensory, corporeal aesthetics) form of seeing, a merging between the viewer and the image seen. When villagers encounter divine images, he writes, the power of the image derives from the visual and bodily performances of the viewers. Images need to be "seated"—allowing them to be seen—so that they become something more than a mere piece of paper: "by placing them before our eyes, . . . *shakti* (energy) has come into them" (Pinney 2002: 363). The face is a core feature of the body that brings this aesthetics of presence into being: the face of a new god picture or statue remains covered until the proper moment of worship and gains its power only when the face is revealed and people behold its image. As Pinney notes, worshipers cup their hands after a blessing of fire in front of an image and "wash the blessing from the deity onto their face" (365). The prominence of the face in South Asian film similarly suggests the tactile mutuality of seeing. In the film *Jai Santoshi Ma* (1975), "intercut shots of the Satyavadi's and Santoshi's faces are used repetitively to inscribe the mutuality of vision that binds the devotee to the goddess" (Pinney 2002: 360). This mutual binding of one person to another, or of a person to a god, makes the act of seeing a face so powerful in Nepal and in other parts of South Asia.

The mutuality and tactile seeing of *mukh herne* and *darśan* pose important challenges to dominant theories of visuality and their attendant models of personhood. The corpothetic merging that occurs in *mukh herne* and *darśan,* runs counter to dominant Western traditions of visuality that "privilege a disembodied, unidirectional, and disinterested vision" (Pinney 2002: 359). In contrast to the contemplative aesthetics that characterizes much Euro-American art, as Pinney argues, this bodily engagement with images occurs in a range of culturally diverse practices, including South Asian practices of *darśan*. These corpothetic forms of seeing offer a broader "counterhistory of visuality" that operates not only in South Asia, but also in other marginal visualities in Europe, America, and elsewhere (Pinney 2002: 359).

Mukh herne practices, like *darśan,* contribute to this counterhistory and push it further to demonstrate that corpothetic visuality is not exclusively in the domain of religious or religiously inspired representations (such as Indian films depicting gods or Hindu chromolithographs) or even devotional practice. Furthermore, as Pinney briefly notes, this zone of mutuality and tactile presence is not exclusively visual; it also occurs through aural modes, as in the unexpected moment during the hijacking of Indian Airline planes when the Sikh hijacker sang popular Hindu film music and passengers asked for more, which Ashish Nandy analyses (Pinney 2002: 361). *Mukh herne* and *darśan* help us extend this observation to show that visual practices, when seen from the perspective of their shared semiotic ideology, reveal links between the voice and the face as two related zones of mutuality.

Many scholars of South Asian cultures have discussed the seductive and sometimes dangerous powers to ignite passion and communion through the exchange of glances. Margaret Trawick writes of the power to excite the passions through the meeting of eyes in Tamil Nadu, which is described as a kind of *darśan:* "Souls are said to mix through the eyes. The first sight of a potential spouse is a kind of *darshan*—a powerful emotional encounter and a transfer of spiritual and sexual powers. A woman could lose her chastity through such a glance" (1990: 95).

Whereas in Tamil Nadu the term for such exchanges of glances maintains the devotional sense of *darśan,* in Nepal the more everyday term *mukh herne* might be used to describe similar mutual gazes between potential lovers. Laura Ahearn recounts how lovers frequently describe the beginning of their romance as deriving from powerful, and often wordless, moments of meeting face-to-face (2001: 120). Such descriptions of erotic love as an external power that afflicts a person abound in South Asian popular representations—film, novels, television series—as well as in people's own descriptions of intimate experiences. A close friend's brother, Rajit, recounted meeting his future wife to me in such a fashion. Following the common trope of a Bollywood film, he described the suddenness with which they fell in love by looking at each other's face. Seeing her first from a window on his way to the Kumbhaswar temple complex (a temple that is notorious for drawing young couples in to furtive meetings), he noticed that she was looking at him. They looked at each other, and according to Rajit, those glances solidified their prospective union. He then began to find out more about her through neighbors and soon proposed to marry her.

While such examples of romantic love may appear to be more egalitarian than previous descriptions of *darśan,* I frequently encountered similar descriptions in the many letters sent to FM radio that implied a relation of subordination and asymmetry between the lovers (see chapter 4). A young man directly addressed his former girlfriend, Rupa, in a letter embedded within his own letter to the FM radio host. "Dear Rupa," he wrote, "Since the dawn of our acquaintance I have looked upon you as a goddess. May I take *darśan* from you in every lifetime."[16] When the term *darśan* is not used, the relation is not as clearly asymmetrical. A young woman writes to one of her favorite radio hosts about the initial stages of her love affair, and as with Rajid, seeing each other's face is the trope used to describe their budding romance: "Suddenly or unexpectedly, I saw a handsome young man near my home. After looking at each other, a strangely beautiful feeling started growing inside of me . . . perhaps that feeling could be love. . . . He used to hang around my neighborhood, and we used to see each other looking at the other's face *[mukh herera dekhchaü]*. . . . I could see clearly on his face that his eyes were looking for me."[17] That "strange feeling" arises *through* the act of looking at each other's face, again emphasizing the constitutive force of these glances in shaping one's subjective world. Desire here emerges through external acts that in turn shape embodied subjectivities (Mahmood 2005). In her analysis of the women's piety movement in Egypt, Saba Mahmood similarly shows that Egyptian Muslim women learn the moral sensibility of shyness only through repetitive acts of veiling. Bodily acts and the face itself are not masks that reflect or deflect an essential interior self; "action does not issue forth from natural feelings but *creates* them" (2005: 157). The tactile contact established in acts of *darśan* and *mukh herne* becomes a means of generating interior feelings. Looking at a face not only incites feelings of attachment and passion; it also points to the mediation and intersubjectivity established by *mukh herne* and *darśan*.

Darśan gains its authority from the religious implications of the term, but it is also used in everyday settings in Nepal. It can be a form of vocal greeting, on the telephone or in person, when Nepalis address an elder or a parent, saying: *"Buwa, darśan"* (Father, *darśan*). As an everyday vocal greeting, *darśan* is only spoken to those higher than oneself and to members of one's kin or caste as a means of signifying their hierarchy and genealogical connection. Among royal and Rana families, members always greet each other with *darśan* to indicate their royal status. A person might greet higher members of their own caste or family with *darśan,* one friend recounted, but all other neighbors are greeted with the more neutral *namaste*. Sometimes a friend might joke with another, if they have not met each other in a while, saying, "Hey, how many days has it been! It has become so hard to take your *darśan! [Ey, kati din bhyo?! Timro darśan pāuna kasto gāro!].*" This jocular tease suggests that the friend has become so busy and important that he or she has had no time to meet their more lowly friends. The teasing remark also reveals the democratic sentiments of this invocation of *darśan*. Its message suggests that *anyone* who works hard enough—not only a person born into a royal position—can become a person worthy of receiving *darśan*. Such statements are intimate greetings that confirm the authority of the person being addressed by invoking a visual practice used to establish authority and express respect.

While clearly related, *mukh herne* and *darśan* are not interchangeable practices. *Darśan* invokes a sacred, devotional relation of hierarchy, whereas *mukh herne* may or may not invoke such hierarchies. They both involve a form of tactile seeing and thereby challenge dominant histories of vision that emphasize the contemplative, objective, distant observer. Closely tied to the voice and part of the same semiotic ideology, the face here is shown to be a tactile, mediating form through which intimate, genealogical connection and morally obligatory relationships are formed and sustained. The face is the medium, like the voice, through which people come to see themselves as social beings. Through the voice and the face people come to feel and inhabit sentiments of intimacy, desire, moral obligation, and devotion.

NATIONAL RECOGNITION AND FACE: *ĀMĀKO MUKH HERNE DIN*

The devotional, religiously inspired practice of *darśan* and the more everyday familial aspects of *mukh herne* come together in rituals like *āmāko mukh herne din* (day to look at mother's face). These holidays were the most common way Nepalis described the idiom of *mukh herne* to me. Though *mukh herne* days are celebrated for fathers and teachers, *āmāko mukh herne din* is by far the most popular of these holidays. On this day, children who live far away return home to give gifts to their mothers. In Kathmandu, many who have lost their mothers make a trip to Mātātirtha pond, just outside the city. There, it is said, a son or daughter can look at her mother's face on the surface of the pond and see the mother's face looking up at them. The fact that the surface of a pond mirrors one's own face is not spoken about, but it does seem to present interesting implications of the practice. Self-reflection and self-distancing—seeing one's mother in oneself and oneself as one's mother face—occur at the same time.

Colloquially translated as "Mother's Day," the holiday evokes sentiments of familial union, presence, harmony, and respect, often amid or in contrast to social disruption and displacement. *Āmāko mukh herne din* is sometimes used as the setting for fictional or journalistic accounts about social unrest. The Kathmandu fiction writer Sulochana Manandhar frames her story "Jhyālkhānā" (Prison) (Manandhar 2058 v.s.) around a series of *mukh herne* rituals.[18] In this story, Manandhar contrasts the ritual of looking at the face of a bride at a wedding and this same bride returning to see her mother's face on *āmāko mukh herne din*. These two *mukh herne* days become the setting for Manandhar's reflection on feelings of constriction and the imprisonment that characterizes marriage (and obedience to one's parents' wishes) for many young Kathmandu women. In a different vein, *Sari Soldiers* (Brigham 2008), a documentary film about six Nepali women during the Maoist civil war, begins with the main character returning to see her mother in their war-torn village on the occasion of *āmāko mukh herne din*. The holiday evokes sentiments of desired connection and familial union amid a social reality of displacement, disappeared family members, and civil war.

. . .

A few days before *āmāko mukh herne din,* I could literally smell a holiday coming on. Sweetshops stacked their counters high with sticky fried breads, donuts, and milk sweets soaked in rose water. White pastry boxes swung from the handlebars of many bicycles and motor scooters through the city. There was a buzz of shopping frenzy in the air. In addition to sweets, people were buying clothing, jewelry, fruit, and nuts. Some even purchased expensive gifts like gas stoves and gold to bring home to their mothers. While some say that the day was declared a national holiday a few years ago, it does not appear as a public holiday on calendars put out by the Maoist government, probably because of its association with Hinduism and the Hindu state. Aside from the increase in sweets in the markets, the day could, in many ways, pass unnoticed.

Most of the older Nepalis I talked with describe the *mukh herne* days as recent celebrations. Middle-aged men and women from Kathmandu often could not recall giving gifts to their parents and looking at their face in their youth. Many said the holiday was growing in popularity. "Some villagers [outside the Valley] are now celebrating the day," one forty-year-old man reported. "Perhaps it is a case of *dekhā-siki* [learning by seeing]." Many described the *mukh herne* holiday as a specifically Hindu practice, but Kathmandu residents who were self-declared Buddhists also celebrated it.

When speaking about the day in conversation, rarely did Nepalis use the language of religion or refer to specific religious doctrine. The *mukh herne* day was instead a time to remember one's mother *(āmālāi samjhane)*, a day to honor her and for children to show their respect by buying their mothers gifts.

The practice of *āmāko mukh herne din* was framed by several intersecting discourses. Many describe the holiday by invoking the popular origin story about an orphaned Nepali cowherder boy who discovers he can see his dead mother's image by looking into a pond. Some describe the day as an expression of the ideal Hindu sentiments toward home, and therefore it acts as a representation of an ideal form of Nepali nationalism (prior to the establishment of the Republic). The origins of this devotion and respect toward mothers, several journalists wrote, could be traced to ancient Vedic texts. These same articles also suggested that the popularity of *āmāko mukh herne din* reflects the alienated condition of modern life in Kathmandu: it was symptom of and cure for the sense of displacement and distance urban residents felt from their childhood homes. In the following pages, I discuss this holiday through each of these discursive sites. In each of these discourses, the face, like the voice, becomes a sign of presence and a medium for intimate attachment, especially to those who are no longer living.

AT THE MĀTĀTIRTHA POND

In the newspapers and in everyday urban lore, most people I talked with explained this holiday to me by repeating the well-known folk story about the boy cowherder. Though there were different versions of this story, the basic plot remained the same and was used to describe one important aspect of *āmāko mukh herne din*. The story went roughly like this.

There once was a cowherder whose mother had died when he was very young. Everyday he would go out to the fields with the cows and goats, and everyday he would cry for his mother. One day, a god who heard his wails called out to him and asked why such a young boy was filled with such sadness *(dukha)*. The boy explained that his mother was no longer *(āmā chainan)*, and that everyday his mother came into his mind and soul *(manmā aunchin)*. "Go to the pond below," the god instructed. "Look into the water, and there you will see your mother." The boy scurried down to the edge of the pond and looked at the surface of the water. In the water he saw the face of his mother, and seeing her image, his grief quickly vanished.[19]

The pond where this young cowherder is said to have looked is located about five miles outside the city border of Kathmandu, a ten-minute walk from the road on a small dirt footpath. Rather than being a naturally formed body of water, the pond is actually made up of three concrete sunken pools, where ten or twelve brass taps pour out clear, cold water from an underground source. People from Kathmandu and surrounding villages and Patan who have lost their mothers go to these pools of water on *āmāko mukh herne din,* in the middle of the month of Baisākh (April and May), just before the rains. Called Mātātirtha, which is also another common name for the holiday, these pools of water conjure up the sense of a journey to a holy place, a return to origins, and a visual encounter that resembles *darśan* in its transcendence of the here and now. The term *mātā* means "mother" in Sanskrit, but it is also a term used to describe female goddesses and it resonates with ideas of the nation in Nepal and in other parts of South Asia.[20] A *tirtha* is a pilgrimage to a Hindu holy site, which often consists of a confluence of three rivers. The name of the pool of water itself therefore implies integration and merging, resembling the practice that takes place there. At Mātātirtha, the boundaries of time and the boundaries of persons, specifically between mother and child, blur in the act of looking into the reflection at the water.

Around 7 A.M. on the *āmāko mukh herne din* in 1998, I arrived at Mātātirtha pond with my Patan friend Gyanisoba Shakya. Already, a thick crowd of people was walking up the muddy path. Although the story about this pond and the cowherder had been repeated frequently to me by many middle-class residents of Kathmandu, very few middle-class professionals were at Mātātirtha on this day. Most people there were farmers from surrounding villages, with some from Kathmandu and Patan, like Gyanisoba, but at least from appearances, they seemed to not inhabit the educated, professional class. As with most folk holidays, the holiday was thought to be practiced primarily by women, but there were quite a number of men also waiting to enter the area of the pond. Separated by yellow ropes that had been put up that year by the police for some unknown reason, the men and women formed distinct lines on the dirt path, where we waited to enter the gated cement area where the pools were located. When we reached the stone entrance, the crowds became an indistinguishable mass and we moved together toward the three concrete sunken pools.

Most of the crowd headed quickly for the smallest and the highest of these pools, for this was the water where one could see one's mother's face. The surface of the water shook from the barrage of coins, flowers, incense, and other typical ritual items that people tossed in the pool. Some people submerged their whole bodies; others placed their heads under the cool tap of water. Most, like Gyanisoba and me, squatted beside the water's edge and put their hands or their entire head into the water. "Do you see your mother?" Gyanisoba asked me, as she bent down. Before I could even look in the pool, she dipped her fingers in and splashed a handful of cold water on my face and her own.

No one sought an image. In actual practice, as opposed to the commonly repeated folk story, there was not even a *pretense* of catching a glimpse of a dead mother's face in one's own mirrored reflection. Quite the contrary, people embraced whatever actual or imagined reflection may have existed on the pond's surface with their hands and their whole bodies. They splashed their own faces with the water, merging with the image of one's mother's face spoken about on the way to the pools (see figure 5, at the beginning of the chapter). This submergence in water is not at all unusual—it is a common aspect of nearly all South Asian practices of ritual honor and purification. Yet this detail is important to note because this particular holiday is framed by a story about the momentary calm of looking at the water's reflection and visual practices of *mukh herne* I described.

Several people described this practice as "taking *darśan* from their mother" *(āmāko darśan linu)*, which further emphasizes the merging, tactile aspect of this seeing and its hierarchical nature. There is an intriguing similarity between the identity presumed in this mother-and-child image at the pond and the identity between the king and subject promoted during the monarchial Panchāyat times (1960–90). Both assume that a person sees oneself in and through the image of a higher authority, and that they are of the same substance. Some people suggested that the *mukh herne* day was actually made into a national holiday in 1987, during the last years of the Panchāyat regime, and was promptly banned, along with many holidays, after the *jana āndolan* in 1990. I was unable to confirm this, but it is worth noting the parallels made between taking *darśan* from one's mother and from the king. Until the devolution of the monarchy in 2008, *darśan* was a central practice in the establishment and recognition of the king's divine and political power. The king of Nepal was compared to the god Vishnu, and when Nepalis saw the king or sought his blessing—regardless of whether or not they believed he was actually a manifestation of Vishnu—they described this meeting as taking *darśan* from the king.[21] Long lines would form outside the palace on the national holiday of *dashain,* as Nepalis waited to take *darśan* and receive *tikā* (red vermillion powder that signifies a blessing) from the king in order to receive some of his powers while also confirming their obligations to the monarch as subjects under his reign. It is this form of visuality that until 2008 helped support the Panchāyat national ideology that Nepal was the world's only Hindu kingdom.

As the ritual practice of *āmāko mukh herne din* suggests, seeing is not always an act of objectification, separation, and distinction from others; rather, like *darśan,* the *mukh herne* ritual implies a visual contact that takes place through the act of looking into the pond. When I invited a young Sanskrit scholar I knew to "ask him some questions about a ritual," he was mildly disappointed that I wanted him to talk about *āmāko mukh herne din.* There was not much written about this holiday, he admitted, and like other people I consulted, he insisted that this was not one of the bigger celebrations *(ṭhulo cāḍ hoina).* Nonetheless, he told me his version of the cowherder story, and explained that what soothes the young herder is the vision of his mother and that her image appears in the reflection of his face. This watchful gaze of his dead mother, embodied in his own image, makes him stop crying and recognize that she is present with him at this very moment. He is brought out of his grief by seeing his mother in himself and himself in his mother. Significantly, the face—imagined and real—is the medium for expressing this familial union. Seeing the mother's face in the pond might be thought of as another way to see oneself, and it therefore has important implications for shaping a son's or daughter's subjectivity. It suggests, perhaps, that one's own perspective of the world should mirror the perspective of one's mother. To see one's mother in oneself, one begins to see as the mother sees.

The tale of the Nepali cowherding boy and the practice of *mukh herne* at the pond are the stuff of a rich cultural imagination that brings together the most everyday experiences with the most ineffable aspects of life. But such myths are not outside of history: they sink below the surface and rise again at different times, their popularity echoing the murmurs of contemporary social life. For this reason, it is important to pursue *why* this practice and the story about the holiday became so popular at this particular time in history. Interestingly, and not coincidently, the two dominant interpretations of the holiday presented in the press stressed either the ancient, ahistorical, and religious roots of the holiday or its significance in the contemporary context of modern, urban alienation.

POLITICAL AND RELIGIOUS RATIONALE

Hinduism was one of the most frequently used rationales for explaining *āmāko mukh herne din*. Many link the holiday to a Nepali nationalist ideology rooted in Hinduism and promoted by the state especially during the Panchāyat regime. One former civil servant for the Panchāyat government, who was also a Brahman priest from a village outside the Valley, lamented the fact that this holiday was no longer recognized nationally. At my request, my close friend and research assistant asked this man (who was the father of the assistant's friend) about the holiday and my friend reported back to me by email: "Mr. Lamichhane told me that these two days [mother and father *mukh herne* days] are momentous Hindu customs and there are some obvious descriptions about the significance of these two events in the Pitri Purana, one of the major Hindu legends. . . . *Āmā/bā ko mukh herne din* are not honored by the national holidays today. Of course they were at one time."

Most people remember beginning to celebrate *mukh herne* days during the 1980s, when the Panchāyat government exerted its most extensive Hindu-centered national programs. No doubt the holiday was practiced among some for many years prior to the 1980s, and possibly it only became a more generalized practice at this time. While the holiday most likely did not arise from Panchāyat policy, the Panchāyat rhetoric that linked Hinduism with Nepali national identity provided a way for people to think about practices like *āmāko mukh herne din* in national terms.

Newspaper articles about *āmāko mukh herne din* also linked the holiday to passages in the Vedas, the ancient Hindu texts.[22] A journalist from *Kantipur,* one of the largest private newspapers in Kathmandu, quoted well-known lines of Sanskrit from the Vedas: "Mother is equal to a Goddess" *(mātā devo bhawa)* and "Mother is ten times greater than Father" *(Pitā dasguna mātā).* The journalist then went on to interpret these ancient lines in today's context. He suggests a telling connection between the "respect" one must give to mothers and patriarchy itself: "Even in a patriarchal society *[pitrīpradhān]* mothers should be respected ten times more than fathers, which is an expression of the existing Hindu respect for women."[23] Given the contemporary significance of *bikās* (development), this comment no doubt responds to accusations by development organizations that Hindu societies denigrate women, as well as to their widespread attempts to "uplift" women's social position in Nepal through development projects. He is right, as feminists have often argued, that this "respect" is a core foundation of patriarchy. But what he does not acknowledge is that this "respect" produces naturalized desires for motherhood in both men and women that make motherhood the source of a woman's value and make it difficult for women to pursue anything else without facing social exclusion. Woe to the woman who does not become a mother in such a "patriarchical society"! Today's celebration of Mother's Day, the same journalist continues, grows directly out of the feelings of devotion to mothers that were evident in ancient times and have existed since that time. "Seeing a mother's face, now [children] give her beautiful clothes, jewels, and sweet food, in the respect shown to mother that has continued since ancient times. . . . Today all Nepalis show their devotion to all mothers by completely submerging themselves in devoted feelings."[24]

In his essay "Nietzsche, Genealogy, History," Foucault (1984) has persuasively argued that histories that declare a continuous and unchanging sentiment as the raison d'etre of any given practice, like the history recounted about this holiday, often read the past through the prism of the present. We must assume that even noble sentiments, like devoted love to one's mother, have a history that is linked to past and present structures of power. Despite the claim that such love derives from "time immemorial," the history of honoring one's mother might be gleaned through a sustained focus on the specific institutions, language, and practices that deeply depend upon and therefore cultivate this particular form of attachment. We might note, for instance, that love and respect for mothers are sentiments that become especially charged with political import as nation-states come to depend upon women to reproduce, train, and cultivate their children to be proper citizens for the modern state (Davin 1978; Mosse 1985). As noted above, in many South Asian contexts, the figure of the mother often aligns with the image of the nation itself, imagined as the motherland and often personified in the figure of a mother goddess (Ramaswamy 1997). These broad-sweeping religiopolitical ideologies, however, only partially explain the importance of the sentiments of devotion and the desire to see a mother's face in today's Kathmandu.

In everyday discourse as well as press representations, the holiday of *mukh herne* also became a way to reflect on the modern sense of alienation and actual displacements from home. It was therefore a holiday especially important for married women, who left their parent's home in marriage. Although it was not a big holiday *(thulo cāḍ),* some Nepali women told me that *mukh herne* day was really just a chance *(bahanā)* for a married woman to "meet her mother," and she could go to her *māitī* without being invited by her brother. In contrast, young men, especially those who lived with their parents, told me that the holiday was not important to them, because "we look at our mother's and father's faces every day." Looking at one's mother's face on this holiday mitigated the absence that married daughters experienced from their *māitī.*

But the emphasis on bridging the distance from home through the holidays of *mukh herne* was not isolated to the experience of married women. Many linked the holiday of seeing a face to broader patterns of movement and migration to and from Kathmandu. Roads were a central motif that almost always emerged in people's descriptions of *āmāko mukh herne din.* One mother of a friend of mine explained that she had been going back to see her mother on this day for about ten or fifteen years, but no longer. "Why?" my friend asked, to which her mother promptly responded that the roads were no good. A middle-aged man, who had worked as a traveling civil servant for most of his life, told my research assistant that the increased popularity of the holiday had to do with "employment opportunities and means of transportation [that] have been growing by leaps and bounds." The same article that linked *āmāko mukh herne din* to ancient texts also went on to describe the contemporary celebration of the holiday using the image a long journey through the mountains. "From far, far away sisters and brothers with sweets and fruits are joined together in friendship, uphill and downhill, to go to the mother's house."[25]

Such explanations themselves point to a contemporary structure of feeling in Kathmandu—one of distance, absence, and lack of face-to-face contact—that is cultivated on this holiday of seeing face. The holiday is predicated on a sense of absence (either through geography or death), which is then temporarily assuaged through the practice of *mukh herne* that cultivates a sense of presence. This is the more general, urban and modern condition of life, several articles about the holiday suggested, a condition that does not only reflect the particular situation of married Nepali women. "People are making a mistake in claiming that this is only a holiday for married women," one journalist wrote in the *Samacarpatra*.[26] Instead, the article went on to describe the sense of alienation and distance from home that many groups experience. By quoting or mentioning how people like Bhutanese refugees—quintessentially displaced people—and an Indian businessman celebrate the holiday, the journalist implies that the day is a more broadly South Asian celebration. The discourse about *āmāko mukh herne din* turns these common stereotypes about these non-Nepali subjects on their head: the refugee and Indian merchant become prime examples of people who celebrate this holiday. The practice of seeing one's mother's face is projected onto displaced persons and imagined to be attractive because the holiday is *about* a return to an original place, to home, and to one's mother. It also marks the holiday as a more broadly regional celebration, rather than exclusively national. The holiday is about creating and recognizing the presence of family members who are often or permanently separated from one another through the act of looking at their face.

The predicament of the refugees and the Indian is presented as virtually the same as the predicament of a Nepali middle-class civil servant. The Nepali civil servant too tells the reporter he only *wishes* he could meet his mother, finding that he has no time.[27] Others describe an increasing divide between life at work and life at home. Mothers were in despair today because their children, particularly their sons, were never at home. The constant outside service *(sevā)* to which a young man must attend on most days merely resulted in his increased debt toward home, the same journalist quoted above suggested.[28] "If one cannot clear one's debt to a mother's life of pure service *(sevā)*, then what good is a single day?" the journalist asked rhetorically. He continued to describe the pitiful condition of mothers, who are depicted as lonely figures in an empty home. "Today's mothers are oppressed *(piḍit)* by their sons. There are distressed mothers who, in spite of having twelve sons, must shed tears in small huts, and they are in a pitiful situation. Nowadays many mothers are forced, crying, crying, to leave their homes, being unable to live a life in which everyone has abandoned their obligations *(tyāgna)* to home."[29]

Although seeing a face on this holiday presumably reestablishes ties of affection and care within the home, this journalist uses the holiday in order to show the lack of familial connection in Kathmandu today. Women do not in fact *wish* to pursue a public life outside the home, the article implies, but they are being forced to do so out of the sheer loneliness in their homes.

What is a home, the article implies, without a mother in it? The journalist blames the sons for this situation, arguing that obligations to home have been replaced by obligations to national or civil service *(sevā)*. This symptom of contemporary urban life in Kathmandu even holidays like *mukh herne* cannot heal. The press discourse about *mukh herne* promotes a rather functionalist explanation of the value of seeing face days as a way to restore a sense of presence, immediacy, and familial connection thought to be lacking in modern, everyday life in Kathmandu.

PHOTOGRAPHS AND POLITICAL INSCRIPTIONS OF FACE

As I have been arguing here, the sense of presence, directness, and intimate and genealogical connection experienced in *mukh herne* rituals deepens our understanding of the related practices of *bolāune* and its connection to voice. To say that the voice and the face are part of the same semiotic ideology is to show the similar mediating work they do in creating intimacy, presence, and a seemingly direct connection between people. The face as a medium gains further traction in the political field. Intimate and political subjectivity, family, and nation come together when we consider the way practices of seeing face work across these fields. Practices around royal portrait photography reveal the political significance of the face, and the resonances between the face and the voice as media that establish political subjectivity.

Largely because of their ability to excite strong attachment, practices of looking at the face have had great political significance throughout South Asia.[30] As noted above, the practice of taking *darśan* from the king was a key strategy of Nepali nationalism, established during the Panchāyat regime, when Nepal was a Hindu kingdom. Photography, as Pinney (2002) argues, enhances (rather than undermines) practices of *darśan* and tactile seeing in India, and the same can be said of Nepal.[31] The capacity to behold the king's image daily, rather than only during the holiday of *dashain,* increased dramatically with the beginnings of mass-produced photography in Nepal. The Panchāyat government (1950–90) made ample use of the photographic medium to enhance the king's power by distributing thousands of photographs of King Mahendra, the first Panchāyat leader, in his coronation robe so that "the image of the King as 'symbol of the nation' is constantly presented to people" (Gupta 1993: 265).

During the Rana period (1846–1950), photography, like all other technologies of the time (radio, telegraph, telephone), was a medium exclusive to the ruling Rana prime ministers and the royal family and a select number of middle-class Nepalis who served them. The ruling families would enlarge the photographic portraits of themselves to life size, treating them like paintings, and hang the photographs on the walls of their palaces. The portraits, hunting pictures, and photographs of political and family rituals were internally oriented—they were meant to be seen by only those within this closed, elite circle and were not circulated beyond this group. The predominant use of photography among the royal and elite families at this time thus worked against its capacity as a technology of mass reproduction. Like the mirrors that adorned their palaces, these enormous photographic portraits enhanced the capacity to see oneself as others see you, creating a relation of both distance and identification (Liechty 1997).[32] Political recognition from within the ruling class is, after all, what is important within an oligarchic polity, and subtle distinctions between members of this class as well as their fundamental distinction from the common subjects over whom they ruled could be conveyed through photography. When photographs were exchanged outside of this closed circle, as Pratyoush Onta notes, they were generally exchanged with foreign monarchs or political rulers, such as governors or high officials in the British Raj (Onta 1998). The photographs not only signified the portrayed individual but also represented oligarchic political power and the broader institution of monarchy (1998: 196). While the practice of taking *darśan* from the king during the national Hindu festival of Dasain was active at this time, the fact that common people seldom had the opportunity to look at the faces of Rana rulers emphasized the different moral and social worlds they inhabited, a central feature of Rana oligarchic rule.

In the later national context, however, royal portrait photography enhanced the power of the king and the institution of monarchy. While the images of royalty and the Ranas were kept largely hidden from the general public during the Rana period, the wide dissemination of the king's image marks a shift to a national sensibility wherein the image of the king—as the representative of the community—*must be recognized* by the general public. Rosalind Morris describes the increased power of the Thai king through his portrait as an effect of the magic of photography. To say that the image *is* the king conflates two distinct things—the person and his image—even as the image simultaneously sustains the duality of the two (2009: 134). More than this, the image also represents the institution of kingship, much broader than any one particular king. Honoring the king and the institution of the monarchy, Morris illustrates, became synonymous with honoring the king's image. Photography appears magical in its ability to transgress the boundaries of space and time, and to produce representations of faces where that same face is absent.

In an ideal world of a monarch, there would be no place in the kingdom where the king was not. Using this logic, the Panchāyat government exploited the technical possibilities of photography as a form of mass reproduction to its fullest in an effort to produce national subjects, who came to recognize themselves as such through the viewing of royal faces. As in the modern Thai context about which Morris writes, the Nepali Panchāyat government (1960–90) established a law that portraits of the king and queen must be displayed in all businesses and state offices. Eight-by-ten color portraits of the king and queen were also spread across the country, and many people hung similar photos in their homes, from which they would take *darśan* as a sign of their respect for the monarchy and the nation. Recognition of oneself as a national subject, then, became entwined with the act of looking at the king's face. Looking at his image in photographs and taking *darśan* from him at national holidays like Dasain established one's connection to the king and the nation. The image of the king's face, as well as the act of looking upon it, became a primary medium for the production of national subjects.

Photographs of the king were also published in the national newspaper, the *Gorkhapatra,* duplicating and representing these important moments of taking *darśan* from the king and his image for the national public to witness. Genevieve Lakier (2009: 221–22) discusses two interesting photographs published in the *Gorkhapatra* that represent how the king (and his image) transformed, through mass media and photography, into a national figure. The first is of King Birendra in 1979 greeting citizens and local leaders in Pokhara during one of his tours of the region, where the citizens praised the king for encouraging development in the area. The second is of the occasion of Unification Day in January 1979, where a crowd carried an image of the first Shah king of Nepal, Prithvi Narayan Shah, through the streets of Kathmandu. As Lakier writes: "This [the photo in the newspaper] is no longer *darshan,* exactly; the reader is no longer graced simply with the divine image but with an image of others receiving that image. The layering of images reinforces the importance of the event. The mediation of the ritual turns the encounter of *darshan*—predicated on the immediacy of the gaze—into a spectacle of national harmony and progress, one which then reflects upon the energies and the potential of the Nepali people themselves" (222).

In such newspaper renditions of the king, citizens witness not only the king, but the faces of other citizens engaged in the act of *darśan* or beholding the image of the king. *Darśan* becomes the ultimate expression of national unity, with the king at the center, but his power is sustained through citizens witnessing other citizens' faces in the ritual acts of looking at the king's face.[33]

The mass reproduction of kingly portraits leads to other representational possibilities that place this image—and the power it represents—at risk. "One can imagine that any technology which can appear to transmit the presence of the king to locations in which his actual body is absent would augment his power," writes Morris, "while also risking it" (2009: 137). Representations of power, Morris elaborates, often require something more—such as the force of the law—to be politically effective. The royal portrait in a "democracy with the king as head of state" (like the Nepali Panchayāt system) is more than an image of the king and his individual and absolute power (Morris 2009: 137). In viewing and honoring these royal images within a national regime, a spectator recognizes the broader system of power and the national community that the king represents. The risk entailed in the mass circulation of kingly portraits is the possibility that these images may be marred or defaced, an act that is essentially an act against the state power represented in the photograph.

To not hang the king's photo and to not participate in practices of *darśan* can be interpreted as an act of disrespect or at times of crisis as a serious challenge to the state. Indeed, the use of photographs and practices of *darśan* to criticize state and kingly power occurred in multiple ways in the years prior to the final demise of the monarchy. After the infamous royal massacre, when King Birendra and nine other members of his immediate family were killed on the evening of June 1, 2001, during a dinner party at the Narayanhiti palace (see introduction and epilogue), photographs became a weapon of critique. This event marked a significant shift in Nepali politics and the beginning of numerous public declarations against the monarchy, particularly against King Gyanendra, who assumed power after Birendra's death. Many people told me that they went to buy a photograph of the entire murdered royal family just after the massacre, but were only able to find portraits of King Birendra and Queen Aishwara. According to the photo archivist at Nepal TV, the photo of the former king's entire family, which soon became

FIGURE 6. Photograph of King Birendra and Queen Aishwara displayed in a Nepali home.
Photo: Cristeena Chitrakar.

a fixture in nearly every home I visited in Kathmandu after the massacre, was only available thirty to forty-five days after the massacre. Many people hung this photograph in their homes, adorned with a marigold garland around the frame to signify the death of the royal family that was represented. Some placed it on the walls, some in the entryway to their house (particularly in the initial days), and some next to the portraits of dead relatives to whom they also did daily *pujā* (worship; see figure 6).

These photos of the former royal family were doing a different kind of cultural work than the mass distribution of royal portraits during the Panchāyat government. Instead of becoming signs of obedience to the royal power, the photos worked as signs of mourning, set beside other objects and photographs that recognize the dead. When asked why they hung these photos, most Nepalis responded that they wanted to remember *(samjhanu)* the king and take *darśan* from the image during *pujā*. Taking *darśan* from the image of the former king, particularly in a moment when conspiracy theories circulated widely about the role the succeeding King Gyanendra played in the massacre, is a silent but powerful way to reject Gyanendra while still honoring the institution of the monarchy and a king who became beloved to many Nepalis because he inaugurated the multiparty system in 1990. These photographs were still hanging in many homes when I visited Nepal in 2007 and 2008, and some are still hanging.

As King Gyanendra came under more severe criticism and was eventually stripped of his royal power, practices of *darśan* became especially charged with political import. While I was residing in Nepal in the fall of 2007, several months before King Gyanendra was officially deposed, rumors circulated in the city about how few people lined up at the palace to take *darśan* and receive blessings from the king. After Nepal officially became a republic, the elected president and prime minister took over the duties of the former king during *dashain,* and citizens went to their homes to take *darśan* from their leaders on the holiday. Yet, monarchists still prefer to see and be seen by the former king, and in 2009, according to a pro-Hindu news source, a few hundred people lined up outside Gyanendra's current residence to take *darśan* from the deposed king.[34] In 2013, just before the November elections, even more people took *darśan* from Gyanendra on *deshain,* and some claim this may have effected the victory of RPP (royalist party) in some areas of Kathmandu.

Activists involved in nonparty politics often criticize the common practice of *darśan* as a way to assert political honor and respect. Basu Shrestha, an activist working under the banner of *nāgarik samāj* (civil society), told me the problems he had with the way activists and politicians treated party politicians. He described alternative kinds of politics and society he envisioned with his friends. Basu exclaimed, with some exasperation: "I have seen that people don't even just say, '*namaste,*' to these leaders; they also do *darśan* (*darśan garne)* (to them)!" In Basu's irritated remark, *darśan* is a visual practice that he clearly distinguishes from a liberal notion of voice. Instead of allowing new voices to be heard, he asserted, greetings of *darśan* simply reaffirm who has the privilege to speak and who must listen.

Noting the contradictions within his own civil society movement, Basu recounted, "Those who speak about the rights of *dalits* (those of the low caste), women's rights, we talk about throwing out Gyanendra, but within us, there is discrimination against women, we oppress *dalits.* . . . All the other people who support us, who distribute pamphlets, who simply listen, they are not given any attention. . . . If we are going to meet Girija or Madav Kumar,[35] we only take those people who can talk, not the others who support us." In these instances, *darśan* signifies who will speak and who will simply listen in the everyday practice of politics, confirming existing hierarchies of speech. Such practices, Basu suggested, are key to understanding why fundamental social and political changes are so difficult.

Basu's comments suggest that *darśan* is bound up with a semiotic ideology of voice that challenges the liberal understanding of voice as freedom, self-expression, and the basis for political democracy that he himself espouses. Such liberal notions of voice assume that all parties should have equal access to "voice" and that this voice expresses the political consciousness of a particular group of people. Liberal notions of voice, implicit in phrases like *āwāj uṭhāune,* are predicated on very different rules of recognition and intimacy than those animated by the visual practices of *darśan* and *mukh herne.* The distinction Basu makes between a liberal formation of voice and *darśan* suggests a split in the ideology that has aligned voice and face in practices like *mukh herne* and *bolāune.* While both may be considered indices of immediacy, intimacy, and presence, in the context of democratic politics people like Basu differentiate between the hierarchical social relations established in practices of seeing face and the assumed relations of parity implied in phrases such as *āwāj uṭhāune.*

MEDIATING FACES AND MEDIATING VOICES

In conclusion to this chapter, I would like to return to Reena and her some-what idiosyncratic definition of *mukh herne* as genealogy. As should now be clear, *mukh herne* does bear some important relation to genealogy, though it is not equivalent. The tactile seeing of *darśan* and the ritual at the pools of water both imply relations of hierarchy and genealogical connection (national and familial) that are secured through the practice of looking at a face. As Nepali citizens took *darśan* from the king, they were recognized and came to recognize themselves as subjects of the king, within the same national geneal-ogy that the king's presence confirms. On *āmāko mukh herne din,* pilgrims commune with their dead mothers by splashing water on their faces, merging with the mother's face that is ostensibly present on the surface of the water. The act of looking at a face in this ritual and practices like seeing the face of a bride are acts of genealogical recognition. Everyday negative iterations of *mukh herne*—such as "I will never see that person's face"—also reveal the term's link to genealogy, for the face, as well as the act of seeing that face, signifies the moral obligations entailed in belonging to a specific family or intimate group. In these acts of refusal, the face becomes a medium of moral censure and affirms several hierarchical relations that underlie the genealogy. Vision and voice are implicitly connected in this phrase: to not see someone's face is to stop talking with them.

While the tactile seeing of *mukh herne* conjures up a sense of immediacy and presence, I have suggested that "seeing face" must be understood as part of broader processes of mediation. Like the voice, the face is a medium through which relations of hierarchy, mutual obligation, and intimacy (often genealogical) are recognized and generated in practices of "seeing face." The face and the voice share a semiotic ideology as indices of presence, intimacy, and genealogy. They are forms of mediation that simultaneous deny their status as mediums. Yet, as I noted above, their function as complementary signs of presence within the same semiotic ideology may be changing during this moment of social and political reform. For some Kathmandu activists, the voice and the face were opposed as media that generated qualitatively different forms of recognition. While recognition through practices of *darśan* reasserts long-standing political and social hierarchies, the act of "raising one's voice" *(āwāj uṭhāune)* has been embraced by activists as a way to reconfigure such political and social authority toward relations of parity.

I first heard about *āmāko mukh herne din* from a Newar woman, Soma, whose daughter was living abroad. She began describing the holiday to me by pulling out a glossy photograph that her daughter had sent her for the day. The twenty-three-year-old daughter was unable to visit her this year, Soma told me; she could only send a picture. Instead of receiving fruit or sweets, clothes or jewelry, this photograph was her gift. It was an indexical trace of her daughter, who remained physically absent from the mother. When I glanced down at the three-by-five print to get a better view of the young woman's face, Soma interrupted my gaze and pointed to the bags beside the daughter's legs. "This is the stuff she was going to send me," she said. "But the boy who came from the United States had no space. The picture was all he could bring." Soma's tangible meeting with her daughter on *āmāko mukh herne din* did not occur primarily through the act of seeing her daughter's face; instead, it occurred through talking with her on the phone. "'If I can't see my mother's face, then at least I can hear her voice'—this is what my daughter said," Soma explained. A technology of voice and the visual technology of photography stand in for the act of meeting face-to-face, suggesting their parallels, if not their equivalence. Instead of rupturing the sense of presence that seeing face practices create, these technologies make the recognition of intimacy and the feelings of presence possible.

The understandings of intersubjectivity established through *mukh herne* and *bolāune* practices inform and are extended into the radio context, where the voice becomes the primary medium of connection and intimacy. While *mukh herne* and *bolāune* practices are primarily between familiars, the voice in the radio context mediates stranger sociality—connections between familiars and strangers. *Mukh herne* and *bolāune* are both practices that incorporate a person into wider social spheres (from the family to the nation) and often mediate a person's relationship to public space. But they are not necessarily about being part of a public. In the following chapters, I explore the faceless, broadcast voice on FM radio as a medium of intimacy, presence, and political possibility that lays the foundation for the formation of urban publics in Kathmandu.

THREE

Making Waves

THE SOCIAL AND POLITICAL CONTEXT
OF FM RADIO

> Wireless, with television, is the last phase of a development that
> was begun by the first seafarers and nomads ... finally, wire-
> less and television enable any number of people to hear and see
> simultaneously what is happening everywhere in the world.

RUDOLF ARNOLD, *Radio: An Art of Sound*, 1936

THE *JANA ĀNDOLAN* (PEOPLE'S MOVEMENT) of 1990 can be aptly called
a revolution of the voice. As it unfolded, personal subjectivities and land-
scapes of political discourse were remade. This reorientation of the political
and intimate voice in Nepali public life has been closely associated with the
rising importance of FM radio as a central cultural medium. The reestablish-
ment of party democracy enabled a host of previously suppressed political
parties to voice their demands in public, and the very idea of free speech
quickly acquired social currency in Kathmandu in realms typically understood to be "political" as well as in public discussion of the personal far more
broadly. New political parties rallied around expressions of public discontent, and such discourse, in all its ramifications, became a vital part of emerging media in Kathmandu. Many of the post-*āndolan* media channels came
to focus on the public expression of personal and social grievance and other
forms of vocal political assertion. Demands for transparency and participation in media that would sustain a healthy democracy lay at the heart of
discussions about the political culture after 1990, and the commercial and
interactive FM radio established in 1996 quickly became a symbol of the
breadth of this new democratic moment.

The next three chapters focus on FM radio as a key technology of voice that
cultivates novel forms of political and intimate subjectivity frequently associated with the figure of the voice. These chapters contribute to a burgeoning
literature on the ethnography of radio that has attempted to reconfigure ideas

FIGURE 7. Radio as the sign of Nepali modernity: studio photograph of a couple holding a radio and dressed in contemporary Nepali styles, ca. 1970. Courtesy of Ganesh Photo Studio.

about ethnographic fieldwork (see Bessire and Fisher 2012). In *Radio Fields,* Lucas Bessire and Daniel Fisher argue that "it is impossible to understand radio sociality without taking seriously the interlocking cultural meanings that radiate outward from any radio field" (2012: 20). Bringing together several ethnographies of radio, they organize the themes that emerge along five conceptual axes: the voice, radio and nation, community radio, transnational circuits, and language and perception. Aside from community radio, the next three chapters address all of these axes. I link radio sociality with questions of "raising voice," *mukh herne,* political and intimate subjectivity, as well as ideas about presence and directness and what it means to be public, which I have addressed in the prior chapters that did not focus on radio.

The figure of the voice here is different than the voice implicit in practices of *bolāune,* and it does not replicate the genealogical or national intimacy of *mukh herne.* Rather, it is more closely linked to the sense of voice implicit in the more liberal notion of *āwāj uthāune* (raising voice) I discussed in relation to the property reform movement (chapter 1). The radio interpellates its listeners into the broadcasts to express their innermost feelings and personal struggles, thereby linking the voice to an idea of personal and interior struggle rather than political reform. As in the prior discussions of *bolāune* and *mukh herne,* I focus on the sense of presence and directness conjured by practices associated with the face and the voice. Here the sense of presence relates to emerging publics in Kathmandu. I trace the cultural history of FM radio and discuss features of its broadcast that make it appear to be a medium that is direct and "more real" than other forms of communication, such as face-to-face interactions or programs on the state-run Radio Nepal.

The mediation that transpires via FM radio is an example of what Asif Agha calls "mediatization" (Agha 2011). In using the term *mediatization,* Agha is drawing attention to the links between processes of communication and processes of commodification (163). All mass media as well as other institutional forms—schools, law, hospitals, libraries, and so on—are examples of mediatization because they all in some ways partake in both communication and commodification. Agha is careful to note that processes of mediatization are "a narrow special case of mediation," and that "mediatized experience are invariably preceded and followed by non-mediatized ones" (165). While the concept of mediatization acknowledges the important role that capitalist economies play in processes of communication, it also disrupts the dominant attention drawn to processes of commodification by scholars of mass media. Such media scholarship ends up producing bankrupt concepts, like "reception," that fail to acknowledge the broader complexities entailed in all processes of semiotic mediation.

FM radio is no doubt a product of increasing liberalization and growth in privatized markets, but I do not focus my analysis on the processes of commodification at work on FM programs. To do so would be to isolate these moments of mediatization from the broader processes of mediation in which they are embedded. Indeed, as Agha argues, "nothing is always or only a commodity" (164); mediation with and through the voice on FM radio must be seen in relation to other forms of mediation that may or may not partake in mediatization.

As a symbol of the moment, FM radio signified both the possibilities and the problems with the emergence of liberal democracy in Nepal. On the one hand, activists and community organizers saw the beginnings of FM radio as the ultimate medium for enabling increased participation in public and political life. Media activists and intellectuals celebrated the possibility of giving "voice to the voiceless" (Dahal 2002: 39), and touted FM radio as the "most democratic medium, because it is cheap and localized" (Onta 2006: 118). While many commented on the possibilities the new medium had for increased participation, FM radio was also subject to significant criticism by those who felt the programs were "ruining Nepali culture" *(sanskritī bigrin-cha)*. Intellectuals, journalists, and cultural purists in Kathmandu criticized FM programming for its exclusive focus on personal stories, individual confessions, and intentionally provocative discussions about sex and romantic love. In its early days in 1996, many with explicitly democratizing political agendas thought the programs on FM radio were overly sentimental, vulgar, and melodramatic and not grounded in the deeper problems that people in Kathmandu face every day. Articles with titles like "FM or Opium?," "My Children Are Already Being Ruined," and "An Accusation against FM for Spoiling Society" appeared in several newspapers. The two most prominent criticisms of FM programs centered on either the language practices of FM radio hosts or the personalized content of its programs.[1]

These critiques echoed a more general malaise among many in Kathmandu who complained about the unfulfilled promises of democracy. By the mid-1990s cynics declared that "democracy" only provided the opportunity for groups to declare how *little* had actually changed. Censorship was built into many of the new media that emerged after 1990. Furthermore, despite the sudden proliferation of new publishing houses just after *jana āndolan* I, more than half of these collapsed due to financial debts. By 1994, there were fewer newspapers than *before* the *jana āndolan,* and the government control of the media was actually expanding (IIDS 1996: 64). This changed yet again in the early 2000s as the privatization of the publishing industry increased, but the discourse about the failed promises of democracy remained. What became standard public and intellectual discourse about the effects of *jana āndolan* I was that democracy simply had not worked in Nepal (Upadhya 2002: 39).

Stepping aside from the issue of whether FM radio does indeed exemplify the forces of a democratic society at work or whether it simply panders to and helps cultivate the desires of the market (by no means mutually exclusive alternatives), I here focus on the broader situation within which FM has come to produce, circulate, and embody what I refer to throughout the book as the political and intimate voice. For activists and progressive intellectuals, FM radio brings about the possibility for a political voice separate from the state that will animate people's consciousness, provide a transparent medium for the discussion of politics, and realize the agency of those previously excluded from public conversations. Indeed, some claim that the success of the *jana āndolan* II in April 2006 was due to the availability of Chinese FM sets that could be purchased for only one hundred rupees. The criticisms hurled at FM programs in its initial stages primarily addressed the intimate voice that has become prominent in the broadcast of many FM entertainment and social reformist radio programs, which in turn often turn out to have strong connections with both commercial marketing and international aid and development projects. Despite their many differences, both formations of voice invoke ideas of agency and directness or transparency, and are clearly an effect of the neoliberal economic forces at work starting in the 1990s. Most significant here, finally, is the fact that both the intimate voice and the political voice are crucial to the formation of an interior self that emerges through such novel forms of media and that is characteristic of both modern and neoliberal subjectivities.[2]

As several scholars have argued, modern interiority is an effect of combining the rational and the sentimental, reason and passion, into a single individuated self (Chakrabarty 2000; Rose 1999; Stoler 2002; Taylor 1989). "For the modern subject to emerge, passions, sentiments, and like have to be located within the mind and within a very particular understanding of the relationship between them and reason," writes Dipesh Chakrabarty. "This is a relationship of struggle between the two because they are of opposed and contradictory character. This struggle is what marks the interiority of the subject" (2000: 131). Amanda Weidman links this struggle between reason and sentiment to the voice. "Modern subjectivity hinges on the notion of voice as a metaphor for self and authenticity, and on the various techniques—musical, linguistic, and literary—by which particular voices are made to seem authentic" (2006: 7–8). Weidman's insightful analysis centers on the musical voice. Here I consider the birth of FM radio as a vital site for exploring these forms of modern subjectivity and the effect of interiority emerging through its entertainment programs and the radio voice. FM radio serves as the prominent media for expressing as well as taming listeners' passions. No doubt, other media, like state Radio Nepal and cultural projects, were actively producing modern forms of self-consciousness far before FM radio. But the FM programs explode these possibilities through their emphasis on participation and the active expression of sentiment, suffering, and internal discontent by their listeners.

The FM broadcasts are involved in the formation of diverse publics and novel subjectivities through the temporal and material qualities of FM radio that shape people's understanding of time, space, sociality, and themselves. Students of radio have spent ample time discussing the change that radio creates in the spatial landscape of a nation or the public sphere, as well as the new temporal orientations created from its programs (Anderson 1991; Douglas 1999; Mrazek 2002; Spitulnik 1993; Weidman 2003). On an everyday basis, for instance, the radio provides a new way of disciplining listeners' ears and arranging the time of the day in relation to the radio programs. FM radio, with its initial twelve-hour broadcast on the single band of FM 100 radio waves, punctuated the lives of different listeners throughout the day, dividing the social landscape of Kathmandu through its programming. "We know our audience," one manager explained to me. "We know who will be listening when." He then took out a list of all the programs and distinguished them through their target audience. *Muna Ghar Pariwar,* airing from 11 to 12 A.M. on Sunday mornings, is a program specifically for housewives, providing "household tips" that a housewife can listen to as she cleans up after her husband has gone to work and her children are in school.[3] Most of the programs that run from 7 to 9 P.M. on weekdays are devoted to teenagers—such as *Close Up Music Jam* and *Sāthi Sanga Man Kā Kurā* (Chatting with my best friend),[4] the latter of which is broadcast on Saturdays on some stations—because they will be home at this time. Tracking the different temporal moments in the broadcast day provides a map of the social world hailed by FM programming.

The approach to the temporal structure of broadcasting on FM radio was a departure from the listening patterns of the state radio, though Radio Nepal of course also had a variety of programming that also catered to different populations. Prior to FM radio, many Nepalis in Kathmandu said they only turned on the radio (Radio Nepal) in the mornings and evenings for the official news. FM programming simply expanded the range of different publics addressed through its programs, including a vast number of language groups that were not represented on Radio Nepal. It also expanded the programs for youth, women, businessmen, urban migrants, laborers, and particular ethnic groups. FM radio first became associated with a particular cosmopolitan and middle-class Kathmandu culture that later was exported and transformed as FM stations began opening around the country in the early 2000s. My focus here is on the cultural history and experience of FM radio in Kathmandu, which, one could argue, largely set the terms for many of the later FM stations around the country.

To view FM radio programs as emblematic of this particular political moment in Kathmandu means to linger a little longer on why so many people listen, write, and talk about FM radio. I was always struck by the fact that Nepalis described their interactions with FM radio hosts and other listeners, who might interact through a listener's club magazine or online, as forms of "meeting" *(bhetne)*. Meeting was not exclusively a face-to-face interaction; one could "meet" through a variety of mediated forms. Like the visits of married women discussed in chapter 1 or the practices of *mukh herne* in chapter 2, FM radio has become another form of "meeting," but one in which strangers are presented as familial others. A place of circulating public gossip, FM programs have become a means to cross social boundaries that otherwise appear impassable. Friends and relatives who otherwise cannot meet each other, as well as close friends and neighbors who form "listener groups," communicate with one another through FM programs and presenters, extending the space of the home and school into the public and faceless arena of the radio waves.

RADIO NEPAL AND IMAGINING THE PANCHĀYAT NATION

FM broadcasts in Kathmandu first took place in 1996 across from the studios of Radio Nepal that are housed in Singha Durbar, a former Rana palace that became the official seat of the government in 1951. During this first year, I accompanied one of the FM managers to the Singha Durbar studios just after the single channel government-sponsored FM station had opened. I recall the decrepit grandeur of the palace I had previously only seen from the street as we were waved through the tall, black, iron gates by a guard dressed in a forest-green uniform with a felt beret. The inside studio had the faint smell of mildew, which was offset by sounds of international pop music reverberating through the shiny glassed-in studio. The studio was brimming with the chatter and youthful energy of several FM presenters (hosts) who occupied the space. They inevitably sought out possible connections and knowledge about the other radio hosts. All of them spoke rapid Nepali slang, with a

FIGURE 8. Singha Durbar wing where Radio Nepal studios are housed. Photo: Cristeena Chitrakar.

sprinkling of English words, which is characteristic of middle-class Nepali youth. A dynamic, heavy-set woman, who prided herself on her many layers of skin, told one of the other hosts: "Ever since I was a baby I was chubby. That's why my husband fell in love with me when I was three." They continued to talk about their pasts and lives, until the woman she was talking with suddenly interrupted. "You're the one!" the other young woman presenter cried. "My mother keeps telling me your story as an example of why arranged marriages are a good thing. You are the woman who was arranged to be married from the time you were a baby. She said you refused and refused and then finally gave in. Now, my mother tells me, you are as happy as can be. Is that true?" Conversations like these echoed the content of programs broadcast from the studio, and they were typical of my visits to the Singha Durbar studios. (See figure 8.)

Singha Durbar, or "the lion palace," is a relic of former Prime Minister Chandra Shumshere Rana, who ruled Nepal from 1901 to 1923. Almost as soon as Chandra Shumshere took office, he began the plan for what he wished to be the largest structure in all of Asia, with an image of Versailles in mind (Sever 1993). Fifty hectares of land were cleared for its construction, more than half the size of the old Kathmandu town. Within three years, this panorama of luxury emerged amid the fields of rice and the thatched-roof houses that stood outside its walls. When completed in 1903, Singha Durbar boasted over fourteen hundred rooms, which, from floor to ceiling, were covered with items that could only be found outside Nepal (Sever 1993). Inlaid parquet floors that squeaked of France lay beneath tiers of Venetian chandeliers. Belgian gilded mirrors reflected images throughout the palace, enabling servants to watch their masters from places out of view. Larger-than-life portraits of the Rana family hung beside paintings of Queen Victoria or King Charles V. Overstuffed velvet chairs and divans, Chinese vases, and Japanese screens cluttered the rooms. It was under Chandra Shumshere Rana's reign that the first radios came to Nepal from England, and one can easily imagine a large Philips radio perched ostentatiously upon one of the Viennese tables that graced the rooms of the palace.

When the first radios arrived in Nepal in the 1920s, access to technology and political power were synonymous. Like photography, which I discussed in chapter 2, radios were the exclusive possession of the family oligarchy of Rana prime ministers and the select Nepalis supporting their rule. For anyone else, listening to the radio was a capital crime against the state. To own a radio required permission of the rulers, and Parajuli notes that during World War II (when the British were being defeated by Japanese) all private radios were seized, kept in Singha Durbar, and then returned (2007: 53). All the broadcasts that the Rana elite could tune in to came from the colonial-supported All-India Radio (AIR), established in 1936.

Rudolf Mrazek writes of radio in late-colonial Indonesia, suggesting that the radio helped "spread the notion of power as largely mechanical" (1997: 33), thereby obscuring the social agency behind the medium itself. In Mrazek's analysis, the radio provided an important metaphor for and transmitter of colonial power, creating a diffuse yet comforting sense of enclosure within colonial homes. The radio became an object of desire that made a modern colonial home complete, similar to its symbolic function in the homes of Rana rulers and other Nepali elite. The comfort of the radio box, Mrazek argues, created an effective shield in the Indies colony from all the political anxiety that existed outside its broadcasts. As a noncolony, radios connected Ranas and elite Nepalis with colonial India, which similarly created a screen and a comfort zone of unchallenged power. The idea that power is embodied in and transpires through machines was equally true in securing state power in Nepal. This convergence of mechanical and political power continued from the Ranas exclusive control over technology to the Panchāyat period I discuss below when more Nepalis began to have access to media that was produced by the Panchāyat state.

Despite the tight control on access to technology, some Nepalis did manage to smuggle in radios and listen to broadcasts from India. Their radio listening stands in stark contrast to the introduction of radio in many colonial settings, where the colonial government aimed to cultivate civil and obedient colonial subjects through its broadcasts. Brian Larkin traces the colonial history of radio in Nigeria, which differs from Mzarek's history of the Indies, but is equally bound up with the production and representation of state power. In the case of Nigeria, radios were not initially domestic objects; rather, the media began as a public technology, in which radio programs were broadcast on public loudspeakers or, if inside the house, between twenty or thirty listeners would gather together to listen. Their programs often discussed the infrastructural achievements of the colonial government (Larkin 2008: 59). The initial public nature of radio listening was widespread throughout colonial Africa (Englund 2012: 25). Radio listening among Nepalis was exclusively a domestic (and often even secret) affair. Within homes many people may have gathered to listen so that the space of the home often served as a semipublic space.

Though radios were not available to the general Nepali public, middle-class Nepalis at least five years before the Ranas were ousted from power began buying radios through agents who would purchase them in India. Satya Mohan Joshi remembers that he bought a radio set from an agent in 2003 v.s. (1946) that cost him 350 rupees, a price that was five times his monthly salary (Joshi 2062 v.s.: 46). He recalls first hearing the radio at a friend of a friend's house and quickly becoming a "radio addict." Kamal Dixit, whose uncle was the principal of Trichandra College in 1995 v.s. (1939), recalls the family purchasing a Phillips radio from London. As a nine-year-old child, he was most fascinated with the radio object, the strange knobs and buttons that he and his cousins would turn repeatedly (Dixit 2062 v.s.: 41).

Prior to the opening of Radio Nepal in 1951, the Nepali Congress established the first underground radio station in Nepal in the Terai city of Birantnagar, which was dedicated to aiding their fight against the Ranas (Onta et al. 2004; Parajuli and Onta 2005). With the dissolution of Rana rule in 1951, the new government created Radio Nepal and a national voice for all who had access to a radio set. Gradually, the ownership of radios increased and was encouraged across the country. As Humagain suggests, Radio Nepal modeled their initial programming and broadcasts on the

Nepali Congress's first underground experiments with radio (2003: 39). Until 1955, all of the programs were broadcast from live musicians or from the few gramophones given by England to Nepal in 1950 as a gift to acknowledge the service of Nepali soldiers during the war (Mukarung 2056 v.s.; cited in Humagain 2003: 55).

After King Mahendra dissolved the multiparty democracy in 1960 and assumed exclusive power to rule, Radio Nepal became the primary ideological mouthpiece of his Panchāyat government, used to promote a national community centered on the Nepali language, a monarchial version of Hinduism, and the ideals of *bikās*. Radios were viewed as signs of modernity and unique Nepaliness (see figure 7, at the beginning of the chapter). By 1962, the government passed the Press and Publication Act 2019, which enabled the government to suspend news, criticism, or any publication it deemed reasonable to ban in the public interest (Humagain 2003; IIDS 1996). In their histories of Radio Nepal and its programs, Devraj Humagain (2003) and Pratyoush Onta et al. (2004) note that the majority of the radio programs in the early years of Mahendra's reign were devoted to denouncing the earlier multiparty democracy and explaining the benefits of the single-party (royalist) Panchāyat government. After the promulgation of a new constitution in 1962 and 1963, a great deal of the radio broadcasting time was devoted to elaborations and discussions about the philosophy of the Panchāyat system itself (Onta et al. 2004: 25).

By 1965, Radio Nepal allowed only the Nepali language for broadcasts of the news and educational programs (25). Radio plays, which began in 1951, were a popular means of paying homage to the king after 1960, and from 1972 to 1973 they became the standard Saturday afternoon entertainment for Nepalis on their weekly break from work (Humagain 2003: 54). Folk songs promoting *Nepalipan* (Nepaliness) were a staple of Radio Nepal programming, and frequently King Mahendra, who had a great interest in music, would go to the Radio Nepal studio to hear the music played live by musicians. In his study of Newar music in Kirtipur, Ingemar Grandin (1989) shows that certain performative genres of folk songs were easily adapted and accepted as mediated forms on Radio Nepal during the Panchāyat period. Becoming mediated, Grandin argues, had some effect on local performance and practice as musicians became increasingly aware of the possibilities of wider circulation. Radio Nepal revised their entertainment programs in 1970 to include regular "Phulbari programs" that broadcast folk songs in different Nepali languages, phone-in programs, and comedy programs (Humagain 2003: 54). As in Larkin's description of colonial Nigerian radio, Nepali Panchāyat programming broadcast the success of the Panchāyat government in terms of development and infrastructural projects.

The power of the media is associated with its ability to carry sounds and stories from other parts of the nation and more powerful places in the world into the sphere of people's houses. With the introduction first of Nepal Television in 1985 and then of satellite TV in the early 1990s, electronic media became increasingly a site of access to places, ideas, and people across the globe. The emergence of FM radio after the collapse of the Panchāyat government was thought to be a more local media than Radio Nepal, due to its narrower range of broadcast. But this localness was centered in Kathmandu, the nation's capitol, and so FM radio programs also cultivated a more cosmopolitan sensibility associated with ideas, music, and people from elsewhere.

PRIVATE FM RADIO AND NEW URBAN PUBLICS

FM radio was established in 1996, forty-five years after the creation of Radio Nepal, and six years after the national People's Movement (*jana āndolan* I). By 1996, approximately 51 percent of Nepali households owned radio sets, including 80 percent of the households in the Kathmandu Valley (Radio Nepal 1997: 24). FM radio was the first nongovernmental electronic media in Nepal to be managed by private businesses. "Freedom of expression after 1990," writes Pratyoush Onta, "coincided with the expansion of the market (and the concomitant greater need to advertise)" (2003: 259). This move toward privatization in radio had begun in the early 1980s, when the government pulled out most of its money from Radio Nepal and the radio station began to survive on advertisements (Humagain 2003: 57). FM stations extended this privatizing trend, and fundamentally transformed the nature of broadcasting.

The beginning of FM radio fit well into broader agendas of international development agencies and the Nepali business community, both of which sought to liberalize the public sphere and the broader political economy after the *jana āndolan* I. Radio Nepal was not replaced by FM radio, but it was among the many state-run industries that were transformed into fully privatized enterprises (Humagain 2003). Just after the *jana āndolan* I, according to many FM managers, a group of Japanese development agents from UNESCO made a proposal to open FM radio waves to the public. The proposal lay dormant until November 1995 when the Nepali government inaugurated an experimental government-run station on FM 100. Six months later, the government held an open auction to rent out blocks of airtime to private companies from 7 A.M. to midnight. Six different companies, many already in the media or communication business, signed a year-long contract with the government that gave them different slots of airtime throughout the day. For the first years of broadcasting, FM stations broadcast from a studio within the government quarters at Singh Durbar, across the hall from Radio Nepal.

The beginning of FM radio was clearly linked to the dramatic growth in mass media, particularly the press, during the 1980s and the 1990s, as well as to changes in the new constitution of 1990. The democratic constitution of 1990 provided legal measures to enforce freedom of expression, the right to establish organizations, and the right of assembly. Most importantly, the constitution emphasized the right to protection from what was colloquially known in media circles as the three black Cs of the press: government censorship, cancelation of registration, and closure. However, perhaps in an ironic spirit suited to the new liberalized consensus, censorship was part of the fabric of the initial FM contract signed between entrepreneurs and the government. At the outset, private stations were prevented from broadcasting news, religion, or any political information.

Most of the managers of the companies did not seem to be uncomfortable with these initial contractual restrictions, as sweeping as they may appear. "The government restrictions from Radio Nepal's point of view were quite liberal and fair, I would say," a manager of one of the largest FM companies told me. "Basically it was political. Only entertainment, no political things, nothing 'antisocial,' that is, against the society. Your messages should not be revolutionary." That is our business, many of FM managers used to tell me, strictly entertainment and fun. One manager from another large FM company did not outwardly complain about these restrictions, but nevertheless implied that the restrictions were a way of maintaining the public circulation of a single public voice, echoing Panchāyat times. In response to my question about why the government would not initially allow FM to broadcast information *(jānakāri)*, this manager diplomatically replied, "They are worried that FM information will contradict the government information, and make people confused." He eagerly waited for the day—which was to come almost two years later—when the government would issue fully private licenses with little or no restriction on broadcasting the news.

The government gave its first private license not to a commercial enterprise, but to a community radio station, Sagarmatha FM in 1997, a station owned by the NGO Nepal Forum for Environmental Journalists (NFEJ).[5] Several commercial stations acquired their licenses after 1998. By July 26, 2001, following a challenge to a government directive that required, among other things, that "independent radio stations ... could [only] broadcast news obtained from the official HMG sources" (Onta 2006: 101), stations were allowed to begin broadcasting their own news. Though the majority of initial licenses were given to Kathmandu stations, by 2008 there were fifty-six FM stations with private licenses (though only thirty-three had begun broadcasting at this time), and only *nine* of them are located in the Kathmandu Valley.[6]

Many of the stations outside the Valley, however, buy programs or news produced in Kathmandu. Program distribution groups like Communication Corner, for example, produce national and local news about events in Kathmandu that is aired on FM stations outside the Valley with the express purpose of bringing listeners from outside Kathmandu emotionally closer to the center (Onta 2006: 96). Within Kathmandu, large mainstream stations like Kantipur FM have acquired additional licenses to broadcast in other parts of the country, but the vast majority of their programming is conducted from Kathmandu and sent via satellite to their connected stations around the country. Despite advertising themselves as a local medium, FM entertainment programs often end up, directly or indirectly, reinforcing the centrality of Kathmandu Valley to national imaginings.

Over the course of the 1990s, FM radio became a desired space for connection and public interaction in Kathmandu. Often contrasted to Radio Nepal, which many described as a "one-way" medium, FM radio quickly became a symbol of the new participatory, democratic moment. Managers and radio hosts promoted FM radio as a "catalyst for discussion" and a place for "questioning authority." FM programs encouraged public interaction with acquaintances or total strangers: people could now easily call up or send a letter to request a Nepali, Hindi, and English song, chat with a radio presenter, or pass on a message to a friend. While request programs were part of Radio Nepal's programming intermittently since its inception and phone-in programs were a regular part of its programming after 1983 (Humagain 2003), broadcasting and interaction with listeners on FM programs were distinctly different. FM radio shows cultivated a sense of familiarity through the distinct vocal "personalities" of the radio hosts, and presenters on FM programs addressed listeners using informal conversational speech, unlike the monotone and Sanskritized speech of Radio Nepal hosts. The FM programs appeared to be so different from Radio Nepal that many thought of them as two different media entirely. "I don't listen to radio," people in Kathmandu frequently told me during the initial years of FM radio, "I listen to FM."

The semiprivate initial FM was explicitly designed for the urban educated elite, and the programs contributed significantly to the making of urban middle-class cultures, especially among youth. Rather than building connections to a national community, the initial vision of FM radio stations was to create a distinct form of local urbanity that would ostensibly connect Kathmandu Nepalis to the rest of the world. The first programs produced a distinctly cosmopolitan and Kathmandu feel that created bonds among a specifically Kathmandu listening community with expressions of personal trouble, intimacy, and affection, and thereby departed in many ways from the national agenda of Radio Nepal. The select group was initially targeted through the use of English and songs that appeared to cross cultural and national borders. "Our basic concept was simple," the manager of Hits FM explained to me in English. "Nepalese people are more exposed to the Western way of life than a lot of people in this part of the world. Even in India they are not so open to, let's say, music. [We'll do] only English and Hindi music. We won't do Nepali because everybody is doing Nepali. So that's how to get people like the urban guys to listen, urban, educated." Though this manager distinguished Nepali from Indian listeners, he nevertheless went to Delhi to "find out how it was done." He invited one of the Delhi FM radio jockeys to come up to Kathmandu for a few days to provide a training course for his presenters. While other FM companies may not have pursued such direct contact with foreign radio hosts, nearly all of them had some foreign connection to help them buy music unavailable in Kathmandu. I, myself, along with several of my visitors from the United States, became a shuttle of CDs more than once.

Much to the chagrin of several FM presenters, the radio waves reached a far broader audience than its initial target audience. It quickly became clear from the letters and the phone calls that more than the urban elite listened to FM programs, though villagers just outside Kathmandu often felt marginalized.[7] An early FM presenter told me that he himself was unsure what the term "urban elite" actually meant when it was used in the contract drawn up between the government and FM radio operators: "Once you open up the airways basically anyone who has got a set, who has an FM set, can tune in. Taxi drivers listen to us, shopkeepers listen to us, schoolchildren listen to us, some expatriates listen to us, you know, housewives. So it's actually reaching out to each and everyone of those people who possesses an FM radio set, which is a whole cross section of the population of the Kathmandu Valley."

The hosts of FM programs play a crucial role in defining the overall style and social messages of FM radio. They aim to speak in an urban vernacular that rings of Kathmandu specifically. They also evoke the immediate sense of presence and distance from the rest of the world. Their role is implied in their title, *prastutakars* (presenters), which gradually transformed over the years of FM broadcasts into RJs (radio jockeys). The word comes from the verb *prastut* (to mention, to present, to note, to propose). *Prastutakar* suggests a double meaning in these faceless voices: they are expected to make themselves appear physically and emotionally present to their invisible audiences through their voices (presenting themselves) as they offer, or present, entertainment and music to these listeners. One presenter felt that his primary role was to create a sense of presence between the listener and radio host: "I want them (the listeners) to feel as if I am in their room with them. So I never address them as listeners *[srotāharu]*, I always address them directly, *tapāīharu* [the formal, plural 'you']." Many of the presenters I spoke with envisioned themselves on the border between Kathmandu and the rest of the world. It was their job to bring that distant world into the intimate space of Kathmandu homes, businesses, and lives. Offering, proposing, and evoking bodily presence through their voice converge in the role of the presenter.

The various urban publics that FM radio produced were enhanced by the extra-FM activities that emerged in its wake, particularly FM listeners clubs and the magazines they spawned. These listeners' clubs occasionally met face-to-face and enjoyed picnics together, but as Pratyoush Onta points out, such contact is transient (2006: 98). Outside the Valley, listeners' clubs of a particular program will gather to listen to that program together or engage in other activities together (often related to the messages of the programs they listen to) in their locale (see Greenland n.d.). Letters sent to particular programs from listeners' clubs frequently make references to their activities or to prior stories that were recently broadcast and add their own commentary, or evaluate prior broadcasts. FM radio presenters will often broadcast the requests from listeners' club letters, as well as read individual letters and requests or take calls, all of which creates "feedback loops that characterize their own space of consumption" (Warner 2002: 71). But unlike the newspaper letters to the editor or comments from the audience about which Michael Warner writes, these commentaries do not always make it on to the broadcast program unless they are fused within the letter itself (as I discuss in chapter 4). The fact that such self-reflexive discourse does frequently appear in the framing of the letters makes it clear that the audience sees itself as part of a broader public of listeners and writers.

Despite the sociality of listener's clubs and the collective listening that occurs frequently outside the Valley, FM radio listening in Kathmandu generally contrasts with the more social way of listening to the news on Radio Nepal, in which the whole family gathers round. Instead, FM listening is usually a more intimate affair within the home or one bound up with commercial and business activities outside the home, in restaurants, taxis, buses, shops, offices, and other work spaces. The listening habits in these different spaces obviously differ: at home, a teenager may take an FM radio set behind shut doors and listen to her favorite program with a few friends or, quite frequently, alone. Some said they even took their FM radio set to bed. In commercial and work environments, FM radio programs blend into the other sounds of people's talking and conducting business, phones' ringing, and outside noise of traffic and horns, becoming a soundscape that pervades much of urban public life in Kathmandu.

The stranger intimacy that constitutes any public is frequently thought to depend upon the condition of anonymity, yet anonymity is frequently subverted in FM programs (Berlant 1997; Habermas 1989; Warner 1990). There is not always a clear division between the FM radio personality and media celebrity and their fans. Listeners' clubs are devoted to organizing events between listeners, and programs like *My Best Friend* (Kantipur FM) aim to put listeners with common interests in touch with one another so that they might meet one another not only on the radio, but also in person. During my visits to various FM radio stations during its initial days, presenters were inevitably on the phone with one of their fans or chatting with them casually in the offices, undermining the stranger quality of most publics. I was always surprised by how easily listeners walked in and out of the radio studios, and how often friendships developed between the presenters and their listeners. In my own research with the radio host Kalyan Gautum (discussed in chapter 4), we went to meet fans of his program in their homes. Kalyan maintained contact with many of these listeners, and some sought him down in his house where they were welcomed with tea or dinner when he was there. I learned later that many marriages (including Kalyan's) were made between radio hosts and their fans. Contrary to much research on publics, anonymity was not an essential or key component of FM radio publics. In this sense, FM radio sociality sometimes resembles the lack of anonymity that characterizes social media like Facebook, as Ilana Gershon has observed (Gershon 2010a; cf. Habermas 1989; Warner 1990, 2002). Perhaps this is not surprising: the prominence of FM radio and the Internet emerged within the same decade in Nepal.

LANGUAGE ON FM: CLASS AND KATHMANDU COMMUNITY

The specifically Kathmandu listening community is based on an imagined sense of emotional proximity between urban residents, combined rather jarringly with a heightened awareness of social class and geographic distance. The juxtaposition of class and geography is especially acute between listeners in the center of Kathmandu and those in the small towns and villages outside the urban center. (Of course, the geography of these listening communities is itself constantly being remade, as, for example, we see the rise of affluent suburban communities in the Valley.) Like all imagined communities, FM radio creates a feeling of temporal and spatial simultaneity, in which listeners envision and actually hear other callers from different parts of the city listening at the very same time (Anderson [1983] 1991: 24). FM radio limits and expands the geographical boundaries of the Kathmandu Valley. In contrast to the written mediums of the novel and the newspaper that Anderson focused on, a voice-based medium like radio makes this feeling of simultaneity even more physically present. Unseen voices provide the effect of immediacy and familiarity along with the illusion of bodily presence as they enter the space of the home, surround people, and encourage them to interact.

The emerging Kathmandu listening communities created through FM radio are also shaped through the imagined and material connections between the middle class in Kathmandu and the rest of the world. With the initial limitation of FM licenses to the boundaries of the Kathmandu Valley and by speaking in styles that resonate with Indian, Pakistani, and even, to some degree, American radio hosts, the first FM radio programs carved sharp distinctions between Kathmandu and the rest of Nepal. The programs continually sought to assert their connection with other FM radio programs across the world, through their style of speaking and the form of the programs. Three months after FM broadcasts began in Kathmandu, *The Kathmandu Post,* the largest English-language daily newspaper, published an article that was written from Lahore titled "Addicted to FM Radio."[8] "The new FM radio stations are a social metaphor of the change sweeping the cities of India and Pakistan," the article ended. It is worth noting that *The Kathmandu Post* is run by one of the largest media conglomerates in Nepal, *Kantipur Publications,* which also opened one of the first and now largest FM stations, Kantipur FM. The publication of this article in *The Kathmandu Post* is a way of indirectly advertising Kantipur Publications's other media, while also implicitly connecting Kathmandu (and the media company) to the other South Asian cities swept up by FM radio.

I recall a conversation I had with one of the FM presenters in the first few months of FM programming, when it was still on the single channel of FM 100. The presenter echoed this aspiration for global cosmopolitanism.

"You are from the United States, right?" he asked me.

"Yes, originally from Philadelphia," I replied.

"Oh yes. Well, you must have an FM there. Tell me about it."

I could not bear to tell him that there are multiple FM stations, and that I only really listened to the radio when I was in the car. But I did offer to bring him some recordings from a few programs, and I am certain I am not the only one who did so. As I discuss in chapter 5, more and more Nepalis are traveling around the world, for study and for work, and no doubt many of them have become informal couriers of music or sample programs for their friends who work at FM radio stations around the country. Now many FM stations have online broadcasts, so FM programs produced in Nepal are listened to by Nepalis around the world. According to some sources, templates of radio programs are now sent to a number of FM stations in Nepal, all generated by a company in Florida.[9] While most of the programs are funded by local industries—Star Beer, San Miguel Beer, or Coconut Tree 100% Mustard Oil—a few are funded by international donors, including USAID and UNICEF, who model their programs on other radio shows they have sponsored around the world.[10]

The explicitly global perspective of such a local media as FM radio in Kathmandu led to many heated arguments during the first few months of FM broadcasts, primarily sparked by religious conservatives, student activists, and journalists. The most common response to the initial broadcasts on FM radio was from those who worried about the destruction or loss of Nepali culture and language. The anger of this small but very loud public against FM radio programs led to a day-long conference at the Blue Star Hotel organized by Radio Nepal two months after the inception of the FM station. The purpose of this meeting was to discuss the issues between FM managers and intellectuals and journalists who opposed the programming. Language became the primary point of contention at the Blue Star conference. Seated around the conference room in this five-star hotel was a select group of journalists, government officials, representatives from each of the six FM stations, and a number of hotel staff serving tea and snacks. I stood out as one of the few women in the room, and one of two foreigners (the other being a British man who was also a manager at one FM station). Each of the FM station managers was given a chance to talk, and most recited the requisite appeal to *bikās* through FM radio programs and said they saw FM as a site for promoting Nepali music.

A striking moment during the conference was when one of the managers of Hits FM decided to give his remarks in English. The effect was similar to the far more public and controversial event, twelve years later, when the newly elected vice president of Nepal, who is from the southern region of Nepal, Pramananda Jha, recited his oath of office in Hindi. In this case, the manager sought to highlight certain ideas and values that were associated with the English language. The manager stressed the importance of "dynamic personalities" and said what very few people were willing to explicitly say: FM radio is first and foremost a business. "Life can only be understood backward," he concluded. "But please remember that we must move forward."

"We don't want to be like the English," one of the journalists yelled out. "This is another form of colonialism!"

Quite clearly, since language always encodes historically specific social values, the debates against English being spoken on FM were more fundamentally debates about the social worlds and values of English speakers. The manager's comments at the Blue Star Hotel specifically linked the idea of business (and notably not development) with the English language, which conveyed a sensibility about private enterprise in ways that the national language, Nepali, did not. Indeed, English is a form of symbolic capital and social power in Kathmandu that carries specific class markers (Bourdieu 1991). English has become the lingua franca of most nongovernmental offices and international development agencies, two of the most popular and respectable occupations among Kathmandu professionals. It is the medium of instruction in almost all private schools, and the language that many elite and a few middle-class Nepalis speak at home. Using English, middle-class Nepalis mark themselves as educated and cosmopolitan, and distinguish themselves from lower-class Nepalis and villagers who have less access to an English education. As in many places, Kathmandu residents (especially youth) refer to English as the "international language"; it is considered and quite practically often serves as a ticket to another place.

FM programs built a very specific middle-class and cosmopolitan idea of Kathmandu, rooted in a connection to English and Nepali, as well as in music from around the world. As in Susan Douglas's comments about the birth of radio in the United States, FM radio in Kathmandu "cultivates both a sense of national unity and, at the same time, a conspiratorial sense of subcultural difference, of distance from, even superiority to that national ethos" (1999: 23). Kunal Lama, one of the first FM radio presenters, embodies this FM-cultivated image of a cosmopolitan Nepali from Kathmandu, and he often distinguishes himself from what he calls the "more Nepali" presenters. Kunal grew up in Kathmandu and attended St. Xavier's school, a renowned private high school run by American Jesuit priests. As the son of an ex-Gurkha soldier, Kunal had the opportunity to travel and live in England for two years. He spoke a mixture of English and Nepali to his Nepali friends, but spoke exclusively in English to foreigners.

I met Kunal at the restaurant he owned, located in the tourist section of town, Thamel. The restaurant vaguely resembles a romantic or trendy joint found in such cities as New York or London with dark wood floors and a daily menu written in chalk on a hanging board. When I began asking Kunal about the beginnings of FM radio in Nepal, he immediately corrected me, saying that it should properly be called Kathmandu FM. His definition of Kathmandu, interestingly enough, developed as we began talking about the language of FM presenters:

> There are always some people who don't understand a word of English. Like, for example, the people in Bhaktapur or even in some of the small neighborhoods of Patan where they might be speaking much of the time in Newari, not even in Nepali. Then it would be a real problem to understand what the English presenters are talking about and to even appreciate their style of presentation or the music, which could be Metallica, for example, or Nirvana. They think radio is meant for all of us, obviously because we can tune into it, but then [they wonder] why can't we understand the programs, why are they

not catering to us? So we have a huge problem. Number one complaint has been basically the language. Too much English is being spoken.

Strikingly, Kunal does not include Kathmandu in his description of the places where English cannot be understood. Both Bhaktapur and Patan are predominately Newar towns; however, many of the people who live there travel back and forth between Kathmandu quite frequently, if not daily. These middle-class Newars are deeply entrenched in the Kathmandu economy; and while most speak Newari at home, many speak English quite fluently. The towns, however, are primarily associated with those Newaris who maintain ties to their fields, who remain at the edge of the middle class. Furthermore, there are many places *within* Kathmandu where people do not speak English. Through FM radio, Kathmandu is largely being imagined as a particular class of people—distinguished from the nearby towns and from the many manual laborers and servants within Kathmandu (many of whom were avid listeners and sent many letters to FM stations)—through the values and social relationships embedded in English.

The battle over who should and should not listen to FM radio was a battle about defining the boundaries of the middle class and the changing definitions of Nepaliness this entailed. Its aim to reach only the urban elite never completely worked. Kunal later expressed his frustration about calls he was receiving on air from listeners whom he felt were inappropriate for his program. "We have to have some selection in who we direct our programs to," he complained. "We can't just broadcast to everyone. I mean, I don't want some Bhaktapur farmer calling up or even listening to my show!"

Debates about defining a specifically Kathmandu audience took shape primarily over the issue of language, but this issue was not limited to a battle between English and Nepali. The FM radio also became a stage for striking debates about what constitutes "good" Nepali. In newspapers and on the street, people complained that FM presenters did not speak correct Nepali. The erosion of the language, critics asserted, signified an erosion of cultural values. Some even went so far as to suggest that the presenters were not even really Nepali. Significantly, the most disturbing issue for many of these critics was incorrect use of hierarchical pronouns and kin terms, and the mispronunciation of the word *Kathmandu*. Pronouns and place names are indexical signs; that is, they are terms that shift depending on where, to whom, and when one is speaking and they point to particular people who inhabit those terms. As Judith Irvine has argued, indexical signs are often particularly contentious forms of language because they effect social distinctions between different groups of people (1989: 252–253).

The heated contests around the word *Kathmandu* took place after one of the main FM stations decided to broadcast its advertisement using the voice of an Englishman who helped manage this station and who pronounced *Kathmandu* with a heavy English accent. In English, the aspirated *th,* a sound distinctive to Nepali, transforms into a long *a* and hard *t* sound. The voice of an Englishman mispronouncing *Kathmandu* signified one of the sharpest critiques of FM radio in its early days: it seemed to be relying too heavily on foreign tastes. The accent clearly identifies the speaker as a foreigner, yet also as a representative of this newly popular media; it therefore spoke blatantly, for some, of the overwhelming foreign presence in Kathmandu and its pronounced effect on political decisions. Moreover, it marked a very specific social landscape in Kathmandu, not just of foreigners living in the city but also of those Nepalis who most frequently mingle with such accented people. The capital city of Kathmandu is at once the seat of governmental power, the center of the most extensive capitalist endeavors, and the place where Nepal most densely interacts with the world outside its borders. The only international airport in Nepal is located in Kathmandu. As home to the government and the king since the late eighteenth century, the place and name of Kathmandu have carried for some time now the ring of political power. To pronounce the name of this significant city as a foreigner would pronounce it—particularly on the public media of radio—presents something of a challenge to the Nepali political power that Kathmandu signifies. It also suggests that the actual site of production, the place where such programs truly originate, is not really in Nepal but some place far outside its borders. One journalist complained about the "drawling twangs" of the FM hosts' accents that made them seem as if they were not Nepali.

This reliance on foreignness, many complained, led to a corruption in key Nepali concepts, like hierarchical kin terms. At the Blue Star conference, one man passionately complained that presenters often addressed male callers who could be clearly identified by their voice as younger than the presenters with the term *older brother (dāi)* instead of *younger brother (bhāi)*. I later conducted an interview with a journalist and staunch critic of FM who also attended this conference, and he similarly felt that the basic problem with FM radio was the misuse of standard Nepali grammar. He explained his complaint to me:

In English you say, "He came." "You came." "She came." It's finished. For a person's *status,* for one's own individual style, expressions, our language has certain rules. For example, if you come in, [I would say] "You *[tapāi]* come in. You sit down *[basnuhos].*" If a brother younger than me comes in, [I would say,] "You *[timi]* sit down *[basa].*" And then if a very close friend came, "You *[tā]* sit *[bas].*" In our language, there is a lot of *diversification*. But FM came, and they say, "*Timi* [the informal pronoun] *basnuhos* [the formal verb ending]." Why are we protesting against FM? The main thing is that FM is ruining our language.

The voices blaring through FM radio collapse the social hierarchies inherent in the Nepali language, this journalist argued, or mix pronouns with inappropriate verb endings and therefore destroy a specifically Nepali consciousness. It is entirely possible, of course, that some of the presenters did not grow up using standard Nepali grammar. The affront has to do with the effect of making such variations in Nepali grammar public, and thus challenging the state-enforced ideas of a proper and standard Nepali language. The trouble with inappropriate use of kin pronouns has to due largely with the context in which they are spoken. Such deitic pronouns rely on context to determine their form and establish the relationship the speaker has with another person at this particular time. To refer to a young boy as if he were the same age or older is a way of humorously presenting their conversation, as if the host and the listener spoke from equal positions. Part of what troubles many in Kathmandu perhaps has to do with the informal nature of conversations on FM programs ("just rubbish," "pure gossip," some remarked), coupled with the use of formal pronouns. By referring to a younger person with a more formal pronoun, the presenter effectively creates a relationship of equality and social distance, even when their conversation otherwise appears as familiar and intimate as everyday gossip. In changing the commonly used forms of hierarchy through these deitic pronouns, the novel context of FM radio effectively produces new social relationships in public that threaten the existing hierarchies expressed in the Nepali language. Despite the fury that initially erupted around FM, many programs do draw upon and help to sustain national narratives, such as the quest for development and the ideals of Nepaliness inherent in the Nepali language. Programs like Kalyan Gautum's *Mero Kathā, Mero Gīt* are spoken exclusively in Nepali and produce a form of public intimacy characteristic of many programs that I discuss in the following chapter.

The tangibly felt presence of the faceless voice combined with the informal speech style created the conditions for what was felt by many to be a more authentic, truly real connection between people, distinct from and in tension with the practices of seeing face that I discussed in chapter 2. Music was certainly part of the huge appeal of this new medium, but music alone was never enough.[11] Hundreds of letters sent to FM radio channels spoke of the power of the voice to make the presenter appear before the listeners' eyes, as well as the way FM programs helped to make connections between themselves, the city, and other strangers they heard or imagined listening along with them. Most of these listeners spoke about the immediacy, presence, and emotional directness that characterized FM programs, thus reiterating the sense of direct, transparent "contact" that the media suggest. One must wonder: what material qualities of FM radio make its mediating powers seem to disappear?

FACELESS TECHNOLOGIES: CALLING IN

The material technology of FM radio enhances those feelings of presence, intimacy, and interiority generated by FM presenters and their programs. Frequency modulations, in contrast to amplification modulations, are achieved through more direct radio waves. While AM radio sound can travel greater distances, the sounds of FM are clearer, with more distinct resolution, but are limited to a range of about fifty miles. FM radio waves are therefore not subject to the same kind of disruption as AM channels, either from nature (for example, lightening storms) or from solid boundaries like concrete buildings (Douglas 1999). These higher frequencies and the better resolution of sound create a much more tangible aura of voices and a more direct sense of participation and engagement with radio voices themselves.

What, then, are features of the voice that Nepalis associate with directness? On FM radio, a fast-paced, verbose, chatty speaker, who peppers his or her speech with new slang, laughter, several different tones, and English, immediately conjures up the image of a young, urban, middle-class hipster, a common host of many FM programs. It is also this person who is regarded as a more direct speaker, someone who has learned to say what they want to say and not hide their intentions within poetic, metaphorical, or literary words. The highly regulated, monotone voice of the Radio Nepal announcer, by contrast, uses many Sanskritized or literary phrases, is usually male, and conjures up an image of a high-caste civil servant whose words echo the sound of the state. These prosodic and semantic features of the voice serve to mark the difference between FM and Radio Nepal broadcasts. While Radio Nepal broadcasts are often interpreted as conveying a hidden state message, FM broadcasts are thought to be more direct and transparent. Despite the pretense of transparency and immediacy, this direct speech actually requires multiple forms of mediation, ranging from FM radio waves themselves to specific styles of speech and ways of modulating one's own voice.

The faceless voice of FM radio conveys both presence and absence simultaneously because of its obvious connection to the body and its ability, through technology, to circulate widely. As Steven Feld (1996) demonstrates, the sound of the spoken voice and the fact of listening suffuse the entire body. "This is why hearing and voicing link the felt sensations of sound and balance to those of physical and emotional presence," writes Feld (1996: 97). The radio combines the emotional presence of voicing with the physical presence of the radio machine, an object as common as a sofa in most Kathmandu middle-class homes. In many histories of the senses, sound perception is considered to be more "present" and "immediate" than other sensory data because it is assumed to surround the person rather than being a directional sense like vision. As Jonathan Sterne points out, "people are used to treating things that they can hear but cannot see, smell, or taste as 'present,' and, therefore, it would make sense that the first sense of a kind of intimate, distant immediacy would be accomplished aurally" (2003: 153). Certainly, with this logic, it would make sense that FM radio would become a key media in generating the sense of directness, immediacy, and intimacy. Yet, as Sterne continues, these histories ignore the affective imagination that people put into writing, and the intimacies that writing generated, which precede sound technology. Copresence is imagined, Sterne concludes, and therefore cannot be determined by any hierarchy of the senses. In the case of FM radio, as we will see in the following chapter, both writing and voice coproduce the sense of directness and public intimacy associated with the media.

One of the powerful effects of radio, like other forms of media, is its extension of specific parts of the body into technological forms (Kittler 1999; McLuhan 1964). The radio extends the voice and ears such that speaking and listening can be experienced across great distances in space. As Frederick Kittler (1999) has demonstrated in his study on *Gramophone, Typewriter, Film,* the phonograph was first used in Europe as a device to take testimonies as well as to simply record and immortalize the human voice. The technology itself helped produce the very notion that voice was the locus of truth and the most direct route back to the past. Kittler quotes the German poet Ernst von

Wildenbruch, who wrote in 1897: "The fawning face can deceive the eye, the sound of the voice can never lie; thus it seems to me the phonograph is the soul's true photograph" (cited in Kittler 1999: 79). Often the appeal of speaking on FM radio in Kathmandu is to have one's voice circulate throughout the city and, quite simply, to hear one's own voice. One thrill of speaking on the radio is that a person can be in two places at once, in what seems like an almost disembodied experience. As one of the presenters explained to me: "It doesn't matter what you say. People just want to talk and to hear their voice broadcast next to them." At the same time, many people told me that the meaning of this talk was important: for this was a place where they could express their most real *(bāstavik)* thoughts. As one of the managers said, "People trust you soooo much. A voice."

In Kittler's analysis of sound technologies, there is a contingent relationship between sound and meaning. Only when human sounds are transposed into technology like the gramophone, radio, or telephone, he argues, does speech become the historical and cultural construct of "the voice," a medium of directness, authenticity, and truth. In semiotic terms, such technologies have an indexical relationship to the voices they record or broadcast, that is, they have a direct relationship to that which they represent. They do not require a human being to record sound, and they therefore record not only meaningful language but also "noise," any background sounds that might be in or around the radio studio or even the sound of the recording device or radio technology. "The phonograph does not hear as do ears that have been trained to filter voices, words, and sounds out of noise," writes Kittler, "it registers acoustic events as such" (Kittler 1999: 23). The radio form was well suited to become a medium of directness and presence.

Kittler's analysis suggests several effects of technologies of the voice. Recorded sound no longer has contact with the body, and it thereby appears to create a "perfect" record of the voice that seems to lie outside the human consciousness and body.[12] Unlike in face-to-face conversations that rely upon visual, aural, and gestural cues, the radio and the telephone rely on a single sensory mode, distilling all messages into the voice alone. The disembodied quality of recorded sound makes its messages appear to be transparent, unmediated, and direct. When discussing the potential of FM radio, listeners frequently invoke social concepts like "true self," "direct emotion," or "transparency," concepts that are integrally tied to the indexicality of the voice and to the radio's reliance on a single sensory mode. Recorded voices appear to be "more real" and "more pure" than language spoken face-to-face, with its multiple sensory registers and gestures. A secondary effect is that recorded voices draw both listeners' and theorists' attention to the conventions of everyday language and the fact that all language is mediated through human consciousness and cultural categories. Recording technologies make it possible for people to imagine ineffable or transparent messages that seem to defy the symbolic quality of words.

Many listeners describe their enchantment with a radio voice as having a power to channel emotions that the listeners themselves cannot express in words. Radio hosts encourage their listeners to "speak your minds and hearts," and fan letters repeat such messages, nearly verbatim: "I really like your program because it helps *you* reveal all *our* true emotions."[13] Frequent references to a listener's inability to articulate what he or she feels are also described in terms of authentic emotions. If the lilts and tone of the radio voice become a route to stardom for the radio host,[14] for the listeners these prosodic features of the voice articulate messages that seem to transcend the symbolic quality of words. Media like radio "do not have to make do with the grid of the symbolic," writes Kittler. "That is to say, they reconstruct bodies not only in a system of words or colors or sound intervals. . . . It refers to the bodily real, which of necessity escapes all symbolic grids" (1999: 11–12). Recording technologies that transmit people's voices ironically make it possible for people to imagine "real" messages without words and for the voice itself to be perceived as the medium best suited for the ideals of transparency and direct connection.

But the material qualities of electronic radio do not alone determine its recognition as a medium of directness (*pace* Kittler). These semiotic properties of technology exist within a social world and historical genres of narratives that affect the media's significance. In contrast to histories of technology that take their cue from McLuhan, Jonathan Sterne has argued that the human desires and social concepts embedded in any technology set the stage for technical innovation and are not derived exclusively from the material properties of that new technology. In the case of FM radio, its emergence during a moment of a transitioning democracy, its contrast to the state Radio Nepal, and its frequent use of other technologies of voice within its broadcasts—such as the phone, digital and tape recorders, and disc players—all contribute to its significance as a medium of directness and often of more credible information and truth.

The idea that FM speech is more direct than Radio Nepal derives from the language and media ideology promoted by and associated with FM programs. The analytic term *media ideology* draws upon the work of linguistic anthropologists studying language ideologies. We can understand a media ideology by focusing on the metalanguage used to describe our technologies of communication and the assumptions imputed to these technologies (Gershon 2010b: 283). Media ideologies are part of a broader focus on semiotic ideologies that involves a consideration of the material dimensions of any sign (284). As I discussed in the previous chapter, the semiotic ideologies of the face and the voice often overlap in that both often work as indices of immediacy, presence, and intimacy. To understand the media and language ideologies of FM radio, we must look at the assumptions made about the kind of language spoken on FM radio as well as assumptions about the medium of FM radio. It also requires us to think about the semiotic ideologies of voice, body, and sound to show the ways in which they all are mediated by language and the medium of FM radio as well.

Of course, language and media ideologies are never exclusively about language and media; they are also about particular constellations of power, the creation of stereotypes about individuals or social groups, and the production of subjects in particular cultural and historical contexts. In Nepal, ideas about directness as an ideal of speech and media transmission are shaped by the world of international development, the emergence of new media and publics, neoliberal economic policies, and the democracy movements that have prevailed in Nepal, particularly since 1990 (Kunreuther 2010). Direct speech and having a direct voice critically shape radio listener's subjectivity, from the technology's form to the content of its programs. We will discuss the implications of this in programs that emphasize public intimacy in the following chapter.

The stage was set for this notion of a direct and authentic faceless voice not only by Radio Nepal, but also, and more effectively so, by the increased availability and use of the phone. The telephone, in many ways, laid the social groundwork for many FM programs. Telephone and telegraph technology was initially introduced by the British Residency in 1872,[15] and was used in specific Rana family homes by 1935. The first private lines became available only after the Ranas were removed from power in 1951, though there were only one hundred lines put in place at that time (Nepal Dhursanchar Sansthan 2056 v.s.). When I first traveled to Nepal in 1989 and 1990, telephones were still a rarity in most urban middle-class homes. The most common way of reaching a person within the Valley was simply to go to their house or call from a corner shop. As a material object, telephones entered most homes after televisions and along with refrigerators; they signified a level of middle-class domesticity and disposable income often associated with those who traveled or had contacts overseas. Telephones became a common household technology in Kathmandu in the mid-1990s, though many families shared a single telephone line. By the summer of 2004, nearly every middle-class family I visited had a telephone, and many young professional Nepalis carried cell phones either in addition to or instead of their landline.

The telephone is a medium of locality in Nepal, frequently thought of as connecting distant places as much as distant people. Common greetings on the telephone suggest the way in which the voice is conceived of as a material, embodied part of oneself that can travel to another place. When telephones first became a regular part of Nepalis' homes, a person would often answer the phone by asking, "where is this call from? *[kāhā bāta phon garnu bhayeko?]*" Similarly, the caller usually asked, *"kāhā paryo?"*—an idiom difficult to translate, but roughly meaning "where have I landed" or "where have I entered?" The greeting quickly became the subject of many Kathmandu jokes, such as the common reply *"Mero kānmā paryo"* (You've landed in my ear). Now this telephone greeting—"where is the call from?"—is a sign of class position; it is no longer used by cosmopolitan Nepalis, who mock the greeting as a particularly "villagey" form of address. Most middle-class Nepalis now have caller ID and address their callers immediately by name.

Even without caller ID, though, I found that many Nepalis were especially attuned to the subtle differences in voice of specific people on the phone. Inevitably, when I received a phone call at home, the person on the other line would simply begin talking, asking me how I was doing and what I was doing, without introducing themselves. I frequently became frustrated by the assumption that I knew who was talking and would ask, perhaps too directly, "who is speaking?" On more than one occasion, I was met by a rather perplexed silence or laugh, after which the person would point out the minor offense I had committed by stating, "You don't know me? You don't know this voice?!" The voice was like a signature, a sign of the uniqueness of a person. To ask who was speaking, I discovered, was taken as a lack of familiarity—even among people whom I truly had only met a few times—and thus a lack of intimacy and respect. After a few of these embarrassing episodes, I learned to simply follow along with the conversation until I gradually pieced together who was speaking through the context of their talk.

The phone, like FM radio, is one of the more desired ways for middle-class youth to "meet." As the first interactive technology of the faceless voice, the phone was one of the few places, many told me, where true relationships flourished, completely and comfortably out of view. Letters sent to favorite radio hosts frequently describe relationships that were born over the phone. During the mid-1990s, youth began using the phone to "connect" with otherwise inaccessible acquaintances through what is colloquially known as a "bluff call" *(blaf kal)*. The friendships that develop through a bluff call are often between two people who are introduced by a mutual friend or the result of a misdialed or randomly dialed number.[16] A twenty-three-year old daughter of a family I frequently visited often invited a young man to her house and to family events. He lived close to the apartment where I was staying, and on one evening, while we were traveling home together, I asked him how he and Sarjana had met. Matter-of-factly he replied, "On the phone." He had apparently misdialed his friend's number and reached Sarjana instead. They began to talk and quickly became regular "phone friends." After a year or so of this phone relationship, they began to meet each other in person.

I recall meeting one young radio presenter at her home, and was struck by the number of times the telephone rang and interrupted our conversation. Her house seemed little different than the radio office or studio, where the phone would ring every minute or so with fans calling for their favorite presenter. Each time she answered the phone, she would inquire casually who was calling, how this person got her number, and appeared to be deciding whether or not to continue the conversation. More often than not, she would hang up the phone in anger and exclaim to me with feigned aggravation, "Oh, these *bluff calls!*" It was clear to me, though, that she at least partially enjoyed this playful game.

The purpose of these bluff calls is to engage a stranger (usually a member of the opposite sex) in conversation and, it is hoped, reestablish this "connection" again and again. Several letters sent to FM radio stations describe the phenomenon of bluff calls. "She . . . started [a] bluff call about four years ago. Gradually we became phone friend[s]. . . . We used to talk about several topics such as music, cinema, education, love etc. . . . I couldn't forget those golden moments when we shared our views about everything."[17]

Engagement over the phone in these "bluff calls" is powerful because it appears to be an unencumbered relationship and to circumvent the usual pressures of family and social control, echoing the introduction of telephone technology in many places (see Barker 2000). One popular radio presenter told me about a phone relationship he had had with a young woman for two years, whom he never met, which he fondly remembered as the only "real" relationship he had ever had. The ability to connect through the phone becomes a context that many young people in Kathmandu describe, in subjective terms, as a more "free" and "real" emotional attachment. Bluff calls are quite different than the common crank calls among US youth, in which the purpose is simply to tell a joke and hang up. The sociality of bluff calls more closely resembles Internet sociality, which encourages continued intimate conversation between strangers. In Kathmandu, FM radio and the Internet emerged as popular media within a few years of each other, producing similar forms of sociality. Like FM radio participation, bluff telephone calls begin as a meeting between strangers who become intimate in part because of the sound of their voice and their conversations about a shared public world. The phenomenon of bluff calls, like FM radio, relies on an audience-oriented subjectivity in which a person constitutes him- or herself by addressing a stranger in intimate terms.

In both FM broadcasts and bluff calls, the voice is not only an index of intimacy but also an index of temporal copresence, a feature of FM broadcasts that adds to the overall effect of presence and directness. This illusion of copresence is enhanced by FM radio's almost exclusively live programming (which is now a small part of its overall programming, but still commands a great degree of authenticity). Indeed, when asked about the main difference between the state Radio Nepal programs and those of the commercial FM, listeners reply that FM is "live." In contrast to the scripted monotone of Radio Nepal, a live FM broadcast foregrounds the seeming directness of its transmission, through, among other things, a poetics of spontaneity, accident, and technical mishaps. Combined with frequent references to the voice, live broadcasting and use of the telephone add to the overall ideology of directness and transparency that came to be associated with FM programs (see chapter 5).

Media, and particularly voiced-based media like radio, often appear to be neutral transmitters that mask their own role in shaping people's subjective knowledge about themselves. The invisibility of FM seems to allow words and narratives that are unsanctioned in other social spaces, adding to the sense of directness and sometimes truth. Several listeners would tell me that FM radio was, as one friend put it, "a place for secrets," a place where people could say things they would never dare say to someone face-to-face. A manager for one of the first and biggest FM companies attributed the eagerness with which listeners exposed themselves to the sheer invisibility of the radio medium itself. "FM is like a curtain," he told me. "People trust us [the radio] more than their own relatives. It's not only a matter of writing to us, but using us to pass on a message to others."

This trust in an FM radio voice was secured not only through the veil-like qualities of an invisible radio voice, but also through the way the medium served as a viable channel to reach others whom one may or may not actually be able to meet in person. Indeed, much of the excitement around FM radio in its first days came precisely from the fact that it was the first public medium built around constant participation from the public. It made the notion of free speech appear to be a reality, despite the government restrictions imposed on FM radio speech. Moreover, the fact that people were saying things that they may never have said out loud, or possibly even to themselves, helped enforce the notion that all speech was possible, especially on FM radio.

POLITICS OF AND POLITICS ON THE RADIO

On October 21, 2005, Nepali government officials attacked Kantipur FM, one of the oldest and largest commercial FM stations in Kathmandu. This attack took place eight months after King Gyanendra assumed sole control of the government, through an unprecedented control and censorship of media around the country, as described in the introduction. The government official's mission in the October attack was to seize satellite equipment that enabled the station to broadcast programs outside the Kathmandu Valley. This seizure was necessary, the Ministry of Information and Communication declared, because Kantipur FM refused to comply with a new government ordinance that forbid the transmission of programs in one location from another location and the broadcast of news (rather than "informational programs"). Put into place on October 9, 2005, the ordinance eerily evokes similar laws during the thirty-year royal regime of the Panchayāt government (1950–90) that severely regulated the content of any media production.[18] But given King Gyanendra's coup nine months earlier (February 1), such state action against a private media house was not entirely surprising.

By this time, it had been four years (from 2001) since FM commercial stations were granted fully privatized licenses as well as the right to broadcast the news, a moment that many managers from the early days had eagerly awaited. FM programs were also broadcast throughout the country, either from small FM stations or, in the case of Kantipur, through programs produced in Kathmandu that were transmitted via satellite to smaller cities throughout Nepal. The wish to stop these transmissions was perhaps part of the old strategy of isolating the Valley from the rest of the country, which had been practiced by prior governments in Nepal.[19] The government had worked hard to keep the Valley without full knowledge of the ongoing Maoist civil war, which was fought primarily in villages far from Kathmandu, but which continuously threatened to enter the Valley. Particularly after February 1, the government sought to isolate villagers from the antiroyal sentiment that had become, by this point, endemic in the Valley.

To protest the October 21 attack, journalists and media personnel gathered together with black cloths around their mouths to signify their stifled voices. The symbol of black cloths is a classic symbol of protest in Nepal (often worn around one's arm) and elsewhere, which allowed this protest to resonate clearly with other similar protests against censorship and governmental measures in general (see figure 2 in introduction). During the height of the *jana āndolan* in 1990, for example, over two hundred writers and artists gathered silently in front of the Trichandra College, in the middle of Kathmandu, with black scarves tied around their faces to signify "how they had been gagged by the government" (Raeper and Hoftun 1992: 62).

After February 1, such protests again became commonplace, particularly among FM radio community. Prabhat Rimal, one of the managers of Kantipur FM, described two humorous protests staged particularly against the king, in what he called "mission journalism." In one incident, media activists and FM personnel went to the most holy Hindu temple, Pashupathinath, where cremations take place regularly. With them, they carried a radio set upon on a *puja* (worship) plate, and decorated the radio with a *mālā* (garland of flowers) and other usual accouterments used to worship gods and goddesses. "We just handed over that radio to Lord Pashupatinath," Prabhat told me, "saying, 'See the king cannot handle this. You better teach him something.'" A similar event was staged at the Buddhist temple of Syambunath, known to tourists as "the monkey temple" because of the packs of monkeys that gather there. "Again we gave a monkey the radio. He looked at it and didn't know what to do with it, and ended up just throwing it away. In this way, we were considering the king as just like a monkey, who didn't know what to do with radio." Both of these events were televised, since television could still broadcast the news.

During this time, FM radio took on a political function that had been largely ignored or censored during the early years of FM radio. Despite restrictions on broadcasting the news after February 1, FM stations found creative ways to get news to their listeners. Some began increasing the "information programs," which served as disguised news updates. A Pokhara FM station, a few people told me, played the news through song. Kantipur FM started running their "bulletins" about local happenings in the area every hour, and then increased them to every half hour. Several students told me that they would carry handheld FM radio sets with them at all times during the movement in 2006 in order to learn where the next demonstration was, where the police were located, and where not to go. During the elections in 2008, people similarly listened to the results via portable FM radios.

Nepal Radio was one of the few FM stations that, having won a Supreme Court case against the government banning their news, unabashedly criticized political leaders and the king. "They would blow and blow (words), scold and scold, scold the king, and also scold the leaders," said Basu Shrestha, one of the leaders of the civil society movement that was particularly active during the *jana āndolan* II in 2006. Speaking specifically of the success of the movement, Basu gave much credit to FM radio:

> Where should the credit go? It should go to FM radio. FM radio, not only in Kathmandu, but in lots of districts, started to broadcast all of the speeches from *nagārik samāj* [civil society] in Kathmandu, all over. People heard. It multiplied by many times. In the fifteen years of (the) multiparty system, there were schools established, FM radio opened, and newspapers and magazines.... Gyanendra thought of ruling in an autocracy, but it was too late to be an autocrat.... Gyanendra did not think of the network of media, and he didn't have anyone advising him on this.

These direct interventions into the political life of the nation paralleled the general feeling among media activists and journalists that FM had become a space to "hear people's voices"—a form of *awāj uṭhāune*. This notion certainly seemed to contrast with the general rejection of politics that was so prominent in mainstream FM stations in its early years. I recall that in the first year of FM broadcasting the Kantipur FM office was plastered with eight-by-ten computer printouts, taped around the periphery of the walls, that bore slogans in English which spoke out defiantly against political expression or the expression of any discontent. "No Politics Please"; "Silence is the great art of conversation"; or "Accept pain and disappointment as part of life." Some echoed a distinctly Weberian Protestant ethic: "Discipline yourself to save money; it's essential to success" or "Arrive early to work and stay beyond quitting time." On the wall facing the door read the most prominent sign, "Say No to Politics, We prefer Love. Say Love, Not Politics." Most of these managers I talked with insisted that the "free expression" of personal concerns—as well as music from around the world—was also crucial for the nation's progress and development *(bikās)*. The expression of love and personal life stories was something necessary, they declared, to realize the ideals of post-*āndolan* free speech. "FM means freedom of expression," the presenters used to tell me. "It means saying what you always wanted to say." What you always wanted to say is, in part, created anew through the very genres of speech and letter that flourish on FM radio. The emphasis on personal subjects is largely determined by the genres in which people are encouraged to speak and write. And these novel genres are themselves overlaid by the medium of FM radio and the medium of the voice itself.

Scholars of media tend to seek out connections between seemingly apolitical broadcasts—such as the televised series of the Hindu epic of the *Ramayana* (Rajagopal 2001) or popular melodramas in Egypt (Abu-Lughod 2004)—and the messages emanating from the programs that resonate or support broader political agendas. Here I am concerned less with the particular political agendas FM programs support than with the kind of subjectivity FM broadcasting cultivates that ultimately paves the way for a particular kind of political and intimate subject. This is a central part of FM politics. Within the turn toward explicitly political subjects, the politics of FM radio is simultaneously bound to the listeners' display and to a performance of their wish for an intimate connection via public media. Many of the letters and notes sent to popular FM presenters refer to past friendships, often cultivated through the phone, to describe their ultimate breakdowns. FM radio programs have become a place to reconnect to these broken relations and to lament their failure. This might be considered an example of modern (imperialist) nostalgia, in which a person mourns that which they've lost by participating in the activity that destroys these connections (Rosaldo 1989: 69). And yet their laments are not about losing a connection to one's family, caste, or ethnic roots, the typical content of such nostalgia (Boym 2001; Ivy 1995). Rather, it suggests a wish for intimate recognition distinct from the joint family and from one's parents. FM radio has become a site to display such desires and rekindle or create such relations with strangers.

．　．　．

In this chapter, I have discussed the cultural and political context in which FM radio emerged as a symbol of participatory "democracy" and "free speech." We have seen the limits of this designation, but also the material properties of FM broadcasting (more distinct sound, "live" programs, more interactive programs) that helped shape this image. The idea of a "political voice" that media activists and intellectuals hoped might emerge from FM radio is coupled with the prominence of the "intimate voice" that is central to many programs. In the following chapter, I follow the explosion of public intimacy and affective publics through FM programs, which, like the discourse about political expression, was closely associated with the figure of the voice. As we will see, ideas about the directness of the voice as a medium and form of expression recur, now associated with the intimate content and affective texture of FM broadcasts.

FOUR

Mero Kathā, Mero Gīt

AFFECTIVE PUBLICS, PUBLIC INTIMACY, AND
VOICED WRITING

At its root intimacy has the quality of eloquence and brevity.
But intimacy also involves an aspiration for a narrative about
something shared, a story about oneself and others that will turn
out in a particular way ... the inwardness of intimacy is met by
a corresponding publicness.

LAUREN BERLANT, "Intimacy: A Special Issue"

Before I heard Kalyan Gautum, I didn't even know I had a story.

LAXMI DEVI, fan of *Mero Kathā, Mero Gīt*

BEGINNING IN THE SPRING OF 1997, every Thursday at noon, college
students, factory workers, taxi drivers, bronze casters, and housewives in the
Kathmandu Valley would turn on their FM radio and listen to Kalyan
Gautum's soothing voice. Among the most popular programs on FM radio
during the late 1990s and early 2000s, Kalyan's *Mero Kathā, Mero Gīt* (My
story, my song) exemplifies the talk and writing about one's personal life that
has become ubiquitous on Kathmandu's FM radio stations, in some ways
similar to mass media around the world. Kalyan begins *Mero Kathā, Mero
Gīt* with instructions to his listeners, repeated every week, that urges them to
"write a letter" and to "spill their *dukha*" (suffering, physical hardship,
remorse, sadness) so that they might free themselves from their desires or
longings:

Please put down your longings. . . . Sometimes it's *dukha,* sometimes it's *sukha*
[happiness]—that is how life turns about. But *dukha* is like mustard seeds.
Wrapped in a bundle of cloth, the mustard seeds are toward the bottom.
When a little hole forms, then the mustard scatters all over the floor. *Dukha*
is also like that. One must spill *dukha.* . . . Therefore, tell your *dukha* freely.
Tell whoever is close to you. If you don't have anyone, I am here together

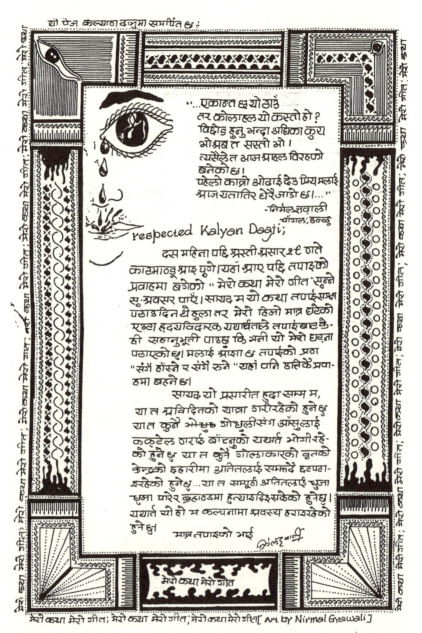

FIGURE 9. Voiced writing: first page of an eight-page letter sent to *Mero Kathā, Mero Gīt*, "My Story, My Song". Courtesy of Kalyan Gautum.

with you. For each of your sufferings, I am here. For all of your happiness, I am here. I am just like you. Therefore, I will give the address. Remember me yourself and write a letter, okay? All songs are mine.[1]

After this prologue, Kalyan reads a "true life story" sent to him in the form of a personal letter by one of his many listeners. Read in a tone that highlights the writers' suffering *(dukha),* and interspersed with Nepali folk and pop songs, the story-letters usually tell a tale of unrequited love or ruptures in the family through death or betrayal. Like several other FM programs in Kathmandu, *Mero Kathā, Mero Gīt* has captivated an urban community of listeners (now expanded to village and overseas Nepali communities) that is brought together by their public expression of desired intimacy, domestic conflict, and individual distress. Beginning in 1997 and continuing through the present with the same host, *Mero Kathā, Mero Gīt* (now called *Mero Kathā*) has become a model program, syndicated and replicated on many other FM stations, including the New York online radio *Himali Swarharu,* where it continues to air.[2] Now it is broadcast through several Internet sites worldwide.

Radio Nepal intermittently ran a similar program called *Gītī Kathā* as early as 1951, which became a standard program on Radio Nepal after 1973 and continued to air intermittently through the early 2000s. The public expression of intimacy and melodramatic expressions of romantic love through song and story connect these programs. *Gītī Kathā* used lines from popular Hindi and later Nepali songs to create a fictional story told by the host and interspersed between songs (Humagain 2003). Madan Das Shrestha, host of *Gītī Kathā* starting in 1978, described the program as a place where love between young girls and boys could blossom through listening to stories and the broadcast of their letters (also read on air). But Kalyan and FM radio hosts of similar programs emphasize that the stories they broadcast are *real* and *true* (obscuring their own editorial hand in the production process), and therefore quite different from the imagined plots created on *Gītī Kathā*. This emphasis on the real was not a planned feature of the program. When Kalyan began the program, he initially thought he would write the stories himself, but then listeners began sending their own stories to him. When talking with me, Kalyan recalled the many letters he immediately started receiving after the program aired. "They started doing my job for me!" he chuckled.

In this chapter, I address the affective public emerging on FM radio and its relation to voice through a detailed discussion of *Mero Kathā, Mero Gīt.*

I argue that the interior quality of radio discourse is made possible by its public nature, the quality of voice and tone of affect that express a person's interior desires, and the presence of an imagined, though not always anonymous, audience. The stories are meant to accomplish both meanings of affect: its meanings as a verb (to stir emotions or influence somebody or something) as well as its meaning as a noun (a conscious, subjective aspect of an emotion). The story-letters are appealing to most because they are presented as "true" stories of "real" people. They are celebrated as authentic forms of self-expression, and in this sense they bear some resemblance to a notion of *āwāj uṭhāune,* "raising voice." The mark of authenticity, though, does not come through the fan's direct voice modulated on the radio; rather, their voice is indexed in the writing and its subsequent presentation in Kalyan's deeply resonant reading. As noted in previous chapters, *āwāj uṭhāune* does not necessarily indicate direct self-expression. It usually refers to a discourse that articulates an individual's or group's perspective to an authority who might be able to effect change. In this case, the authority is Kalyan and the affective public of FM radio. By calling his fans to write ("Remember yourself to me, and write a letter, okay?"), Kalyan interpellates his listeners into the field of FM radio, inviting them *(bolāune)* to engage in a form of self-expression through which they will be recognized by the FM radio, Kalyan, and other FM listeners. Together, he and his listeners create a distinct radio genre—"voiced writing"—that gives the program authority and sentimental form. By focusing on the qualities of voice that substantially contribute to the program, this chapter complicates the textual focus of most scholars of the public sphere (Cody 2011; Berlant 1997, 2008; Habermas 1989; Povinelli 2002; Warner 2002).

Like many similar FM programs, this program encourages listeners to write about themselves in ways that often depart from and even contradict ways of talking about oneself in other settings. FM radio is envisaged as a place to experiment with ways of speaking that are not necessarily used in face-to-face contexts. *Mero Kathā, Mero Gīt* provides a place to voice opposition to the dominant structures of home through the letters that listeners send to (and hope will be aired on) the program. It offers a place to express the virtues of romantic love in contrast to arranged marriage, a place to declare caste hierarchies unacceptable, a place to pass on a difficult message to family members or friends about a divorce, a property dispute, or an unacceptable marriage. These stories, notes, and letters to the radio address contemporary concerns, such as the importance of having a story of loss and a true life story to tell as well as the discourse on individual justice and proof, all subjects that stamp the letters as products of 1990s and early 2000s Kathmandu.

In focusing on the production and listener-author interpretations of the show, I avoid the distinctions made in some ethnographies of media between production and reception (Abu-Lughod 2004; Ganti 2012; Ginsburg 2002; Mankekar 1999). Listeners who consume the program (that is, its reception) are also the authors and letter writers whose stories become critical to its production. So here we see the important interdependence between production and reception and the friction that emerges between Kalyan's final broadcast production and the listeners' own expectations of the show. The listeners and the host of the program are clearly not on an equal footing; I do not intend to evade issues of power and agency by blurring the distinction between production and reception. Rather, the wide circulation of the program—its popularity at a certain moment and the genres it draws upon and produces—reveals an important interplay *between* reception and production. I engage specific listeners' views on the program, but the broadcast of their narratives is always in relation to Kalyan's own editorial choices, his preferred genre, and his voice, which are crucial to the narratives' circulation. The overall effect of the program is the achievement of an aura of smoothness and harmony that erases the tensions evident through ethnography. The aim of this chapter is to use ethnography to engage the question of affective publics on FM radio and reassess some of the theoretical assumptions made about publics by other scholars.

Who are letter writers and the audience of this program? The letter writers might be seen as autonomous modern subjects marked by the self-expression of their lives and interior desires. But they are only realized as such through processes of mediation and recognition that necessarily circuit the interior through the exterior.[3] Kalyan insists that the letters must be written by the listener's own hand, and if he feels the letter is written by someone else (because of tone, style, vocabulary, or even handwriting) he will not broadcast it or will send it back. While the self-generated narratives are what make the program feel "real" or "true," the program's main appeal occurs through the mediation of Kalyan's voice, the varied timbre and cadences that seem to accurately capture others' sentiments. This form of self-expression or "voice" – often associated with interiority, autonomous judgment, and individual desire – only emerges through

There have been many other programs that have similarly asked people to publicly discuss their intimate lives since the very beginning of FM radio, such as Maria's *Heart-to-Heart* (in English) or the early sex advice program *Panther Hotline* (in Nepali). I chose to focus on this program specifically because, contrary to other programs, *Mero Kathā, Mero Gīt* created very *little* controversy. While many stories broadcast on *Mero Kathā, Mero Gīt* challenge local notions of acceptable relationships and ways of talking about one's life face-to-face, the program as a whole does not fundamentally challenge local forms of acceptable public discourse. Its popularity aroused so little disturbance because the program follows seamlessly from prior models of narration and contemporary popular forms like Bollywood film, despite its novel focus on the self and the "real stories" of actual listeners. *Mero Kathā, Mero Gīt* may serve as a kind of boundary-case that reveals the continuities and ruptures between existing and emerging modes of subjectivity.

The public expression of intimate suffering on this program bears resemblance to other popular programs around the world, such as confessional programs in the United States like *Oprah, Donahue,* and *Dr. Laura,* or the therapeutic Russian radio programs *We Will Solve Everything with Doctor Kurpatov* and *For Adults about Adults* (Illouz 2003; Lofton 2011; Matza 2009). Analyses of these programs tend to emphasize the links between confessional speech, therapeutic discourse, and neoliberal politics. Eva Illouz and Kathryn Lofton both discuss Oprah's creation of a global community of sufferers. The therapeutic, confessional narratives Oprah elicits are well suited to the "interface of high velocity capital, information technology, and expert knowledge" (Illouz 2003: 172). In the case of Russian talk shows, Tomas Matza similarly discusses the two programs mentioned above as an effect of the burgeoning prominence of psychotherapeutic discourse in post-Soviet Russia and the neoliberal political rationality that emphasizes an autonomous, choosing, and socially unobligated subject (2009: 508).

Kalyan's connection to the advertising industry and his use of this program to "earn himself a name" *(nām kamāune)* accord well with the neoliberal subjectivity described in these other cases. But the relative paucity of therapeutic discourse in Nepal and on this program makes the subjects produced within it distinct. The goal of this program is not the explicitly neoliberal incentive of "working on the self"—only Kalyan is really working on himself through the program. Rather, what is sought is recognition from Kalyan and the listening community, the recognition of being suffering individuals with thwarted desires and of being on morally and socially acceptable grounds.

Listeners' appeals for moral recognition often undermine or at least desta-bilize the modern, autonomous subjectivity articulated in their narratives of desire and suffering. It may be that on a program like *Mero Kathā, Mero Gīt* listeners are able to reassemble the boundaries of sentiment and collective morality in ways that are impossible in a more formal public sphere.[4] Much of this complicated dynamic arises from the productive function of the host, Kalyan, and from the imperatives of the FM medium itself. The fascinating complexity of *Mero Kathā, Mero Gīt*'s production reveals an overlapping dynamic between a subjectivity centered on interior desire, affect, and indi-viduality and a subjectivity that emphasizes the centrality of familial roles, duties, and moral obligations.

AFFECTIVE PUBLICS AND PUBLIC INTIMACY ON FM RADIO

What kind of public does the program *Mero Kathā, Mero Gīt* create? How do FM publics shape the intimate subjects recognized by and projected over the radio? And how do writing and voice figure into the production of this public? In the literature on publics, stranger intimacy, a mass subject, and anonymity are central to understanding what makes it possible to have a public (Berlant 1997; Calhoun 1992; Cody 2011; Habermas 1989; Warner 2002). Scholars of publics usually draw upon the seminal work of Jürgen Habermas on the bourgeois public sphere and of Benedict Anderson on nations. As Francis Cody notes "both theorists [Habermas and Anderson] insist on the centrality of a form of stranger sociability that arises with the conjuncture of print-mediated discourse and new modes of imagining public life enabled by capitalist production" (2011: 39). Many analyses of publics are concerned with the emergence of political subjects through print or elec-tronic media that create conditions for mass subjectivity and for a function-ing liberal democracy. In this program, rather than a strictly rational subject, we see the emergence of an intimate subject characterized by expressions of affect, who is interpellated by Kalyan's voice on air.

I use the notion of an "affective public" to distinguish the overall tone and texture of this public (and many FM publics) from the rationalized public sphere Habermas describes. The intimate subject produced here is closely related to the political subjects of democracy insofar as the will to publicly express one's personal and social desires is central to both. The affective publics produced on FM radio programs also echo the tone and content of development narratives that compel their subjects to produce narratives of suffering, which can then be assuaged through development efforts.

Public intimacy characterizes much of *Mero Kathā, Mero Gīt* letters and provides the content for the broader affective tone of many FM radio programs. The program relies upon the intimate recognition that Habermas deems essential to a modern, bourgeois public sphere, yet it also suggests important challenges to the rational, dispassionate subject Habermas assumes is central to the working of all publics.[5] While the personal story-letters sent to *Mero Kathā, Mero Gīt* are part of a public of letters forming in Nepal, the personal content of the program would, for Habermas, represent a degradation of the political function of the public sphere. To achieve a properly functioning democratic public sphere, Habermas insists that the personal and intimate content of such letters should remain private. One could easily argue that *Mero Kathā, Mero Gīt* is a clear example of this process of degradation and depoliticization insofar as the program turns people's lives into "marketable forms for the public services provided in a culture of consumption" (Habermas 1989: 171). And one aspect of the program's politics certainly is to turn people's attention toward their own personal struggles to create a marketable narrative. Yet something more subtle is happening that cannot be neatly summarized as "depoliticization." I instead suggest that *Mero Kathā, Mero Gīt* provides an accessible and playful way for many listeners to engage with politically charged subjects, particularly those who do not feel they can gain access to the more "serious" public sphere. The intimate subjectivity emerging through this and other programs, I contend, is continuous with and may even be enabling of the kind of democratic, political subjectivity emerging in other fields.

The content of *Mero Kathā, Mero Gīt* letters frequently engage in fundamental questions about the dominant structures of home, intimacy, and society, forming what Lauren Berlant (1997) terms an "intimate public sphere." As one of a few early Nepali-only programs on FM radio, it immediately evokes a sense of Nepaliness and the specific challenges of romance, marriage, and general personal trials for Nepali citizens. Citizenship in an intimate public sphere is not imagined through the abstracted, nondomestic public sphere Habermas envisions; rather, as Berlant argues, national citizenship becomes perceived and largely intertwined with the public presentation of "personal acts and values, especially originating in or directed toward the family sphere" (1997: 5). Like many Bollywood films, which serve as a visual model for the program, most of the letters sent to Kalyan present "suffering individuals" who desire a romantic relationship that transgresses lines of caste, religion, class, or urban-rural distinctions, falling outside the boundaries of a socially sanctioned marriage (see Ganti 2012). *Mero Kathā, Mero Gīt* letters, like many privatized media programs throughout South Asia, vacillate between directly challenging and reinforcing hegemonic domestic relations like the joint family or prescribed ties to caste or ethnicity.

The public intimacy of this program, like Berlant's analysis of the intimate public sphere in the United States, does little to disturb hegemonic relations of love.[6] Writing of Reagan-era publics in the United States in the 1980s, Berlant argues that intimacy is *useful* for institutions to "normalize particular forms of knowledge and practice, and to create compliant subjects" (1998: 288). The intimate public sphere displaces political questions onto the sphere of private life (Berlant 1997: 3), suggesting anxieties about the economy, citizenship, and nationality. More fundamentally, it impairs an actual discussion of intimacy, in all its different forms (9). The normative politics of public intimacy, according to Berlant, is to create "a life" (or in the case of *Mero Kathā, Mero Gīt* "a life story") that aligns with the compulsory heterosexuality in society. When there are so many different people, asks Berlant, why does only one story count as "a life," a story that essentially discredits intimacy or lives that do not fall along heteronormative sexual lines?

Kalyan's program similarly produces one dominant plot, but it is important to note that unlike the programs Berlant examines, he (like many FM hosts) imagines his program as being a challenge to the status quo. He would often talk about the needed "freedom" people had on his program to reject romantic relations based on caste, ethnicity, religion, or gender. He was proud to broadcast what he claimed to be one of the first public confessions of a lesbian, and strategically placed that story in his first book, *Dear Kalyan: Mero Kathā, Mero Gīt* (Gautum 2059 v.s.: 150–66). Even though this story was possibly the first lesbian story broadcast on air, it is far from condoning same-sex love. The story ends with the protagonist criticizing not only her pursued lover, but also herself, and warns women to avoid such relationships at all costs. As my research assistant, who read and discussed these stories with me, put it, the story "sounds like a moralizing tale of a homophobic society, where even homosexuals tend to be homophobic." Despite the radical nature of simply speaking in public about women-only love, compulsory heterosexuality remains its core message.

There are other ways that FM radio programs contests many social hierarchies, such as by broadcasting in languages other than Nepali (though not on this program) or by broadcasting programs that discuss and even promote romantic relations across caste, class, and religious lines. These expressions of intimacy are transgressive of dominant social relations even as they are generative of other emerging hegemonies associated with privatization, the rise of the individual, romantic love, and the nuclear family. For Kalyan, there is no "story" to broadcast without the expression of one's desires that contrasts or expresses conflict with the dominant, socially acceptable hegemonic route. Yet this wish of the producer is complicated by the fact that often letter writers conclude their letters by choosing to follow the well-trodden path, the hegemonies of caste, religion, or class, a fact that Kalyan occasionally edits out.

The sheer volume of letters, stories, and notes of affection sent to FM programs and hosts is testimony to the fact that FM radio is not only a place for speaking publicly, but also a forum for popular writing about the self.[7] The letters circulate through the public, constituting it by addressing both a personal and an impersonal audience (Warner 2002: 57). In the early days of *Mero Kathā, Mero Gīt,* when Kalyan was broadcasting on a single channel, his program received between two hundred and five hundred letters every week, and they were on average around eight handwritten pages long. Other programs may not receive such long letters, but they too have stacks of letters that some stations have begun to archive and that others simply throw away due to a lack of space. The program *Sāthi Sanga Man Kā Kurā* receives between twelve hundred and fifteen hundred letters over the course of a month, and they have hired two full-time people devoted exclusively to reading and responding to these letters. In contrast to *Mero Kathā, Mero Gīt,* the content of this program is more in line with the neoliberal project of working on the self in that the program advocates that listeners learn a set of important "life skills" to improve themselves that can be applied to numerous situations (Greenland n.d.; Kunreuther 2010).

One effect of public intimacy is the universal humanity it encodes. Kalyan tries to emphasize that anyone can send a letter, that the program is open to all; as he puts it tellingly in one of his many introductions to the show, "all songs are mine." While *Mero Kathā, Mero Gīt* is decidedly a Nepali program, with all the letters written by fans and all broadcasts in Nepali, Kalyan often refers to its general humanistic appeal. The "need to spill *dukha,*" Kalyan once told me, "is not specific to Nepalis, but this is true for *all peo-*

ple." Several scholars have noted the humanistic appeal of "love" as a senti-ment that is professed to be both individual and universal, the ultimate sign of "humanity" (for example, Povinelli 2002; Siegel 1995). The letters do pri-marily focus on love, but this is paired with the South Asian concept of *dukha,* arguing for its universal significance. *Dukha* (suffering, physical hardship, or sadness) is frequently associated with women, yet it is also thought to be a general description of a difficult life. Despite this ideal to incorporate everyone, Kalyan's choice of whose letters to broadcast fre-quently subverts this ideal.

The fiction that the program can and does incorporate everyone is made possible by Kalyan's own social position as a Brahmin man who presents everyone's stories. Critics of Habermas often point out that even though the bourgeois public sphere seems to allow any person to submit rational, disem-bodied public opinion without personal risk, only certain bodies count as unmarked.[8] As Warner argues, it is just white men who can transcend their bodies and be abstracted away from being "white" or "male" (2002: 382–83). In Nepal, even in a moment of radical ethnic nationalism and identity poli-tics, the unmarked public persona remains Brahmin and male.[9] Furthermore, letter writers to *Mero Kathā, Mero Gīt* are not offering "public opinion" in the same way that Habermas or Warner discuss, for Kalyan is the shaper and ventriloquist of their stories. Nor are they in the same social position as the program's host and speaker. Their stories gain authority through being voiced by Kalyan and all that his social position conveys.

For this reason the medium of Kalyan's voice plays an important role in constituting the affective public of *Mero Kathā, Mero Gīt.* Even though Kalyan never mentions his own caste—he is only "Dear Kalyan" (a phrase that he has now adopted as his public name and uses to introduce himself)— or that he is not from Kathmandu, his background as a Brahmin man, from outside the Valley, is known immediately to most listeners through the sound and specific cadence of his voice. He speaks softly and slowly, with the authority of someone versed in literature, using precise gendered verb end-ings that rarely appear in common speech. That his speech is devoid of virtu-ally any English or the fast-paced banter that characterizes many of the hip urban radio presenters indicates that he is probably from somewhere outside the Valley, but it is hard to attach a specific geographical origin. He simply sounds like the typical unmarked public persona of Nepali media. The medium of his voice, which is more distinct and amplified on the FM radio waves than it would be on Radio Nepal broadcasts, enables him to realize the ideal of universal humanity. That Kalyan reads the letters aloud, week after week, transforms each one from a story rooted in a specific person's life (with all the markers of caste, ethnicity, religion, or other social ties) into a more generic, neutral form that circulates alongside a vast number of other letters. Their significance derives from the melodramatic tones Kalyan employs as he reads. In his reading, listeners experience the social distance between Kalyan, his fans, and the writer, and this becomes an especially appealing feature of the program. Kalyan might be thought of as a "master empathizer,"[10] whose empathy is conveyed by incorporating others' words and mediating them through his own voice. While *dukha* stories are by no means unique to this program, being read through Kalyan's voice gives feelings like *dukha* and tragic domestic tales an added degree of cultural authority. Listeners repeatedly told me they were moved to write by Kalyan's voice alone. An older woman, began her letter by referring to the quality of Kalyan's voice: "Namaskār. I have not met you yet, [but] even so, listening to your heartfelt voice it seems that you understand the sorrow that you read. For that reason, I write you my own life story."[11]

Recent scholars of modern publics like Berlant or Warner give us excellent models for the analysis of an intimate public in terms of the content of its widely circulating narratives, the material properties of texts, and their mediation in the press, but very few focus on the qualities of the voice and the affective tone as a key feature of the publics they describe. The task is, as Debra Vidali-Spitulnik has set out in her analysis of Zambian radio, to attend to the "ways of hearing and sounding—and ways of being an acoustically attuned being—[that] may be much more central as organizing and orienting cultural logics than many scholars have yet to give them credit for" (2012: 258).

Charles Hirschkind's work on Islamic cassette sermons and Amanda Weidman's work on ideologies of the voice in Indian music are examples of acoustically attuned analyses. As Weidman discusses, the ideal, voice associated with mid-century Karnatic women singers was one that seemed to transcend the body, be unmediated by any performance, and come naturally from within. This emerged as nationalist ideals of womanhood and domesticity became particularly pronounced in South India. Kalyan too represents one national ideal expressed through his voice, though in this case the national ideal is decidedly male and high-caste and merges village and urban lives. In the context of *Mero Kathā, Mero Gīt,* it is a reading voice, not a singing voice, that expresses the nation. Unlike the Indian playback singers whom

Weidman discusses in her later work, the appeal of Kalyan's reading is not about performing different styles or identities through his voice (Weidman 2014). It is the consistency of his tone that gives his voice such authority.

Charles Hirschkind also focuses on the affect created through the sound of the Islamic *khatib's* voice. He uses the term *counterpublic* to distinguish his analysis of Islamic cassette sermons from the assumptions built into the idea of modern publics, namely, the fiction that all publics are self-organized and therefore free from any institutional or external forces (Warner 2002: 50).[12] As Hirschkind points out, the idea of a self-organized public obscures the material conditions and speech forms that make any discourse understood to particular people (2006: 106). To get at these material conditions, Hirschkind focuses on "the figure of the ethical listener—with all its dense sensory involvements—that founds and inhabits the counterpublic" (107).

Though *Mero Kathā, Mero Gīt* is not explicitly religious, Hirschkind's idea of the "ethical listener" is useful here for considering the important role of the listeners in the letter writers' quest for recognition. Hirschkind links the informal affective practices of listening to the ethical bodily dispositions these sermons aim to create. Listening is a central feature in the interpretation of Quranic sermons; it is not the speaker but the hearer who becomes central in the transmission of the words of God (2006: 34). This understanding of "the miraculous word of God" is based on a language ideology that views godly speech as performative in its capacity to reform an open and receptive heart. But it is also clear from Hirschkind's rich ethnography that the *khatib's* voice *does* affect the active reception of the sermon. The rhetorical, stylistic, and sonic features of the *khatib's* sermon along with the material cadences of his voice (see Hirschkind 2006: 143–72) inform the audience's vocalizations that constitute the sermons' success and power. Kalyan is not a religious leader ostensibly transmitting the words of God. Yet, like a religious leader, his particular voice and its connection to broader ideologies have a sensory force that shapes his audiences' listening and the broader affective public of *Mero Kathā, Mero Gīt*.

VOICED WRITING AND THE MASTER EMPATHIZER
OF *MERO KATHĀ, MERO GĪT*

Kalyan and I met for the first time in the busy office of Hits FM in Naya Baneswar, an expanding business and industrial area that is home to many students and migrants in Kathmandu. He arrived wearing what I soon

FIGURE 10. The FM host Kalyan Gautum in the studio. Photo: Cristeena Chitrakar.

discovered was his everyday attire—dark slacks, a button-down, light-colored cotton shirt, and heavy shoes—clothing that distinguished him slightly from the younger, jeans-wearing radio hosts of Hits FM. He directed me away from the bustle of people, music, and chatter that filled up the office space, upstairs to the serene rooftop that afforded us an expansive view of Kathmandu houses, where his voice was heard every Thursday at noon. During our first meeting, Kalyan offered to assist me with my research; he too was interested in "social work and service *[sevā]*." I quickly jumped at the opportunity, and from that day on Kalyan and I spent many days together, reading through letters and discussing their connections to Nepali society, culture, and history. In addition to our readings, we visited many of the letter writers, often in their homes, but sometimes at work or in one of the bustling teashops that mark nearly every Kathmandu corner. These meetings provided rich ethnographic arenas to see the way Kalyan was viewed by his audience as well as to explore the varied meanings the stories had for writers and listeners. (See figure 10.)

Though Kalyan speculated that his program was enjoyed primarily by those of the "standard class"—by which he meant the educated middle class—his listeners and writers are surprisingly diverse.[13] They are generally Nepali migrants from villages, college students, civil servants, and illiterate urban or village residents who had others write for them. I also met a few lawyers and one doctor who were avid fans. On Thursdays at noon, near the few remaining fields on the edge of Kathmandu, I would often see two or three older women crouched in a huddle around a battery-run radio, listening to *Mero Kathā, Mero Gīt* while they relaxed from their work in the fields.

Kalyan's changing representation over time of what his intentions were for the program exposes a collusion between the world of privatized commercial business and the world of *bikās* and national *sevā* (social service) that both participate in shaping the publics of FM radio in Kathmandu and across the nation. Initially, Kalyan claimed that *Mero Kathā, Mero Gīt* was a form of *sevā*, aligned with the importance of national service, which helped his listeners express their suffering hearts. He spoke about his program and its success as a form of "social work" that contributed to *bikās* rather than as a product of his masterful entrepreneurship and privilege, both of which run several generations deep. The fact that two motorcycle companies engaged in a bidding war to become the sole sponsor of *Mero Kathā, Mero Gīt* after two years of being on air, offering Kalyan nearly six times the salary he received from Hits FM (from 10,000 rupees per month to 60,000 rupees per month), reveals the program's close ties to the wider market.

Ten years after the first broadcasts of *Mero Kathā, Mero Gīt,* Kalyan opened his own advertising business (a common route for many FM hosts) and began to embrace the fact that he works squarely within the commercial sector. While Kalyan distinguished *sevā* to one's nation (including *bikās*) from the work of business, his claim that the same program could serve the interests of both suggests that the line between the two is blurry at best. With increasing possibilities for private business and neoliberal practices that now encompass much development work (Leve and Karim 2001), the cultural currency attributed to *sevā* and *bikās*—both national prerogatives since the late 1970s—has been slowly shifting toward the embrace of a less state-centric, more capitalist mode of production. Indeed, Kalyan's career trajectory embodies these economic transformations that Kathmandu residents witnessed and (in diverse ways) participated in from the late 1990s to the early 2000s. The narratives of self in development-sponsored programs often require a similar reflection on inner desire and affect as the narratives produced in a fully commercial enterprise like *Mero Kathā, Mero Gīt,* a point I return to below.

Kalyan is, in many ways, the quintessential neoliberal subject and entrepreneur, who imagines himself as a bundle of skills that he is honing through his radio program and advertising agency (Gershon 2011; Harvey 2005; Rose [1990] 1999; Uriciuoli 2008). A neoliberal self, writes Ilana Gershon, establishes a "reflexive relationship in which every self is meant to contain a distance that enables a person to be literally their own business" (2011: 539).

Kalyan has produced new markets based on his program through a range of mass cultural products—advertisements, several volumes of story-letter books, an unfinished TV serial based on the stories, and most recently a historical novel about radio in Nepal.[14] In October 2011, he opened a Facebook page under the name Mero Khata [sic]:-Dear Kalyan that expands the reach of this affective public. Here, many of the stories are published; he posts links to the online radio station, photographs, and promotions for his latest novel, and many of his fans respond to specific episodes or photos. His listeners' letters are the raw material through which Kalyan can achieve this neoliberal subject position. He remains always already distant from himself, always strategically managing his alliances, his presentation, and his social strategies in a reflexive manner. Kalyan has effectively turned himself into a brand by personally introducing himself to strangers, fans, and friends as "Dear Kalyan" and authorizing books with this name, epitomizing the sense of literally *being* his own business, like many public personas and celebrities (cf. Illouz 2003; Lofton 2011; Shipley 2013).

As both a personality on the radio and a person living in Kathmandu, Kalyan also embodies the issues of dislocation and the complex dilemmas of home that his program seeks to address. Kalyan was a single man in his late twenties when he began the program. A son of a wealthy Brahmin family of landowning *jamindārs,* Kalyan spent his childhood in a village in the western region of Dang. Dang is the site of a well-known Sanskrit school that Kalyan briefly attended as a child at the urging of his grandfather, which no doubt influenced his later love of Nepali literature. As the youngest son, he stayed in his village home longer than his brothers and sisters, and he did not attend an English-medium school, as his siblings did. He moved to Kathmandu, where his older sister and brother resided, to complete his high school education. Like many of his listeners and other Nepalis from villages who reside in Kathmandu, Kalyan has made a permanent life for himself in the urban metropolis, but he nevertheless describes Dang as his home. Dang was a stronghold of Maoist power during the recent civil war (1996–2006), and the site of one of the most violent Maoist attacks in 2001. During the ten years when the Maoists controlled much of the area, Kalyan's family experienced very little trouble aside from the usual extortion tactics of the Maoists. Like many landowning families in the region, they simply paid off the Maoists, who then left them alone.

It is not entirely surprising that Kalyan has so quickly and easily found a place for himself in the current political economy of Kathmandu, for his father and grandfather adjusted themselves to the shifts in the economy and politics for generations. Their elite position as landowners and Brahmins made these transitions quite smooth. Kalyan often affected a slightly distanced, self-mocking stance about the social inequalities that his family helped sustain and that enhanced their wealth and position. He described his grandfather as a benefactor of the oligarchic Rana regime, who actively encouraged erecting a "curtain" between India and Nepal so that common people would not learn about what they did not have (particularly education), while at the same time he sent his own sons to study in Benares. As large landowners, his family had *kamaiyā* (bonded laborers) working their farms for generations, and many of the same former *kamaiyā* families currently remain employed on their land. Kalyan said he always felt fondly toward the *kamaiyā,* and he recalled giving an extra handful or two of rice beyond their allotment when he had the opportunity. When I traveled with Kalyan to observe an FM station in Nepalganj (a border city in the south) and to visit his family in Dang, there were numerous occasions in which Kalyan presented himself as a successful Kathmandu radio host, as well as a Brahmin and a son of a Dang landholder. These social positions provided him with easy access to help from many willing parties.

I recount this familial background to provide some social context that helps explain Kalyan's keen ability to capitalize on the specific structures of feeling and the ideas of personhood that he has cultivated in his program and that echo broader social sentiments outside the radio field. While not of the academic bent, he is part of an emerging class of mass-culture producers who have benefited greatly from the expansion of the publishing industry and the privatization of the media (Hutt 2012). Kalyan's story and many like it show us that while there are important changes in the political economy of an emerging liberal democracy, there are equally important ways in which the social relations may not have changed all that much. Though FM radio is touted as bringing "freedom," "free speech," and democratic ideals to people throughout Nepal, it is as important to remember that these changes also serve to reproduce unequal social relations and obscure these inequalities (Kunreuther 2012; cf. Berlant 1998).

Despite (or perhaps enabling) these reproductions of class and status, the program is publicly advertised as something for and about common people. Kalyan promotes the notion that the everyday life of common people, especially the tragedies of love, can be transformed into a story that people should want to document and circulate on FM radio. The program does more than elicit stories; it provokes their creation. A widow, whose story I recount below, told me after her story was broadcast, "Before I heard Kalyan Gautum, I did not have the wish to write. Even if I did, who would I tell? Who would I tell? *I did not even know I had a story."* In the process, listeners are encouraged to begin seeing their lives as a narrative with discrete, identifiable moments that can be captured neatly within the bounds of a five- to eight-page written, personal letter. Here we see the making of an individual self through the writing of a narrative life story, a self that is complicated by multiple and overlapping social ties inscribed in the texts and the writers' frequent appeals to a moral community of listeners.

Kalyan's program has remained a relatively popular FM program, among a select group of people, since its beginnings.[15] But it is by no means enjoyed by all. Left-leaning intellectuals, who prefer political or discussion programs on FM radio's community stations, criticize *Mero Kathā, Mero Gīt* as an example of mass manipulation that turns people's lives into sentimental, commodified narratives. Others do not give it much thought, for it is simply too kitschy and melodramatic to take seriously. Some professional Nepalis I talked with laughed when they found out that I was doing research on "such a meaningless program," and others dismissed the program as being "too villagey" *(gāūle)* or "too feminine" to be a subject of study. The gendered dimension of this program has less to do with the fact that only women write or listen to the program—this certainly is not the case—and more to do with the fact that the program emphasizes people's *dukha* (suffering), marginality, and isolation and the sentimental aspects of their personal lives. One Nepali, who attended the US college where I teach, read one publication of these story-letters, and told me he would much rather read Laxmi Prasad Devkota, the famous national poet who is known by all Nepali schoolchildren. He drew a clear distinction between the "high literature" of Devkota and "popular" literature, like the stories sent to *Mero Kathā, Mero Gīt*.

Kalyan often smoothed over distinctions between "high literature" and his own popular genre by readily comparing the story-letters to Devkota's poems, particularly the well-known love tragedy *Munā-Madan.* The comparison to this particular poem is striking because though it was written in 1936, the plot and moral message of *Munā-Madan* parallel many aspects of the story-letters Kalyan presents (see Hutt 1991). Based on a folktale, the epic poem depicts the story of Madan, who travels to Lhasa to get rich. He becomes seduced by the city's beauty and then falls sick en route to his home and returns to find that both his wife (Muna) and his mother have died. As Michael Hutt discusses, the poem's primary message is that "loved ones are far more precious than material wealth," but it also rejects caste hierarchy in that Madan is nursed back to health by a beef-eating Tibetan Buddhist (1991: 42).[16] These story-letters too, Kalyan implied, were forms of legitimate literature and had national significance.

That Kalyan *reads* these stories enhances their literary quality, and effectively removes them from the author's hand. The scene of Kalyan reading a moral story to an audience is reminiscent of other spheres of Nepali social life, such as groups of people listening to a *guru* (religious teacher) reading from a text under the shade of a tree or on the verandah of a temple, a practice that has now also become popular on FM radio. Obviously, the context and experience of listening are quite different over the radio, for not only do urban residents often listen alone or in small groups of two or three individuals, but the reading lasts for only one hour rather than a whole afternoon. Nevertheless, Kalyan often seemed to take on the role of a modern *guru* who maintains the authority and credibility of a religious authority by reading not from a religious text but from an everyday person's story that is transformed, through this reading, into a *kathā,* a modern short story.

At the inaugural party of Kalyan's first book of story-letters, he invited one of Nepal's poet laureates, Madav Prasad Ghimire, to give the inaugural address, during which Ghimire spoke about Kalyan's keen ability to create a truly literary text. Kalyan also invited me to give a speech, and together our presence seemed to validate the book as a literary and globally relevant achievement. There was little mention of the fact that these stories were sent to Kalyan by another author or that he presented them on air as unedited testimonies of a person's suffering life. In the setting of promoting the book, the emphasis was on Kalyan's own literary skills in gathering these stories. The flourishes that Kalyan adds to people's letters, the Nepali proverbs and turns of phrase that read like poetry, the grammatically precise verb endings, and the use of all three hierarchical pronouns *(tapāī, timi, tā)* echo the tone of literary Nepali and signify a "more perfect" language than is commonly used in everyday speech. Some listeners associated the power of Kalyan's voice with the fact that it *sounds* like literature, comparing the stories, as Kalyan did, to familiar plots of tragic and romantic Nepali literature.[17] Like literature, the stories are meant to move people to a place of reflection outside the here and now, while examining the exigencies of everyday life. Though they conveyed the power of literature, the stories had an added measure of authenticity in being "real" or "true," and this is where Kalyan associated himself with me. After leaving the book promotion party, I remember

Kalyan's excitement as he boarded his motorcycling, declaring, "Now, I am just like you!" *(Ma ahile tapāī justai bhaē).* Since I am someone who takes everyday tales and transforms them into another written text, perhaps he is right. Of course, our intentions and strategies are quite different, not to mention our sales!

This genre of voiced writing combines the corporality and seeming immediacy of the voice with the distant, authoritative qualities of a written text that can circulate in absentia of the author and addressee (Derrida 1988). In his well-known critique of the logocentric focus in the philosophy of language, Derrida argues that voice and speech are not sites of presence, the original condition of language, nor markers of the intentionality of the speaker.[18] Instead, Derrida argues that *both* speech and writing depend upon the ability of signs to be recognized and iterated outside the context of their production, always in ways that do not exactly reproduce any original meaning. Reversing common distinctions made between speech and writing, Derrida argues that the principles we attribute to writing more aptly structures all language. All language depends, after all, on words that have been uttered and are recognizable by someone else who is not present (Bakhtin 1981; Volosinov [1929] 1973).

In Kathmandu, many FM programs are examples par excellence of Derrida's reversal of the speech-writing dichotomy. In their reliance on written texts (such as listeners' letters and stories), programs like *Mero Kathā, Mero Gīt* produce a form of voiced writing in which the written word does in fact structure speech (Kunreuther 2004). Rather than rejecting out of hand the qualities of voice that appear to be nostalgic referents of presence, it is important to see the way speech and writing, voicing and listening, work together to create an authoritative and authentic story. Voiced writing merges the seemingly present-centered qualities of the voice with the absence, circulation, and authority attributed to a written text. The voices and letters broadcast on the FM radio are signs of each person's agency and presence, but they are powerful precisely because they circulate unattached to the person whose story or voice is heard over the radio (Derrida 1988). When recontextualized over the radio, the personal written letter is no longer a form of communication between two people. It becomes instead a *performance* or display of intimacy to an invisible public of listeners.

Kalyan's place within the stories is central, for all the stories are written in the form of a personal letter to "Dear Kalyan." Kalyan is the animator, sole mediator, and the embodiment of transmission through which these expressions of suffering must travel to be heard. The fact that these letters are *voiced by Kalyan* and *heard by an invisible audience* transforms their significance greatly from simply being a written text. Kalyan's voicing and public performance are large parts of the story-letter's message. The soft, slow, and breathy quality of Kalyan's voice, the lilts and tone he uses as he reads, and the "expressive function" of his message convey "his attitude toward what he is speaking about" and therefore his attitude toward the writer and his audience (Jakobson 1987: 66). For this reason, the distant, self-mocking tone Kalyan adopted when speaking to me about his family would never work on this program. His voice conveys compassion and empathy and gushes with melodramatic sincerity.

Contrary to the dominant tradition in modernity (against which Derrida writes) that views written texts as deferrals of presence and authenticity, the written text produced by listeners is what gives the voicing on the radio both authenticity and legitimacy. To speak too much about oneself or one's own life is considered arrogant *(ghamaṇḍī)*.[19] "Sometimes there is this situation," Kalyan once explained. "You cannot find the *environment* to tell people about an event. . . . Also people cannot say it. So they send it here." Through this voiced performance, listeners are able to hear their own words and sentiments spoken by someone other than themselves. Along with several other radio hosts, Kalyan has created a notion of empathy and compassion rooted in listening, so that the practice of listening and hearing, rather than solely the practice of writing or speaking, remains at the heart of the program's appeal.

BIKĀS RHETORIC AND EFFECTIVE LISTENING

As Kalyan's own personal trajectory reveals, *Mero Kathā, Mero Gīt* intertwines the vast expansion of private business with the "*bikās* (development) industry" (Des Chene 1996; Pigg 1992), an equally powerful force within Kathmandu's cultural and political economy. The *bikās* industry includes the proliferation of nongovernmental organizations (NGOs) that support a vast number of middle-class salaries in Kathmandu as well as the forms of knowledge and development personnel who actively promote and circulate *bikās* ideas at various levels. Rather than narrowly referring to international development projects, *bikās* describes the idea of progress and the ability of personal narrative to affect it that profoundly structure a Nepali experience of modernity.[20] It refers more generally to the improvement of individual skills and learning, as well as to Nepal's increasing national engagement with foreign governments and aid since the 1960s (Pigg 1992: 497). The implicit connection between *Mero Kathā, Mero Gīt* and the *bikās* industry is perhaps one key reason why the program remains uncontroversial.

The importance of *bikās* to the formation of Nepali publics registers an important difference from the arguments about publics in the United States or Europe. Lauren Berlant's argument about the intimate public sphere, for example, examines the specific political economy and backlash against the multicultural identity movement that characterized America in the 1980s. To understand public intimacy on FM radio in Nepal, we must consider Nepal's long-standing links to Western liberal democracies and other industrialized nations, most notably through the context of the enormous international development aid industry that has shaped and transformed the country's economy over the past fifty years.

The effects of the global economy are obviously experienced quite differently by Nepalis than by those in the United States or Europe, since people leave the country for work to send home remittances and the aid community continues to dominate the world of middle-class Nepalis in Kathmandu. The content of public intimacy is therefore also quite different than the abortion debates or live sex acts that Berlant discusses—and clearly its politics differs. Public intimacy generated by programs like *Mero Kathā, Mero Gīt* must be situated within similar attempts by development organizations and by other media sources to generate personal narratives that focus on internal struggle.

In 2001, UNICEF sponsored a new "youth program" that began broadcasting on radios throughout Nepal. Initiated by the NGO Equal Access Nepal (EAN), the program—*Sāthī Sanga Mankā Kurā*, which is translated by the program as *Chatting with My Best Friend*—started with the objective of preventing drug use and HIV from spreading among Nepali youth (see Greenland n.d.).[21] Its broader agenda, as stated on their website, is to provide a "confidential and open platform . . . where anyone can open their heart out on issues deeply related to them" (SSMK website). By talking with the radio hosts of this program about intimate matters, people will learn to "deal with problems on their own," the program's designers suggest. *Sāthī Sanga Mankā Kurā* (SSMK) seeks to create a person who can speak directly and intimately with strangers on a radio program, with friends and family that they meet regularly, and most importantly with themselves. In short, the program creates the ideal neoliberal subject implicit in international aid organizations like UNICEF: a subject who is self-sufficient and can make their own choices. For such a subject, one's personal life becomes the paradigmatic site of political transformation (Kunreuther 2010).

Though it is notably different in content and style than Kalyan's program, when SSMK first aired several listeners described it as a program that resembled *Mero Kathā, Mero Gīt*. What they were referring to, I believe, is the emphasis on expressing one's personal struggles and feelings through the public medium of radio, particularly on matters of love and family. The comparison also indicates the currency associated with narratives of suffering and interiority in both the commercial and the development world. While Kalyan felt his program was quite different than SSMK, he too initially spoke about the success of his program as contributing to *bikās*.

Kalyan would often, for example, explicitly use the prestigious language of the development industry and align his program with educational rather than entertainment programs. He drew parallels between the letters he received and documents of suffering produced by humanitarian organizations and NGOs, such as the pamphlets and books about AIDS victims or the recently freed *kamaiyā* (bonded laborers).[22] The letters were a form of "education" *(sikchyā)* for other listeners, he claimed, and could inspire productive social change. Letter writers too reiterated the educational value of their stories. One woman mused about whether she should share the fact of her divorce from a long time ago, a fact she had not yet shared with her own daughter; she used education as an explanation for her writing: "It could be that my life's bitter truths should not be broadcast on air. But if my past could be an education for someone else, why then retreat, right?"[23] The writer's ambivalence about publicly sharing such a tale of sorrow (particularly on the subject of divorce, which is often viewed as a sign of personal failure for women) is quickly overcome by framing the story as an "education for someone else." In aligning her story with the discourse of education, she also aligns it with much development talk and practice.

Kalyan told his listeners, journalists, and other social commentators (including myself) that the broadcast of these stories would "raise consciousness" *(chetnā jagāune)*. The idea of gaining or "raising consciousness," like education, is a central motif in development projects across Nepal and speaks broadly to how development agencies imagine what they do (Fujikura 2001). Like on many FM programs, consciousness is often attributed to education, referring not to skills a student learns in school, but rather to the possible means through which one can construct a better life (2001: 272).[24] Tatsuro Fujikura suggests that talk about "consciousness" among both development planners and recipients of development aid frequently refers to an *internal* realization that suddenly inspires a desire for improvement and change. The "consciousness" described in development circles points to several practices that instill a notion of individual agency—"such as, the ability to sign one's own name on paper, or stating one's own name and making a speech in front of a group of people" (2001: 271)—which is often linked to writing or speaking about oneself in public as listeners are encouraged to do on FM radio. In both the world of development and the discourse of FM programs like *Mero Kathā, Mero Gīt,* "coming to awareness" and "consciousness" have to do with recognizing and *making public* one's personal story. The personal story, complete with expression of affect and desire, becomes currency that enables participation in emerging publics.

Statements about "awareness" that are rooted in ideas of personal transformation need not be interpreted as either "distorted reflections of the real (political economic) processes that were happening elsewhere, or . . . [as the confined] idealism of liberal progressivist narrative" (Fujikura 2001: 276). Rather, they are evidence of how people's personal stories can *mean something* in a public world by maintaining a link with the dominant social discourse of development. The stories show the way "development consciousness" has become a mediating discourse throughout Nepal (and elsewhere around the world) that enables a double relation of self-distance and self-recognition, precisely the dynamic that Mazzarella argues is characteristic of all mediation.

Bikās creates a sense of contributing to a national project while also participating in the world beyond Nepal's borders. Kalyan actively cultivates this sense of the global and national significance of *Mero Kathā, Mero Gīt* by making special efforts to broadcast stories from Nepalis overseas (particularly those he published in his first book of story-letters). While travel abroad suggests the global significance of his program, it also becomes a way to reassert the importance of the nation, for in many tales being overseas is quite simply a terrible place to be.

This feature of the program quite literally came home to me when Kalyan sent me several articles that had been published in local newspapers after I had returned to New York. All of the articles featured photographs of Kalyan and spoke warmly of his capacity to feel sympathy for his listeners around the world. Most took note of the fact that letters from Nepalis around the world had been sent to Kalyan from as far away as Japan, America, Germany, and India. One of the articles went so far as to incorporate me into the global landscape of *Mero Kathā, Mero Gīt*. "*Dear Kalyan* is the Subject of an American Woman's PhD in Anthropology," the headline read. After indicating the national *and* global importance of this program by describing my research with Kalyan, the journalist, Shyam, told his readers not to worry that Kalyan might leave like so many of men of his generation: "These days Laura sends 'Dear Kalyan' emails just about everyday. She says to come to America. She requests him to start a radio program and live over there." (Off the record, I might add, none of this is true.)

The article continues: "But, Dear Kalyan is not in the mood to go to America so quickly and says [to me], 'Shyamji, I first want to do something for my country. Only after I do something here will I go over there.'"[25]

Such discourse about Kalyan serves to highlight both the global reach of his program and his nationalist sentiments, sentiments that Kalyan also ascribed to his program. As the program became incorporated into many FM stations around Nepal, this global image of a clearly national program became a more prominent feature of the program. In the fall of 2008, Kalyan did come to the United States and arranged with an online Nepali radio station in New York, *Himalī Swarharu* (Himal Voices), to broadcast *Mero Kathā* weekly on the online program. Each week, Kalyan advertises on his broadcast inside Nepal that *Mero Kathā* also airs on an online radio program in New York.

VOICED WRITING AS INTERTEXTUAL GENRE: FORM AND TIME OF THE STORY-LETTER

What are the more specific features of the genre that play such an important role in shaping people's participation in *Mero Kathā, Mero Gīt*'s public? As personal letters, the stories rely on a familiar genre for making and sustaining distant yet emotionally close social connections to create a novel form of attachment through the radio. The letters are always addressed to "Dear Kalyan," an address that recurs many times throughout the letter and is the only consistent English terminology, which adds a sense of global significance to the story. The story-letters usually center on an episode of unrequited love or a tragic event in the writer's past, and they combine aspects of a formulaic love letter (Ahearn 2001) with features of a typical Bollywood film. Many story-letters make frequent reference to their own practice of writing and exchanging love letters. "Brother Kalyan," writes a young man, who sent more than one story-letter to the program, "this is not my pride, but I don't think anyone has ever written as many love letters as I wrote to Rupa, even within the context of Nepal" (that is, where people exchange love letters frequently).[26] Like the exchange of love letters, which sometimes leads to marriages or long-lasting friendships, many writers express hope that the broadcast of their letter will effectively repair broken relations. But contrary to common love letters, the story-letters sent to Kalyan almost always end with a sense of isolation, loneliness, and suffering. This compulsion toward tragic endings expresses the desire for such intimate recognition as it confirms the power of the family, caste, or class. (See figure 9 at the beginning of the chapter, which shows the ornate aesthetics that some letter writers strive for.)

Most stories describe a romance that happens unexpectedly, often beginning with a sudden "meeting of the eyes" (dekhā-dekh), a moment of tactile seeing that I described in chapter 2.[27] Many of these romances transgress the social boundaries of either caste, class, ethnicity, or religion. An equally sudden crisis then occurs that forces a separation. The conflict usually centers on either the writer or the beloved deciding to succumb to social pressures of family, caste, or class. As one letter writer put it, "I sacrificed [balidān dinu] my love because I was a good son in the family and a member of a respectable [ādarnṭiya] family."[28] Sacrifice was a key aspect of expressing one's dukha and also a means of asserting one's respectability.

Toward the end of the letter, the writers usually turn their address away from "Dear Kalyan" and toward the larger imagined audience, which often includes the lover or family member the writer has lost. "Dear Rupa," writes Kiran, after a lengthy letter about their separation. "May I see you and be seen by you [darśan linu] in every lifetime. . . . I want to ask you, also, not to get angry with me for broadcasting our story."[29] Not all letters end so apologetically, but many make reference to the addressed listener potentially hearing the story. It is as if writing and broadcasting the story add a certain gravity to the writer's love and become yet another marker of the writer's "true suffering." The stories are always framed as "true" (satya) and "real" (vāstavik) tales, yet as Kalyan advised one avid fan, "even if the story is real, it is an added plus if it is like a Hindi film."

Kalyan plays on the trope of the village by playing the sounds of birds in the background and interspersing folk songs between their stories of woes to create a sense of community among listeners. He begins many programs with the loud moo of a cow, the quintessential sound of village life and a metonym for a pure Hindu world. These sounds contribute to the feeling of a generic village scene filled with a familiar sensibility. In *bikās* rhetoric, the village has come to stand for the place of "real Nepal," which has the dual effect of marginalizing actual villagers from centers of power and declaring them central to a national program (Pigg 1992). To set these stories within the frame of village life portrays them as the stories of *real* Nepalis, even if the writers are urbanites. The village is conceived of as a place of suffering, where people feel social constriction more intensely, yet it is also a space of desire and nostalgia. Indeed, village life has become almost inseparable from representations of the past and, in particular, the past of Kathmandu (Pigg 1992: 499–503). Through the broadcast of village sounds, Kalyan evokes an imaginative, nostalgic space of harmony associated with village life, as opposed to the social differentiations of the urban capitol.

Love stories are not the only kinds of letters sent to Kalyan. Widows wrote about relinquishing their rights to property when legal debates about women's rights to property raged in the city (as shown in a story below). Former Gurkha soldiers wrote tales about their treatment in the Indian army when this issue was being reexamined by the Nepali state. Former Maoists soldiers wrote about their often fraught and ambivalent relation to the conflict and their lost loves. Yet for both Kalyan and the writers, social commentary was rarely at the center of the tales—their pathos was precisely in their tragic and personal nature. Much of the social value attributed to these stories was not in their ability to stir people into political or social action, but rather to provoke empathy and compassion for a person who has suffered. Though centered on a single individual in ways that dovetail with the ideals of individualism, the desired effect of the stories, particularly for listeners, was to generate a moral community and an affirmation of social belonging.

The cultivation of this moral community and belonging is made possible through the letters' intertextual form (Briggs and Bauman 1992). In transforming the handwritten letters into his preferred genre, Kalyan told me that he edited the story-letters so that they more closely resemble the melodramatic plots of popular films. "I make [the stories] like a film, because I am a *scriptwriter*.[30] The things about (lovers) meeting the first time, I *picturize* for them. They are not really like films. But some are, because even if you say [sic] a film, the things that people imagine, they imagine through society.

Otherwise, how would they imagine anything! Every person is born in society, lives in society. Society and film—it's not so different."

The nonvisual medium of radio provides an opportunity for Kalyan to "write a script," to use sound, song, voice, and text that will evoke imagery and resemble the visual medium of film. This is not unusual in many aural commodities. Hirschkind describes the style of one particularly popular *khatib* as a "word as camera" style, and notes the overlaps between Quranic imagery and the cinematic imagination that is so central to the experience of modernity (2006: 153–57). Parallels to popular Indian film are common in *Mero Kathā, Mero Gīt* stories, and as my research assistant pointed out, nearly all the stories published in Kalyan's first book resemble the typical plotlines of any Bollywood film. Kalyan even claimed that one of his broadcast story-letters may have inspired the production of the Bollywood film *Kya Kehna* (2000, dir. Kundan Shah) about a pregnancy out of wedlock, produced seven months after this story was aired. Not surprisingly, this was one of the stories that he included in the first published book of story-letters. It is unlikely that the well-known film director Kundan Shah was inspired by this broadcast in Kathmandu. Yet in Kalyan's view the intertextual nature of the program is a key to its success, and is enhanced by Kalyan's own entrepreneurial activities of producing other texts based on the program.

Dukha is the leitmotif of most letters Kalyan reads, as it is in many forms of South Asian entertainment—popular films, Nepali literature, and television serials. As noted above, *dukha* is a sentiment that is often associated with women, because they do so much of the household labor and have to leave their parents' home in marriage; but in contemporary Kathmandu, where many have left their homes, it is a condition that characterizes modern life more generally. Voicing and listening to these stories, Kalyan argued, provides a means for people to express *dukha* and possibly alleviate the pain. Inspiring sentiments of compassion for other people's *dukha* is the task Kalyan sets up for himself in *Mero Kathā, Mero Gīt:* "When I read over the *air* and *give it very deeply* and when I *rewrite* it very *deeply*, at the time I read it, that *dukha* everyone will keep. Everyone will be listening to it. I think the writer feels he or she will pull themselves *free*."

Others collect the *dukha,* Kalyan suggests, releasing the author from its hold. Kalyan's melodramatic, soothing tone of voice is crucial, for he is the medium to pass on the *dukha,* his voice an index of his compassion. The prominence of *dukha* and the realism of the tales also connect them closely to the *bikās* industry that has infiltrated so much of Nepali consciousness about the self.[31] While Kalyan seeks the melodramatic effect of popular film—a form that many middle-class Nepalis condemn as terribly unrealistic (Liechty 2003: 169)—he also draws upon the conventions of time and causation promoted by the *bikās* industry and the genres of realism that emphasize a linear narrative in which one's life progresses through a series of clearly defined stages.

The notion of a changed future is central to the rhetoric of *bikās,* suggesting that time moves ever forward, away from the activities and events of the past, and will always bring something better and brighter. This temporality promotes an evolutionary view of society whereby, as Stacy Pigg discusses at length, "everyone's tomorrow will (or should) look like some people's present [that is, the middle-class Kathmandu Nepalis]" (1992: 501). Through this notion of linear time we can begin to see how such stories work to maintain and secure certain crucial social asymmetries across class, gender, caste, and region. Ideas of a changed future frequently frame many letter writers' tales to Kalyan. "*Kalyanji,*" begins one letter by a man in his early thirties. "I am fully convinced that the program *Mero Kathā, Mero Gīt,* which you present, will discourage, to a certain extent, our social wrongdoings, our superstition, and narrow-mindedness."[32]

The letter writer then links his letter to the recent broadcast of Laxmi Devi Joshi's letter (discussed below), and suggests that both of their letters will effectively transform people's "traditional" attitudes. Listening becomes a key agent of change, as the letter writer (like Kalyan) calls upon other listeners to appropriate the message into their own attitudes and practices.

During one of our meetings with a fan, Dipesh, Kalyan explained the formula for an appropriate story-letter, which emphasized the linear, progressive narrative structure. Dipesh had invited us to meet him in the army barracks where he worked as an assistant to a radiologist in the army hospital. Why had his letter not been broadcast? he asked. Kalyan explained: "The story that you sent just now, what happened with that is that there were no events *(ghatnā).* . . . It is written like an application *(nibedan).* It is not a story. It is not a story."

In comparing Dipesh's story to a bureaucratic form—an "application"— Kalyan implies that it did not have the appropriate sentiments conveyed in narrative form, though he says the problem is with its lack of events. For a story to be "a story" it needs to have a set of crucial events around which a person narrates their life. Kalyan then went on to describe to Dipesh the type of plotline and the kind of sentiments he wished to read over the radio. The army civil servant listened attentively, making mental notes for his future letter, as Kalyan continued: "What I need is this: first, one is born, right? Because when writing a story, people should give the whole thing. [One] is born, then which place [they] grew up. There are ordinary/simple *(sādhāran)* events. Then one comes to college.[33] Very *fast*, ok. Because people of today look for the events and happenings *(ghatnā)*. Literary writers who go around and around, they don't have any appeal anymore. . . . Now people look for events. 'Now what?' *'What happened?'*"

The word Kalyan uses for event—*ghatnā*—is most frequently invoked in the news to describe the incidents of the day and in historical narratives to describe the events in Nepali history. It carries within it the sense of facticity and conflict involved in the notion that something has happened, something that is assumed to interrupt the flow of everyday life.[34] Yet the events in a *Mero Kathā, Mero Gīt* story are not large-scale political or social events that fundamentally disrupt one's life; instead, they are events of everyday intimacies, familial injustices, or personal struggles that disrupt one's personal well-being. Even so, Kalyan's focus on events in the form of true stories bears some relation to a way of imagining the past and one's life in time that is linked to a broader form of historical consciousness.[35]

The most pervasive metaphors Kalyan adds to stories center on the passage of time—"life's/time's roller-coaster ride" *(jindagika/samaya ka roteping)*, "time like flowing water" *(samaya bagi-rahane pāni jastai)*. Kalyan contrasts the form of story-letters he broadcasts with a story form that is more circular, or "goes around and around," which he indicates with a gesture of his hands. These more winding tales he associates with a previous, outdated model— and ironically one that he associates with literary writers. In his reconstruction of the story-letters, he seeks to maintain the sense of time moving forward through factual events while adding his own poetic flourishes to create a "literary" feel.

This way of packaging time within the narrative, as a plodding movement forward between one or two critical events in an individual's life, does not come readily to many of his listeners. Kalyan sends back or rejects the vast majority of the story-letters sent to him because they do not meet this standard narrative form. This way of understanding one's life in time in terms of progress, an everyday popular Nepali form of the bildungsroman, means that by the end of the story the person has literally and metaphorically, spatially and temporally, moved from one place to the next. Time and history appear together as complementary projects that an ordinary person can shape and even create. For the most part, however, the stories tend to be unfinished bildungsromans, for usually they end in unrequited love, a longing for something else, a possibility in the past that was never realized. In the act of writing the story down—and, most importantly, having it heard and listened to—the story achieves completion.

The notion of time embedded in these story-letters parallels a modern understanding of one's inner "voice," the voice with which one accounts for one's own life that emphasizes inner struggle and consciousness. In modern linguistic ideology, as Richard Bauman and Charles Briggs argue, "voice" is perceived to be the means to express an already constituted interior self, rather than a medium actively shaping that self (Bauman and Briggs 2003; see also Keane 1997, Weidman 2006). This notion of voice is implicit in Kalyan's insistence that the letters must be written in the author's own hand, such that their handwriting serves as an index—a signature, if you will— binding the content to the legitimacy, sincerity, and interior desires of the writer-author (Keane 2002).

But this modern ideology of voice is complicated by the fact that these letters are ultimately shaped and publicly spoken not by the writers themselves, but by Kalyan. They are not direct utterances of inner consciousness. The letters are what Mikhail Bakhtin calls "double-voiced" discourse. In *Mero Kathā, Mero Gīt*, we see Kalyan, the animator of the letters, making use of "someone else's discourse for his own purposes by inserting a new semantic intention into a discourse which already has, and which retains, an intention of its own" (Bakhtin 1984: 189; cited in Morson and Emerson 1990: 150). Double-voiced discourse is not a specifically performative genre, though it is especially prominent in performance. Everyone's individual speech in daily life is shot through with double-voiced discourse. By reporting what someone else said, by taking on the language of a profession or the style of a particular type of speaker, by imitating the tone of an authority, we constantly make use of other's discourse. Here, the performed letters literalize this sense of double-voicing, for Kalyan presents the letters as a direct report of someone else's words, not his own. This is not the active double-voicing that Bakhtin celebrates, the parody or ironic discourse in which the use of someone else's speech becomes a means to critique, mock, or contest that speech. Rather, this is a more passive double-voiced discourse in which Kalyan's recitation of the letter writer's words and sentiments and his own voice appear not to conflict. The genre of story-letter maintains the modern ideology of voice through its double-voicing, for the program would not carry the same appeal if it were presented as Kalyan's words alone. The program's popularity rests on the absent writer, whose words gain authority, circulation, presence, and the status of "real" or "true" through their animation in Kalyan's voice.

This complex notion of voice is inscribed in the way the story-letters are composed and shape the specifics of its genre. Genres, as Mikhail Bakhtin has described them, do not only relate to literary works or works of writing; rather, they exist in daily speech to "establish ways of seeing" and conceptualizing reality (Morson and Emerson 1990: 275). When Kalyan is training his listeners to produce a certain genre of life story, he is training them to see and hear their lives in ways that resonate with new realities. They are urged to emphasize certain events and not others, to focus on certain sentiments and not others. To get a better sense of this process, I turn to a story-letter and a visit with an older widow, whose broadcast letter was frequently referred to by many other listeners as a frame for their own story-letters.

A WIDOW'S LETTER: JOURNEYS BETWEEN HOMES

Perhaps one of the most suffering figures in fiction and in lived social life is the South Asian widow. It is not a surprise, then, that widows sometimes sent letters about their lives to Kalyan. In late-nineteenth- and early-twentieth-century Bengal, widows figured centrally in writing by Bengali middle-class men, who wished to display their compassion (Chakrabarty 2000). This urge to document the suffering lives of widows was due in part to the fact that widowhood became an important political issue at the time. Debates between colonial rulers and Indian nationalists were often staged around the question of *sati* (widow self-immolation) in the early nineteenth century and the controversial Widow Remarriage Act of 1856 (Mani 1998). *Sati* and widowhood did not carry the same political weight in Nepal as in India, for there was no colonial power regulating the practice or the legal code. But neither was Nepal separate from these debates: widowhood was one of the key issues of social reform in Nepal in the 1920s. While the Nepali state legal code of 1854 had not abolished *sati*—thus mirroring traditionalist arguments put forth by Indian nationalists against their colonial rulers (Mani 1998)—in 1920, the Rana Prime Minister Chandra Shumshere outlawed *sati* completely from the legal code, an act that was part of his more general strategy of securing closer political relations with the British (Sever 1993: 283). In the popular imagination, the widow is still considered a general figure of suffering in Nepal. Though they are not the most common stories sent to the program, Kalyan readily broadcasts letters written by widows because of the affect their stories generate. In contrast to nineteenth- and early-twentieth-century Bengali tales of widowhood, Kalyan expects widows to write their own stories.

When Kalyan received Laxmi Devi's story, written neatly on five sheets of lined notebook paper, he returned it immediately. He told her that she ought to elaborate on the section about her journey to her husband's house in Benares and her return, three years later, to Kathmandu—a strategy that would anchor the idea of time passing to concrete movement in space. The emphasis on journeys across borders, as noted above, captures not only the global and national significance of the program, but also a sense of displacement, *dukha,* and desire that Kalyan wishes to highlight. While we tend to think of memory as a movement back in time, quite often it also marks a movement in space (Boyarin 1994). In Nepali as well as other South Asian languages, the death of a relative or friend is usually represented as a spatial rather than a temporal distance between the living and the dead. In Laxmi Devi's case, the death of her husband coincided with her journey to another place. Laxmi Devi dutifully agreed to embellish her journey, and Kalyan read her life story on the air soon after her revisions.

Even after her revisions, Laxmi Devi's narrative was not entirely typical. Though it is a story of loss, it is not a tale of unrequited love like the stories many of the younger listeners sent, nor is it a tale that devotes great detail to her desires in contrast with the desires of her family. She writes about her feelings upon joining her husband's family, but these brief interludes are eclipsed by her quick return to confirming her place within the family. It is a story that conveys great affect, and in this way represents the affective public that Kalyan cultivates. Her revised letter draws out the feelings of loneliness and abandonment after her husband's death, particularly at such a young age, asking listeners acknowledge her situation. While she does not directly address the subject of property reform, which was hotly debated at the time of her writing (see chapter 1), it hovers within the margins of her prose. Like many other letters, Laxmi Devi's story is a call for recognition from a moral community of familiar neighbors as well as the invisible audience of FM programs. I turn to it to consider these aspects of the story-letters more generally.

Her second letter reads as follows:

Dear Kalyan Bhāi! [younger brother]

Namaskar.

I have not met you yet, [but] even so, listening to your heartfelt voice it seems that you understand the sorrow that you read. For that reason, I write you my own life story.

In 2003 v.s. [1946], in the month of Jetha [June-July], when I was around eighteen years old, I got married. My husband was twenty-four years old. According to the traditions of that time, no one checked with my wishes. I did not tell anyone of my wishes [that is, I had an arranged marriage].

After marriage I stayed at my *māitī* for two years, and one day I received a letter from my husband, in which he wrote that *Sāsu* [mother-in-law] had become sick and therefore with his heart he invited/called *[bolāune]* me to Benares. At that time there was no *airplane* and no cars at home *[ghar]*, there was no one to go together with. Then later, we arranged that Āmā [Mother] and I would go. One of Āmā's relatives was studying in Benares, and we arranged to go to Benares with him and went.

From Kathmandu, [we] stayed in Bhimkedii by Ulinkot [and] reached Birganj, and from Birganj we went by *train* and reached Benares. On the road, thoughts about my husband's house were turning in my heart-soul. "How is my husband's house, maybe? How would the people of this home use [me]?" A kind of fear was in my heart. But at the home *[ghar]*, I found good home relations *[byabahār]*, and also a lot of love. My brothers-in–law called me *bhāuju* [brother's wife] and were very dear and respectful. The next day my brother-in-law walked [me] around the city of Benares, our house being near to Imalighat. Having done that, each day I spent enjoyably, and one week later Āmā returned to Kathmandu. And so the days were spent, through my husband's dearness nothing made me inferior. In the end, [he] is the householder of the *ghar* [*grihasti*, second stage of a Hindu man's life], but there was nothing, nothing [to do]. But being together with my husband, even all the suffering *[dukha]* resolved into happiness *[sukha]*.

Living in a foreign country, he did not make my *māitī* inferior.

At that time, he was doing a *specialization* in making *spectacles* and the *government* sent him to America for *further studies*. "I will summon [you] out in one week," [he] said and went to Kathmandu. At that time there were no *phones,* and it took around one month for letters to arrive.

One month later, his letter came and he summoned me *(bolāune)* to come to Kathmandu. One month's time after [his] departure seemed like one *yug* [twenty-four thousand years, or a cycle of one epoch in Hindu cosmology] to me, and after that peace would be returned to my dear world. But my happy days couldn't be very long. When I was at my *māitī* a message came that my husband is sick, they said, but I didn't know what kind of disease.

When I arrived at his [house] then I found out that the "black fever" had grabbed him, called *malaria*. Nepal, at that time, was very behind *medically* and he became more and more *serious* each day. While he was sick he said [to me]: "Don't go to Benares and as much as is possible relinquish the property of the *ghar*. I cannot understand why God cut my fate/luck so short." In 2007 v.s. [1950], on the fourteenth day of *Āshwin* he left me.

You do know: there is no right for a daughter in her *māitī,* and according to my husband's order, I should relinquish [deny myself] the property of the *ghar*. In that way, I was an eighteen-year-old young woman,[36] and on this hillside of the world, I was alone. My only accompaniments were, except for his memory and dearness, nothing else. But in front of everyone I assured them I would not be a responsibility/burden and I made my decision that I would do work to be independent. My *dewar* [brother-in-law] at that time was the Secretary of Health and I requested that he arrange for some job for me. At first, *dewar* did not agree because at that time there wasn't a custom of putting [married] women in jobs. But after making up my mind he said, "whatever *bhāuju*'s wish is okay" and arranged a *post* for me to be *in charge* of at the Praśutī Griha Thapathali hospital *hostel*.

Even without the accompaniment of my husband, the clock of life brought me forward. For that reason, I *concentrated* all of my *energy* on my work. In the *hospital,* I received love and affection and everyone called me *didī* [older sister] and [we] began to relate in that relation. In that way, I spent my own thirty-two years in that hospital. Now, I have already retired.

I only was able to have three years of my own [life] with my husband, but in those three years I received love that I depended on for my whole life. I am living in the frame of that love *[māyā]* and affection *[prem]* and the memories up until today. Today it has been forty-five years since he went to heaven. And accompanying my life I received affection from the hospital. In this world I have seen love from the hospital, and the affections of the world.

Yours sincerely
L. D. Joshi[37]

About two months after this letter was broadcast, Kalyan and I went to meet Laxmi Devi. To reach her house, we descended a long dirt path carved between brick and concrete buildings that have recently sprouted up in the center of old Kathmandu. I chuckled at the thought that Kalyan and I physically traced the paths of the radio waves with the tires of my scooter as we rode from the radio office to Laxmi Devi's house. Laxmi Devi, a graying woman of about sixty, dressed in a muted cloth sari, stood waiting for us at the edge of the red corrugated gate in a middle-class neighborhood close to the center of the city. She greeted us warmly and escorted us down the concrete steps, onto a long balcony that connected several rooms. From the balcony, we entered a shadowy room made dark by the heavy drapes and carpet. This drab place, in her brother's house, her *māitī,* had become the place where Laxmi Devi lives, only three years after she retired.

Laxmi Devi's entire narrative centers on a series of remembered homes, describing both her dispossession and her independence from the conventional life of a woman and a widow. These places are personally important to Laxmi Devi and also help locate her socially. Two of Laxmi Devi's homes are well known to all of her fellow Nepali listeners, as I discussed in chapter 1: her natal home, or *māitī,* and her husband's house, or *ghar.* These two homes represent what Bakhtin calls the "chronotope," the spatial and temporal context around which a story is woven, which expresses the inseparability of time and space to understand experience. The chronotope is the ground that makes particular plots and activity possible (Morson and Emerson 1990: 369). As chronotopes, the *ghar* and *māitī* help the listener feel the sense of time moving forward (initially, in the *ghar*) or always waiting to move (in the *māitī*) since these two homes represent two different narrative tracks in Laxmi Devi's represented life. They also give the narrative a feeling and a tone that are useful in expressing Laxmi Devi's desires and feelings. The silent disinheritance that *māitī* implies is what Kalyan and I feel when we enter Laxmi Devi's room.

Almost as soon as we arrived at her *māitī,* Laxmi Devi reached into the black zippered suitcase beside her bed and pulled out a pocket-sized photo of herself and her deceased husband, encased in a delicate silver frame. The tiny photo, worn with years, was a testimony to her story, and to the social landscape against which she, as a widow, narrates in her present-day life. Placing the frame down beside her, Laxmi Devi began to recall her life story, written initially on four pages of notebook paper, in round, legible print, which she then sent to be broadcast on Kalyan's program *Mero Kathā, Mero Gīt.* As she told it, her life was a series of journeys that initially appeared to progress in a linear fashion, but then brought her back to where she began, to her *māitī.* Like other stories, hers is a bildungsroman cut short and finished to some degree with her letter to Kalyan.

That Laxmi Devi narrated her life story from within these perpetual journeys was not something only requested by Kalyan. In fact, it parallels the dislocation that still organized Laxmi Devi's contemporary life. Married women's visits to and from their *māitī* are always brief, as discussed in chapter 1, but they are important performances of memory that act as unwritten records of a daughter's absence in her parents' and brothers' house. While doing so was somewhat unconventional, it is not surprising that Laxmi Devi moves back to her *māitī* after retirement. In the Hindu ideology that Laxmi Devi's family follows, widows should live at their *ghar* with their husband's parents, but in practice, many widows return to their *māitī* for long periods of time. Nonetheless, Laxmi Devi is well aware of the fraught tension this creates with her brothers, and tries carefully not to make herself too much at home.

I noticed after a few moments in Laxmi Devi's room that it appeared as if she had just moved in: she kept her clothes and valuables in a light-weight green metal chest, and her black suitcase, where she took the photo from, was zipped up tight, ready and patiently waiting to be carted off again. Some of this is not so unusual; many Nepalis store everyday items in locked chests beneath their beds. But Laxmi Devi's situation seemed a bit peculiar. Where were the material items that immediately indicate that this is a middle-class Kathmandu home: the tall, two-door mirrored cabinet for hanging clothes or the brightly colored chromolithographs of smiling Devis, Krishnas, Sai Babas, or the Buddhas that normally stare down at you from the walls? There was only a TV humming softly in the background as we talked. Laxmi Devi told us that indeed she planned to move again. "They need the house, my brothers' sons," she explained. "'Leave,' they tell me. After saying that, what to do? I should go. It's someone else's house—it's not mine—its theirs, they need it. 'Leave,' they say."

The reality of Laxmi Devi's dispossession, from her *ghar* (through her husband's pressure) and from her *māitī* (through Nepali law and her nephews' request), is something she expressed for the first time in the letter she sent to *Mero Kathā, Mero Gīt*. At the climax of her written story-letter, Laxmi Devi narrates her husband's last words to her, spoken in Kathmandu while he was dying of malaria. Directly quoting his words, Laxmi Devi wrote: "While he was sick, he said to me, 'Don't go to Benares and as much as is possible relinquish the property of the *ghar*.'" As a widow without sons, Laxmi Devi did have a legal right to this property, and her husband acknowledges this by directing her to not claim this right. With a quick shift from her storytelling voice to the explanatory voice of the narrator, Laxmi Devi then addresses Kalyan and the audience directly. She wrote, "You do know: there is no right for a daughter in her *māitī*, and according to my husband's order, I should relinquish the property of the *ghar*. Thirdly, I was an eighteen-year-old young woman and on this hillside of the world, I was alone."

This statement, which directly addresses the listeners via Kalyan, is a call to a moral community to recognize her plight, but it is also an expression of *dukha* that makes her story all the more heroic and appealing. The public debates around *angsa* and a daughter's inheritance (see chapter 1), touching so closely on Laxmi Devi's personal situation, may have provided a language for her voice. It set her narrative in dialogue with an already deeply politicized discourse about the past and women's relationship to their parents' genealogy. In Laxmi Devi's letter and broadcast, the political public sphere comes together with the politics of the affective public of FM programs. The proliferation of discourse about women's property rights at the time of this broadcast prepares the general Kathmandu population to hear and to listen to such stories, to evaluate her situation, and perhaps to imagine this situation with different possible endings in mind. Set within the narrative frame of a letter to "Dear Kalyan," however, it does not directly engage the political issues implicit in her plight. It is presented as a sentimental story that compels listeners' compassion.

When I returned to Laxmi Devi's house for a second visit, this time without Kalyan, she told me that in her original letter (which had been discarded) she had only described the parts of her story she felt were important: first, the words her husband spoke to her, and second, her life in the hospital. That Laxmi Devi singled out these two moments as the essence of her life story intrigued me. Being written out of her *ghar* and *māiti* by the rule of law and by her husband's command, Laxmi Devi sought another place of belonging significantly away from both places, in the state hospital where she lived and worked for thirty-two years. Yet, for Kalyan, that Laxmi Devi managed to put her life together and create another home in her work at the hospital does not adequately capture the sense of *dukha* he wishes to broadcast. He asked instead for more details on the journey to and from Benares to capture the sense of displacement, loneliness, and later grief that this journey ends up creating for Laxmi Devi.

Laxmi Devi's report of her husband's words is what she felt was an important part of her story. Reported speech is a prime example of Bakhtin's double-voiced discourse, and it is the most obvious places to see various social perspectives intermingling in the story. When a person uses reported speech, she conveys important information without being responsible for its message. By placing her husband's imperative between quotation marks, Laxmi Devi distances her present voice as a widow and her past voice as a wife from these words (Bakhtin 1981; Volosinov [1929] 1973). As the narrator, Laxmi Devi stands outside her husband's cited words; she is looking in and engaged with the command. Both voices dialogically resound with authority and index his hierarchical position within the *ghar*. The quotation is doubly double-voiced because it is articulated to a public through Kalyan and not Laxmi Devi herself. At least four different social positions and three distinct times emerge in this single utterance on the radio broadcast: the dead husband, the former wife (Laxmi Devi as a young woman), the present-day widow rewriting those words, and the present-day radio host, Kalyan, who later broadcasts them to an audience.

When I asked Laxmi Devi whether she ever wanted to disclose her husband's request that she not claim her share of the property before, she replied with a simple, matter-of-fact answer: "Who should I tell? That also came into my heart. It is not right to tell my younger sister, it is not right to tell my younger brother, cannot tell over there [in the *ghar*], cannot tell over here [in the *māiti*]; who should I tell? Before hearing Kalyan Gautum, the urge to write was not in my heart. Even if I wanted to write, but who should I tell?" Such a command safely nested between quotation marks gives the husband's voice authority in culturally appropriate ways but also calls out for an evaluative response from imagined listeners. As the first animator of her husband's words, Laxmi Devi implicitly asks the listeners to judge his demand. To be able to write requires that one have a listener. This is precisely a dialogic understanding of the word and language itself: nothing can be uttered without the concrete knowledge that these words will continue in a response. "To some extent," writes Bakhtin, "primacy belongs to the response, as the activating principle: it creates the ground for understanding, it prepares the ground for an active and engaged understanding" (1981: 282). In Laxmi Devi's case, there may never have been an appropriate social setting for her to voice her husband's words. *Mero Kathā, Mero Gīt* provides a partial solution, simply because the listeners are invisibly present as sympathetic listeners within the broadcast itself. Most story-letters, like Laxmi Devi's, are shot through with the expectation of response.

Laxmi Devi told us that she did receive many responses to her broadcast story. The day before Kalyan's program aired, Laxmi Devi phoned her husband's relatives, telling them to listen. They immediately called her after the program, she told us; they wanted her to visit. She also received many warm greetings on the street from people who knew about her story, but had never heard it directly. And this was not unusual among letter writers. "It was not only a question of writing to us," the manager of Hits FM (Kalyan's boss at the time) told me, referring to Kalyan's program, "but using us to pass on a message to other people." Through his program, Kalyan traffics information and stories between those who no longer see one another. Unlike the messenger of important family letters or love letters, a person always well known to both parties, Kalyan is a faceless voice who gives the stories additional caché and authority, and the texture of his voice makes his fans feel that he is as close as family. When Kalyan and I left on that afternoon, Laxmi Devi presented Kalyan with a jar of homemade *achār* (pickles), affectionately saying, "This is for my *bhāi* [younger brother]." Kalyan tells me that he still occasionally visits Laxmi Devi in her home.

ACHIEVING SMOOTHNESS: AN INTERLUDE

This program, an exemplar of an affective public, is characterized by an aura of smoothness. Smoothness describes the overall tone and texture of this affective public, which are achieved by the composition of the program itself and Kalyan's presentation, the genres of voiced writing, the composition of listeners' responses, and the multiple expectations and ideas of efficacy brought to bear both by Kalyan and by his listeners. Yet within the aura of smoothness there are notable differences between Kalyan and his listeners, particularly in terms of their expectation of what the program offers. The variations between Kalyan and his listeners are not usually a source of tension or contest. Indeed, this is one of the key hallmarks of the program—its content and form evoke a sense of harmony and union between and among the host and listeners. The harmonious quality of the program is also marked by the lack of public debate that constituted its entry into the newly privatized FM radio market. Taking seriously the variations between the listener-authors' and Kalyan's view of the program, which was evident in our meetings and in the analysis of letters, can productively contribute to our understanding of publics more broadly.

The literature on publics, particularly on liberal public spheres, suggests that the expression of differences of opinion or contested ideas between members of the public is central to what it means to be part of that public; in Habermas's view, a public sphere is constituted through rational debate and deliberation on a subject of common interest. What unites the participants is their common "audience-centered subjectivity," cultivated through the practices of solitary reading and personal writing that serve as a basis for this subject position. Even those works that challenge Habermas's model, such as Michael Warner's or Charles Hirschkind's work on counterpublics, assume that producer and audience share the same subjectivity and similar views on the significance, purpose, and intention of any given public, though their opinions about the content may differ. In this affective public, by contrast, the variations between Kalyan and many (though not all) of his listeners are not sources of deliberate debate on the program nor in letters to and about it, unlike what much of the literature on publics would suspect. One might reason that this is merely proof of Kalyan's authority over the genre and the program in general. Smoothness and harmony are simply expressions of his dominance. But I think this explanation is too simple. There remain implicit, unstated assumptions about what the program offers to people that expose differences in Kalyan's and his listener's views and at times differences in their subjectivities that are crucial to its working and its politics.

These differences only became clear to me through ethnographic research: the multiple meetings I had with listeners throughout the Valley, reading their letters and the revisions of the letters with Kalyan, listening to the broadcasts, and my frequent, long conversations with Kalyan. The variations in expectation and even in subjectivity, I argue, are essential to the configuration of any public and the social complexity that any public seeks to address, perhaps acutely an affective and an "intimate" one. We might acknowledge, for example, the diversity of assumptions about what a given public is doing, and the potentially diverse subjectivities involved in producing a program that appears quite smooth. Smoothness allows us to take seriously the texture and tone of the narratives, voiced writing, and performances that necessarily create any public.

To not attend to these variations risks flattening the social complexity of publics into well-worn analytic categories that fail to acknowledge how intimacy, affect, and the sense of a public are achieved. I turn now to several other revealing ethnographic moments through which we can see how such tensions between Kalyan and his listeners are erased or disregarded to achieve the overall aura of smoothness.

RECOGNITION AND LEGITIMATION THROUGH STORY-LETTERS

Kalyan often told me that the reason so many people wrote to *Mero Kathā, Mero Gīt* was to justify their existence to others, to search for a community of sympathetic listeners, and to provide a moral message for others through their actions. Drawing on a vision of social awareness that has become the stomping ground of political activists, development agencies, and the state alike, Kalyan explained to me that these stories presented possible opportunities in one person's failed past that other listeners might act upon in the future. For the program to work as a form of recognition, the letter writers must assure Kalyan that they do indeed exist and that their stories are true. Writers use a host of indexical signs that function in other spheres of life in Kathmandu as proof of their existence and that speak to the radio's profoundly intertextual nature. FM radio has become its own "media ecology" (Fuller 2007), a host to several different media, such as letters, bureaucratic forms, photographs, and telephone calls, that shape its programs. Many are indexical signs used to establish and recognize the listener's identity by state institutions (such as schools and hospitals). Listeners often sprinkle their letters with legal and bureaucratic terms, emphasizing words like "proof" *(pramāṇ)* and "evidence" *(sabut)*. One young man sent along a hospital diagnosis that recorded his brief stay in the hospital. Another sent a photocopy of his diploma. Several listeners sent photographs of themselves to complement their life story. (See figure 11.)

Here we can see the ways in which "the personal" comes to be authenticated through its confirmed connection to broader social institutions, along the lines that Berlant argues. By sending indices of institutional recognition, listeners affirm their presence as part of a broader Kathmandu public that they hope facilitates recognition from the FM radio host. The letters are forms of testimony that implicitly call upon other listeners to become sympathetic judges of their predicament. When taken together with Kalyan's own hand in editing the letters, a picture emerges in which sometimes the basis for recognition is quite different for Kalyan and for his listeners.

Consider the case of Raju, a young man who lives in a small village just outside Kathmandu's periphery. Raju heard himself referred to in his former girlfriend's story, which recounted her failed relationship with Raju and her subsequent marriage to another man and divorce. After listening to this story of the radio, Raju promptly wrote his own version of the story to Kalyan. Toward the beginning of his letter, he addresses Kalyan and the wider audience:

Though your program *Mero Kathā, Mero Gīt* is not a place for arguments, I deem it my moral duty to scribble a few words in response to *Mero Kathā,*

FIGURE 11. Photograph of a couple sent to *Mero Kāthā, Mero Gīt,* ca. 1998. Courtesy of Kalyan Gautum.

Mero Gīt of Chaitra 21.... After the story of my downfall, a lot of my close ones and classmates accused me of being the chief antagonist and perhaps you also thought the same. But anyone who reaches a decision after hearing one version of a story is deemed an unsuitable judge. So, Dear Kalyan, if you are really moved by the authenticity of the stories you receive on *Mero Kathā, Mero Gīt* and if someone's *dukha* makes you sad, then let me cry out my heart by giving my tragedy an opportunity on your program. If possible, please announce my full address and request from those people who have negative ideas about me after hearing *Mero Kathā, Mero Gīt* on Chaitra 21 to write me a few words and tell me *who was to blame?*[38]

The broadcast of one's story, Raju suggests, is an "opportunity" *(maukā)* to be recognized and justified by both friends and strangers outside the radio context. Even though Raju openly acknowledges that the program is not "a place for argument," he frames his own story as a forum for deliberation and debate. Raju inaugurates an almost legalistic correspondence with anonymous listeners and friends to determine, as he puts it, "who was to blame." Kalyan's program has become a forum for listeners to seek public recognition from invisible listeners in ways that may not be possible, or authorized, by other channels.

This theme that the program is a novel forum for recognition is present in nearly all the story-letters published in Kalyan's first book. In the preface to this book (see the introduction), Kalyan directly compares his program with a court of law and place of justice, suggesting there is no place else to go "if one's feelings have been shattered" (Gautum 2059 v.s.: 10). Phrases within the published stories echo this preface—likely through Kalyan's editing—and emphasize the lack of an appropriate listener for this tale: "Where is the person whom should I tell, where should I go to have my anguish listened to?" *(Khai kaslāi bhanu, kāhā gayera sunāu yo mero bedanā?)* (Gautum 2059 v.s.: 87). Put into the frame of a personal letter and an entertaining radio broadcast, these voiced writings might be thought of as a more acceptable and certainly more accessible means to pronounce judgment on social strictures than in a legal court.

Kalyan acts, in a certain fashion, like a lawyer who voices and represents his listener's tales, altering their words, editing the tales, and monitoring his voice in such a way that adequately expresses their feelings. Or, as some have suggested to me in earlier versions of this work, Kalyan might be viewed as a Nepali Oprah, who through his reading, his voice, and the songs interspersed throughout the program gives these everyday tales of love and *dukha* a weighty pathos such that "misery" becomes glamorous (Illouz 2003). But unlike a lawyer or Oprah, most of the time Kalyan does not seek to do anything other than to broadcast the stories in his own melodramatic voice— there is no negotiating, no advice, no fines paid, no punishment or attempt to suture people's open wounds.

Kalyan's theory of justice is, not surprisingly, bound up with the act of listening to his program. He is, therefore, not only cultivating a particular genre of voiced writing, but also promoting a way of listening through the affective tone that emphasizes moral issues in the story-letter. The work is left to the listeners, if it is to be done at all, and Kalyan becomes the vehicle—a medium—through which people like Raju gain a listening public. In Raju's case (and many others), this listening public is not primarily connected to the ideals of a liberal democracy, with its emphasis on individual freedom and privacy; rather, Raju seeks to be recognized by a moral community through his expression of public intimacy and to be justified by them for his actions.

Given the centrality of the listener in effecting change, Kalyan's active interest in Raju's story intrigued me. Unlike with other stories, he was clearly interested in directly mediating the relationship between Raju and his former girlfriend, Tara, a fact that appears in the small edits he makes to the broadcast letter. Kalyan focused his editing on the ending of Raju's story, in which Raju directly addresses Tara and writes, "you are welcome in my little home," a phrase that Kalyan told me was essentially a marriage proposal on air. This is all the more exciting because Tara's tale tells of her eventual divorce with another man. Eager to broker such an uncommon match that breaks with social convention in multiple ways—an intercaste, interclass marriage to a divorced woman—Kalyan suggested that we visit Raju in his village just forty minutes south of Kathmandu proper. We set out on my scooter on a Saturday, knowing only Raju's village and his name, in the hope that he would be home on the weekly day off. Once we arrived in the village, we were immediately directed to a small mud-packed farmhouse, where we were informed that Raju lived with his widowed mother and that Raju would be home soon. Two young children, who overheard our conversation, ran out to the dirt road a few minutes later, and yelled to a young man, informing him of our arrival.

"Oh Kalyan!" Raju said enthusiastically, as he approached us from the road. "I tried to visit you in the studio. I wanted to get in touch with you. Come in, come in!"

We spent the afternoon in Raju's small room, listening again to his saga and to his wish to clear his name after the broadcast of the story of Tara. Enacting the self-reflexive discourse that Warner (2002) claims is necessary to any public, Raju inscribes her story and its broadcast within his own letter. The effect of Raju's story is at once confusing and intriguing, for there was never actually any direct condemnation of him in Tara's original letter. In fact, Tara does just the opposite. Toward the end of her letter, she wrote: "I admit that I am more guilty than you in the failure of our love.... Even today, she [Tara] is ready to bow down before you and beg your pardon." Raju's real name was not broadcast, but apparently many of Raju's friends knew the tale well enough, detected him, and accused him of being the true culprit of this breakup. Listeners' interpretations of the story, which contradicted the content of the story, illustrate yet again the power of Kalyan's voice to evoke sympathy and align him with the writer. It also illustrates the veiled messages inherent in Tara's gushing apology.

Despite Raju's focus in clearing his name during our conversation, Kalyan tried to turn his attention to the ending and the possibilities it presented. "There's one mistake you made in the broadcast," Raju complained. "You forgot to say that I must talk things over with my mother first." Indeed, when I returned to the letter later, the last line read: "If there is no possibility of reunion with him [Tara's former husband], then you are welcome in my little home. After talking things over with my family, I am ready to let you into my heart." The omission of this small phrase—"After talking things over with my family"—radically changed the message. Despite his professed love and inner turmoil that he recites in florid language, Raju remained adamant that the decision to marry is not his alone. Within the story-letter as well, Raju frequently recites and then rejects his own feelings, writing of the expectations his family has of him and noting that at the time he was too young to do anything but follow the "formula of a common Hindi film that said there was no partiality of class and creed in true love." Raju frequently mentions their class differences in the story-letter, and then in our conversation he asserted that his mother would never let him marry a divorced woman. To marry Tara, Raju told us, would be to leave his widowed mother alone. He was not prepared to do this.

Kalyan shrugged the complaint off, and returned to the idea of a reunion to no avail. As we rode home on the scooter, I asked Kalyan why he had not broadcast that final phrase. He responded curtly and without explanation: "There was no time." It is clear that Kalyan wishes to capture an individual's break from family and social pressure in his stories. An individual acting purely out of his own passionate will is, for Kalyan, an ideal hero and a clearly marketable idea, particularly if this person is a man. That Raju remains unconflicted and essentially unchanged in his love toward Tara adds to the melodramatic flavor of the tale. But as Raju made clear during our meeting, such clarity does not in fact exist.

This discrepancy between Raju's and Kalyan's interpretation of the broadcast story tells us something about the complex workings and social politics of this affective public that appears so harmonious. On the one hand, Kalyan seeks to challenge, albeit in conventional ways, the pressure of family, class, religion, ethnicity, and caste by presenting the story of an individual heroically defying social pressure by expressing his conflicting desires. While the expression of these desires is crucial, it is equally important that the desires not be completely realized for the story to have its full sentimental effect. Both Kalyan and his listeners imagine the program as a place where people negotiate their relations to others outside the radio context, but their view of what this might entail is sometimes quite different. For listeners, the program provides a platform to be recognized and evaluated on moral terms by an audience of intimates who are both familiar and strangers. Kalyan imagines that the expression of these desires might actually lead to a different set of relations in the world outside the radio broadcast.

Kalyan sees these story-letters as a means for people to gain recognition for their suffering, and, following liberal logic, he tends to place an emphasis on the individual desire in contrast with societal prescriptions, even though many of the stories end with conservative messages. Here, even as Raju reaches out to his former love, he also criticizes his own misguided ideas about their attachment. These differences are smoothed out through Kalyan's editing and do not become a source of conflict on the program or even in subsequent letters to Kalyan. Yet they are important to recognize because they are critical to the formation of this affective public. Somehow Kalyan addresses enough of the writer's desire for recognition by a moral community that his own wish to broadcast stories of individual suffering does not completely efface this desire. Public intimacy remains at the core of what Kalyan perceives to be appropriate content for the program, and expressions of affect through the content of the listeners' letters and the tone of Kalyan's voice when reading the letters contribute to the overall texture of the program. Yet listeners like Raju imagine themselves and the effect of this affective public in quite different ways than Kalyan does. Raju's subjectivity is not first and foremost one of an individual acting against his family; to the contrary, this is a space for him to clear his name and be recognized and justified by other familiar listeners through expressing his compassion for his former girlfriends' plight while also noting his necessary alignment with his family's interests.

EFFECTIVE POWER OF LISTENING

The social politics of the program becomes even more clear as we consider more closely what people imagine may transpire beyond recognition through listening. By looking at stories that have been excluded, we can begin to see some of the differences between Kalyan and his listeners' understanding of the program.

Lulu Lama was a fan who had hoped for significant changes in his familial and state position via the broadcast of his letter, but was disappointed when it was not chosen. Lulu was, at the time, an eighteen-year-old Tamang man from a village outside the Valley who spent his days in a Tibetan Thanka painting workshop in northern Kathmandu. Tamangs are an ethnic group of Nepalis who have historically supplied much of the manual labor for the Kathmandu Valley throughout the twentieth century (Holmberg 1989; March 2002). From the beginning, Kalyan seemed to take little interest in Lulu or his story, but I was interested in understanding what kind of stories were rejected by Kalyan, so we agreed to visit Lulu at his painting workshop. Lulu's father had abandoned him and his mother as soon as Lulu was born, and when Lulu arrived in Kathmandu in the early 1990s he began to search for his absent father. Through a network of villagers he learned that his father had remarried and lived in Kathmandu. It was then, he told us, that he considered writing to *Mero Kathā, Mero Gīt:*

> At that time, I was in the tenth class; at that time we [father and I] had not met yet. It seemed that everyone was sending letters, it was like a kind of message through this program. Since I had not met him in so many years, perhaps doing it this way—not by searching—his heart might change and he would come looking for me? He might want to meet? After sending a message, he might say, "Until today, my son exists." And for that I wrote a letter. That's the most important reason.

As we talked in the musty back room of the factory, I became more and more intrigued with this story while Kalyan became more and more absorbed in his newspaper. Lulu seemed to feel that the expression of affect might lead to real effects. The affective powers of Kalyan's voice and the radio medium, Lulu suggested, had the power to "change someone's heart." Like many other listeners, Lulu suggested that voiced writing conveys an aura of authenticity and truth that "moves" listeners, not only emotionally, but also, potentially, into some kind of social action. He began to talk about his childhood in his mother's village.

Shifting his weight from side to side with some discomfort, Lulu described his mother's village to us—his mother's *māitī* and Lulu's *māmāko ghar* (maternal uncle's home). He talked about how this home was oppressive because it did not belong to him. In a soft voice, Lulu recalled the distance created between him and the other villagers because of the mere fact that he was living in his uncle's home.

"To stay with one's mother's people is not very good," Lulu explained, looking at me.

I asked him to be more specific: was it not okay to stay with his mother's brother, his *māmā*?

"No," he replied, and then to clarify he added, "my mother's brothers—my mother's landlords *(gharpatī)*."

"Why was it difficult for you to live with your *māmā* in the village?" I asked, already knowing the answer.[39]

"For me, it was, what should I say, contempt. Also there's this rule if there is a mother and a father. Now, there's a saying, what do people say, "Eh, it's not your father's address, it's your mother's!... In this village, you *[tā]*, in the village, you are just like a *batuwā*."[40]

Looking up from his newspaper, Kalyan exhaled a deep breath of sympathy, "*Bāf*... oh my god!"

Batuwā is a slang term that refers to a person who is orphaned, wandering, rootless, or perhaps drunk. It evokes the sense of being without a place and aimless. Clearly, as Kalyan's reaction itself illustrates, this was a terrible insult to a young boy.

Lulu continued: "I felt like, this doesn't seem like it's my own house, why stay in this place? Instead, I'll go."

"It didn't feel like your own house?" I repeated his words.

"It's *not* my own house," he answered matter-of-factly. "My house... actually, my mother's, ummm, my home *(ghar)* is in *Bethān* [where his father is from].... But I didn't even know [then]."

More than sympathy, Lulu actually imagined that material, political consequences might transpire from this letter to *Mero Kathā, Mero Gīt*. After repeating his entire life story with his eyes fixed to the ground, he looked up at me and said: "To make a citizenship card, you also need one's own *Thar* [a caste or ethnic name], a name in order to show your identity. For *that* also, I needed to search for my father. For later, well, to get a job in an office, or to do some small work. Well, after saying you are Nepali, well, one needs proof, and for that one's citizenship card is important. For that, I needed to meet my father. For that, also, I wrote a letter."

Lulu ostensibly sent a letter to gain recognition not only from his father, but more importantly from the state. In Lulu's words, the proof *(pramān)*—a technical term that usually implies a piece of bureaucratic documentation—

is the requirement of the state, but one that can only be granted through a socially recognized father. At the time that we talked, one's citizenship was granted through proof of paternity, a law that changed in 2006, enabling mothers to be recognized for proof of citizenship. Citizenship was also a central political issue for many ethnic minority parties, but for Lulu, who is outside the political elite, it becomes a problem that he imagines could be solved through the affective public of FM radio. Lulu did eventually find his father, but not because of the letter he sent to Kalyan. Kalyan felt this letter was unsuitable, and never broadcast the story.

As we left the workshop, I asked Kalyan why he never broadcast the story, and he replied quite matter-of-factly: "It was not well written." His decision was based on an aesthetic choice. Yet, it is clear the subject of Lulu's letter is immediately provocative; it not only confronts the failure of a father toward his son, but also implicitly confronts the failure of the state. The power of Kalyan's voice, a sign of public legitimacy that Lulu otherwise lacked, seemed in Lulu's analysis to be directly related to the ethics of how people listened. In contrast to many of the other letters Kalyan broadcast, Lulu had a quite practical solution to his problem in mind. We might wonder: would Kalyan have broadcast the letter if it had been written instead by Lulu's mother? My guess is he would have. Lulu's story exposes patrilineal authority and the role of the state in a way that conventional tales about women's *dukha* paradoxically do not. As a son, he is not supposed to be the one who suffers from familial, domestic trouble—his *dukha* would be more presentable if it were about a lost love or a relative's suicide (like a story sent by a young boy Lulu's age that Kalyan published) or the death of a family member. It reveals that the problems with patrilineal citizenship affect not only young women, but also young men whose fathers have left.

As feminist scholars have long shown, patriarchal forms of power are not just about gender inequality (for example, Butler 1990; Rubin 1974); they affect all subject formations. Criticism is perhaps most unsettling and pointed when it focuses on relations between men (for example, Lulu and his father)—the unmarked categories of a patriarchal system—rather than the marked position of women. Lulu's story in so many ways defied the genre of *dukha* and the politics of the program, but Kalyan dismissed it on aesthetic grounds, revealing the clear connections between aesthetic form and political content. Lulu's unread story exposes the conventions and limits of *dukha* on the program—the specific kind of suffering that Kalyan looks for, that he imagines fans will find appealing, and that will elicit compassion. Confirming

Berlant's analysis about the one life that counts as "a life", rejected stories like Lulu's reveal at once the aesthetic boundaries of a life story on this program *and* the political aspirations of listeners to gain both state and familial recognition through this nonpolitical, affective public.

MODERN LISTENERS OF SUFFERING: ETHNOGRAPHY AND AFFECTIVE PUBLICS

The effectiveness of listening and the necessary expression of *dukha* have set the tone for many programs on FM radio. While this turn toward the personal may be helpful to a good number of Nepalis, it is important to keep in mind that the impulse to confess is produced by the large financial institutions that fund the FM radio, from businesses like Hero Honda, which initially funded *Mero Kathā, Mero Gīt,* to aid organizations like UNICEF and USAID, which fund, directly or indirectly, other FM programs. Bound up with such enormous global capital, expressing one's *dukha* or one's personal story is not an innocent act.

Public intimacy on *Mero Kathā, Mero Gīt* is bound up with the necessity to express suffering. That in these stories one must suffer in order to have a story—through love, grief, or heartache—gives these tales a certain cultural caché that links them directly with the motives and significance of a development state. Within the development state, as Ferguson and others have shown, properly articulated suffering leads to material consequences (Escobar 1995; Ferguson 1994). Institutions of *bikās* are in the business of alleviating pain and suffering and shaping subjects who might begin reflecting differently on their *dukha*. The trope of *dukha* cannot be reduced to a mere effect of the development industry; but rather, it is a more complex, long-standing sociocultural concept that has a gendered component (often associated with women) and describes a more general experience of sadness and suffering (emotional, physical, social). That "love," particularly the *dukha* of love, is a form of redemption when broadcast on *Mero Kathā, Mero Gīt* presents certain challenges to the development state. Whereas within the discourse of development all suffering can be potentially alleviated through the right changes in attitudes, institutional projects, and infrastructure, this program suggests that suffering in and of itself is part of being human. Within a modernist order, there is no prescription for this suffering, and it can never be completely eradicated, despite efforts by the *bikās* industry.

As we have seen here, expressions of *dukha* and love are packaged within the genre of the life story narrative. *Mero Kathā, Mero Gīt* produces what listeners express as a novel sense of having a story to tell that enables them to participate and gain access to a public. This public is not the rational public that Habermas describes as necessary to a functioning democratic polity, but an affective public built on the recognition and expression of appropriate sentiments and forms of intimacy. Several existing forms contribute to the achievement of this affective public and the ideas of voice and listening that emerge from it. The first is the melodramatic plots of popular Indian film, which most FM listeners are quite familiar with and which play a role in shaping the kinds of narrative Kalyan seeks and broadcasts. Second, and related to popular film, is the expression of *dukha*. The third is the genre of "voiced writing" and particularly the tone and texture of Kalyan's voice (itself indexing a particularly powerful social position) that lend to the production of a seemingly true and authentic tale.

As Dipesh Chakrabarty (2000) has argued, the capability and urge to document and to notice suffering (even one's own) are crucial markers of the modern self. With proper training and education, anyone—not merely the extraordinary witnesses of suffering and exemplars of compassion like Buddha or Christ—can learn to notice suffering and therefore feel compassion. In cultivating this modern sensibility, the aim is not simply to assuage the suffering; rather, the recognition of suffering becomes the mode through which one human being recognizes another, particularly people with whom the recognizer would otherwise not relate. Suffering becomes a desired state of being, for it is within this field of sentiments that one gains a place in a wider, public world. Furthermore, as Chakrabarty's analysis suggests, it is not simply voicing one's suffering but disciplining one's ear to hear and listen to the suffering of others that constitute this modern sensibility. Lynn Festa (2010) has similarly argued that the recognition of the suffering of others during the late-eighteenth-century abolition movement in England depended upon sentimental tropes encouraged by new epistolary novels (Hunt 2007). These created the possibility of the "sentimental sympathy" that lies at the root of contemporary human rights discourse.

What is different about Kalyan's program is that the listeners and writers of suffering are not exclusively from the literati class about which Chakrabarty writes nor is the suffering they depict or respond to centrally concerned with social justice as Festa describes. Instead, this is a profoundly personal and affective suffering linked to relations of romantic love and heartache. As we can see from the example of Lulu, only certain types of suffering are considered worth listening to; others that too radically challenge existing social forms are cast away as aesthetically unappealing. Despite this, the broadcast of this program nevertheless seems to convince people like Lulu that they too have a story to tell and that this program could be an avenue for gaining broader public recognition from absent family members or even the state. Programs like *Mero Kathā, Mero Gīt* become forums for training people in the art of listening to strangers' personal stories of suffering and love and performing sentiments of care, a training that has become a key part of the fabric of modern subjectivity.

. . .

I have argued that the texture and tone of this program can be characterized by an aura of smoothness, despite the different intentions, ideas about the program, and even subjectivities it engages and cultivates. We have seen these diverse perspectives in Laxmi Devi's different idea of an ideal story, in Raju's complaint about the changed ending of his story, and in Lulu's rejected tale. To recognize the variations between the FM radio station, the radio producer, and the diverse audience members in an affective public like *Mero Kathā, Mero Gīt* is not exclusively to recognize of the power differentials between the various actors involved. Nor can it be adequately explained through the familiar dichotomies of tradition and modernity or communalism and liberalism. Rather than tag Kalyan's listeners as a homogenous group, primarily bound to traditional notions of communal life, or Kalyan as the quintessential neoliberal entrepreneur, here I attended more closely to interpretations of the program that show how these different outlooks appear without explicit contest or even tension. To be clear: this is not a call to reexamine the reception of media in contrast to its production. Kalyan's intertextual production, inspired by multiple popular genres, can itself be seen as a kind of reception and interpretation of the forms that surround him. Instead, I am suggesting that the variations in the expectations of the program among the listeners and between the listeners and Kalyan crucially exist within the aura of smoothness that the program achieves, and even further, I would wager that this is true for many (or most) publics when examined ethnographically.

As Anna Tsing (2005) has productively shown, through ethnography we usually find "friction" that enables global "flows." Responding to the popular language of descriptions of globalization and "global motion" from the 1990s, Tsing uses the metaphor of friction to suggest that in fact the motion of commodities, goods, ideas, and people does not proceed unimpeded because "motion is socially informed" (2005: 5–6). Taking a cue from Tsing, I aimed to show the friction we encounter between different subjects and intentions that allows for the overall sense of smoothness that characterizes the program. As in the previous chapters, I do not to reduce the subjectivities in play by deploying a single rubric like tradition, modernity, or neoliberalism. Instead, I use ethnography to help us rethink some of the assumptions we carry about what it means to be part of a public.

To study a public is to study what Raymond Williams called the "structures of feeling" of a given moment, "a social experience which is still *in process,* often indeed not yet recognized as social but taken to be private, idiosyncratic, and even isolating, but which in analysis (though rarely otherwise) has its emergent, connecting, and dominant characteristics, indeed its specific hierarchies" (1977: 132). The affective public of *Mero Kathā, Mero Gīt* reveals prevailing structures of feeling—*dukha,* romantic love, authenticity, and the truth of personal tales—that characterize Kathmandu in the mid-1990s and early 2000s. In the next chapter, I move from the local context of *Mero Kathā, Mero Gīt* to a more focused discussion of how these structures of feeling are linked to and mediated by broader global forces: the growth in the diaspora population, the remittance economy, and the important "presence" of the global Nepalis in Kathmandu through FM radio waves.

FIVE

Diasporic Voices

SOUNDS OF THE DIASPORA IN KATHMANDU

A generation ago, the horizon of speech was very limited.... Today all this has been changed. The telephone has vastly extended the horizon of speech. Talking two thousand miles is an everyday occurrence.

"Your Telephone Horizon," 1912, quoted in Sterne
2003: 168

When I first used a telephone, I shouted very loudly, and the shop owner laughed. "How can they hear me all the way across the river in Bhimsenthan?" I thought. Now I know I can call you in America and speak normally.

GYANISOBA SHAKYA, Patan

TECHNOLOGIES OF THE VOICE ALLEVIATE and aggravate Nepali dreams of contact across great distances. Fantasies of escaping the Maoist civil war and of earning enough money to support a middle-class life in Nepal are constantly belied by stories about the difficult and sometimes outright horrific conditions of work abroad. This contradiction produces anxieties that loom large, making the material and symbolic presence of the Nepali diaspora increasingly important to urban sociality in Kathmandu.[1]

In this chapter, we turn to another affective public constituted by FM radio and by broad social and economic transformations that have dramatically affected the landscape of Kathmandu: the remittance economy and the growing Nepali diaspora. Kathmandu streets have multiple signs of Nepalis working and living abroad. Western Unions and advertisements for Nepali banks abroad are ubiquitous (see figure 12, at the beginning of the chapter). Numerous unfinished renovations and building projects perforate the cityscape, many of which are financed by money sent from family working abroad (see figure 13). Corner telephone shops

FIGURE 12. Diaspora connections: texting at a money order outlet in Kathmandu. Photo: Siddartha Baral.

advertise their cheapest rates to some of the most common destinations for Nepalis: Dubai, Malaysia, Australia, Japan.

I focus on the effects of the diaspora for those Nepalis who stay at home by asking how the mediated and vocal production of an urban Nepali subject is shaped by the figure of the diaspora. This Nepali diaspora is made "present" in Kathmandu and becomes a distinctive part of urban Nepali subjectivity primarily through two technologies of the voice: the FM radio and the telephone. Here I discuss the *hearing* and *voicing* of telephone calls made between Nepalis in Kathmandu and those abroad that were broadcast on one of Kantipur FM's popular radio programs, *Rumpum Connection*. Unlike many analyses of diaspora, I do not focus directly on a particular community of Nepalis living abroad, but instead on the mediation of a diaspora within Kathmandu. Nor do I discuss place as the primary category through which diasporic communities emerge. Temporality and affect, rather than shared territory, shape the way in which this diaspora and its public are produced (Axel 2002). These categories

FIGURE 13. Unfinished high-rise construction in Kathmandu is linked directly or indirectly to the enormous remittance economy generated by Nepalis working abroad. Photo: Daniel Karpowitz.

are themselves produced by the voice projected over the radio and telephone.

In the previous chapters, I discussed the ways in which urban Nepali subjects are interpellated into social positions by various practices, such as *bolāune,* in which a brother calls his married sisters home (chapter 1), or practices of *mukh herne,* which instantiate a hierarchical relation between parent and child, king and subject, and higher and lower politicians or colleagues (chapter 2). In this chapter, through a discussion of *Rumpum Connection* (sponsored by Rumpum Noodles),[2] I show the ways in which the FM radio interpellates a Nepali diaspora and urban subject, creating discursive forms through which the diaspora and urban subjects are recognized by others as well as by themselves. Interpellation occurs not only through the discursive structures of "excitable speech" (Butler 1997), but also through technology. We have already seen that media, such as television, film, and radio, constitute the social entities, such as "society," "nation," "culture," and "romantic love" that they claim to merely represent on air (Mazzarella 2004: 357). FM radio is not simply the medium for broadcasting conversations between distant Nepalis. Rather, the very idea that "urban Nepalis" and a "Nepali diaspora" exist prior to their mediation (through radio, telephone, and, earlier, newspapers) is one persuasive effect of technologies of voice.

In the last chapter, I discussed the production of an affective public on FM radio through the genre of "voiced writing" and the medium of Kalyan Gautum's melodramatic voice. Here I also ask how the modulated voices of the telephone and radio become media for producing affect, subjects, and diverse temporalities. More specifically, how do these technologies of the voice configure a contemporary urban sociality in Kathmandu that centers on Nepalis living abroad? To answer these questions, I continue the exploration of voice as a medium of immediacy and transparency, alongside its materiality, or what I have referred to as the "sonic voice." The "sonic voice" conveys messages at the level of sound, through intonation, rhythm, or musical song and helps create the texture of affective publics like those of *Mero Kathā, Mero Gīt* or *Rumpum Connection*. On *Rumpum Connection* as well as many other FM programs, callers often refer to the voice as an indicator of presence as well as one's internal state of being. And this register of feeling is particularly important for Nepalis whose loved ones are working or studying far away in distant lands.

Rumpum Connection must be understood as part of the broader history of FM radio and its programs as well as of the political and economic conditions that have led to the presence of a Nepali diaspora in Kathmandu. Over the past two decades, money sent from abroad has become vitally important for supporting the state and middle-class life in Kathmandu. Life abroad is increasingly associated with material and symbolic possibility, and is thought of as a source of social redemption and financial success. Like Shanghai Chinese, about whom Mayfair Mei-hui Yang (2002) writes, Kathmandu Nepalis increasingly identify with overseas Nepalis, who are appearing in more and more Nepali films, TV shows, and popular songs. Yang suggests that this "subjective mobility" presents challenges to state modernity and to the regulations of the state that determine how to be Chinese. In the Nepali context, the Nepali state encourages Nepalis to work overseas, and the state has become increasingly dependent on these overseas Nepalis.[3]

There are three main points about the mediation of voice and the Nepali diaspora that I make here. First, FM programs generate particular temporalities, such as the simultaneity of "live" broadcasts, and forms of intimacy and feeling that are key to the making of an affective public in Kathmandu. Here there is more continuity between expressions of intimacy toward family members, friends, and romantic partners than in *Mero Kathā, Mero Gīt,* but the voice is still central to the texture of this affective public. Second, I continue my argument about the mutual emergence of the figure of the voice and neoliberal discourses of democracy through connections made between transparency and directness in descriptions of voice. This occurs at the level of emotional immediacy and at the level of democratic governance that hovers in the background of these exchanges. Finally, I engage in an "ethnography of forms," moving between the particular "things" animated on the FM radio—the figure of the voice, urban Nepali subjects, and a Nepali diaspora—and the discursive and technological forms that generate these "things" (Gaonkar and Povinelli 2003: 391).

This attention to technological and linguistic form follows, on the one hand, a McLuhan-like emphasis on technology and media that are incorporated within FM programs, such as the telephone, letters, and email, which, I noted in chapter 4, make the FM radio into its own "media ecology" (Fuller 2007). On the other hand, I examine the discursive form of *Rumpum* conversations, which are replete with references to potential telephone calls, to sent photos and emails, and to possible letters. The excess of this discourse about technology I refer to as "technological phatic" speech. Like other forms of phatic speech, references to possible communication do not convey any information, but simply reiterate the strange fact that people seem to "connect" through technology. Attention to the material and discursive forms of FM radio suggests links between the figure of the voice and the figure of diaspora in contemporary urban Nepali subjectivity.

NEPALI DIASPORA ON AIR

Rumpum Connection engages in a dynamic that echoes the work of the media consolidator Communication Corner, which is described in chapter 3; but rather than seeking to affectively draw villagers into urban life, the program aims to evoke the presence of Nepalis abroad, figuratively drawing them into the public space of the nation's capitol. The program began in 2001 and ended nearly a year after King Gyanendra's coup in 2005. *Rumpum Connection*'s format was a broadcast of telephone calls between Kathmandu Nepalis and their friends or relatives abroad. A day before the program aired, *Rumpum*'s host, Anamika, arranged several phone calls with Kathmandu residents who had written letters or emails requesting a specified call abroad. At noon on

Saturday, a day when most Nepalis are at home, Anamika made a series of conference calls from Kantipur FM's radio studio. These calls ostensibly "connected" Kathmandu residents with their friends or families abroad. *Rumpum Connection* does not actually make a connection between disparate parties, as its name suggests. Instead, the very notion of connection constructs the subjects of "urban Nepali" and "Nepali diaspora," which come into being through the show. They become social categories through which callers and listeners recognize others as well as themselves.

The conversations on *Rumpum Connection* were only public to listeners in Kathmandu.[4] Although the speakers from abroad may have been expecting a call from their family or friend, they did not hear their phone calls or voices broadcast throughout the city. The program's popularity during its four years is a broader sign of the desire among urban Nepalis to communicate in public with their friends and family abroad. Listeners of *Rumpum Connection* commended the program because, they said, it enabled them to speak *for free* to their relatives abroad. The callers largely consisted of a growing consumer class that is increasingly dependent on the remittance economy and the forms of consumption this new wealth enables.[5] If the calls appear to be gifts from Kantipur FM, they mask the ways in which the program constitutes, circulates, and publicizes the social relations that enable this transnational consumer economy to flourish. The program goes further in actually cultivating desires for further consumption and public conversation as it seems to ease the personal and familial losses upon which this consumer economy depends.

As on *Mero Kathā, Mero Gīt*, rarely did the conversations on *Rumpum Connection* discuss political subjects. Instead, they centered on personal and familial affairs that do not immediately appear political. This may be due to the government restriction that forbids FM programs from engaging in public discussions of religion or politics, as well as the government ordinance in October 2005 that made it illegal for any media program to speak directly against the monarchy. In spite of the personal nature of the calls, the program is clearly a politically charged arena that produces "Nepaliness," first by creating the distinct categories of urban, at-home Nepalis and the Nepali diaspora, and then by seeming to unite these Nepali subjects within a broadcast of the program itself. The political and economic context in which this Nepali diaspora emerges is important to briefly outline, since it helps reveal the political implications of radio conversations that often appear to be without any direct political content.

Travel to and from Nepal, accompanied by many years of work in other lands, has been a vital part of Nepalis' lives for over two centuries. The nature of this travel, the kinds of work pursued, and the people's relation to Nepal as a nation-state within the context of travel abroad, of course, have changed in different times. As many scholars of the South Asian diaspora have argued, colonialism—specifically, the institutions of indentured labor—set the context for the vast number of migrations from the subcontinent, creating categories like "migrant," "overseas South Asian communities," and "people of South Asian descent living outside South Asia" (Axel 1996; Chatterjee 2001; Shukla 2003; Van de Veer 1995). Though Nepal was not an official colony of the British, colonial systems in British India also became the context in which Nepalis moved across borders. After the Anglo-Nepali Treaty of Sagauli in 1816, which set the current borders of Nepal as a nation-state, a significant number of agriculturally based Nepalis left their villages to escape the new taxes (converted from payment in kind to cash after this treaty) in search of work in British India (Hutt 1998). Many of these Nepalis traveled eastward toward Northeast India, Bhutan, Assam, and Darjeeling to work on tea plantations or as laborers, and still today there are many Nepalis in Nepal who will marry people residing in these regions (Chatterjee 2001; Hutt 1998). These Nepalis tended to stay in India for many generations, becoming "Indian Nepalis" and seeing themselves as distinct from other Indians and from Nepalis in Nepal (Subba 2001). More fortunate Nepali villagers left Nepal throughout the nineteenth century and into the twentieth to become the famed "Gurkha soldiers" (or *lāhures*) in the British Army (Caplan 1995; Des Chene 1993). In addition to the many Nepali villagers who pursued work abroad, elite Nepalis from Kathmandu often traveled to India for education throughout the late nineteenth century and early twentieth, and frequently returned with nationalist sentiments for Nepal inspired by the anticolonial nationalism they encountered in India.[6]

While Nepalis have been traveling abroad for two decades, it would be a misnomer to group them together as a "Nepali diaspora." Either as soldiers, migrant workers, or those traveling for an education, these different Nepalis did not maintain much contact among themselves *as Nepalis* who shared a mutual connection to the nation of Nepal. Sandhya Shukla (2003) points out that movement to and from the diaspora must be distinguished both from immigration (a one-way, permanent move to another nation) and from migration: "If migration describes movements of peoples and ideas that have constituted subjects in the eyes of the (national) law . . . then diaspora conjures forth a form of belonging that is global" (2003: 13). The point is not to define a migrant as fundamentally distinct from those who live in the diaspora. A single person might claim to be part of a diaspora *and* to be a migrant. But in using these different concepts, we evoke a distinct set of ideas and sentiments. Migration tends to focus primarily on patterns of work and movement that constitute subjects through state laws, whereas diaspora forces us to contend with the relations of affect, temporality, and global belonging that stretch across national borders. Technologies like radio and telephone, as well as the Internet, of course make possible these affective and temporal ties to home that appear to link disparate Nepalis together.

Diaspora—a word that stems from the root "dispersal"—must include a minimum of two different destinations from which different groups of people connect to one another and their national homeland (Butler 2001: 192). Most studies of diaspora focus especially on people's relation to place, with an emphasis on the "place of origin." As Brian Axel points out, the emphasis on place unwittingly contributes to "an essentialization of origins and fetishization of what is supposedly to be found at the origin (for example, tradition, religion, language, and race)" (2002: 411). Implicitly or explicitly, this attention to place of origin aims to reveal a particular *diasporic identity*. While studies of diaspora seek to problematize narratives of nationalism by including nationalists who reside *outside* the homeland, the conflation of place with identity paradoxically has the effect of reinscribing the significance of territory to national imaginings.

A specifically diasporic identity has been emerging among Nepalis around the world, and much of this identity is informed, at least partially, by a mutual connection to place. My emphasis is not on describing this identity or discussing the explicitly political program of Nepalis abroad (see Hangen forthcoming). Drawing upon Axel's work, I suggest instead that the cultural category of diaspora emerges through the temporality and relations of affect produced on media like FM radio. Conversations over the telephone on *Rumpum Connection,* for example, generate a temporality of simultaneity as well as affective connections through which urban Nepalis and the Nepali diaspora converse and appear present to one another. Technologies of voice obscure this process and project a fantasy of presence and immediacy that

FIGURE 14. Father blessing his eighteen-year-old daughter before she leaves to work in Dubai through a Manpower Agency. Photo: Daniel Karpowitz.

enables newly constituted subjects to imagine themselves "connecting" through the radio and the telephone.

The emergence of a Nepali diaspora has been heavily influenced by state agendas. Over the past decade, the Nepali state has actively encouraged Nepali citizens to pursue work outside the country, in part because the national economy increasingly depends upon remittances sent from abroad. Since the mid-1980s, the Nepali state has entered into contracts with other states through foreign employment agencies—colloquially known as "manpower agencies"—to send Nepali laborers to foreign countries.[7] For a fee incurred by the Nepali citizen (which can be as high as 80,000 rupees [$1150] and much more when taking into account additional moving expenses), the agencies interview, select, and ultimately arrange to send a specified number of workers to a particular job abroad with official work visas. Often the agencies find ways to circumvent the Ministry of Labour for additional fees, thereby shortening the process but also making these laborers "unofficial" (Seddon, Adhikari, and Gurung 2001: 69). (See figure 14.)

Stories abound about the large-scale corruption, bribery, and deception carried out by the manpower agencies in Kathmandu. One of the most traumatic incidents that involved a manpower agency's deception occurred in late

August 2004 when twelve Nepali laborers, who were initially sent to Jordan by Moonlight Manpower Agency, were captured and killed by the militant group Ansar Al-Sunna after being redirected to Iraq.[8] The mediation of this tragic killing abroad, through videos of the killing circulated over the Internet and graphic newspaper reports, became the ground upon which to critique political and economic hardships inside Nepal. Heated Nepali protesters in Nepal and around the world used these deaths abroad to address ills at home: government failures and the corruption of manpower agencies. The Nepali diaspora emerges as a social category through its mediation here, becoming an integral part of public life in Kathmandu that is called upon to further clarify and discuss local and national tensions.[9]

RUMPUM CONVERSATIONS

The state's endorsement of its citizens' movement abroad points to some of the unique features of the diaspora that arose on *Rumpum Connection*. Callers on *Rumpum Connection* ranged from migrant villagers living in Kathmandu to middle-class Kathmandu families. Given that the vast majority of requests were for calls to Malaysia or to the Gulf—where currently the least-educated Nepali laborers are employed through manpower agencies—most callers are clearly not part of the political or cultural elite (Gurung 2000). Unlike NRNs (Non Resident Nepalis), who have "made it" in another country, the diasporas that arise from manpower employment consist of neither the poorest villagers nor the wealthiest professionals. Nepalis in these diasporas have managed to get just enough cash together to leave the country, harboring dreams of achieving middle-class respectability and a prospective comfortable life *in Nepal*. Such diasporic fantasies are implicit in many *Rumpum* conversations, which, in many ways, can be seen as extensions of state interests.

The idea for *Rumpum Connection* itself emerged from transnational flows of people and language. The program was conceived of by the only British manager of Kantipur FM, after he heard a similar program broadcast in London. The program's host, a young, energetic woman named Anamika, explained that she and another young man were first chosen for the program because they could understand and speak good English. After a year, Anamika became the sole host of the program. "You don't know if the person who answers the phone will speak Nepali," she told me, in a mix of Nepali and English, typical of most young, educated Nepalis. "I need to be able to speak English so I can *reach* the Nepalis abroad."

According to Anamika, the program was explicitly conceived of as a "Nepali space" that transcends the political borders of the nation-state. But the fact that only subjects within Nepal heard *Rumpum* conversations suggests that the program actually reinforced the territorial claims of the nation-state. Phone calls spanned across the globe primarily to family members, but also to girlfriends, boyfriends, and simply good friends. Since many Nepalis abroad live with other Nepalis, if the requested person is not at home, often the caller would simply converse with a person he or she had never met. As Anamika explained to me, she *never* entertains phone calls between Nepalis and non-Nepali foreigners living abroad. The main premise of the show, Anamika reported, was to cultivate ties between Nepalis around the world. "There are a lot of Nepalese people around the world, but even so, we are not able to reach them. Therefore, why should one converse with foreigners? Very many numbers of foreigners come [to this program]. But I cut those out. I don't honor those. Those are not allowed. It's not really that foreigners are not allowed, but there are a lot of people, Nepalese people, around the world who want to talk. . . . 'Instead, speak with another Nepali,' I tell people."

The program brings forth the categories of Nepaliness, a Nepali voice, and a Nepali diaspora voice as it implies the need for radio and telephone to materialize these social relations. The national premise of the program suggests that it might be considered a quintessential example of long-distance nationalism (Glick Schiller and Fouron 2001).[10] Yet, despite its attempt to create a virtual "Nepali space," *Rumpum Connection,* unlike other forms of long-distance nationalism, did not engage a diasporic subject reaching *back* toward the homeland; instead, it publicized Nepali subjects in Kathmandu reaching *out* toward the diaspora and ostensibly bringing those voices of diasporic Nepalis' *back.*[11] The diaspora, the Nepali voice, and sense of Nepaliness are effects of *Rumpum Connection,* which make Nepalis who are dispersed around the world appear like ghostly presences within Kathmandu.

A vast majority of *Rumpum* conversations were spent envisioning who exactly is listening in Kathmandu and who is sitting beside the speaker abroad. The speakers indicate the public nature of the program by referring to invisible but known listeners, and by implication to other listeners both potential and anonymous. At the same time, direct reference to relatives and personal friends seems to subvert the publicness of the conversation, enclosing it within already familiar intimates. In most conversations broadcast on *Rumpum Connection*, there is an explicit tension between the host's wish to emphasize the public format of the program, and the personal, domestic, and familial forms of the speakers' conversations.

Consider the following *Rumpum* conversation between Anup and his older female relative, Meena, who lives in Canada.[12] After Meena initially tried to establish exactly where Anup was calling from, Anamika, the host of the program, interrupted and explained: "Meenaji, this is being broadcast over the radio. Everyone can now hear your conversation. If you have anything to say from your side, you may say it."

> ANUP: *Didī* [older sister], *māijuharu* [uncles' wives] are listening upstairs…
>
> MEENA: Oh really? *Dāi* [older brother] and *bhāuju* [sister-in-law/his wife] are listening?
>
> ANUP: *Māmā* [maternal uncle], my oldest *māmā*, went out to the fields and mommy is not here. She went to Balaju. But *māiju* and Ananda are listening upstairs.

A few minutes later, their conversation falls into a lull and Anamika urges Anup to continue talking. Anup returns again to describing who is listening and Meena continues to envision the scene of listening.

> MEENA: And Sambhu? (referring to another relative)
>
> ANUP: Sambhu is over there listening to the radio. He doesn't want to talk. He's listening at Arav's place.
>
> MEENA: Why not?
>
> ANUP: He's over there listening.

Anamika interrupts and again tries to explain the public nature of their exchange, saying, "He's too shy to speak on the radio."

> ANUP: My younger brother is shy, but not me.
>
> MEENA: Arav is also there?
>
> ANUP: Yes, Arav is also listening over there. La, say something to Arav.
>
> MEENA: Arav—we also remember you. We remember your mommy and daddy. Send [us] an email sometime.

Anup then attempts to conjure up the scene from which his *didī* is speaking.

ANUP: Is uncle [referring to Meena's husband] there?

MEENA: Yes, he is here.

ANUP: Let me talk to uncle.

One striking feature of this and many *Rumpum* conversations is the profoundly domestic setting and content of the talk, as listeners try to imagine their relatives listening inside their homes. Conversations are replete with references to everyone in the home and where they are listening, from both within Nepal and abroad. The sense of affect, intimacy, and interiority of the conversation is based on a spatial model of interiority (rather than a model of interior consciousness), in which little outside the home or domestic setting is discussed. The home often serves as an apt metaphor for sentiments of the nation, and in South Asia, this has been a trope of anticolonial nationalisms (for example, Chakrabarty 2000; Chatterjee 1993; Tagore [1916] 2005). While the political implications of this may not be directly obvious to listeners or the host, the domestic and interior settings of the conversations no doubt add to the overall sense of national affect that the program cultivates.

It is worth noting that this conversation is typical in its preoccupation with identifying the invisible listeners by name and relation. The constant references to who is listening are a way for those Nepalis abroad to become part of the urban space of Kathmandu, marking their presence and subjectivity in a field where they are otherwise invisible. If naming is form of "hailing" (Butler 1997), then to call out a name interpellates that person into a given social space, in this case, into the world of the family, the diaspora, and urban Nepal. Through interpellation, Meena emerges as a subject who is Nepali and a member of a particular family, yet also, as part of the diaspora, a subject who is simultaneously included and excluded from these social worlds. In naming and locating these silent listeners, callers bring forth and constitute an invisible and affective public as *really there*. This process establishes a relationship between the diaspora and urban Nepalis that becomes a vital part of the urban publics established through FM radio.

MATERIAL AND TRANSPARENT VOICES

Anamika told me that she thought the possibility of reaching many family members at once—and especially the possibility of hearing their loved one's voice together—was one of the program's great appeals. There is something particularly evocative about hearing a loved one's *voice,* not just over the telephone, but circulated widely over the radio. "Everyone wants to hear the voice of everyone else," Anamika suggested. She continued to explain why: "How are they? What is going on? Because from the voice one can figure out many things: Whether that person is happy or not. How it is there. What is there. All of the family has the opportunity to listen at the same time. If I'm the one person speaking, and if the radio is on, then everyone else can hear that person's voice. Whatever conversation is going on—it's very transparent. Everyone can listen to it."

The voice is viewed here as an index and measure of a person that can be easily interpreted, indicating their personal satisfaction or discontent. The sound of the voice, Anamika suggests, registers one's internal state, bringing those interior feelings out into the public where "everyone else can hear that person's voice." The figure of the voice also creates a sense of immediacy and direct connection, which Anamika refers to as "transparent," a quality largely made possible by electronic technology like the radio and telephone (Kittler 1999; Morris 2002; see also chapter 3). The materiality of the voice that Anamika refers to is frequently spoken of directly by FM listeners, who refer to the voice as a material thing transported over great distances through the radio waves or telephone wires. One woman, for example, began and ended her conversation on *Rumpum Connection* by profusely thanking the "FM family" for allowing "my phone and my voice to reach Nepal" *(Mero fon ra swar Nepalmā pugyo).* The sense of the materiality of the voice may be closely tied to a lower-class position (see chapter 3), which suggests who is speaking in *Rumpum* conversations.

While the discourse of transparent government is not explicit in Anamika's reference to the transparent voice on *Rumpum Connection,* it is clear that she and her listeners are drawing on a broader understanding of the voice among a wide audience of FM listeners. The "voice" and "transparency" are both used to describe better governance and a form of political agency that enables civilians to participate in politics and speak against the state. As William Mazzarella points out, "the desire for immediacy ha[s] become embedded in contemporary hypermediated governmentality" (2006: 500). Ironically, then, "immediation" (Mazzarella 2006) is pursued through elaborate systems of mediation, such as the FM radio, the telephone, and the technology necessary to facilitate connection between these two networks. As in discussions about political transparency, the voice serves as the locus and medium associated with direct, unmediated expression. The transparency on

FM entertainment programs invokes spatial and emotional presence that is frequently attributed to the sound of the voice.[13]

Recall the powerful figure of Kalyan's sonic voice that we encountered in the previous chapter, which I argued was key to the creation of an affective public. "Your melancholy voice tells someone's real life story, in which there is a little bit of pleasure and a little bit of happiness," writes one fan of *Mero Kathā, Mero Gīt* (My story, my song). "When I hear those words in your voice, it seems as if you are really crying, or as if you are feeling pleasure."[14] The very notion of reality and authentic emotion that this woman describes strikingly depends upon the appropriate representation and prosodic features of a voice that will adequately convey "a real life story." In this and many other letters, listeners describe the material and sensuous quality of the voice as the raison d'etre of their listening, the invocation that calls them to participate in FM programs. In *Rumpum Connection*, too, it is also the powerful sound of the voice—not the host's voice but the voice of intimates and family—that calls people to participate with the program. From these voices, suggests Anamika, the reality of the diaspora becomes affectively real and present within Kathmandu.

Rumpum Connection helps to create what Brian Axel calls a "diasporic imaginary" within Kathmandu. The diasporic imaginary is a social process that constitutes a specific diasporic community, not primarily through a relationship to place, but through formations of temporality and affect (2002: 412).[15] The circulation of public conversations on *Rumpum Connection* effectively makes the diaspora and urban Nepali subjects appear to be already-established social entities, linked together in this performance of intimate attachment between Nepalis in Kathmandu and abroad. The diasporic imaginary produced on *Rumpum Connection* is different than Axel's example of the Sikh diaspora, not only in content, but also, and primarily, because it engages those *not living in the diaspora*. The *diasporic imaginary* shows how important the context of the diaspora is for those who may never leave Kathmandu.

Anamika believed that so many people are interested in hearing these personal conversations between familial intimates because it gives them information on what it is like to live and work abroad, and reminds them of their own connections with Nepalis overseas. Listeners I talked with thought the program was primarily about communicating with relatives or friends, and the conversations I heard always centered on family affairs and events in Nepal. They only discussed what it is like to live abroad in the most general terms. If the program's content does not discuss life in the diaspora explicitly, its form does work to establish the existence of a Nepali diaspora, presenting it as fundamental to Kathmandu life. Disparate voices produced through the FM program are considered "Nepali" voices separated around the world. Condensed into a single hour, these "voices of the diaspora" are presented as connected yet distinct from those listeners in Kathmandu. In this sense, as Anamika surmised, the program reminds people of their own connections with Nepalis overseas and, in the process, constitutes the Nepali diaspora as a spatially separate yet integral part of Kathmandu public life.

LIVENESS AND TEMPORAL SIMULTANEITY

During our interview at the FM office, Anamika drew attention to the fact that *Rumpum Connection* was live, emphasizing its ephemeral qualities: "You have to be very quick. Because with a live show, this is the difficult part. You cannot edit. Once it goes on it's gone." Anamika felt her most important role in this program was to become an on-the-spot editor and censor, who listened carefully for provocative questions about the government and especially about the king. She claimed that the program's "liveness" was crucial to its success. In these brief live conversations broadcast on air, Nepalis separated across the world seem to exist, momentarily, together at the same time. On programs like *Rumpum Connection*, temporal simultaneity is fundamental to the programs' creation of a shared space of Nepaliness.

Liveness was a key feature of FM radio that initially distinguished it from Radio Nepal and, as I noted in chapter 3, contributed to the overall media ideology of directness and transparency associated with FM radio. The scene projected by live broadcasts is one in which the radio host and listeners appear physically distant from one another but are nevertheless talking to each other at the same time. The "liveness" of FM broadcasts encodes a temporality that is immediate and instant, in which individualized subjects are brought into simultaneous and intimate "connection" via the apparent miracle of broadcast technology. The constitutive links between the technology, its temporal features, and the subjects it invokes are obscured by this fantasy of copresence. This is particularly appealing in a program that attempts to bring together Nepalis in the urban capitol with Nepalis living abroad.

Live programs, according to some radio hosts, also seem to add to FM programs' authenticity. One radio host from Radio City FM 98.8, Uma, clearly distinguished her program, *Jindagi ka Āyamharu* (Dimensions of life), from other similar programs by claiming that she *always* broadcast her program live. Compared to the more long-standing program *Mero Kathā, Mero Gīt* (My story, my song), discussed in chapter 4, Uma declared that her program was more "real" and more direct.

"Kalyan sometimes records his reading [of listeners' letters], I know he does," Uma told me, as if she were revealing something she thought Kalyan would rather not be known. "Do you know how I know? I sometimes hear the whir from the tape recording machine over the air."

"Why does that make a difference?" I asked Uma, curious about this particular contrast.

"If you read it live," Uma explained, "you give all the feelings *as if you were there with the person*. People tell me this: 'I feel that you are with us.'" A live program produces temporal simultaneity between the radio host and their listeners, making them feel as if "you [the host] are with us." This temporality is subverted, according to Uma, in a recorded program when one hears the hissing of a machine. Recording a live program as it plays did not present a problem for Uma, though. She recorded every program and kept these cassettes at home, "in case anyone wishes to hear them again."[16]

The potential for both live and recorded live programs—particularly those based on phone calls or listeners' letters—enhances the self-recognition and self-distancing effects of the media (Mazzarella 2004: 357). By hearing their own letters read through the radio host's voice or their voice mediated through the radio machine, listeners come to recognize themselves and their words reflexively, as if from a distance (see chapter 3). The self-distancing aspect is doubled in *Rumpum Connection* conversations. On the one hand, there is the spatial distance that defines a diaspora and, on the other hand, there are the effects of the technology (radio and telephone) that create and simultaneously seek to subvert the spatial distance through the temporal simultaneity of a live broadcast.

The reflexive circulation of a public's discourse by reading fan letters or referring to other moments of consumption (like in the conversation quoted above) creates new ways of organizing time, a temporality marked by punctuality rather than by a continuous stream of time (Warner 2002: 66). This punctual temporality divides the day into distinct segments of listening hours and then combines with the live broadcasting of FM radio to create the "flow" (Williams 1974), the ephemeral nature of broadcasting that conveys the here and now. People experience the ephemeral "thinning of time" as a loosening of social controls, argues Arvind Rajagopal, while also evoking "feelings of closeness and reciprocity to unknown participants who may exist only in imagination" (2001: 5). In particular, electronic media, like television and radio, seem to have the capacity to subvert or reach beneath political or cultural constraints and reveal underlying, essential truths of politics, society, personhood, and emotion. In discussions about the potential of media itself, everyday and face-to-face social and cultural practices appear to be the most mediated and inauthentic forms of interaction. The temporality that the radio medium encodes, particularly in "live" broadcasts like *Rumpum Connection,* provides the conditions for people to experience radio conversations as *unmediated* transactions.

But simultaneity is never fully achieved. "Noise" from the phone call abroad frequently interferes with the fantasy of presence and simultaneity generated by the radio and phone. Because the program is broadcast at noon in Kathmandu, Nepalis who live abroad receive their calls in the middle of the night. One can often *hear* the differences in time through their groggy voices and yawns. "How is your son? Is he asleep?" one caller asked his cousin, who resided in North America. "Yes, of course," she replied, "it's 3 A.M.!"

Because Nepal uses a non-Roman calendar, quite often the failure of temporal simultaneity centers on the differences in dates. "I will go with my daughter to Jhapa[17] on Magh 15," a husband tells his wife. His wife responds with some confusion: "Magh is very far away. But what is today's date anyway? Today is November 1 over here, what day is it over there?" These intrusions subvert the intended portrayal of simultaneity on the live broadcasts, accentuating the temporal and spatial divides that separate the speakers, a separation that is the basis of technological communication and that technology then aims to "bridge."

The desire for temporal simultaneity through a live conversation eventually led to the downfall of *Rumpum Connection.* I assumed that the reason the program had stopped had to do with difficulties that ensued at Kantipur FM after King Gyanendra's coup in February 2005. But Anamika corrected me, explaining that the real problem had to do with technological issues and the fact that they often could not reach the correct person overseas during the hour of broadcast. Sometimes the program would be temporarily shut down due to load shedding, when certain parts of the city lost all their power and the FM stations had to rely on a generator. If they were on the telephone with someone overseas, it was often very difficult to reconnect that call. More often than not, though, the problem was that the designated recipient of the phone call abroad was not at home. Their absence heightened the fact that these Nepalis lived in different spaces, and particularly in different time zones. Despite being told by their relatives that the phone call would be coming from Kantipur FM at a particular hour, the timing did not always translate well. Nepal's time is fifteen minutes ahead of India, and both India and Nepal are off the global standard time set by Greenwich Mean Time. Thus calculating the hour of the phone call was never simple. Anamika summed up the reasons for the program's demise: "Technology was difficult and basically our timing was often off." Temporal simultaneity and the illusion of "presence" relied upon technology that could not achieve its task.

TECHNOLOGICAL PHATIC

Perhaps the failure of complete simultaneity is one reason why so many conversations on *Rumpum Connection* centered almost exclusively on the various media—letters, emails, telephone calls—through which the speakers imagine they will or have "connected." In a context where electronic recording technologies have become hegemonic, Rosalind Morris suggests that a common wish is to achieve "a transmission so pure that it requires no medium" (2002: 383). Morris writes of the Thai fantasy of spirit mediums that are thought to be so powerful that their voice can be heard without incarnating within a human body. Ironically, in everyday conversations on FM radio, the emphasis on different technological media actually reinforces the seemingly pure transmission and "contact" enabled by technology. Like Thai spirit mediums, many FM conversations frequently center exclusively on the sheer fact that this elusive "connection" can occur at all.

Roman Jakobson's analysis of the six functions of speech helps us understand the social importance of immediacy and why listeners' enchantment with the medium itself appears so often in their conversations on FM radio. In order to relay a message over the radio or in any conversation, a speaker must convey a referent and a context that the listener can grasp; they must share a lexical code; and they must be able to make contact through "a physical and psychological connection [which] . . . enables both of them to enter and stay in communication" (Jakobson 1987: 66). Speech that centers on this ability to make contact is what Jakobson, following Malinowski, refers to as the "phatic" function of language. Phrases like "how are you?" and "you know?" are often used simply to prolong communication without exchanging any information (see Jakobson 1987; Malinowski 1953).

Consider a standard exchange on an FM call-in show during its early days:

HOST: Hello, do you hear me?

CALLER: Yes, I hear you. Hello.

HOST: Where are you calling from?

CALLER: I'm calling from Baneswar.

HOST: And you're name?

CALLER: I'm Raju from Baneswar.

HOST: Okay, Rajuji, have you eaten rice?

CALLER: Yes, I've eaten. And you?

HOST: Yes, I've eaten, eaten. And what would you like to say, Raju *dāi?*

CALLER: I like your program very much. And I would like to say hello to my sisters and friends. Okay—I'm putting [the phone] down.

HOST: Goodbye, a big thanks for calling.

This typical conversation functions primarily in the "phatic mode." The actual information these two speakers share is minimal. Their exchange centers on checking whether the channel of communication clear: "Hello, do you hear me?" "Yes, I hear you. Hello." Both host and caller repeat a common colloquial greeting, "Have you eaten rice?" *(Bhāt khānubhayo?),* which seems to ask for specific information, but in fact is a phrase used to begin a conversation or simply to establish contact between acquaintances passing each other on the street. It is inflected with a sense of familiarity and habitual meeting. Such conversations resemble the kinds of conversations frequently heard on trains in the United States when passengers instinctually reach for their cell phones "just to connect."

I learned that phatic speech is especially important when beginning a conversation with most Nepalis outside the media context. I recall being reprimanded once by one of my close friends, who told me that I always began conversations too fast. "You can't just come in here and start talking right away," she told me, with a little laugh. "First, you have to come in, ask *"bhāt khānubhyo?"* and tell what time you ate, and other things. That's the way we talk." Phatic phrases figure centrally in metalanguage about proper speech; they are part of a shared language ideology about how to gradually and politely approach conversation. It may be that the evisceration of phatic speech on many more recent and scripted FM programs is what contributes to the media ideology of directness associated with FM radio (see chapter 3).

In between the phatic phrases quoted above, the radio host attempts to identify the caller through two key indicators of place ("where are you calling from?") and name ("what is your name?"). Both of these questions transform an anonymous voice into a particular person with a social identity ("I'm Raju from Baneswar"). At the same time, the question "where are you calling from?" may also work to veil the fact that true temporal simultaneity is impossible. It draws listeners' attention to the stated spatial distance between host and caller, and in so doing callers engage in a fantasy of presence by repeating the simple fact that they can "connect" through the telephone and the radio.

By referring to the various channels of communication, phatic speech draws attention to the voice as a *mediating tool* of social relations. Such discourse becomes the link between technology and voice by highlighting, in a single phrase, the concurrent mediation of the two mediums (voice and radio). The phatic speech that characterizes much talk on call-in FM radio programs becomes a marker of coeval presence between the radio host and listeners that appears to be neutrally facilitated by the channels of voice and radio. Drawing attention to the medium of contact may at first glance seem to subvert the fantasy of copresence, which rests on an ideal of unmediated, direct communication. But I would argue the opposite: the emphasis on the "channels of communication" actually turns one's focus *away* from the specific material and mediating properties of the voice and the radio, presenting them as neutral media that simply facilitate connection between two or more speakers and allow them to feel, in the words of one radio host, "as if we are all together." This presumed neutrality relates to broader ideologies of voice and FM radio as two media of directness.

On *Rumpum Connection,* the various media that course through any given conversation invoke the speakers' relation to Nepal and to the diaspora, for themselves as well as for the listening public. Conversations that often begin with "Did you receive that email? or "Have you spoken on the phone to so-and-so?" reiterate the fact that Nepalis in Kathmandu and abroad seem to "connect" through technology, without directly referring to the content of those messages. Such frequent references to the various media of communication might be thought of as "technological phatic" speech. The excess of phatic speech on *Rumpum Connection* reveals the mediating qualities of the voice that are simultaneously obscured by the sense of presence and immediacy. Phatic speech also becomes a poignant expression of intimacy. Using technological phatic speech, *Rumpum* callers draw attention to the media through which they communicate between Kathmandu and the diaspora, as they construct a dialogue that is largely about contact itself.

Here is an excerpt from a conversation broadcast on *Rumpum Connection* between Indira, a Nepali woman working in Israel, and a male relative, Purosattam, presumably her husband, in Kathmandu, which illustrates the use of technological phatic speech.[18] Particularly striking in this exchange is the overlap between the visual and the voiced in the conversation, as speakers try to picture their loved ones on the other end of the line. After the requisite statement of their names, the conversation begins with Indira asking about her young daughter, whom she eventually talks to on the phone.

PUROSATTAM: Is everything okay there?

INDIRA: Everything is fine. How is everything there? How is my daughter?

PUROSATTAM: She is listening right now. I told her that her mother's phone would come here today. She's sitting right here.

INDIRA: Oh ho! How happy am I! A big thank you to Kantipur FM, from my side.

PUROSATTAM: I want to thank them too. Did you get the email? Ritu called me from America on the eleventh, and said, "I will call my *sāsu* [mother-in-law] in Israel." Did she call you or not?

INDIRA: She hasn't called. When are you going to call again?

PUROSATTAM: After three weeks.

Presumably, the content of that missed phone call was about money, as Indira switches the subject immediately.

INDIRA: Send money? How should I send money? Sending money involves many, many problems. What to do?

Purosattam quickly tries to change the subject away from money, perhaps avoiding such a personal subject on this public medium, and replies.

PUROSATTAM: First I will talk to my family, and then we will talk on the phone [about sending money].

INDIRA: You promise to call me on Saturday. I will wait all day at the phone.... Tell my well-wishers that I miss them a lot and remember them. Nobody sends any letters to me. I check the mailbox every day, and nothing comes. Everyday the mailbox is empty. I have looked everyday.

PUROSATTAM: Listen, listen, did the letter from Dangol reach you yet or not?

INDIRA: I received one letter only, the one of October 26, to which I replied. Did you receive that yet?

PUROSATTAM: That letter hasn't reached here yet.

A few minutes later, Indira asks to speak to her daughter, who has been sitting by the radio listening in. A little girl, probably between six and eight years old, gets on the phone.

DAUGHTER: What will you bring me from there?

INDIRA: Oh, pants, dolls, cloth, everything for my princess. . . . Did you receive anything from your father for Dashain?

DAUGHTER: Yes, shoes, clothes. That's all.

INDIRA: Take a photo of yourself and your father in your new Dasain clothes and send it to me.

This conversation, like many on *Rumpum Connection,* begins almost immediately with a discussion of money, the main reason Indira traveled to Israel and a key medium through which Nepalis abroad relate to their families in Kathmandu. The veiled and sometimes explicit discussions of money reveal the complex issues of class in this diaspora. Most callers on *Rumpum Connection* managed to get enough money to travel abroad, but once there, they become part of the vast laboring class, struggling first to pay their debts back home and then to earn enough to contribute to their family's income. As in many *Rumpum* conversations, the discussion of money indicates the failure of this medium to adequately "connect"—Indira only notes how difficult it is to send money.

The subject of money in *Rumpum* conversations simultaneously connotes the affection implied by sending money, and its use as a medium of intimacy between distant families. As Danilyn Rutherford (2001) has argued, the exchange of money does not only homogenize values and erode intimacies; it often serves as a vehicle of social identity and intimacy even among strangers in a market. Of course, when considered among family members this point seems obvious. In the context of an FM radio program, which is a form of consumer exchange, direct reference to the intimate connotations of money works in two ways. On the one hand, it refers to the broader consumer culture of FM radio and the affective public it creates, and on the other hand, it refers to money and other commodities sent as tokens of affection between

Nepalis in Kathmandu and abroad. With her daughter, Indira returns to the subject of commodities offered as evidence of intimate attachment, and asks for a photograph that depicts the father's affectionate giving on the national holiday of *Dasain*. Like their voices over the phone, the photo indicates that the daughter *is really there*. The indexical properties of the voice and a photograph create dreams of direct access to the person on the other line or the person pictured in the photograph.

But clearly too much talk about money is somewhat taboo, particularly in such a public setting as FM radio. As we have seen here, Purosattam quickly turns the conversation away from the exchange of money to the exchanges they engage in through other mediums: telephone calls and letters. Here again, the focus is on the possibility of "connecting" and its failure: "Did [Ritu] call you or not?" "She hasn't called." Or "Did you receive the letter from Dangol?" "I received only one letter . . . to which I replied. Did you receive it yet?" "That letter hasn't reached here yet." Even more poignantly, Indira remarks on her constant checking and disappointment at seeing an empty mailbox day after day.

Each medium has its advantages and disadvantages in achieving "contact." While the radio generates temporal simultaneity, letters delay contact and are often discussed in terms of a potential future. In another *Rumpum* conversation, a young man discusses the benefits and problems with chatting over the Internet. "Nowadays we cannot even do 'voice chat,'" the young man says to his cousin in North America. "Whenever I go online you are not there, and whenever you go online I'm not there." Little information is actually exchanged in these references to other technologies. Such technological phatic discourse evokes the pathos and affection of the program by highlighting the desire and possibility of "connection." Technological phatic speech, along with the spatial interiority of the conversation, draws in an audience of listeners who are not speaking on *Rumpum Connection,* providing the overall affective tone of national unity across borders.

Like many FM hosts, Anamika herself becomes a fetish of connection, a medium that is magically endowed with a special power to facilitate connection between people living far away. In this sense, Anamika is like the Thai spirit mediums referred to above. The difference is that Anamika is not a "voice without a body"; instead, she seems to embody the affective power of connection made possible through her program, and a voice that incarnates the various powers and possibilities produced by technology. Anamika told me that she frequently receives gifts—chocolate, perfume, jeans, bags, cards, decoration pieces for the home—from her listeners in Kathmandu and around the world. Sometimes listeners come to meet Anamika at the studio, as they do with many FM hosts. More often, however, as she explained, "It's only over the phone, and over the mail. That person hasn't seen me, and I haven't seen that person."

The form of attachment people express toward Anamika is somewhat different from the aura of a celebrity. It is assumed that listeners can and will enter into gift transactions with her in ways that strikingly resemble the acts and desires discussed on her program. As the callers discuss the emails and letters they write, the photos they hope to receive, or the telephone calls they are waiting for, they incorporate Anamika into these same exchanges. Like all radio broadcasts, these conversations are, importantly, *performances* to an invisible audience. As a fetish of connection, Anamika's very presence in the radio performances represents the forms of exchange that are expected to flow between the diaspora and Nepalis in Kathmandu, obscuring the process by which such social categories emerge on the radio.

MEDIATED SUBJECTS

As in many places, recent contests over political power in Nepal often involve gaining control over the media to communicate with subjects or citizens. Given the significance of "voice" and media in this context, the royal seizure of media on February 1, 2005, and the raid on Kantipur FM's studio in October 2005, which I discussed in previous chapters, are not at all surprising.[19] My interest throughout the book lies with the constitutive processes enacted by technology and other forms of mediation, rather than with the alignment of sides in the current political conflict. Most of the conversations explored here do not refer explicitly to the politics of the nation, but their forms of mediation and the meanings they generate register some of the national anxieties produced in Kathmandu during the mid-1990s and early 2000s. The sheer and persistent desire for "contact" and communication across borders, for example, when it may be taken away at any moment, is perhaps one key symptom of political and economic distress in Kathmandu at this time.

The emergence of a Nepali diaspora by way of technologies of the voice is a key feature of contemporary urban Nepali subjectivity. Echoing the presence of a "diaspora" in Kathmandu publics generated by programs like

Rumpum Connection, the Nepali diaspora is becoming a common subject of representation among Nepali intellectuals and writers.[20] As Nepal increasingly becomes a site of political instability and economic crisis, life abroad appears to offer the only promise of escape. Daily life in Kathmandu is riddled with numerous difficulties that require additional resources: during the dry months, there is so little water coming from the taps that those who can afford it buy water from private companies. Those who cannot buy water create elaborate storage facilities for water. During these same months, hydropower generates only a limited amount of electricity, creating the necessity for load shedding across the country, when electrical power runs only at select hours throughout the day in specified areas. Everyday tasks like bathing, doing laundry, cooking, and washing dishes become far more complicated work. Life in the diaspora seems to offer both financial resources to cope with these everyday difficulties and a refuge from them. Yet Nepalis in Kathmandu also are confronted with the extremes of material wealth associated with this promise and with stories about the difficulty of working abroad and the frequent encounters with brute oppression. The emergence of this diaspora occurs not primarily through attachment to place, but rather through specific temporalities and relations of affect, each of which is an effect of technological mediation.

Dreams of "contact" and the excess of phatic speech on FM programs both allay and express the contradiction between a desire to flee and the failed promises of the diaspora. More than this, it is in such moments of political and economic crisis that something normally concealed—the power of technology to create illusions of realness—is revealed through technological phatic speech. Unlike discourses that attempt to make a technological apparatus vanish so that "the voice" appears all the more real, this phatic discourse emphasizes the agency of technology involved in satisfying the seemingly antecedent desire for "connection." In technological phatic speech, subjects appear as individuals who exist prior to the broadcast or telephone call, whose needs and desires are met by the miraculous interventions of technology.

By looking closely at the form of radio and telephone, along with the discourses they produce, the voice can be seen more clearly as an effect of technology and a medium rather than only as a metaphor and seat of consciousness, agency, and intentionality. This formulation requires us to consider the materiality of the sonic voice—the lilts and tones that people refer to as particularly evocative—as well as the cultural and historical construct of "the voice" as a sign of transparency, emotional directness, and a key element in democratic discourse. It requires us to consider the overlaps of different media within any given technology of voice, and to ask how these overlaps are productive of the "voice" as well as of the subjects that the radio and telephone seek to represent. And finally, it requires us to consider the significance of diasporic voices that emerge as a ghostly presence in Kathmandu. This ghostly presence of the diaspora, constituted through technologies of voice, evokes a pervasive sense of what it means to be Nepali within urban Nepal today.

Royal Victims, Voicing Subjects

ROUGHLY A DECADE AFTER THE first *jana āndolan* (People's Movement), King Bir Birendra Bikram Shah Dev, Queen Aishwarya, and their entire immediate family were murdered. The massacre occurred on the evening of Friday June 1, 2001, during a family dinner party at the royal palace in the heart of Kathmandu, where ten members of the palace's inner circle were shot to death. Reports emerged in the days that followed declaring that Crown Prince Dipendra was the killer, who after single-handedly having murdered most of his family finally turned one of his many deadly weapons on himself. The official version of events held that the Crown Prince Dipendra, intoxicated on the drink and drugs he was known to consume, had quarreled yet again with his mother, Queen Aishwarya, about his desire to have an unarranged "love marriage" with Devayani Rana, over the Queen's objections. At the time (and still today), most Nepali citizens categorically rejected this widely circulated explanation of the murders. By the next morning, Nepal had become the center of an international media spectacle, with the event appearing immediately as major news headlines on the BBC, *The New York Times,* Indian national newspapers, and many other news media throughout the world.

Inside Nepal, on the morning after the massacre, all state media were shut down. Radio Nepal and Nepal TV were silenced. One friend, then a girl living in a far western village, told me that her father thought there was something wrong with the radio set and sent her to the store to buy new batteries. As they were to discover, the meaning of the technical "breakdown" was rather different, and they only learned the news of the disaster, like many of those living outside the Valley, through the Nepali-language BBC report at 9 A.M. the next day. Radio Nepal played solemn religious mourning songs,

FIGURE 15. Portrait of King Birendra and family that circulated widely after the massacre. Courtesy of Photo Concern.

and the government-controlled Nepal Television showed shots of Pashupathinath Temple, and images of Vishnu, reiterating the purported divine genealogy of the king. Virtually no daily papers were released.[1] Even the FM radio—a symbol of democratic "free speech"—played mourning music for days on end, framing the event as one of traumatic personal and national loss, suited only for the ineffable modes of music and ritual. Most Nepalis in Kathmandu learned about the incident via telephone calls, often from the diaspora, and rumors that reverberated throughout the city during the night. By Saturday morning, people clustered around Internet cafes to read reports from abroad and the web bulletins published by *Nepali Times* throughout the next day, since all satellite television transmissions were also blocked. Gyanendra Shah, the widely disliked younger brother of the murdered king, who had been conspicuously absent the night of the massacre, was hastily crowned king and conspiracy theories quickly circulated about his role in the murders.

Who, in this moment of silence, were the voicing subjects of Nepal?

. . .

I end with this unsettling and unresolved incident in Nepali history because the event juxtaposes so many of the themes of this book: the complex relationship between mediation, technology, and transparency; the politics of public intimacy and affective publics; the deep interconnection between personal subjectivity and the experience of having, raising, and losing "voice"; and the relation between genealogy and political subjectivity. The events at the royal palace and the swirl of mass mediation, uncertainty, censorship, and performance that emanated from it speak to the complex contradictions involved in an ongoing process of creating what I call voicing subjects.

The events of the massacre, including their mystifying mediation, represented a rupture on several levels. The initial terrifying silence about what happened in the palace provoked serious questions about the ability of ordinary Nepali citizens to know anything transparently through mass media, particularly when it concerned the palace. It was a shock to a social system that, since the liberal revolution of 1990, had become increasingly self-conscious about its freedom of speech and the often dizzying links between the powers of increasingly pervasive technologies of the voice and the liberation presumed of such agency. This disruption in the public sphere itself revealed and resonated deeply with a persistent discomfort that went to the heart of political subjectivity. The massacre at Narayanhiti palace and the rich context of both its censorship and its mediation revealed a profound tension felt by many between their position as national subjects of the king and their position as national citizens of a democratic state. This tension was particularly acute for journalists at the time and other participants in *nagarik samāj* (civil society) who self-consciously performed their subjectivity through acts of speaking in a social field characterized as both public and personal.

In her insightful analysis of the massacre, Genevieve Lakier quotes the words of Kapil Kafle, the chief editor of the daily paper *Rajdhani,* who reflects on the profound difficulty of speaking at that moment: "The problem was that, after the king had died and we found this out, that he had died, who could speak? Could we write simply that the king had died? Who could write this? Tell me! 'It was said that the king was dead': who can write that? . . . For those of us citizens inside the country, it was very hard" (quoted in Lakier 2009: 212). Kafle's words recall the speech of my former Kupondol landlord, whom we met at the beginning of this book. Recall that my landlord, as a member of the increasingly outspoken middle classes of Kathmandu, had condemned King Birendra as "crazy," linking a disorganized or unhealthy self with what the speaker considered to be an improper royal place within the national body politic or its constitution. Then, a few days later, the king acquiesced to a multiparty system, and my landlord expressed this momentous event as a watershed moment for speech, and for a new constitutional order in which speech and personhood emerge in tandem: *"balla, balla bolna sakchaũ"* (finally, finally, we can speak).

In the wake of the palace massacre eleven years later, Nepalis were faced again with a crisis over public speech. In an age characterized in part by the explosion of political, hotly contested, and frequently deeply personal public speech, the royalty reemerged in all of its past grandeur as a topic that could not be addressed; king and queen and the whole royal family were beyond the law and beyond the scrutiny of public speech and analysis. In contrast to the habitual censorship that defined the Panchāyat period, this time the state silence was all the more frightening and uncanny. It exposed an inability to handle the situation with the instruments of liberalized media, both of the state and privately held. As if to complete the complex irony of the situation, however, the return of the most heavy-handed censorship and the crisis in the public media were argued to be caused by the most intimate, personally idiosyncratic event that had ever linked the "private" lives of the royal family with the fate of the nation.

Who was to speak for the nation in this moment? Existing between the status of subject and citizen, how was one to voice oneself? As discussed in the introduction, changes in the political role of the king had been marked in the changing Nepali terms for "democracy" from *prajātantra*—which constituted "the people" as subjects of the king (*prajā,* "subject" of a ruler)— to *loktantra,* a term that invoked "the people" or "folk" *(lok)* rather than subject. In *loktantra,* national citizens are perhaps dissociated from their king, but only to be reconstituted by their relationship to an ethnic folk. While this could be a homogenized national "Nepali," it also could take on even greater power if located within a more local, deeply felt, and even separatist identity. These changing appellations for democracy register profound shifts in the relationship between speech and the nation. Who could speak in and to the public at this moment? Not the dead king, who had long been the sole speaker of the nation during Panchāyat times and retained the national role of unifier after democratic reforms. But neither could Nepali citizens, who increasingly saw themselves as speakers and active participants in democratic processes. Only the sounds of Hindu mourning songs reverberated through the televisions and radio broadcasts.

In discussing the figure of the voice throughout this book, we often turn to the theme of metalanguage, speech about language or speech itself. Speech, for Kafle and many throughout this book, is about being public and officially recognized through writing and the media. When Kafle asks, rhetorically, "who could speak?" he follows this question with his own reflections on writing for the press and the self-censorship that all journalists felt as Nepali citizens:[2] "who could write?" Clearly people were speaking at the time, but Kafle is not referring to the rapid circulation of rumors that spread through the nation.[3] The stunning poetic complexity of Kafle's plea reveals numerous subject positions and contested social dynamics at the heart of "voicing subjects." Kafle's passage is striking for its frequent repetition of metalinguistic speech that poignantly conveys the social dilemmas journalists faced: "Who could speak?" "Who could write that?" "Tell me!" "It was said that the king was dead." Like Anita in chapter 1 imagining her brothers' speech should the property reform law be passed or Lulu in chapter 4 imagining his father's words should his story be broadcast, these discrete moments of metalinguistic speech highlight the contest over different social positions and subjectivities—citizen, subject, brother, sister, father, son, media presenter, and audience—who are all defined through their relation to speech and the effect that others' speech has on them. *Voicing Subjects* argues that we ought to attend more closely to these moments when people talk explicitly about voice or speech, for it is here where we see social conflicts and diverse subjectivities at play. In Kafle's case, talk about speech is about what it means to be part of a public, and particularly the connection between the figure of the voice and one's position within the polity.

PUBLIC INTIMACY AND FAMILY AND NATIONAL GENEALOGY

The official story about the massacre being rooted in the crown prince's dispute with his mother and the public's reactions against this explanation reveal the largest and most garish possible staging of the public intimacy that I have traced throughout the book. Even as the official story about Prince Dipendra's failed love affair was uniformly dismissed by most Nepalis, it nevertheless called to mind changing ideas of marriage, inheritance, love, and intimacy that lay at the center of public reforms and discourse during the 1990s and early 2000s. The dispute Prince Dipendra allegedly had with his mother reiterated disputes that many young Nepalis have with their parents—or that they imagine having in the future—around the issue of romantic love and "love marriage" (Ahearn 2001). Indeed, the official narrative of the massacre converges remarkably with the popular, democratic fascination with narratives of individualized love frustrated by "cultural" conventions. Such conflicts are broadcast widely on FM radio programs and in programs like *Mero Kathā, Mero Gīt,* as well as in tabloids, weekly newspapers, television series, and films. The dominant representation of this event resonates with a pervasive theme of the popular media in the 1990s and early 2000s: namely, that love is a significant and desired form of democratic free speech. The alleged dispute between Prince Dipendra and Queen Aishwara ultimately was bound up with contested issues of agency, choice, and voice—specifically whose voice would determine a son's or daughter's future—that remain key issues animating many different publics in Kathmandu.

The official explanation of the killings echoes FM radio's motto about broadcasting "love not politics." It is difficult to say whether this official story represents the dramatic failure to separate "love" from "politics" or the apotheosis of doing so. For many Nepalis, the love narrative was nothing more than an attempt to use a fairy tale of precisely the sort one might hear on FM radio entertainment programs to conceal a hidden political truth about the motives of the new king, the army, or the omnipresent foreign intelligence agencies. In these widely circulated and popular interpretations, the familial drama was in fact a violent dynastic conflict, such as those that wracked the prior Rana regimes for generations. Dipendra should and would have become king, his beloved Devayani Queen. Intimate matters within the palace have always reverberated with the politics of the Nepali state.

The palace massacre may have hastened the already-shifting Nepali national genealogy, or as one book written about the incident declared, the event appeared at once to be the "end of a line" (Misra 2001). A cameraman for Nepal Television, who filmed Gyanendra's coronation, told me that he knew this reign was doomed when the newly crowned king entered the palace grounds in his processional as the clock tower struck 12 noon, a time that is said to be particularly inauspicious. Gyanendra's inauspicious coronation was followed, several years later, by his bungled attempt to seize power from the democratic government. The failed coup in 2005 (see chapter 3) provided much energy to fuel the *jana āndolan* in 2006, the toppling of the monarchy, and the declaration of a Nepali republic in 2008. The sentiment that many felt in the days after the Naryanhiti incident—that the massacre presaged the dissolution of the two-hundred-year monarchy in Nepal—proved to be correct.[4]

The royal massacre, with its eruption of familial passions, and the later dissolution of royal patrimony into a new republic bear uncanny echoes of the first major reform campaign after 1990, the conflict over *angsa,* family genealogy, and inheritance. Recall that the legal activists we encounter in chapter 1, who seem far from popular culture representations in their quest to secure property rights for daughters, advocated that a shift in this law would lead to more equitable, more compassionate, and more "authentic" marriages, ones based on love rather than economic dependence. While the conflict over *angsa* centered on daughters gaining a birth right to their parent's inherited property, it raised deeper issues about how this change would affect the entire family genealogy. Much of these concerns were expressed through the idiom of *bolāune*—the intimate callings of a brother to his sister, or his invitations home (literally, "to cause to speak")—which I argued laid a foundation for gendered subjectivity and its relation to state laws. In tension with the activists' liberal notion of *āwāj uṭhāune* (raising voice), *bolāune* presents a different paradigm of voice and self that aligns with a national genealogy that maintains the king at its apex.

Just as the legal reformers sought to dramatically change the gender relations that underwrote state inheritance law by keeping a traditional institution *(angsa),* so, too, did citizens critique the misuse of power and hierarchical social relations sustained by the palace by invoking their ongoing respect and grief for the murdered king.[5] In a nationwide wave of grief, tens of thousands of Nepalis shaved their heads and mourned for King Birendra, the leader who became beloved after his death, hailed as the king who had bowed to the popular liberalizing movement of 1990 and accepted a multiparty democracy. Nepalis in the Maoist army apparently performed public death rituals in King Birendra's honor.[6] Two days later, crowds of Nepalis from all walks of life carried photos of the dead king and queen, and wept together at the royal funeral. All of these mourning practices were quickly understood to also be forms of protest against the new king (see chapter 2).

The mass circulation of photographs of King Birendra and his family after the massacre played an especially important role in this public outcry against

King Gyanendra. During the funeral procession and cremation ceremony at Pashupatinath Temple, portraits of King Birendra and Queen Aishwara and photographs of King Birendra's whole family were carried by mourners and placed in public arenas throughout the city and nation, so that citizens could pay proper respect to the murdered royal family. Photos were also left at worship sites throughout the city for the fifteen days of official mourning.

The photos of King Birendra and his murdered family served two purposes that went beyond the devotional work of *darśan*. First, they highlighted the conflation between family and national genealogy, with the face becoming a medium through which political and intimate attachments were recognized and expressed. While the photos commemorated the king as king—upholding citizens' lower status as subjects of the king—they also facilitated the work of mourning one might engage in for a family member. Such photos became staples in many Nepali homes, integrated into household *pujā* corners where citizens could engage in *darśan* or a tactile connection with the dead king alongside other gods and dead relatives (see chapter 2). Second, public and household displays of King Birendra's photo became a means of political critique. Security forces immediately recognized the subversive nature of these photographs and raided shops selling pictures of Birendra or Dipendra (Rademacher 2010: 95). The striking absence of Gyanendra's photo in places other than the required state institutions and businesses revealed Nepali citizens' dissatisfaction with the palace.

The Narayanhiti massacre enabled a reaffirmation of a national public that Genevieve Lakier argues both remembered and forgot the king, recalling one monarch and condemning another in an outstanding show of national unity that this mysterious death was felt to threaten (by the palace, at least) (2009: 228). The martyred King Birendra became a key symbol of national sentiment; the dead king was all that the living King Gyanendra was not. The monarchy was appropriated to serve the democratic moment: valorizing the former king became a means of serious political critique of the palace.[7] In so doing, Nepalis could simultaneously validate overlapping forms of voice and subjectivity, that of loyal royal subject and that of democratic citizen.

MEDIATION AND TRANSPARENCY

The fury many Nepalis expressed toward the government and their suspicion of the army and surviving royal heirs speak to the third theme this book has addressed: the quest for transparency and its relationship to mediation. The profound public doubt of the official representation of the Narayanhiti event captures some of the complexities inherent in the vast growth, scope, and depth of the mass media and its publics during the democratic moment after 1990.[8] The emergence of this incident as a "media event" (Papailias n.d.) illustrates the relation between the growth in mass media and the quest for transparency that mass media generate.

Transparency has become a term ubiquitous across the world, signifying "good governance" and the ability to see the workings of power clearly. As Harry West and Todd Sanders have argued, the ideology of transparency is often paired with the related though seemingly opposite discourse of conspiracy. "Amid all this talk of transparency," they write, "many people have the sense that something is not as it is said to be—that power remains, notwithstanding official pronouncements, at least somewhat opaque" (2003: 2). Conspiracy and doubt are the alter egos of transparency; when there is a crisis in the ideology of transparency, as was the case after the palace massacre, conspiracy theories and rumors emerge as mainstream reason. In response to the shoddy representation of the massacre, Nepalis confronted the limits of the transparency that people aspired to during the eleven years of democracy—limits at the level of government corruption and of media representation—giving rise to a host of rumors and conspiracy theories that quickly circulated around the nation.

In his first official statement to the nation, King Gyanendra announced that there would be a commission to investigate what actually happened at the palace during the dinner party of June 1. The eventual Probe Commission produced a 140-page, minute-by-minute report of the fatal evening, which placed full and exclusive responsibility in the hands of Crown Prince Dipendra. The Probe Commission report was a state performance of the ideals of a transparent public sphere, in which the government ostensibly revealed the truths of the event it faithfully investigated to inform its citizenry. However, it came across as a mockery of a transparent process.[9] All Nepalis I talked with after the event felt that the government's minute-by-minute account of all the prince's movements and actions had substituted precision for accuracy about the event. The Probe Commission report used the formal qualities of a transparent document: a detailed narrative rendition of the evening, complete with maps of the scene of the crime marking where each person was killed, and a detailed description of all the weapons that were used. And yet, for everyone I spoke with, it was an empty form. The report revealed the power of details to obfuscate any reasonable explanation of what happened or the broader issue of the political motive that many felt underlay the murders (cf. Mazzarella 2006). More than this, the commission was received as a travesty, in which the ostensible transparency of a full-fledged democracy was not possible while the old royal and Panchāyat ways were absurd—and transparent—in their manipulations. They stand revealed, on the television screen, as liars and manipulators. According to most Nepalis, only the palace's attempt to hide the truth is clearly revealed through the Probe Commission. In this sense, the Probe Commission is a moment of true clarity, if not transparency.

Rumors proliferated. And each rumor was given more authority as it recirculated in newspaper articles, novels, and other literature that emerged in the aftermath of the event (Hutt 2012; Lecomte-Tilouine 2012). The press and the market for mass literature became forums for publicizing doubt, particularly about the palace (Hutt 2012; Lakier 2009; Lecomte-Tilouine 2012).[10] Interviews and stories by the citizens questioned the official account or offered thoughts about Dipendra's good character, even though the press never itself directly challenged the government's story (Hutt 2012).[11] Reversing the logic of voiced writing that I discussed in chapter 4, the widely circulating and anonymous rumors passed from person to person and voice to voice, and were touted by many as the most credible source of information. The press had to harness these rumors, creating what Marie Lecomte-Tilouine calls "written rumors" to assert their own legitimacy among their publics.[12] The movement between written and voiced form here, as in my discussion of voiced writing, suggests an important alliance between the written and the oral as two mutually constituting forms in many contexts of Nepali public life. Both appear implicit in the figure of the voice.

The rumors and conspiracy theories that circulated widely in the aftermath of the incident are undoubtedly an effect of a public constituted by mass media and the ideology of transparency, rather than the uniquely Nepali response that some foreign journalists suggested (Greenwald 2001; cited in Lakier 2009: 207). Such theories point to what Ann Stoler (1992) refers to as competing, diverse, and polarized "hierarchies of credibility." With fragmented knowledge about the event, people attempted to fill in the gaps with culturally reasonable conjecture. The hierarchies of credibility in this event reversed many existing authorities of knowledge discussed in this book—writing, FM radio, and state law—and thereby exposed the vulnerability of the press, the palace, and the government itself. In widely circulated (and often anonymous) emails and on blogs that appeared right after the event, the dominant sentiment became "we will never know," producing an ironic moment of national unification around the politics of disbelief (Lakier 2009).[13]

In this moment of crisis within the ideology of transparency, the mediated quality of all media became all the more clear, just as the sources of credibility shifted. As we have seen, particularly in the chapters on FM radio, there is a persistent contradiction between the ideology of transparency espoused by mass media and the very fact of mediation. In order to achieve transparency, something needs to be revealed—a secret, a life, something that provides an image of unobstructed and previously unknown knowledge. We have seen a celebration of mass media's potential to reveal previously unknown truths in FM radio programs, such as Kalyan's *Mero Kathā, Mero Gīt* when listeners wrote to him declaring that they had never told anyone their story before or when listeners celebrated the program for presenting "real," "true" stories. Public intimacy supports the will to transparency. In representations of the palace massacre, however, these ideals of transparency failed, and we see more clearly the mediated nature of all social relations, particularly, but not limited to, those that emerge through mass media.

Within the ideology of transparency, I have argued, there is a strong association between the direct conveyance of information and direct social relations, both of which appear to depend on mass media. Desire for the transparency of media and a tendency to obscure the mediated quality of all social life interestingly correlate with the assumed or aspired equality of all people and the emergence of an autonomous self in a democratic state. FM radio advertises itself as a place to reveal that which cannot otherwise be said and as a place that enables direct social connection that is otherwise impossible, because the other person or people live abroad (as discussed in chapter 5) or because social pressure makes it difficult for young couples or friends to meet. The revelation of intimate lives, secrets, sorrows, and social relations that seem unobstructed by cultural forces appears to be newly realized and realizable through new technology and mass media. The quest for transparency and unmediated social interaction therefore becomes the promise of a growing public sphere constituted through new media forms.

In light of these associations, it is interesting that among the most galvanizing evidence offered by the government's Probe Commission were Dipendra's calls to his beloved Devayani, made on his cell phone. According the Telecommunications Office and palace records, Dipendra called his lover only thirty minutes before the killings. In a compulsory interview from Delhi, after Devayani quickly left the country for "health reasons," the bereaved lover was forced speak to the public about something she called "personal" (Raj 2001: 75). Devayani repeated that her boyfriend's speech was slurred, and her published interview focused almost exclusively on the phatic nature of their conversation, the seeming failure of their connection: "He had called on my mobile phone and I could not hear very well. So I told him, 'I don't understand.' Then he hung up before I could answer" (cited in Raj 2001: 76). When asked if she found anything different in the crown prince, or if he seemed to be his usual self, Devayani replied: "His voice was slurred and as I said earlier he might not be [sic] feeling well" (cited in Raj 2001: 76). It is as if the media have not so much displaced as consumed the monarchy.

At the center of this ritual of exposure lies the "slurred voice" of the crown prince, a perfect metaphor for the broader historical moment in which this book is set. The voice, as I have argued throughout, is a leading figure of the political and intimate discourse in the years following the democracy movements in Nepal, its features revealing the complexities of the mediated subject in a moment of profound political and social transition. This has led me to several reflections on the materiality of the voice, its association with selfhood and sentiment, and the way the voice serves as an index of social origins and position. Dipendra's slurred speech might be read as a metaphor for the dissolution of the monarchy and its ability to hold and embody national identity. It also offers a fascinating and uncanny representation of the voice as an index of an individual young man "breaking down," reinforcing the idea of voice as the medium of the true self, even as it enacts its disintegration. As such, Dipendra's slurred voice stands in contrast to the voice of "Dear Kalyan," a master empathizer, whose voice homogenizes and refashions the dreams, sentiments, and conflicts of his listener-writers. In the wake of the palace massacre, Dipendra's slurred voice becomes evidence, a forensic fact submitted to the public by the government's official Probe Commission, in their attempts to determine the truth.

. . .

This ethnography takes its start from the connections that link contemporary democratic politics and distinctively public modes of intimacy. At the heart of the material lies a tension between the desire for directness and transparency and the dependence on processes of mediation to achieve "immediate" effects. In the wake of the royal massacre, the figure of the voice emerged as a solution to the corrupt and violent politics signified by the palace. Yet here as elsewhere, conflicting ideas of governance and subjectivity complicated the redemptive agency ascribed to the voice. Differing formations of the voice as encountered in practices of *bolāune* or *mukh herne* are not easily subsumed within liberal and neoliberal rubrics. This is in part due to their not being predicated on a direct identity between the voice and an autonomous self. By exploring these tensions, I have sought to show the power, limits, and interconnections across divergent notions of voice in the fields of democratic politics and public intimacy.

This book looks toward a theory of mediation that is as broad as possible. It associates mass media with other forms and practices that mediate and configure subjectivity. In each of the fields explored, from FM radio narration to a brother's hailing, the voice exemplifies processes in which we come to recognize ourselves through something or someone outside ourselves. This may lead us to reimagine the boundaries between the authentically human and the technologically mediated, as much as it reaffirms the intersubjective nature of the self. The voice is commonly interpreted as an index of self and desire. But it also appears as a medium outside of oneself, a prosthesis that can be recorded, broadcast, and circulated away from the body and self. At its broadest level, then, *Voicing Subjects* approaches the mediation of subjectivity through modes too often and too easily opposed—the technological, the virtual, the present, the authentic, the human.

NOTES

INTRODUCTION

1. The other word for voice, *swar,* is used in everyday speech to refer to the sounds of the human voice and animal sounds, and is defined in dictionaries both as "sound" and as "speech." In this book, I rely on *āwāj* because it is used more frequently in both political and intimate contexts.

2. While in English the "voice" exclusively refers to a human agent who speaks, *āwāj* is not always tied to human agents, and more broadly refers to *anything* one can hear. To raise one's voice, in other words, is to speak and to have oneself heard.

3. The Kathmandu Valley consists of three adjacent cities—Kathmandu, Patan, and Bhaktapur—which together have a population of more than 2.5 million according to the 2011 census (Central Bureau of Statistics 2012).

4. *Karobar National Economic Daily,* "Nepal Third in Receiving Remittance in terms of GDP," October 4, 2013, www.karobardaily.com/news/2013/10/nepal-third-in-receiving-remittance-in-terms-of-gdp.

5. Z-Net Asia. "Notes from Nepal: On the Royal Takeover," 2005, www.zmag .org/southasia/southasia1.cfm#Nepal. Z-Net Asia is an Internet site that publicizes recent political incidents, reports, and critical thinking about social issues around Asia.

6. On the relation of Nepali Panchāyat government (meaning five wards or village councils) to the Basic Democracy system in Pakistan, see Gupta 1998: 255.

7. The Rana rule might be thought of as "colonialism on the cheap," since unlike early-twentieth-century colonial regimes, the Ranas never upheld any liberal ideology that would have required them to invest in schools, colleges, or infrastructure that sought to connect rather than isolate people.

8. *Sāthi Sanga Man Ka Kura* (SSMK) [Chatting with my Best Friend]. Home page. Ssmk.org.

9. Susan Hangen, personal communication.

10. By "subjectivity," I mean the way that people come to see and identify themselves as a youth, a national citizen, an intimate person, a woman or man, or an

activist. As I argue throughout the book, this recognition of subject position is often felt to be derived from an exterior source described as making people finally see who they really are.

11. As Asif Agha has argued, Althusser assumes too much from the act of hailing, and not all moments of interpellations are successful to the same degree (2011: 168).

12. In drawing on Pascal, Althusser was well aware and explicit about the theological aspects of his theory.

13. I would argue that Althusser does not imply this in his argument, but Butler's point draws out important perhaps unstated assumptions about the discourse of voice.

14. See chapter 2 on connection between face and voice.

15. See chapter 2 and Sterne 2003 for critique of the dichotomy of vision and sound.

16. See Papailias 2005 on how new technologies of documentation—such as the voice recorder and photography—have entailed "a new conception of historical truth" (97).

17. See Larkin 2008 on relation between formal qualities of media and urban infrastructure.

18. There is a significant body of interesting scholarship on the relation between media and culture in South Asia. See, for example, Ganti 2012; Liechty 2003; Mankekar 1999; Manuel 1993; Mazzarella 2003; Rajagopal 2001, which have all, in different ways, served as inspiration for this book.

19. See, for example, among the many semiotic ethnographies, Agha 2006, 2011; Daniel 1984, 1996; Hull 2012; Keane 1997.

20. Here I follow the analytic move toward practice, discourse, and performance, drawing on thinkers such as Pierre Bourdieu, Michel Foucault, and Judith Butler, who center their analysis on the way identities come to be known and inhabited by people, without reifying that identity.

21. Clearly this is not exclusively a recent phenomenon, for many scholars have noted the importance of creating native identities to secure colonial rule (for example, Cohn 1996; Dirks 2001; Mamdani 1996; Stoler 2002). This is a specifically democratic version of the prominence of identity.

22. There are also many recent ethnographies of Nepal that do not use caste or ethnicity as the main frame of analysis. See, for example, Ahearn 2001; Liechty 2003; Rademacher 2011; Rankin 2004.

23. At the time of Lévi's writing, Nepal referred exclusively to the area of the Kathmandu Valley. Ranas began to refer to the area of their rule as the realm of Nepal only in the 1930s, when Nepali also became the official language. This terminology derived from a misnomer by a British grammarian, who wrote a grammar and dictionary of language of the Gorkha kings, and called it Nepali. The definition of the current national territory and language was clearly affected by British cultural and political acts in relation to Nepal.

24. That Nepal represents a pure version of India is an argument that has survived in both foreign scholarship and the history of the Nepali state itself. In the

first wave of foreign development in the mid-1950s, rather than being a test site to discover the pure nature of Indian Buddhism, Nepal was now looked upon as a development laboratory opportunity for trying out theories of development on a blank slate (Fujikura 1996: 271).

25. My argument about public intimacy and affective publics could be easily situated within broader discussions of recognition. See Beth Povinelli's (2002) argument on the "impasses of late liberalism," in which she argues that the contradictory forms of recognition are generative forces that continue to motivate liberal thought and action. The most pervasive tension is between cultural recognition demanded by the law and those based on different evidentiary claims and different moral sensibilities. Such competing forms of recognition lie at the center of this book as well, though I do not focus exclusively on formal institutions (like the law).

26. Of course, interior life existed among Nepalis prior to 1990; but the *discourse* about interiority and intimate lives proliferated profoundly after 1990 and the vastly expanded private market of media. As I argue here, the political and the intimate mutually constitute each other in this context of neoliberal, democratic reform.

27. See Habermas 1989 for an example of the equality and universal access to the public sphere found in liberal humanist ideals that have been widely critiqued (for example, Calhoun 1992; Warner 2002).

28. Most of my interviews were conducted in Nepali, except on occasions like this one, when the person refused to speak Nepali to me and we conversed in English.

29. The Nepali suffix of emphasis, *ni,* added to his English description stressed the universal timeless nature of love, suggesting that such relations always, in all places and times, exist.

30. For discussion Nepali short stories that emphasize an interior world in conflict with dominant societal values, see Hutt 1991: 175.

31. Voice, for Burghart, does not indicate simply a form of speaking, "but rather the way one *ought to speak* if one is to be heard" (300, emphasis added). Burghart tracks the way Nepali activists of the 1980s gradually create a moral space to publicly criticize that at once recognizes the body politic established by the monarchy, and also indicates the failure of that body politic. Voice does not exist without a listener, Burghart argues (like Bakhtin), and public critique is not an autonomous action (Burghart 1996: 318).

32. During the teacher's strike of 1984–85, for example, the teachers wore black armbands—a longstanding symbol of political repression in Nepal—and went to their classrooms but refused to speak (Burghart 1996: 310–11). During times of censorship and political agitation, both before and after *jana āndolans,* newspapers often published blank editorial pages to signify government censorship and the paper's critique of that censorship.

33. To be sure, indirect speech and irony continue to be the prevalent modes of criticizing authority and discussing uncomfortable subjects.

34. For a detailed analysis of press just after 1990, see IIDS 1996. A few interesting statistics to note here: There was a sharp rise in the number of newspapers, from

eighty-four newspapers in 1980 to 459 in 1985, following a national civil disobedience movement. In the mid-1990s, after a sharp rise and decline in private newspapers (due to cost), two-fifths of these newspapers were distributed exclusively in the Kathmandu Valley.

35. In 2000, there were at least one hundred thousand Nepali workers in the Middle East alone (Gurung 2000: 9), a number growing due to the political instability in Nepal and the war in Iraq, where Nepalis were being channeled to from other Gulf states to help with the work of reconstruction.

36. In Nepal, these transformations also gave rise to an alternative vision of modernity with the Maoist movement.

37. In Germany, for example, the use of glass in the renovation of the Bundestag (state capitol) after the unification of Germany signified the transparent nature of the new government. See Strassler 2004 on the Indonesian "dream of transparency" and photography.

38. See Amin 1995. See Stoler and Strassler (2000) for critique of this model of "voiced memory."

39. Thanks to Sanjib Baruah for pointing this out.

CHAPTER ONE

1. I have used the popular pronunciation of this word for my transliteration, as noted by Turner (1931: 7), with one minor alteration. Instead of using *aṅsa* to indicate the nasalized sound, I have used *angsa* to better represent the pronunciation of the term for an English audience. The short *a* sounds like the *u* in the word *up*. The Sanskrit version of the term is commonly transliterated as *aṁśa*.

2. The recent Maoist civil war (1996–2006) and the ongoing push for a federalist state structure, organized along ethnic and caste lines, are two key examples of radical attempts to restructure the state from the outside.

3. The southern group of Madheshi Nepalis has been at the forefront of arguing for federalism along ethnic lines and, more radically, for separation from the state of Nepal. Its radical aim is to expose deep inequalities in political representation and the ownership of property and land.

4. See Cameron 1998 for a detailed analysis of lower caste Nepalis' relations to property.

5. The campaign was a national campaign and many of the activists traveled throughout the country advocating the reform. Here I focus only on the debates within the capitol city.

6. Due to the repressive nature of the Panchāyat regime, the legal code had never been subject to a constitutional debate, even though ostensibly a Supreme Court existed during Panchāyat times as well. In the 1970s, most of changes to existing inheritance laws were conducted through Parliament.

7. Although much of this coverage opposed the bill, activists agreed that the oppositional talk about this bill helped their cause enormously by publicizing it.

8. See Tuladhar and Joshi 1997, for a discussion of the international agencies involvement in this reform bill.

9. See Ahearn 2001: 49, for a detailed discussion of the term *māyā*.

10. In Indonesian, the word *pangil* has similar connotations (Ann Stoler, personal communication); however, in Nepali, the tone of authority is often hidden within expressions of tenderness, care, and love that *bolāune* implies.

11. These practices appear to relate exclusively to married women, but even women who never marry experience some of the pull of such practices such as *bolāune* that produce gender hegemonies in Nepal.

12. See Povinelli 2002; Weiner 1992; and especially Verdery and Humphreys 2004 for an overview of this literature and relevant articles.

13. See Hunt 1992; Davin 1978; Stoler 1995: chaps. 5–6; Stoler 2002. For South Asia, Chakrabarty 1997, 2000: chap. 5; Chatterjee 1993: chaps. 6–7; Rajan 2003.

14. See Majumdar 2009 for feminist interpretations of Engels's idea as a form of "political romanticization" that failed to consider deeper roots of gender hierarchies that preceded the advent of capitalism.

15. These emotions were assumed to be universal, Janet Carsten points out, "a matter for psychological rather than sociological study" (2004: 11).

16. After *angsa* is divided among brothers, it is sometimes possible to literally see the division between the brothers' property within the house through markings on stairwells or partitions put up between rooms to distinguish households.

17. More middle-class men in Kathmandu are now attempting to establish their own homes away from the familial home, and many Nepalis say that daughters do as much, if not more, of the caretaking.

18. Working as a linguistic anthropologist, Kockelman identifies a class of nouns that usually appear in grammatically possessed form among speakers of Q'eqchi'-Maya in Guatemala, and when they do not, they seem odd (for example, body parts, kin terms, clothing, land, and names). *Angsa* does not carry that same grammatically possessive form, but does suggest links between inalienable possessions and personhood.

19. The Mulukī Ain of 1854 was modeled on a Hindu caste hierarchy, such that ethnic minority groups and Buddhists were considered to be castes. This affected such groups only in criminal cases, not in inheritance law. See Gilbert 1990; Hoefer 1979; Tamang 2000.

20. Some suggest that the initial law code of 1854 was actually less strict about women's sexuality than the revised law: it did not require unmarried women to return any inheritance they had received upon marriage. These restrictions were imposed around the 1920s when several amendments were made to the Mulukī Ain in response to veiled social criticism against the Rana regime (Hoefer 1979).

21. Since the mid-1990s, there has been a growing movement among ethnic nationalists and other minority groups to reevaluate their religious affiliation and declare themselves to be Buddhist as a means of contesting state-imposed Hinduism (Hangen 2005).

22. See Sangroula and Patak 2002 for a critique on the underlying Hindu bias of this law.

23. Several middle-class men referred back to this amendment of 1975 to point out that women do have rights to inherit *angsa* either through their marriage or, if they remain unmarried, after thirty-five. The difference between a birthright and a right granted through marital status was almost never remarked upon.

24. In addition, a woman could only sell or dispose of more than half of inherited immovable property—land and houses—with consent of either the father (for an unmarried woman) or adult sons (for married women living separately or widows). If a married woman was living within her in-laws' home, she could enter into any contracts on the basis of her expected share and could demand partition of the property.

25. Many of the women activists involved in this legal reform movement are Brahmin or Newar and proud of their connection to Hindu "tradition."

26. Documentation of this is available at the archive of the Legal Aid and Consultancy Center.

27. Echoing colonial, Victorian moral logic (Burton 1994), one friend of mine declared that men would become lazy if women gained a right to *angsa*. A woman's lack of property rights in her parents' home was a key factor in keeping her husband's in line, and women's morality (that is, *not asking* for property) was crucial for maintaining one's class status.

28. This sentiment may have changed somewhat during the decade-long Maoist "People's War" against the state (1996–2006). During these ten years, many wealthy families who had undivided land in Maoist-controlled regions decided to separate their land in order to protect themselves from Maoist accusations of their being a single wealthy landlord.

29. The reference to a woman's loose sexuality comes through implicitly in such statements.

30. There are, of course, several exceptions to this rule in Nepal, particularly among Tibeto-Burman ethnic groups such as the Sherpa (Adams 1996; Ortner 1989) and Tamang (Holmberg 1989; March 2002).

31. This term is often pronounced in the more Sanskritized form, *bamsa* or *vamsa*. Because I wish to show connections between the concepts, I have chosen to transliterate it in a way that shows its linguistic relation to *angsa*. Despite this relation, the connection in concepts is rarely discussed in public articles about the debate. When the occasional article appeared, *vangsa* was quickly dismissed as an impossible wish or, as Khagendra Sangroula (2053 v.s.: 6) writes, "a silver platter."

32. Until recently, Nepal was one of the few South Asian countries where married daughters did not have a legal right to inherit some portion of their parents' property, though in the countries that did have the legal right, the portion was not always equal (Agarwal 1994).

33. Bina Agarwal translated the first and the third verse, and the second verse, Agarwal quotes from a translation by Veena Das (1994: 1).

34. "Killing the love" is usually translated as "to forget." When I suggested that the "love" between brother and sister would not necessarily disappear but simply be different, all Nepalis agreed.

35. When I delivered a version of this chapter in Nepal to a group of students and activists, nearly everyone in the audience burst into laughter when I read the quotations about this imagined effect in Nepal. Their laughter at the absurdity of this scenario, like that of Anita and Gita, suggests how fundamental practices of *bolāune* are to producing gendered subjects.

36. I thank Mark Liechty for helping me clarify this point.

37. Lakshman Pandey, "Personality Profile: A Reformist Rebel!," *Weekend*, November 30, 1992.

38. For some women, performing *the kriyā-kāj* was a way to prevent all of their parents' *angsa* property from being consumed by other male relatives. This suggests there are informal, unofficial means by which daughters do gain access to *angsa* when there are no sons. But in the context of the legal reform movement, this fact never arose.

39. Though Indira felt the Hindu texts justified her performance of mourning, she also paradoxically admitted that she was indeed acting "against" her religion.

40. For Chirmei, who is a Newar and who speaks primarily Newari, the relation to *māitī* is even more intriguing. The word for *māitī* in Newari is *Twa:chien,* which means "own home." In Newari the significance of *māitī* is heightened: it is only after marriage that a Newar woman gains her "own home"—the place that she has left.

41. One Nepali anthropologist complained to my partner, Daniel, and me that the advocates "did not know about traditional Nepali social structure." Provocatively, Daniel asked him, "Aren't the advocates themselves Nepali?" The anthropologist declared with some exasperation, "Yes, can you believe it! They are *even* Nepalis and they don't know about our social structure!"

42. No doubt, this is related to the fact that India poses a more visible financial threat to Nepalis, who view Indians as clever *(calākh)* entrepreneurs. Foreign governments like the United States, Japan, and European nations, by contrast, appear in the popular imagination to be helping by granting NGOs and His Majesty's Government large sums of money.

43. The easy slip from *angsa* to dowry property was not uncommon, with some claiming that a dowry was a woman's form of inheritance. Described as "given by wishes or love," a dowry is one aspect of the love that forms the second half of the common adage quoted above. The difference, of course, is what advocates were arguing for: a dowry is secured through the precarious love of one's parents, whereas *angsa* is secured through rights to the law.

44. See Des Chene 1997: 166, for this argument in relation to these debates about the property reform in Nepal.

45. Mughlan refers, negatively, to the Mughal Empire (Burghart 1996: 268). The Court of Nepal did maintain religious and political ties to India, but in these cases India was termed Hindustan.

46. See Tharu and Lalita 1993 and Mitra 2006 on similar images of an immoral sphere of sexuality among *devadāsī* (temple dancers) in the court in nineteenth century.

47. See Chakrabarty 1992 on Bengali "split" consciousness, and particularly the Bengali home *(griha)* that embodies a split between past and present.

48. See Agarwal 1994 for details and discussion of its remaining inequalities.

49. In an earlier, condensed incarnation, I called this chapter "Between Love and Property" (Kunreuther 2009). Such a title requires us to think about the relation between two concepts that are often thought of as being in opposition, or at least occupying two extremes of a spectrum of exchange.

50. But the women's legal activist organization, Legal Aid and Consultancy Center (LACC), has compiled an archive on cases by daughters who sought to claim their rightful share of property after the law passed.

51. For example, in the build up to the 2008 elections, several organizations began new projects that were devoted to enabling the "expression of the people's voice" during the elections. One such organization, funded by Canadian International Development Agency, adopted the Nepali phrase *Jana Awāj* (People's Voice) as their project name. The director of Jana Awāj, Yosodha Shrestha, wrote in anticipation of the elections, "There seems to be no end to different groups coming forward, calling for strikes to have their voices heard. . . . A concrete strategy is needed to make sure all stakeholders have an equal say in formulation of a new constitution that respects the voices, issues and concerns of all."

52. While this liberal model of government was a prominent mode of reimagining the Nepali state during the 1990s, it was certainly not the only one. But even the Maoists and the Communist parties embraced some liberal and even neoliberal economic policies (Lakier 2007).

53. See Ahearn 2006 for analysis of Nepalis' elopement narratives in which individual agency is associated with elopement at the level of grammar (through use of Nepali suffix of action *-le*).

54. The very idea of *āwāj uthāune* was clearly distinguished from the illiberal forms of protest that also characterized the democratic moment after 1990. See Lakier 2007.

55. The two figures of voice activated in this debate suggest connections between the patterns of recognition established within the subjects of *bolāune* and the relations emerging between citizen and state during this period.

CHAPTER TWO

1. I voluntarily taught English to a group of Patan girls from Reena's courtyard community in 1992–93, as part of a German NGO (GTZ) project targeted to young girls called Self Help. The project was meant to inspire communal trash collection and public sanitation. To compensate the girls for their participation, GTZ offered English lessons, karate, and knitting (at the girls' request), and I was one of the English teachers.

2. Editorial, Kāntipur, Jeth 13, 2053 v.s.

3. The meanings for *vangsa* span from the most clearly power-laden terms to more neutral terms: "a dynasty, lineage, race, family, clan, offspring, descent, descendent, side of a generation" (Singh and Singh 1971: 415).

4. Throughout this chapter, I translate the phrase *mukh herne* as both "seeing face" and "looking at face." *Hernu* is translated as "to look at," "gaze upon," or "consider" (Turner 1931: 642), and the translation "looking at face" best expresses the intersubjective social relations implied in the practice. I have also used the phrase "seeing face," because "looking at face" is more unwieldy in English, and because this translation helps draw out *mukh herne*'s connections with and distinctions from Euro-American philosophies of seeing.

5. The phrase resembles the English saying, "I am seeing someone" or "I am not seeing him or her anymore," as an indication of a dating relation. In Nepali, however, the phrase does not have a specifically romantic meaning as in English. Thanks to Karen Strassler for pointing this out.

6. There are other commonly used words to denote a face—*anuhār* and *swarup,* which mean overall features, but will often refer to facial features. While people use *anuhār* and *swarup* to discuss particular facial features, *mukh* is consistently used to discuss social relations between people as exemplified in the phrase *mukh herne.*

7. See Ihde 1976: 181 on links between face, voice, and silence.

8. Writings against modern "ocularcentrism" begin with Nietszche and Bergson, Jay suggests, and continue with Surrealists and later Foucault in France (1994: 174).

9. See Weidman 2006 for discussion of voice, oral culture and modernity in India.

10. See Florida 1995 and Strassler 2009 for discussion of the Javanese word *semu* ("allusion"), which means "face" or "facial expression."

11. Levinas's discussion replicates the audiovisual litany that Sterne describes, yet also reverses common associations made between aural speech and vision. Levinas describes the face as maintaining "a relation with me by *discourse*" (1969: 195, italics added), not primarily through vision.

12. See Benson and O'Neill 2007 for fascinating discussion of Levinas's metaphor of "face" in relation to the ethics of ethnographic fieldwork.

13. Robert Levy glosses *ijjat* as "face" (1990: 185); however, the English meaning for face he uses does not fully capture the idea of *mukh herne* I describe here.

14. A South Asian concept of death is often thought of as a displacement in space rather than a distance in time.

15. For Benjamin, photography creates an "optical unconscious" that facilitates contact and presence as it establishes obvious distinctions between the viewer and viewed. Though clearly different from *darśan,* both describe a form of perception that relies on the "unstoppable merging of the object of perception with the body of the perceiver and not just the mind's eye" (Taussig 1994: 208).

16. Letter to *Mero Kathā, Mero Gīt,* 4/5/2054 v.s.

17. Letter to *Mero Kathā, Mero Gīt,* no date.

18. Thanks to Anil Bhatterai for translating this story for me.

19. There are some resemblances between this Nepali folk tale and Freud's "Mourning and Melancholia." From a psychoanalytic point of view, a projected, objectified image—outside of oneself—is important to properly mourn, to recognize

the dead as separate from oneself and to make a radical break between the dead and the living in order to continue living in this world. The practice at the pond resonates more closely with "melancholia," in which the lost love is but a mirror of oneself and "the shadow of the object [falls] upon the ego" (1917: 249), as illustrated most clearly through the tale of Narcissus. Unlike Narcissus in Ovid's story of *Metamorphosis,* the Nepali cowherder boy is not destroyed by his own vanity and staring at his own reflection in a pool of water. Instead, he finds relief, suggesting an ideal self in which a person knows themselves not by separating from others, but by seeing oneself in another's look.

20. See Ramaswamy 1997 for connections between mother (also referred to as *mātā*), goddess, and language in early-twentieth-century Tamil nationalism.

21. Most Nepalis in Kathmandu will say they do not "believe" the king is a manifestation of Vishnu, but they still may wish to take *darśan* from the king on national holidays. *Darśan,* like most Hindu practices, is not bound up with the category of belief as in Christian practices.

22. The Vedas are ancient Hindu texts that give clues about Vedic society, beginning around 1500 B.C., though there was not a uniform "Hindu" practice. Many argue that the idea that Hindu practice was bounded by a distinct set of religious (and nonpolitical) ideas was largely a strategy of control and order used by the British.

23. Tulsiram Kandel, "Mātātirtha Aunsi Purba ra Mātātirtha" [Before Mother's Day and Mother's Day], *Kantipur,* 22 Baisākh, 2057 v.s.

24. Tulsiram Kandel, "Mātātirtha Aunsi Purba ra Mātātirtha" [Before Mother's Day and Mother's Day], *Kantipur,* 22 Baisākh, 2057 v.s.

25. Tulsiram Kandel, "Mātātirtha Aunsi Purba ra Mātātirtha" [Before Mother's Day and Mother's Day], *Kantipur,* 22 Baisākh, 2057 v.s.

26. Swagat Nepal, "Āmā Khushi Parera Phal Khāne Purba Mātātirtha Aunsi" [Mother's Day: the festival to reap the fruits of making mothers happy]. *Samacharpatra,* 13 Baisākh, 2057 v.s.

27. Swagat Nepal, "Āmā Khushi Parera Phal Khāne Purba Mātātirtha Aunsi" [Mother's Day: the festival to reap the fruits of making mothers happy], *Samacarpatra,* 13 Baisākh, 2057 v.s.

28. The concept of *sevā* (service) is linked to a deliberate national strategy of the Panchāyat government, promoted in schools as well as in radio and television broadcasts.

29. Swagat Nepal, "Ama Khushi Parera Phal Khāne Purba Mātātirtha Aunsi" [Mother's Day: the festival to reap the fruits of making mothers happy], *Samacharpatra,* 13 Baisākh, 2057 v.s.

30. See Amin 1984; Charkarbarty 2000; Pinney 2002 for discussion of *darśan* and anticolonial nationalism, particularly among Indian peasants.

31. Several scholars of South Asia have noted the enhanced effects of *darśan* through mechanically produced images, but many have misread this enhancement as an example of Benjamin's "aura" (Benjamin 1968). See, for example, Lutgendorf 1995, which suggests the "religious aura" around *Ramayana* videocassettes echoes

Benjamin's notion of the aura. In Benjamin's "utopian fantasy" (Pinney 2002: 357), he imagined a *shattering* of the bourgeois aura with mechanically produced images, rather than the enhancement that Lutgendorf implies. What might be rescued in Benjamin's argument, Pinney notes, is the form of perception captured in the notion of "optical unconscious" that Taussig calls "tactile seeing" (Pinney 2002: 357).

32. See Liechty 1997 for a discussion about the Ranas consumption of objects that expanded one's capacity for seeing, such as telescopes, mirrors, photography.

33. The image of the king's face and his subjects beholding his image highlights the identification of the king with his portrait, and resonates with the idea that the face, founded on resemblance and identity, is "the very ground of representation" (Doane 2011: 224).

34. Sarkar, Sudeshna. "Dashain Festival Keeps Nepal's Last King in Spotlight," *Thaindian News*, September 28, 2009, www.thaindian.com/newsportal/politics /dashain-festival-keeps-nepals-last-king-in-spotlight_100253331.html.

35. Girijad (Girija) Prasad Koirala was the former prime minister of Nepal (1991–94; 1998–99; 2000–01; 2006–08) and former president of the Nepali Congress. He died in 2010. Madav Kumar Nepal was the former prime minister of Nepal (2009- 11) and former general secretary of UML Communist Party of Nepal.

CHAPTER THREE

1. Dhaomya Ayod (Nirmal), "FM Ki Aphim?" [FM or opium?], *Shri Sagarmatha*, 6 Jeth, 2053 v.s., 4; Harikla Adhikari, "Mero ta Chorachori Bigrina Lagisake" [My Children are already ruined], *Gorkhapatra*, 19 Magh, 2055 v.s., 7; Bikas Bhatterai, "F.M. Radiomāthi Samāj Bigāreko Ārop" [An Accusation against FM radio for ruining society], *Ājako Samacharpatra*, 28 Saun, 2055 v.s., 3. See also Ram Chandra Kushwaha, "Ketā Khojāune F.M" [The FM that searches boys (or girls)], *Jana Āstha*, 15 Magh, 2054 v.s., 6.

2. Whereas modern discourses emphasize an always-present interior self that simply needs to be recognized, a neoliberal self needs to be cultivated and worked on in order to fully emerge (Gershon 2011; Matza 2009; Urciuoli 2009). See Kunreuther 2010 for discussion of this distinction in the FM program for youth sponsored by UNICEF.

3. The workweek in Nepal begins on Sunday and ends on Friday afternoon.

4. This is the translation its sponsor, UNICEF, gave to the program. A literal translation would read "Heart-to-heart talk with a friend."

5. Based on the model of public broadcasting in North America, the programs tend to focus on specific ethnic groups and their particular cultural productions (songs, drama, and so on), educational programs, and programs focused on a development issue that differs in politics and content from commercial FM programs.

6. The Maoists also ran an unlicensed FM station that could be heard outside of Kathmandu and in the far west and east of Nepal.

7. See K. C. Sriram, "Gauleherulai Gijyairahecha—FM Radio" [Scoffing at the Villagers—FM radio], *Jana Dhāranā*. 25 Ashad, 2055 v.s., 3, on the FM's focus on urban Kathmandu population and the marginalization of villagers.

8. Beena Sarwar, "Addicted to FM Radio," *Kathmandu Post*, July 10, 1996.

9. Sanjib Baruah, personal communication.

10. For example, U.S. Agency for International Development indirectly funded one of the early FM programs, Panther (later CRS) Hotline, the first sex advice program in Nepal, an experiment in "social marketing." Because of the success of a similar program broadcast in Uganda, USAID provided funding to a Nepali NGO that specialized in contraception to directly support the program.

11. The one hour-long music-only program on Kantipur FM, sponsored by Marlboro cigarettes, failed miserably because listeners wanted to converse with the popular host.

12. See Weidman 2003 on the appeal of the gramophone in early-twentieth-century South India as a way to "hear" the music more perfectly than one's guru.

13. Letter to *Heart-to-Heart*, July 1996, my emphasis.

14. Cf. Barker 2002 on the power of a modulated voice on an Indonesian intercom to generate local stardom.

15. According to a popular rumor recorded in the history of the Telegraph Ministry, the place where the British Residency was located, *Lainchaur* (pronounced "line chaur," meaning "field"), got its name from the fact that it housed the first telegraph "line" out of Nepal (Nepal Dhursanchar Sansthan 2056 v.s.).

16. With the introduction of caller id and the increased use of mobile phones, there has been a significant drop in phenomena of bluff calls.

17. Letter sent to *Friends and Trends,* on Hits FM, October 6, 1996.

18. See Bhatterai 2005 for the details of the ordinance and its effect as a form of "legal cover" for media censorship.

19. During the Rana oligarchy (1846–1950), for example, people needed passports to enter and exit the Valley.

CHAPTER FOUR

1. Thanks to Prakash Thapa for the initial translation of the letters in this chapter. All other translations are mine.

2. By the summer of 2004, nearly every FM station in Kathmandu had some version of this program such as *Mero Shabda, Mero Bhāwanā* (My words, my thoughts/feelings) that clearly mimics *Mero Kathā, Mero Gīt*. Kalyan likes to contrast his program to the others by insisting on the "reality" of the stories he reads.

3. This is an example of a "site of mediation ... at which we come to be who we are through the detour of something alien to ourselves" (Mazzerella 2004: 356).

4. I thank William Mazzarella for helping to clarify this point.

5. See Habermas 1989: 43–51 on domestic practices of intimate recognition and writing that paved the way for the audience-centered subjectivity Habermas deems is necessary for critical, rational discourse.

6. Even in the more controversial sex advice programs, FM radio programs promote dominant ideas of heterosexual love like most mainstream media in South Asia and elsewhere.

7. Kalyan compares the letters he receives to diaries, a relatively infrequent practice in Kathmandu, but nevertheless widely portrayed in South Asian popular culture. See bollywoodhungama.com's video "Bollywood's Love Affair with the Diary," www.bollywoodhungama.com/celebritymicro/videos/id/85042/type/view /videoid/1389446.

8. While some wholly reject the inequalities built into Habermas's model, others suggest that a shift in a new liberal economy makes "the disembodied, rational public imaginary only one moment in an expanded public sphere" (Lee 1992: 407). See critiques of Habermas, particularly of the gendered nature of his claims: Calhoun 1992; Göle 1997 (on the public sphere in the Muslim context); Hirschkind 2006; Lee and LiPuma 2002; Negt and Kluge 1993; Robbins 1993; Warner 2002.

9. In recent years, the dominant castes of Brahmins and Chetris, feeling profoundly threatened by the power of the *janajāti* (ethnic national) movement, have declared that they too are an ethnicity, and have demanded a place within the debates about federalism. The situation resembles the crisis in US citizenship following the rise of multiculturalism that Berlant describes, when "many formerly iconic citizens who used to feel undefensive and unfettered feel truly exposed and vulnerable. . . . They sense that they now have *identities,* when it used to be just other people who had them" (1997: 2).

10. I thank Hajime Nakatane for the notion of a "master empathizer."

11. Letter to *Mero Kathā, Mero Gīt,* November 1997. Not all letters include a date such as this one. Where the letters do include a date, I cite it as the writer inscribes it.

12. Hirschkind's use of the term *counterpublic* differs from Nancy Fraser's (1992) discussion of "subaltern counterpublics" and Warner's (2002) elaboration on the same concept. Hirschkind's Islamic counterpublic operates on very different assumptions about a public than the liberal model that Fraser and Warner both presuppose.

13. To appeal to the middle class accords with the initial goals of Kathmandu FM (see chapter 3) and is a way of validating his program both morally acceptable and "suitably modern" (Liechty 2003).

14. In this novel, an anthropologist (who happens to be named 'Laura Kunreuther'), who studies radio sets up the frame narrative for the novel's story. It is sometimes hard to tell who is writing about whom.

15. Though many suggest its popularity has diminished over time and with the proliferation of similar programs.

16. This poem echoes themes in the play *Mukunda Indira,* discussed in chapter 1.

17. For discussions about such literature, see Chalmers 2002; Hutt 1991; Pradhan 1984; Subedi 1978.

18. See Morris 2002 for a similar argument about the simulation of presence through voice. Derrida's translator, Gyatri Spivak, also draws on this sense of voice in her much-debated essay "Can the Subaltern Speak?"

19. But in recent years, there has been a surge in the production of biography—from Maoist memoirs to individuals publishing with their own personal funds—particularly among those who have never formally written before, like the letter writers to this program. See Hutt 2012; Rai n.d.

20. See classic critiques of development, such as Escobar 1995; Ferguson 1994; Gupta 1998, as well as critiques that focus particularly on Nepal, such as Ahearn 2001; Fujikura 1996, 2001; Pigg 1992; Rademacher 2011. Many nonanthropological, scholarly discussions of development in Nepal can be found in the journal *SINHAS* (Studies in Nepali History and Society).

21. As noted earlier, this is the translation UNICEF gave to the program. Literally translated as "Heart-to-heart talk with a friend," its title resonates with my larger argument about affective publics.

22. Programs oriented toward *sevā* and *bikās* (development) have been central to Radio Nepal broadcasting, particularly during the Panchāyat times (Humagain 2003: 47–52, 58). Educational programs jumped from 23 percent of the overall programming on Radio Nepal in 1968 to 35 percent of Radio Nepal programs in 1984 (42).

23. Letter to *Mero Kathā, Mero Gīt,* no date.

24. If, as Bakhtin suggests, all words "taste" of a profession, a genre, a tendency, a party . . . [that is,] the context and contexts in which [the word] has lived its socially charged life" (1981: 293), then "raising consciousness" and "education" are words that "taste" of development, modernity, and Nepali's encounters with the world outside Nepal's borders.

25. *Nepal Samachar,* Push 9, 2056 v.s./December 24, 2000.

26. Letter to *Mero Kathā, Mero Gīt,* 4/5/2054 v.s.

27. Echoing my discussion of *mukh herne,* this exchange of glances is an extremely common way for Nepalis to describe the beginnings of their courtships, and is often represented in many love letters (Ahearn 2001: 120) and popular Indian films (see chapter 2).

28. Letter to *Mero Kathā, Mero Gīt,* 1998.

29. Letter to *Mero Kathā, Mero Gīt,* 4/5/2054 v.s.

30. I have indicated when English was spoken in interviews by italicizing the words spoken in English here and elsewhere. Unless noted, all conversations are in Nepali.

31. See Liechty 2003: 171 on relation between "realism" and *dukha* in South Asian films. *Dukha* is what links this program to the morality associated with realism. As Liechty argues, the convention of realism in film is not so much about creating the illusion of reality as about portraying a world that seems plausible (2003: 179–82). The effect of realism is to shape the way people think about their own lives:

reality itself becomes increasingly a mediated experience (180). Kalyan's program extends this one step further. In imagining their lives and representing them in a way that is appropriate for a mediated form, people's lived reality and the reality of the radio program appear to merge.

32. Letter sent to *Mero Kathā, Mero Gīt*, 6/11/2053 v.s.

33. Implicitly, Kalyan suggests that a person leaves his home in the village and comes to Kathmandu. This is not always the case, but more often than not the trajectory of many writers resembles Kalyan's stated trajectory (this is one of their few similarities) that Kalyan tends to focus on.

34. As Nietzsche has argued, this notion of an event juxtaposed to an assumed continuity has framed an entire historical tradition. Foucault, following Nietzsche, suggests that we look more carefully at the category of event that has structured much of history: an event is bound up with the "reversal of a relationship of forces" (1989: 88).

35. See White 1987 on history as a moral narrative, distinguished from other forms of historicity. To shape an event into a story, as Kalyan asks his listener to do, "is intimately related to, if not the function of, the impulse to moralize reality, that is, to identify it with the social system that is the source of any morality that we can imagine" (1987: 14).

36. The inconsistency of Laxmi Devi's age of marriage and the age when she was widowed is not unusual. Only present generations celebrate birthdays, and most Nepalis do not speak much about their age. Middle-aged women tend not to like admitting that they were married much before seventeen or eighteen. Yet here, in order to inspire an appropriate dose of sympathy from her listeners, she needed to present herself as a child-widow.

37. Letter to *Mero Kathā, Mero Gīt*, November 1997.

38. Letter to *Mero Kathā, Mero Gīt*, 1998.

39. *Māmāko ghar* (mother's brother's or uncle's house) is a term that refers to a child's mother's *māitī*, and like the *māitī, māmāko ghar* embodies ambivalent feelings of unbounded affection and distance. Just as Laxmi Devi was well aware that her *māitī* was not hers to claim, Lulu was aware that he did not have a right to stay long in his mother's village.

40. *Tā,* the lowest pronoun form, is used to address a child, a wife, or a servant, or is an expression of anger against a lower-status person, as this case indicates. *Tā* is also used between close friends or relatives to express intimacy. When seen as a social tool, pronouns are used in different ways to negotiate specific social contexts.

CHAPTER FIVE

1. When I discuss "Nepali," "the diaspora," and "the voice," I am referring to social entities and concepts that arise largely as an effect of the technologies of voice I discuss here.

2. Rumpum Noodles is a product sold by Asian Thai Foods Ltd., which is primarily distributed in Nepal, India, and Bhutan.

3. The recent movement among the NRNs (nonresident Nepalis) to create dual citizenship points to the collaboration expected between overseas Nepalis and the Nepali state.

4. *Rumpum Connection* is an early example of a Nepali radio program that was broadcast over the Internet and could be heard abroad, but was not public in the same way as FM radio in Kathmandu.

5. See Liechty 2003.

6. The field of "Nepali" literature was born from the efforts of Nepalis educated and living in India, Nepal's first diaspora. Nepal's revered poet, Bhanubhakta, lived much of his life in Calcutta and Darjeeling, where he translated the *Ramayana* into Nepali, making it accessible to ordinary Nepalis (Onta 1996b).

7. See Gurung 2000 for statistics on Nepalis working abroad, many of whom are employed through manpower agencies. Manpower agencies employ Nepalis in the Gulf, Malaysia, Thailand, Japan, China, Australia, and some countries in Western Europe.

8. See, for example, Chandra Shekhar Adhikari, "All 12 Nepalese Hostages Killed in Iraq," *Gorkhapatra,* September 1, 2004.

9. See Axel 1996: 427 for similar use of "Overseas Indians" by Indians within India to critique colonial rule and forward a program of anticolonial nationalism.

10. See Schiller-Glick and Fouton 2001: 20–23 on three key features of long-distance nationalism that center on developing a new state beyond territorial borders.

11. This echoes many representations of diaspora around the world. See Mei-Hui Yang 2002 for similar presence of overseas Chinese in popular Shanghai television programs. Similar programs are broadcast in Greece as well (Penelope Papalias, personal communication).

12. While it is unclear exactly how they are related, it seems that Meena is either Anup's paternal aunt or a distant cousin. Anup refers to Meena as *Didi,* which means "older sister," and is a generic term of respect and intimacy for a woman older than oneself, but it is clear from their conversation that they are not actual siblings.

13. See Leder 1990: 103 on voice as a medium of both presence and absence.

14. Letter to *Mero Kathā, Mero Gīt,* November 1997.

15. Axel includes corporeality as central to his understanding of the diasporic imaginary, an issue I do not address here.

16. Undoubtedly listeners of Uma's program also recorded programs, though I did not find them. Many listeners of *Mero Kathā, Mero Gīt* recorded the program when their story was read and replayed it for their friends and family.

17. A town in eastern Nepal.

18. While many more young men than women travel abroad to work, according to a recent government survey, there were more than double the number of women working in Israel than in any other country. This may be due to the Government of Nepal's ban on women working in the Gulf from 1998 to 2010, a period when this

program was broadcast. Subsequently, the government has imposed a ban on women under the age of thirty from working in the Gulf.

19. Media and technology are central to struggles over state power from a range of different political positions. Compare, for example, the seizure of media during Chavez's coup in Venezuela or the recent shutdown of state media in Greece to the use of cell phones during the civilian-backed overthrow of President Estrada in the Phillipines in 2001 (Rafael 2003).

20. See, for example, Sharad Adhikari's book *Bideshma Nepali Saphaltaka Katha* (Success stories of Nepalis abroad), published in 2011.

EPILOGUE

1. In Genevieve Lakier's analysis of this event, she notes that there were only two daily papers—*Samacharpatra* and *Spacetime Dainik*—that dared to publish the event and neither mentioned the culprit or cause of death (2009: 209). *Kantipur,* the largest national daily newspaper, published a special edition that evening.

2. See Hutt 2006 on self-censorship among journalists, particularly regarding matters of the palace.

3. Note these rumors are no more "free" than the censorship journalists imposed on themselves.

4. See Rademacher 2010 for a discussion of some Nepalis' presaging the king's death.

5. As I noted in the introduction, many defamed the now beloved King Birendra in the protests of the *jana āndolan* in 1990. During this same *āndolan,* people burned images of Prithvi Narayan Shah, the first Shah king and so-called father of modern Nepal, who conquered the Valley in 1769 (Ogura 2001: 112–13, cited in Lakier 2009: 208). In the emerging aftermath of the Narayanhiti massacre, similar slurs were hurled at the newly crowned King Gyanendra.

6. Dhana Laxmi Hamal, personal communication.

7. Glorification of the king appears at first to echo the earlier Panchāyat nationalism that places the king at the center of the nation. Yet here the sentiment is importantly different because the martyred king is used to denigrate (not uphold) the palace.

8. Many, in a mood alternately desperate and ironic, amassed newspaper clippings that they hoped might one day be assembled into a coherent and more truthful historical narrative than what was presented in any one official representation.

9. The opposition leader M. K. Nepal, who was initially part of the Probe Commission, called the commission "unconstitutional" since it was organized by the palace, not the Parliament, and promptly resigned, calling for more "transparency" (Lakier 2009: 207).

10. See Hutt 2012 for a discussion of the two most provocative editorials published after the incident, which were by one of the primary leaders of the Maoist

party, Baburam Bhattarai (who subsequently became prime minister in August 2011), and a Kathmandu intellectual, Khagendra Sangroula.

11. In his analysis of the best-selling novel *Raktakunda* by Krishna Aviral, Michael Hutt suggests that the book's popularity comes from its confirmation of rumors and conspiracy theories circulating on the streets, combined with a claim that it is based on research and the testimony of two former palace employees.

12. These written rumors, writes Marie Lecomte-Tilouine, consistently blurred the boundaries usually maintained between the anonymous rumors circulating on the street and the profession of journalism, which requires definitive evidence (2012).

13. As Lakier argues, the social fact of disbelief that the massacre generated is "intrinsic to the social practices of mass mediation itself" (2009: 200).

REFERENCES

Note to Readers: Nepali texts are often dated using the Nepali calendar year, Vikram Sambat, or v.s. Vikram Sambat is a lunisolar calendar that is approximately fifty-seven years ahead of the Gregorian calendar.

Abu-Lughod, Lila. 1990. "The Romance of Resistance: Tracing Transformations of Power Through Bedouin Women." *American Ethnologist* 17(1): 41–55.

———. 2004. *Dramas of Nationhood: The Politics of Television in Egypt.* Chicago: University of Chicago Press.

Adams, Vincanne. 1996. *Tigers of the Snow and Other Virtual Sherpas: An Ethnography of Himalayan Encounters.* Princeton, NJ: Princeton University Press.

Adhikari, Jaganath. 2007. "Globalization and the Securitization of Migration: The Context of Nepali Foreign Labour Migrants and Sustainable Livelihood." Talk presented at Martin Chauteri, Kathmandu, December 16, 2007.

Agarwal, Bina. 1994. *A Field of One's Own: Gender and Land Rights in South Asia.* Cambridge: Cambridge University Press.

Agha, Asif. 2006. *Language and Social Relations.* New York: Cambridge University Press.

———. 2011. "Meet Mediatization." *Language and Communication* 31:163–70.

Ahearn, Laura. 2001. *Invitations to Love: Literacy, Love Letters, and Social Change in Nepal.* Ann Arbor: University of Michigan Press.

———. 2006. "Acting in Love: Agency, Development, and Love Letters in Nepal." Talk given at New York Academy of Sciences, February 27.

Althusser, Louis. 1971. "Ideology and the State Apparatus (Notes towards an Investigation)." In *Lenin and Philosophy, and Other Essays,* 121–76. Translated by Ben Brewster. New York: Monthly Review Press.

Amin, Shahid. 1984. "Gandhi as Mahatma: Gorakhpur District, Eastern UP, 1921–2." *Subaltern Studies* III:1–15.

———. 1995. *Event, Metaphor, Memory: Chauri Chaura, 1922–1992.* Berkeley: University of California Press.

Anderson, Benedict. (1983) 1991. *Imagined Communities: Reflections on the Origin and Spread of Nationalism*. London: Verso.

Appadurai, Arjun. 1996. *Modernity at Large: Cultural Dimensions of Globalization*. Minneapolis: University of Minnesota Press.

Askew, Kelly, and Richard Wilk. 2002. *The Anthropology of Media: A Reader*. Oxford: Blackwell.

Axel, Brian Keith. 1996. "Time and Threat: Questioning the Production of the Diaspora as an Object of Study." *History and Anthropology* 9(4): 415–43.

———. 2002. "The Diasporic Imaginary." *Public Culture* 14(2): 422–28.

———. 2006. "Anthropology and the New Technologies of Communication." *Cultural Anthropology* 21(3): 354–85.

Bakhtin, Mikhail. 1981. *The Dialogic Imagination*. Translated by Caryl Emerson and Michael Holquist. Austin: University of Texas Press.

———. 1984. *Problems of Dostoevsky's Poetics*. Edited and translated by Caryl Emerson. Minneapolis: University of Minnesota Press.

Barker, Joshua. 2002. "Telephony at the Limits of State Control: 'Discourse Networks' in Indonesia." In *Local Cultures and the "New Asia,"* edited by C. J. Wan-Ling Wee, 158–83. Singapore: Institute of Southeast Asian Studies.

Basu, Srimati. 1999. *She Comes to Take Her Rights: Indian Women, Property and Propriety*. Albany: SUNY Press.

———. 2001. "Cutting to Size: Property and Gendered Identity in the Indian Higher Courts." In *Signposts: Gender Issues in Post-Independence India*, edited by Rajeswari Sunder Rajan, 249–92. New Brunswick, NJ: Rutgers University Press.

Bate, Bernard. 2009. *Tamil Oratory and the Dravidian Aesthetic: Democratic Practice in South India*. New York: Columbia University Press.

Bauman, Richard, and Charles Briggs. 2003. *Voices of Modernity: Language Ideologies and the Politics of Inequality*. Cambridge: Cambridge University Press.

Bell, Vikki. 1999. "On Speech, Race, and Melancholia: An Interview with Judith Butler." *Theory, Culture & Society* 16(2): 163–74.

Benjamin, Walter. 1968. "The Art of Mechanical Reproduction." In *Illuminations,* edited by Hannah Arendt, translated by Harry Zohn, 217–52. New York: Schocken.

Bennett, Lynn. 1983. *Dangerous Wives and Sacred Sisters: Social and Symbolic Roles of High-Caste Women in Nepal*. New York: Columbia University Press.

Benson, Peter. 2008. "El Campo: Faciality and Structural Violence in Farm Labor Camps." *Cultural Anthropology* 23(4): 589–629.

Benson, Peter, and Kevin Lewis O'Neill. 2007. "Facing Risk: Levinas, Ethnography, and Ethics." *Anthropology of Consciousness* 18(2): 29–55.

Berlant, Lauren. 1997. *The Queen of America Goes to Washington City*. Durham, NC: Duke University Press.

———. 1998. "Intimacy: A Special Issue." *Critical Inquiry* 24(2): 281–88.

———. 2008. *The Female Complaint: The Unfinished Business of Sentimentality in American Culture*. Durham, NC: Duke University Press.

Bessire, Lucas, and Daniel Fisher. 2012. *Radio Fields: Anthropology and Wireless Sound in the 21st Century.* New York: NYU Press.

Bhatterai, Binod. 2005. "Censored: Nepal's Press under King Gyanendra's Regime." *Studies in Nepali History and Society* 10(2): 359–401.

Bourdieu, Pierre. (1979) 1984. *Distinction: A Social Critique of the Judgment of Taste.* Cambridge, MA: Harvard University Press.

———. 1991. *Language and Symbolic Power.* Cambridge, MA: Harvard University Press.

Boyarin, Jonathan. 1994. "Space, Time, and the Politics of Memory." In *Remapping Memory: The Politics of TimeSpace,* edited by Jonathan Boyarin, 1–38. Minneapolis: University of Minnesota Press.

Boym, Svetlana. 2001. *The Future of Nostalgia.* Boston: Beacon.

Briggs, Charles, and Richard Bauman. 1992. "Genre, Intertextuality, and Social Power." *Journal of Linguistic Anthropology* 2(2): 131–72.

Brigham, Julie. 2008. *Sari Soldiers.* Women Make Movies, Documentary Film.

Bull, Michael, and Les Back, eds. 2003. *The Auditory Culture Reader.* New York: Berg.

Burghart, Richard. 1996. "The Conditions of Listening." In *The Conditions of Listening: Essays on Religion, Politics and Society in South Asia,* edited by C. J. Fuller and Jonathan Spencer. Delhi: Oxford University Press.

Burton, Antoinette. 1994. *Burdens of History.* Raleigh: University of North Carolina Press.

Butler, Judith. 1990. *Gender Trouble: Feminism and the Subversion of Identity.* New York: Routledge.

———. 1997. *Excitable Speech: A Politics of the Performative.* New York: Routledge.

Butler, Kim. 2001. "Defining Diaspora, Refining a Discourse." *Diaspora* 10(2): 189–219.

Calhoun, Craig, ed. 1992. *Habermas and the Public Sphere.* Cambridge, MA: MIT Press.

Cameron, Mary. 1998. *On the Edge of the Auspicious: Gender and Caste in Nepal.* Urbana: University of Illinois Press.

Caplan, Lionel. 1995. *Warrior Gentlemen: "Gurkhas" in the Western Imagination.* Oxford: Berghahn.

Carston, Janet. 2004. *After Kinship.* Cambridge: Cambridge University Press.

Central Bureau of Statistics. 2012. "National Population and Housing Census, 2011." Kathmandu: Government of Nepal, National Planning Commission Secretariat.

Chakrabarty, Dipesh. 1992. "Postcoloniality and the Artifice of History: Who Speaks for 'Indian' Pasts?" *Representations* 37:1–26.

———. 1997. "The Difference-Deferral of Colonial Modernity: Public Debates on Domesticity in British India." In *Tensions of Empire: Colonial Cultures in a Bourgeois World,* edited by Fredrick Cooper and Ann Laura Stoler. Berkeley: University of California Press.

———. 2000. *Provincializing Europe: Postcolonial Thought and Historical Difference.* Princeton, NJ: Princeton University Press.

Chalmers, Rhoderick. 2002. "Pandits and Pulp Fiction: Popular Publishing and the Birth of Nepali Print-Capitalism in Benares." *Studies in Nepali History and Society* 7(1): 35–99.

Chatterjee, Partha. 1993. *The Nation and Its Fragments.* Princeton, NJ: Princeton University Press.

Chatterjee, Piya. 2001. *A Time for Tea.* Durham, NC: Duke University Press.

Chun, Wendy Hui Kyong and Thomas Keenan, eds. 2006. *New Media, Old Media: A History and Theory Reader.* New York: Routledge.

Cody, Francis. 2011. "Publics and Politics." *Annual Review of Anthropology* 40:37–52.

Cohn, Bernard. 1996. *Colonialism and Its Forms of Knowledge.* Princeton, NJ: Princeton University Press.

Comaroff, Jean, and John Comaroff. 1989. "Images of Empire, Contests of Conscience: Models of Colonial Domination in South Africa." *American Ethnologist* 16(4): 661–85.

Crary, Jonathan. 1990. *Techniques of the Observer: On Vision and Modernity in the 19th Century.* Cambridge, MA: MIT Press.

Dahal, Dev Raj. 2002. "Mass Media, Trust, and Governance." In *Media and Society,* edited by P. Kharel, Dev Raj Dahal, Sushil Raj Pandey, and Krishna B. Bhattachan, 19–48. Kathmandu: Supravaha.

Daniel, E. Valentine. 1984. *Fluid Signs: Being a Person the Tamil Way.* Berkeley: University of California Press.

———. 1996. *Charred Lullabies: Chapters in an Anthropography of Violence.* Princeton, NJ: Princeton University Press.

Davin, Anna. 1978. "Imperialism and Motherhood." *History Workshop* 5:9–57.

Davis, Richard. 1997. *The Lives of Indian Images.* Princeton, NJ: Princeton University Press.

Deleuze, Gilles, and Felix Guattari. 1987. *A Thousand Plateaus.* Vol. 2 of *Capitalism and Schizophrenia.* Translated by Brian Massumi. Minneapolis: University of Minnesota Press.

Derrida, Jacques. (1967) 1976. *Of Grammatology.* Translated by Gyatri Chakravorty Spivak. Baltimore: Johns Hopkins University Press.

———. 1988. "Signature, Event, Context." In *Limited, Inc,* edited by Gerald Graff, translated by Samuel Weber and Jeffrey Mehlman. Evanston, IL: Northwestern University Press.

Des Chene, Mary. 1993. "Sovereignty and Silences: Gurkhas as Diplomatic Currency." *South Asia Bulletin* 8 (1–2): 67–80.

———. 1996. "Editorial: In the Name of Bikas." *Studies in Nepali History and Society* 1(2): 259–70.

———. 1997. "'We Women Must Try to Live': The Saga of Bhauju." *Studies in Nepali History and Society* 2(1): 125–72.

Dirks, Nicholas. 2001. *Castes of Mind: Colonialism and the Making of Modern India.* Princeton, NJ: Princeton University Press.

Dixit, Kanak Mani. 2006. "Nepal's People Phenomenon." *Himal Southasian* 19(3). www.himalmag.com/2006/may/commentary_1.html.

Doane, Mary Ann. 2011. "Screening the Avant-Garde Face." In *The Question of Gender: Joan Scott's Critical Feminism,* edited by Judith Butler and Elizabeth Weed, 206–32. Bloomington: Indiana University Press.

Douglas, Susan. 1999. *Listening In: Radio and the American Imagination.* New York: Random House.

Eck, Diane. 1981. *Darśan: Seeing the Divine Image in India.* Rev. ed. Chambersburg, PA: Anima Books.

Edwards, Brent Hayes. 2001. "The Uses of Diaspora." *Social Text 66* 19(1): 45–73.

Engels, Fredrick. (1884) 1891. *The Origin of the Family, Private Property, and the State.* 4th ed. Translated by Alick West. New York: Penguin.

Englund, Harri. 2012. *Human Rights and African Airwaves: Mediating Equality on the Chichewa Radio.* Bloomington: Indiana University Press.

Erlmann, Veit, ed. 2004. *Hearing Cultures: Essays on Sound, Listening and Modernity.* New York: Berg.

Escobar, Arturo. 1995. *Encountering Development: The Making of the Third World.* Princeton, NJ: Princeton University Press.

Feld, Steven. 1996. "Waterfalls of Song: An Acoustemology of Place Resounding in Bosavi, Papua New Guinea." In *Senses of Place,* edited by Steven Feld and Keith Basso, 91–135. Santa Fe, NM: School for American Research Press.

Feld, Steven, Aaron Fox, Thomas Porcello, and David Samuels. 2004. "Vocal Anthropology." In *A Companion to Linguistic Anthropology,* edited by Alessandro Duranti, 321–45. Malden, MA: Blackwell.

Feld, Steven, and Donald Brenneis. 2004. "Doing Anthropology in Sound." *American Ethnologist* 31(4): 461–74.

Ferguson, James. 1994. *The Anti-Politics Machine: "Development," Depoliticization, and Bureaucratic Power in Lesotho.* Minneapolis: University of Minnesota Press.

Festa, Lynn. 2010. "Humanity without Feathers." *Humanity: International Journal of Human Rights, Humanitarianism, and Development* 1(1): 3–27.

Fisher, James. 1997. *Living Martyrs: Individuals and Revolution in Nepal.* Delhi: Oxford University Press.

Florida, Nancy. 1995. *Writing the Past, Inscribing the Future: History as Prophecy in Colonial Java.* Durham, NC: Duke University Press.

Foucault, Michel. 1977. *Discipline and Punish: The Birth of the Prison.* Translated by Alan Sheridan. New York: Pantheon.

———. 1978. *History of Sexuality.* Vol. 1. New York: Pantheon.

———. 1982. "Afterword: The Subject and Power." In *Michel Foucault: Beyond Structuralism and Hermeneutics,* edited by Hurbert Dreyfus and Paul Rabinow, 208–26. Chicago: University of Chicago Press.

———. 1984. "Nietzsche, Genealogy, History." In *The Foucault Reader,* edited by Paul Rabinow, 76–100. New York: Pantheon.

Fox, Aaron. 2004. *Real Country: Music and Language in Working Class Culture.* Durham, NC: Duke University Press.

Freud, Sigmund. (1917) 1986. "Mourning and Melancholia." In Vol. 14 of *The Standard Edition of the Complete Psychological Works of Sigmund Freud,* 243–58. Translated by James Strachey. London: Hogarth.

Fujikura, Tatsuro. 1996. "Technologies of Improvement, Locations of Culture: American Discourses of Democracy and Community Development in Nepal." *Studies in Nepali History and Society* 1(2): 271–311.

———. 2001. "Discourses of Awareness: Notes for a Criticism of Development in Nepal." *Studies in Nepali History and Society* 6(2): 271–313.

———. 2007. "The Bonded Agricultural Laborers' Freedom Movement in Western Nepal." In *Political and Social Transformations in North India and Nepal: Social Dynamics in Northern Asia,* vol. 2, edited by Hiroshi Ishii, David Gellner, and Katsuo Nawa, 319–59. Delhi: Manohar.

Fuller, Matthew. 2007. *Media Ecologies: Materialist Energies in Art and Technoculture.* Cambridge, MA: MIT Press.

Ganti, Tejaswini. 2012. *Producing Bollywood: Inside the Contemporary Hindi Film Industry.* Durham, NC: Duke University Press.

Gaonkar, Dilip Parameshwar, and Elizabeth A. Povinelli. 2003. "Technologies of Public Forms: Circulation, Transfiguration, Recognition." *Public Culture* 15(3): 385–97.

Gautum, Kalyan. 2059 v.s. *Dear Kalyan: Mero Kathā, Mero Gīt* [Dear Kalyan: My Story, My Song]. Kathmandu: Ebharestra Graphik Press.

Gellner, David. 1992. *Monk, Householder, and Tantric Priest: Newar Buddhism and Its Hierarchy of Ritual.* Cambridge: Cambridge University Press.

———, ed. 1998. *Nationalism and Ethnicity in a Hindu Kingdom: The Politics and Culture of Contemporary Nepal.* London: Routledge.

———. 2009. *Ethnic Activism and Civil Society in South Asia.* Delhi: Sage.

Gershon, Ilana. 2010a. *Break-Up 2.0.* Ithaca, NY: Cornell University Press.

———. 2010b. "Media Ideologies." *Journal of Linguistic Anthropology* 20(2): 283–93.

———. 2011. "Neoliberal Agency." *Current Anthropology* 52(4): 537–55.

Gilbert, Kate. 1990. "Nepali Family Law: An Annotated Translation of the *Muluki Ain* of 2022 V.S. and V.S. 2035." American Bar Foundation Working Paper 9023.

———. 1992. "Women and Family Law in Modern Nepal: Statutory Rights and Social Implications." *New York University Journal of International Law and Politics* 24:729–58.

Gilligan, Carol. 1982. *In a Different Voice.* Cambridge, MA: Harvard University Press.

Ginsburg, Faye. 2002. "Screen Memories: Resignifying the Traditional in Indigenous Media." In *Media Worlds: Anthropology on New Terrain,* edited by Faye Ginsburg, Lila Abu-Lughod, and Brian Larkin, 39–57. Berkeley: University of California Press.

Ginsburg, Faye, Lila Abu-Lughod, and Brian Larkin, eds. 2002. *Media Worlds: Anthropology on New Terrain.* Berkeley: University of California Press.

Gluckman, Max. 1963. "Gossip and Scandal." *Current Anthropology* 4(3): 307–16.

Göle, Nilüfer. 1997. "The Gendered Nature of the Public Sphere." *Public Culture* 10(1): 61–81.

Government of Nepal. 1975. *"Mulukī Ain.* 2032 v.s." [The Law Code of Nepal].

———. 2013. "International Economic Cooperation Report, Fiscal Year 2011–2012." Kathmandu: Ministry of Finance, Foreign Aid Coordination Division.

Grandin, Ingemar. 1989. *Music and Media in Local Life: Music Practice in a Newar Neighborhood in Nepal.* Linkoping: Linkoping University.

Greenland, Natalie. n.d. "Yuba: Making Modern Youth, Making New Nepal." PhD diss., University of Adelaide, Australia.

Greenwald, Jeff. 2001. "Murder and Intrigue in Kathmandu." *Salon,* June 12. www. salon.com.

Grewal, Inderpal. 1996. *Home and Harem: Nation, Gender, Empire and the Cultures of Travel.* Durham, NC: Duke University Press.

Guha, Ranajit. 1996. "The Small Voice of History." In *Subaltern Studies, 10: Writings on South Asian History and Society,* edited by Bhadra, Gautum, Gyan Prakash, and Susie Tharu, 1–12. Delhi: Oxford University Press.

Gupta, Akhil. 1998. *Postcolonial Developments: Agriculture in the Making of Modern India.* Durham, NC: Duke University Press.

Gupta, Anirudha. 1993. *Politics in Nepal, 1950–1960.* Delhi: Kalinga.

Gurung, Ganesh. 2000. "Patterns in Foreign Employment and Vulnerability of Migrant Workers." Paper presented at the Workshop on Migrant Workers, Nepal Institute for Development Studies, November 15. aidsouthasia.undp.org.in /publicatn/6TH%20ICCAP/pdfs/Nepal.pdf.

Habermas, Jürgen. (1962) 1989. *The Structural Transformation of the Public Sphere: An Inquiry into a Category of Bourgeois Society.* Translated by Thomas Burger. Cambridge, MA: MIT Press.

Hangen, Susan. 2005. "Race and the Politics of Identity in Nepal." *Ethnology* 44(1): 49–64.

———. 2009. *The Rise of Ethnic Politics in Nepal: Democracy in the Margins.* London: Routledge.

———. Forthcoming. "Global Gurungs: Ethnic Organizing Abroad." In *Facing Globalization in the Himalayas: Belonging and Politics of the Self,* edited by Gerard Toffin and Joanna Pfaff-Czarnecka. New Delhi: Sage.

Hardt, Michael. 2011. "For Love or Money." *Cultural Anthropology* 26(4): 676–82.

Harvey, David. 2005. *A Brief History of Neoliberalism.* Oxford: Oxford University Press.

Helmreich, Stefan. 2007. "An Anthropologist Underwater: Immersive Soundscapes, Submarine Cyborgs, and Transductive Ethnography." *American Ethnologist* 34(4): 621–41.

Hirschkind, Charles. 2006. *The Ethical Soundscape: Cassette Sermons and Islamic Counterpublics.* New York: Columbia University Press.

Hodgson, Brian. 1874. *Essays on the Languages, Literature, and Religion of Nepal and Tibet.* London: Trübner.

Höfer, András. 1979. *The Caste Hierarchy and the State of Nepal: A Study of the Muluki Ain of 1854*. Innsbrück: Universtätsverlag Wagner.

Holmberg, David. 1989. *Order in Paradox: Myth, Ritual, and Exchange among Nepal's Tamang*. Ithaca, NY: Cornell University Press.

Hull, Matthew. 2012. *Government of Paper: The Materiality of Bureaucracy in Urban Pakistan*. Berkeley: University of California Press.

Humagain, Devraj. 2003. "Radio Nepalkā Kāryakram: Adharshatābdiko Samikshā" [Radio Nepal's program: a review of half a century]. *Studies in Nepali History and Society* 8(1): 37–66.

Hunt, Lynn. 1992. *The Family Romance of the French Revolution*. Berkeley: University of California Press.

———. 2007. *Inventing Human Rights: A History*. New York: W. W. Norton.

Hutt, Michael. 1991. *Himalayan Voices: An Introduction to Modern Nepali Literature*. Berkeley: University of California Press.

———. 1998. "Going to Mugalan: Nepali Literary Representations of Migration to India and Bhutan." *South Asia Research* 18(2): 195–214.

———. 2006. "Things That Should Not Be Said: Censorship and Self-Censorship in the Nepali Press Media, 2001–02." *Journal of Asian Studies* 65:361–92.

———. 2012. "Reading Maoist Memoirs." *Studies in Nepali History and Society* 17(1): 107–42.

———. n.d. "The Royal Palace Massacre, Conspiracy Theories, and Nepali Street Literature." Presented at the workshop "The Creation of Public Meaning in Nepal." SOAS, London, July 2012.

Ihde, Donald. 1976. *Listening and Voice: A Phenomenology of Sound*. Athens: Ohio University Press.

Illouz, Eva. 2003. *Oprah Winfrey and the Glamour of Misery: An Essay on Popular Culture*. New York: Columbia University Press.

Inoue, Miyako. 2002. "Gender and Linguistic Modernity: Toward an Effective History of Japanese Women's Language." *American Ethnologist* 29(2): 392–433.

———. 2006. *Vicarious Language: Gender and Linguistic Modernity in Japan*. Berkeley: University of California Press.

Institute of Integrated Development Studies (IIDS). 1996. *Mass Media and Democratization: A Country Study on Nepal*. Kathmandu: Institute of Integrated Development Studies.

Irvine, Judith. 1989. "When Talk Isn't Cheap: Language and Political Economy." *American Ethnologist* 16:248–67.

Ivy, Marilyn. 1995. *Discourses of the Vanishing*. Chicago: University of Chicago Press.

Jain, Kaijri. 2007. *Gods in the Bazaar: The Economies of Indian Calendar Art*. Durham, NC: Duke University Press.

Jakobson, Roman. 1987. "Linguistics and Poetics." In *Language in Literature,* edited by Krystyna Pomorska and Stephen Rudy, 62–94. Cambridge, MA: Belknap Press of Harvard University Press.

Jankowiak, William, ed. 1995. *Romantic Passion: A Universal Experience?* New York: Columbia University Press.

Jay, Martin. 1993. *Downcast Eyes.* Berkeley: University of California Press.

Joseph, Suad. 1994. "Brother/Sister Relationships: Connectivity, Love and Power in the Reproduction of Arab Patriarchy." *American Ethnologist* 21(1): 50–73.

Joshi, Satya Mohan. 2005. "Jindagikā Dhun Harumā Radio" [Radio in the tunes of life]. In *Radiosanga Hurkdā: Tinpuste Nepaliko Anubhab* [Growing up with radio: the experience of three generations], edited by Shekhar Parajuli and Pratyoush Onta. Kathmandu: Martin Chauteri.

Karpowitz, Daniel. 1998. "Alternative Perspectives on Property Rights." Fulbright presentation at United States Educational Foundation, Kathmandu.

Keane, Webb. 1997. *Signs of Recognition.* Berkeley: University of California Press.

———. 1999. "Voice." *Journal of Linguistic Anthropology* 9(1–2): 271–73.

———. 2002. "Sincerity, 'Modernity,' and the Protestants." *Cultural Anthropology* 17(1): 65–92.

———. 2003. "Semiotics and the Social Analysis of Material Things." *Language and Communication* 23:409–25.

Khadka, Navin Singh. 2004. "Open Secret: Everyone, Even the Government, Knew Nepali Workers Were Going Illegally to Nepal." *Nepali Times,* August 27– September 2.

Kittler, Friedrich. 1990. *Discourse Networks 1800/1900.* Translated by Michael Metteer, with Chris Cullens. Palo Alto, CA: Stanford University Press.

———. 1999. *Gramophone, Film, Typewriter.* Translated by Geoffrey Winthrop-Young and Michael Wutz. Palo Alto, CA: Stanford University Press.

Kockelman, Paul. 2007. "Inalienable Possession and Personhood in a Q'eqchi'-Mayan Community." *Language in Society* 36:343–69.

Kondo, Dorinne. 1997. *About Face: Performing Race in Fashion and Theater.* New York: Routledge.

Kunreuther, Laura. 2004. "Voiced Writing and Public Intimacy on Kathmandu's FM Radio." *Studies in Nepali History and Society* 9(1): 57–96.

———. 2006. "Technologies of the Voice: FM Radio, Telephone, and the Nepali Diaspora in Kathmandu." *Cultural Anthropology* 21(3): 323–53.

———. 2009. "Between Love and Property: Voice, Sentiment, and Subjectivity in the Reform of Daughter's Inheritance in Nepal." *American Ethnologist* 36(3): 545–62.

———. 2010. "Transparent Media: Radio, Voice, and Ideologies of Directness in Post-Democratic Nepal." *Journal of Linguistic Anthropology* 20(2): 334–51.

———. 2012. "Aurality under Democracy: Cultural History of FM Radio and Ideologies of the Voice in Nepal." In *Radio Fields: Anthropology and Wireless Sound in the 21st Century,* edited by Lucas Bessire and Daniel Fisher. New York: NYU Press.

Lakier, Genevieve. 2007. "Illiberal Democracy and the Problem of Law: Street Protest and Democratization in Multiparty Nepal." In *Contentious Politics and Democratization in Nepal,* edited by Mahendra Lawoti. London: Sage.

———. 2009. "After the Massacre: Secrecy, Disbelief, and the Public Sphere in Nepal." In *Censorship in South Asia,* edited by William Mazzarella and Raminder Kaur, 206–34. Bloomington: Indiana University Press.

Larkin, Brian. 2008. *Signal and Noise: Media, Infrastructure, and Urban Culture in Nigeria.* Durham, NC: Duke University Press.

Lawoti, Mahendra. 1990. *Towards a Democratic Nepal: Inclusive Political Institutions for a Multicultural Society.* New Delhi: Sage.

———, ed. 2005. *Contentious Politics and Democratization in Nepal.* New Delhi: Sage.

Lecomte-Tilouine, Marie. 2012. "Rumours and Printed Media about the Royal Palace Massacre." Presented at the workshop "The Creation of Public Meaning in Nepal." SOAS, London, July 2012.

Leder, Drew. 1990. *The Absent Body.* Chicago: University of Chicago Press.

Lee, Benjamin. 1992. "Textuality, Mediation, and Public Discourse." In *Habermas and the Public Sphere,* edited by Craig Calhoun. Cambridge, MA: MIT Press.

Lee, Benjamin, and Edward LiPuma. 2002. "Cultures of Circulation: The Imaginations of Modernity." *Public Culture* 14(1): 191–213.

Leve, Lauren. 2011. "Identity." *Current Anthropology* 52(4): 513–35.

———. 2014. *Ethical Practice, Religious Reform, and the Buddhist Art of Living in Nepal.* London: Routledge.

Leve, Lauren, and Lamia Karim. 2001. "Privatizing the State: Ethnography of Development, Transnational Capital and NGOs. An Introduction to the Symposium 'Power, NGOs and Development.'" *POLaR* 24(1): 53–58.

Lévi, Sylvain. 1905. *Le Népal: étude historique d'un royaume hinou.* Vol. 1. Paris: Leroux.

Levinas, Emmanuel. 1969. *Totality and Infinity.* Pittsburgh, PA: Duquesne University Press.

Levy, Robert. 1990. *Mesocosm: Hinduism and the Organization of a Traditional Newar City in Nepal.* Berkeley: University of California Press.

Lewis, Todd. 1999. *Popular Buddhist Texts from Nepal: Narratives and Rituals of Newar Buddhism.* Albany: SUNY Press.

Liechty, Mark. 1997. "Selective Exclusion: Foreigners, Foreign Goods, and Foreignness in Modern Nepali History." *Studies in Nepali History and Society* 2(1): 5–68.

———. 2003. *Suitably Modern: Making Middle-Class Culture in a New Consumer Society.* Princeton, NJ: Princeton University Press.

Lofton, Kathryn. 2011. *Oprah: The Gospel of an Icon.* Berkeley: University of California Press.

Ludden, David. 1992. "India's Development Regime." In *Colonialism and Culture,* edited by Nicholas Dirks. Ann Arbor: University of Michigan Press.

Lutgendorf, Philip. 1998. "All in the (Raghu) Family: A Video Epic in Cultural Context." In *Media and the Transformation of Religion in South Asia,* edited by Lawrence A. Babb and Susan S. Wadley. Delhi: Motilal Barnasidass.

MacLeod, Arlene. 1992. "Hegemonic Relations and Gender Resistance: The New Veiling as Accommodating Protest in Cairo." *Signs: The Journal of Women in Culture and Society* 17(3): 533–57.

Mahmood, Saba. 2005. *Politics of Piety: The Islamic Revival and the Feminist Subject.* Princeton, NJ: Princeton University Press.

Majumdar, Rochona. 2009. *Marriage and Modernity: Family Values in Colonial Bengal.* Durham, NC: Duke University Press.

Malinowski, Bronislaw. 1953. "The Problem of Meaning in Primitive Languages." In *The Meaning of Meaning,* edited by C. K. Ogden and I. A. Richards, 296–336. New York: Harcourt and Brace.

Mamdani, Mahmood. 1996. *Citizen and Subject.* Princeton, NJ: Princeton University Press.

Manandhar, Sulochana. 2058 v.s. "Jhyālkhānā" [Prison]. *Asmita,* 25–30.

Mani, Lata. 1998. *Contentious Traditions: The Debate on Sati in Colonial India, 1760–1833.* Berkeley: University of California Press.

Mankekar, Purnima. 1999. *Screening Culture, Viewing Politics: An Ethnography of Television, Womanhood, and Nation in Postcolonial India.* Durham, NC: Duke University Press.

Manuel, Peter. 1993. *Cassette Culture: Popular Music and Technology in North India.* Chicago: University of Chicago Press.

March, Kathryn. 2002. *"If Each Comes Halfway": Meeting Tamang Women in Nepal.* Ithaca, NY: Cornell University Press.

Matza, Tomas. 2009. "Moscow's Echo: Technologies of the Self, Publics, and Politics on the Russian Talk Show." *Cultural Anthropology* 24(3): 489–522.

Mazzarella, William. 2003. *Shoveling Smoke: Advertising and Globalization in Contemporary India.* Durham, NC: Duke University Press.

———. 2004. "Globalization, Mediation, Culture." *Annual Review of Anthropology* 33:345–67.

———. 2006. "Internet X-Ray: E-Governance, Transparency, and the Politics of Immediation in India." *Public Culture* 18(3): 473–505.

McLuhan, Marshall. 1964. *Understanding Media: The Extensions of Man.* New York: McGraw Hill.

Misra, Neelesh. 2001. *End of the Line: The Story of the Killing of the Royals in Nepal.* New York: Penguin.

Mitra, Royona. 2006. "Living a Body Myth, Performing a Body Reality: Reclaiming the Corporeality and Sexuality of the Indian Female Dancer." *Feminist Review* 84:67–83.

Morris, Rosalind C. 2002. "A Room with a Voice: Mediation and Mediumship in Thailand's Information Age." In *Media Worlds: Anthropology on New Terrain,* edited by Faye Ginsburg, Lila Abu-Lughod, and Brian Larkin, 383–97. Berkeley: University of California Press.

———. 2009. "Photography and the Power of Images in the History of Power: Notes from Thailand." In *Photography's East: The Camera and Its Histories in East and Southeast Asia.* Durham, NC: Duke University Press.

Morson, Gary Saul, and Caryl Emerson. 1990. *Mikhail Bakhtin: Creation of a Prosaics.* Palo Alto, CA: Stanford University Press.

Mosse, George. 1985. *Nationalism and Sexuality: Middle Class Morality and Sexual Norms in Modern Europe.* Madison: University of Wisconsin Press.

Mrazek, Rudolf. 2002. *Engineers of Happy Land: Technology and Nationalism in a Colony.* Princeton, NJ: Princeton University Press.

Mukarung, Bulu. 2056 v.s. *"Nepali Sangītko Bikāsma Radio Nepal ra Salgan Kalākārharu Jhangkār (Swarang Mahotswa Smārikā)."* (Radio Nepal and the Artists Involved in the Development of Nepali Music) Ṭṛek Prasād Ghimire, S.Pr. Kathmandu: Radio Prasār Sevā Bikās Samiti.

Negt, Oskar, and Alexander Kluge. 1993. *Public Sphere and Experience.* Minneapolis: University of Minnesota Press.

Nepal Dhursanchar Sansthan. 2056 v.s. *Nepal Dursanchar Sansthan: Ātit Ra Wartaman* [Nepal Telecom Private Limited: the past and the present]. Kathmandu: Nepal Dursancchar Sansthan.

Ogura, Kiyoko. 2001. *Kathmandu Spring: The People's Movement of 1990.* Kathmandu: Himal Books.

Ong, Walter. 1982. *Orality and Literacy: The Technologizing of the Word.* London: Routledge.

Onta, Pratyoush. 1996a. "Ambivalence Denied: The Making of *Rastriya Itihas* in Panchayat Era Textbooks." *Contributions to Nepalese Studies* 23(1): 213–54.

———. 1996b. "Creating a Brave Nepali Nation in British India: The Rhetoric of *Jati* Improvement, Rediscovery of Bhanubhakta and the Writing of *Bir* History." *Studies in Nepali Society and History* 1(1): 37–76.

———. 1997. "Activities in a 'Fossil State': Balkrishna Sama and the Improvisation of Nepali Identity." *Studies in Nepali Society and History* 2(1): 69–102.

———. 2003. "Critiquing the Media Boom." In *State of Nepal,* edited by Kanak Mani Dixit and Shastri Ramachandaran. Kathmandu: Himal Books.

———. 2006. *Mass Media in Post-1990 Nepal.* Kathmandu: Martin Chauteri.

Onta, Pratyoush, and Radhu Mainali. 2002. *Sthaniya Radio: Sambhadana ra Upayogita* [Community radio: relation and utility]. Kathmandu: Martin Chauteri.

Onta, Pratyoush, Shekar Parajuli, Debraj Humagai, Kamal Bhatt. 2004. *Radio Nepalko Sāmājik Itihās* [Social history of Radio Nepal]. Kathmandu: Martin Chauteri.

Onta-Bhatta, Lazima. 1994. "Street Children: Contested Identities and Universalizing Categories." *Studies in Nepali History and Society* 1(1).

Ortner, Sherry. 1974. "Is Female to Male as Nature Is to Culture?" In *Woman, Culture, and Society,* edited by M. Z. Rosaldo and L. Lamphere, 68–87. Palo Alto, CA: Stanford University Press.

———. 1989. *High Religion: A Cultural and Political History of Sherpa Buddhism.* Princeton, NJ: Princeton University Press.

———. 1995. "Resistance and the Problem of Ethnographic Refusal." *Comparative Studies in Society and History* 37(1): 173–93.

Özyürek, Esra. 2006. *Nostalgia for the Modern*. Durham, NC: Duke University Press.

Papailias, Penelope. 2005. *Genres of Recollection*. New York: Palgrave.

———. n.d. "Media event." Unpublished manuscript.

Parajuli, Ramesh, and Pratyoush Onta. 2003. *Mediya Utpadan ra Untarwastu* [Media production and content]. Kathmandu: Martin Chauteri.

Parajuli, Shekhar. 2007. "Seven Decades of Radio Listening in Nepal." *Westminister Papers in Communication and Culture* 4(2): 52–67.

Parajuli, Shekhar, and Pratyoush Onta. 2005. *Radiosanga Hurkdā: Tinpuste Nepaliko Anubhab* [Growing up with radio: the experience of three generations]. Kathmandu: Martin Chauteri.

Parashar, Archana. 1992. *Women and Family Law Reform in India: Uniform Civil Code and Gender Equality*. New Delhi: Sage.

Parker, Andrew, Mary Russo, Doris Sommer, and Patricia Yaeger, eds. 1992. *Nationalisms and Sexualities*. New York: Routledge.

Pesman, Dale. 2000. *Russia and Soul: an Exploration*. Ithaca, NY: Cornell University Press.

Pigg, Stacey. 1992. "Inventing Social Categories Through Place: Social Representations and Development in Nepal." *Comparative Studies in Society and History* 34(3): 491–513.

Pinney, Christopher. 1997. *Camera Indica: The Social Life of Indian Photographs*. Chicago: University of Chicago Press.

———. 2002. "The Indian Work of Art in the Age of Mechanical Reproduction: Or, What Happens When Peasants 'Get Hold' of Images." In *Media Worlds: Anthropology on New Terrain,* edited by Faye D. Ginsburg, Lila Abu-Lughod, and Brian Larkin, 355–69. Berkeley: University of California Press.

———. 2004. *"Photos of the Gods": The Printed Image and Political Struggle in India*. London: Reaktion; Delhi: Oxford University Press.

Povinelli, Elizabeth. 2002a. *The Cunning of Recognition: Indigenous Alterities and the Making of Australian Multiculturalism*. Durham, NC: Duke University Press.

———. 2002b. "Notes on Gridlock: Genealogy, Intimacy, Sexuality." *Public Culture* 14(1): 215–38.

Pradhan, Kumar. 1984. *A History of Nepali Literature*. New Delhi: Sahitya Akademi.

Rademacher, Anne. 2011. *Reigning the River: Urban Ecologies and Political Transformation in Kathmandu*. Durham, NC: Duke University Press.

Radio Nepal. 1997. "Radio Ownership and Listening in Nepal: A National Study." Kathmandu: Radio Nepal, Audience Research Section.

Raeper, William, and Martin Hoftun. 1992. *Spring Awakening: An Account of the 1990 Revolution in Nepal*. New Delhi: Viking.

Raheja, Gloria, and Ann Gold. 1994. *Listen to the Heron's Words*. Berkeley: University of California Press.

Rai, Kailash. n.d. "Yuddha Sakchi: Maowadi Mahilā Saṁsmaranṭ" [War witness: memoirs of women maoists]. Paper presented at workshop "The Creation of Public Meaning in Nepal." SOAS, London, July 2012.

Raj, Prakash A. 2001. *"Kay Gardeko?" The Royal Massacre in Nepal.* New Delhi: Rupa.

Rajagopal, Arvind. 2001. *Politics after Television: Hindu Nationalism and the Reshaping of the Public in India.* Cambridge: Cambridge University Press.

Rajan, Rajeswari Sundar. 2003. *The Scandal of the State: Women, Law, and Citizenship in India.* Durham, NC: Duke University Press.

Ramaswamy, Sumathi. 1997. *Passions of the Tongue: Language Devotion in Tamil India, 1891–1970.* Berkeley: University of California Press.

Rankin, Kathryn. 2004. *The Cultural Politics of Markets: Economic Liberalization and Social Change in Nepal.* Toronto: University of Toronto Press.

Rebhun, L. A. 1999. *The Heart Is an Unknown Country: Love in the Changing Economy of Northeast Brazil.* Palo Alto, CA: Stanford University Press.

Robbins, Bruce, ed. 1993. *The Phantom Public Sphere.* Minneapolis: University of Minnesota Press.

Rosaldo, Michelle Z. 1980. "The Use and Abuse of Anthropology: Reflections on Feminism and Cross-Cultural Understanding." *Signs: Journal of Women in Culture and Society* 5(3): 389–417.

Rosaldo, Renate. 1989. "Imperialist Nostalgia." In *Culture and Truth: The Remaking of Social Analysis,* 68–90. Boston: Beacon.

Rose, Nikolas. (1990) 1999. *Governing the Soul: The Shaping of the Private Self.* 2nd edition. London: Free Associations Books.

Rubin, Gayle. 1975. "The Traffic in Women: Notes on the 'Political Economy' of Sex." In *Toward an Anthropology of Women,* edited by Rayna Reiter, 157–209. New York: Monthly Review Press.

Rutherford, Danilyn. 2001. "Intimacy and Alienation: Money and the Foreign in Biak." *Public Culture* 13(2): 299–324.

Sangroula, Khagendra. 2053 v.s. "Chorilāi Sampati Adhikār Diye Rāmro Huncha/ Chorilāi Sampati Adhikar Diye Sarbaswa Huncha" [Giving daughters rights to property is good/all will change by giving daughers rights to property]. *Bikās,* 1–7.

Sangroula, Yubaraj, and Geetha Pathak. 2002. *Gender and Laws: Nepalese Perspective.* Kathmandu: Pairavi Prakashan.

Schiller-Glick, Nina, and Georges Fouron. 2001. *Georges Woke Up Laughing: Long-Distance Nationalism and the Search for Home.* Durham, NC: Duke University Press.

Seddon, David, Jagannath Adhikari, and Ganesh Gurung, eds. 2001. *The New Lahures: Foreign Employment and Remittance Economy of Nepal.* Kathmandu: Nepal Institute of Development Studies.

Sever, Adrian. 1993. *Nepal under the Ranas.* New Delhi: Oxford and IBH.

Shipley, Jesse. 2013. *Living the Hiplife: Celebrity and Entrepreneurship in Ghananian Popular Music.* Durham, NC: Duke University Press.

Shneiderman, Sara. 2009. "Ethnic (P)reservations: Comparing Thangmi Ethnic Activism in Nepal and India." In *Ethnic Activism and Civil Society in South Asia,* edited by David Gellner, 115–41. Delhi: Sage Publications.

Shukla, Sandhya. 2003. *India Abroad: Diasporic Cultures of Postwar America and England.* Princeton, NJ: Princeton University Press.

Siegel, James. 1986. *Solo in New Order: Language and Hierarchy in an Indonesian City.* Princeton, NJ: Princeton University Press.

———. 1995. *Fetish, Recognition, Revolution.* Princeton, NJ: Princeton University Press.

Silverstein, Michael. 1981. "The Limits of Awareness." Sociolinguistic Working Paper 84. Austin: Southwest Educational Development Laboratory.

Singh, Chandra Lal, and Matshyendra Lal Singh. 1971. *Nepali-English Dictionary, with pronunciation in Roman Nepali.* Kathmandu: Educational Enterprise.

Singh, Silu. n.d.a. "Existing Laws Which are Discriminatory against Women." SUSS archive.

———. n.d.b. "Legal Position of Nepalese Women in Family." SUSS archive.

Slusser, Mary. 1982. *Nepal Mandala: A Cultural Study of the Kathmandu Valley.* Princeton, NJ: Princeton University Press.

Spitulnik, Debra. 1993. "Anthropology and Mass Media." *Annual Review of Anthropology* 22:293–315.

———. 2002. "Mobile Machines and Fluid Audiences: Rethinking Reception through Zambian Radio Culture." In *Media Worlds: Anthropology on New Terrain,* edited by Faye Ginsburg, Lila Abu-Lughod, and Brian Larkin, 337–54. Berkeley: University of California Press.

Spivak, Gyatri. 1988. "Can the Subaltern Speak?" In *Marxism and the Interpretation of Culture,* edited by Cary Nelson and Larry Grossberg, 271–313. Urbana: University of Illinois Press.

Sterne, Jonathan. 2003. *The Audible Past: Cultural Origins of Sound Reproduction.* Durham, NC: Duke University Press.

Stiller, Ludwig F. 1968. *Prithwinarayan Shah in the Light of Dibya Upadesh.* Ranchi, India: Catholic Press.

Stoler, Ann Laura. 1992. "'In Cold Blood': Hierarchies of Credibility and the Politics of Colonial Narrative." *Representations* 37:151–89.

———. 1995. *Foucault's History of Sexuality and the Colonial Order of Things.* Berkeley: University of California Press.

Stoler, Ann, and Karen Strassler. 2000. "Castings for the Colonial: Memory Work in 'New Order' Java." *Comparative Studies in Society and History* 42(1): 4–48.

Strassler, Karen. 2004. "Gendered Visibilities and the Dream of Transparency: The Chinese-Indonesian Rape Debate in Post-Suharto Indonesia." *Gender and History* 16(3): 689–725.

———. 2009. "The Face of Money: Currency, Crisis, and Remediation in Post-Suharto Indonesia." *Cultural Anthropology* 24(1): 68–103.

———. 2010. *Refracted Visions: Popular Photography and National Modernity in Java.* Durham, NC: Duke University Press.

Subba, T. B. 2001. "Nepal and the Indian Nepalis." In *State of Nepal,* edited by Kanak Mani Dixit and Shastri Ramachandaran. Kathmandu: Himal Books.

Subedi, Abhi. 1978. *Nepali Literature: Background and History.* Kathmandu: Sajha Prakashan.

Tacchi, Jo. 2002. "Radio Texture: Between Self and Others." In *The Anthropology of Media: A Reader,* edited by Kelly Askew and Richard Wilk, 241–57. Oxford: Blackwell.

Tagore, Rabindranath. (1916) 2005. *The Home and The World.* New York: Penguin.

Tamang, Seira. 2000. "Legalizing State Patriarchy." *Studies in Nepali History and Society* 5(1): 127–56.

Taussig, Michael. 1994. "Physiognomic Aspects of Visual Worlds." In *Visualizing Theory,* edited by Lucien Taylor, 205–13. New York: Routledge.

Taylor, Charles. 1989. *Sources of the Self.* Cambridge: Cambridge University Press.

Taylor, Jessica. 2009. "Speaking Shadows: A History of the Voice in the Transition from Silent to Sound Film in the United States." *Journal of Linguistic Anthropology* 19(1): 1–20.

Tedlock, Dennis, and Bruce Mannheim, eds. 2005. *The Dialogic Emergence of Culture.* Chicago: University of Illinois Press.

Tharu, Susie, and K. Lalita. 1993. *Women Writing in India.* Vol. 2. New York: Feminist Press at the City University of New York.

Thompson, Julia. 1993. "Speaking of Dissent, Speaking of Consent: Ritual and Resistance among High-Caste Hindu Women in Nepal." *Contributions to Nepalese Studies* 20(1): 1–27.

Transparency International Nepal (TIN). 2000. "First (Annual) Report 1995–2000." Kathmandu: Transparency International Nepal.

Trawick, Margaret. 1990. *Notes on Love in a Tamil Village.* Berkeley: University of California Press.

Tsing, Anna. 2005. *Friction: An Ethnography of Global Connection.* Princeton, NJ: Princeton University Press.

Tuladhar, Anita, and Bikas Joshi. 1997. "Perspectives on the Failure of the Women's Property Rights Movement in Nepal." *Studies in Nepali History and Society* 2(2).

Turner, Ralph Lilley. 1931. *A Comparative and Etymological Dictionary of the Nepali Language.* New Delhi: Allied Publishers.

Upadhya, Sanjay. 2002. "A Dozen Years of Democracy: The Games That Parties Play." In *The State of Nepal,* edited by Shastri Ramachandaran and Kanak Mani Dixit. Lalitpur: Himal Books.

Urciuoli, Bonnie. 2009. "Skills and Selves in the New Workplace." *American Ethnologist* 35(2): 211–28.

van der Veer, Peter, ed. 1995. *Nation and Migration: The Politics of Space in the South Asian Diaspora.* Philadelphia: University of Pennsylvania Press.

Verdery, Katherine, and Caroline Humphrey, eds. 2004. *Property in Question: Value Transformation in the Global Economy.* Oxford: Berg.

Vidali-Spitulnik, Debra. 2012. "'A House of Wires upon Wires': Sensuous and Linguistic Entanglements of Evidence and Epistemologies in the Study of Radio Culture." In *Radio Fields: Anthropology and Wireless Sound in the 21st Century,* edited by Lucas Bessire and Daniel Fisher, 250–67. New York: New York University Press.

Volosinov, V. N. (1929) 1973. *Marxism and the Philosophy of Language*. Translated by Ladislav Matejka and I. R. Titunik. Cambridge, MA: Harvard University Press.

Warner, Michael. 1990. *The Letters of the Republic: Publication and the Public Sphere in Eighteenth-Century America*. Cambridge, MA: Harvard University Press.

———. 2002. "Publics and Counterpublics." *Public Culture* 14(1): 49–90.

Weidman, Amanda. 2003. "Guru and Gramophone: Fantasies of Fidelity and Modern Technologies of the Real." *Public Culture* 15(3): 453–76.

———. 2006. *Singing the Classical, Voicing the Modern: The Postcolonial Politics of Music in South India*. Durham, NC: Duke University Press.

———. 2014. Neoliberal Logics of Voice: Playback Singing and Public Femaleness in South India. *Culture, Theory, and Critique* 55:2.

Weiner, Annette. 1976. *Women of Value, Men of Renown: New Perspectives in Trobriand Exchange*. Austin: University of Texas Press.

———. 1992. *Inalienable Possessions: The Paradox of Keeping-While-Giving*. Berkeley: University of California Press.

West, Harry G., and Todd Sanders. 2003. *Transparency and Conspiracy: Ethnographies of Suspicion in the New World Order*. Durham, NC: Duke University Press.

White, Hayden. 1987. *The Content of the Form*. Baltimore: Johns Hopkins University Press.

Williams, Raymond. 1974. *Television: Technology and Cultural Form*. New York: Schocken.

———. 1977. *Marxism and Literature*. Oxford: University Press.

World Bank. 2002. *Voices of the Poor*. Washington, DC: World Bank.

Yanagisako, Sylvia. 1979. "Family and Household: The Analysis of Domestic Groups." *Annual Review of Anthropology* 8:161–205.

———. 2002. *Producing Culture and Capital: Family Firms in Italy*. Princeton, NJ: Princeton University Press.

Yanagisako, Sylvia, and Jane F. Collier. 1987. *Gender and Kinship: Essays toward a Unified Analysis*. Palo Alto, CA: Stanford University Press.

Yang, Mayfair Mei-hui. 2001. "Mass Media and Transnational Subjectivity in Shanghai: Notes on (Re)Cosmopolitanism in a Chinese Metropolis." In *Media Worlds,* edited by Faye Ginsburg, Lila Abu-Lughod, and Brian Larkin, 189–210. Berkeley: University of California Press.

INDEX

About Face: Performing Race in Fashion and Theater (Kondo), 94–95
affective publics, 26, 163–73, 193, 257n25; *bikās* industry and, 211–13; effects of listening by, 207–13; following Narayanhiti palace massacre, 242–49; management of tensions within, 201–7; of the mediated diaspora, 216–20, 229–30; recognition of suffering by, 212–13; smoothness and harmony in, 200–201, 206–7, 213–14. *See also* FM radio; *Mero Kathā, Mero Gīt* program
Agarwal, Bina, 68, 260n33
agency, 4–5, 10–14, 28–35, 247; *āwāj uṭhāune* (raising voice) as, 46, 83–86; feminist theory on, 48; indigenous Nepali forms of, 52–53; of political voice, 30–35, 167, 171, 258n36; property reform movement and, 45, 46, 61–62, 83–86, 187; provocative silence and, 29, 257nn32–33; self-conscious identity and, 35–40; in theories of subjectivity, 37. *See also* subjectivity
Agha, Asif, 21, 126, 256n11
Ahearn, Laura, 22, 52–53, 103
Aishwarya, Queen, 6, 57, 118–19, 242–49
All-India Radio (AIR), 132
Althusser, Louis: on hailing, 69–70; theory of interpellation of, 12–13, 16, 70–73, 217–18, 256nn11–13
āmāko mukh herne din (day to look at mother's face), 88*fig.*, 105–15, 122; distance and absence in, 113–15, 122; at

Mātātirtha pond, 88*fig.*, 107–11, 263n19; rationales for, 111–12
AM radio, 148
Anamika (host of *Rumpum Connection*), 224–33, 238–39
Anderson, Benedict, 141, 167
angsa property relations, 42–44, 55–58, 248, 258n1, 259n16, 260n32; *bolāune* practices and, 68–74, 85, 261n35; caring for elders and, 55; class and gender in, 58–62; inalienable possession implied by, 55, 72, 259n18; mourning rituals and, 76–79, 261nn38–39; for unmarried women, 57–58, 260nn23–24; women's movement between homes and, 63–67, 73–75, 79–83. *See also* property reform movement
anonymity, 140, 167–68
Arya Samāj, 82
audience of FM radio, 17, 19–20, 129–30, 138–56, 237, 266n7; as affective public, 26, 163–73, 193, 200–214, 257n25; authentication of truth for, 202–5; diasporic connections of, 39–40, 184–85, 214, 216–20; as imagined cosmopolitan community, 26–27, 141–48; listener clubs of, 139–40; of *Mero Kathā, Mero Gīt*, 164–67, 178, 207–11; radio participation by, 25–28, 104, 127–30, 148–56; of *Rumpum Connection*, 225–27. *See also* listening
aurality, 94, 101, 263n11
Avaaz.org, 33–34
Aviral, Krishna, 272n11

āwāj (voice), 4, 33–34, 255nn1–2. *See also*
voice
āwāj uṭhāune (raising voice). *See* political
voice; raising voice
Axel, Brian, 18, 222, 229, 270n15

Bakhtin, Mikhail, 21–22; on the chrono-
type of a story, 196; on double-voiced
discourse, 191–92, 198–99; on genre,
192; on inter-subjectivity, 91; on words
and contexts, 268n24
Basu, Srimati, 54
Bate, Bernard, 14
Bauman, Richard, 191
Benjamin, Walter, 101, 263n15, 264n31
Benson, Peter, 97
Bergson, Henri, 263n8
Berlant, Lauren: on colonization of the
public by the private, 38; on the intimate public sphere, 168–69, 172, 182,
202; on the life that counts, 211
Berlin Wall, 32
Bessire, Lucas, 125
bikās (development): definition of, 181–82;
dukha discourses and, 211–13; evolutionary view of society in, 189–92; language
use and, 143–45; as national goal, 28, 30,
56–57, 112, 134, 159, 175, 268n22; as
neoliberal capitalist endeavor, 175–77,
181–85, 189; symbol of the village in, 187
biography, 268n19
Birendra, King, 3; murder of, 6–7, 36, 40,
118–19, 242–49; pictures of, 117–19,
244*fig.*, 249; public criticism of, 3, 245,
271n5
birthrights. *See* property reform movement
bolāune (hailing/summoning), 85–86, 248;
brother-sister love in, 68–74, 261n35;
gendered subjectivity of, 36–37, 45, 49,
51, 54, 259n11; general meaning of, 47,
69, 259n10; as honor, 73–74; interpellation and, 69–73, 217; materiality of
brothers' voices and, 73; seeing face
(*mukh herne*) and, 89–91
Bollywood films, 103, 166, 169, 186, 188, 212
Bourdieu, Pierre, 256n20
Briggs, Charles, 191
British Residency. *See* colonial era

brother-sister love, 67–74; *bolāune* (familial summoning) and, 36–37, 45, 47, 49,
51, 54, 68–74, 85, 261n35; sisters' voices
during *tihār* and, 73. *See also* family
relations
Buddhism, 24, 259n21
Burghart, Richard, 29, 80–81, 257n31
Butler, Judith, 256n13, 256n20; on authority
of speech, 72–73; on interpellation, 13,
70, 72, 217, 227

"Can the Subaltern Speak" (Spivak), 33
Carsten, Janet, 259n15
cell phones, 153
censorship, 6–8, 40, 127; colonization of
the public by the private and, 38; of FM
radio, 136–37, 220; on the Narayanhiti
palace massacre, 242–44, 271nn1–3;
under Panchāyat's government, 28–29,
156, 266n18; provocative silence and, 29,
257nn32–33
Chakrabarty, Dipesh, 33–34, 81–82, 212
citizenship: dual citizenship movement
and, 270n3; intimate public sphere of,
168–69; patrilineal basis of, 209–11;
terminology of, 36, 245–46
civil society, 8–9, 120
civil war, 6, 35, 36, 157, 176, 258n2, 258n36
class: in construction of identity in, 96; FM
radio listening and, 129–30, 138–39,
141–48, 237; imagined community and,
141–48; mediation of voice and, 228;
property ownership and, 43–44, 58–62,
73–74, 260nn23–25; radio ownership
and, 132–34. *See also* *ijjat*
Close Up Music Jam program, 129
Cody, Francis, 167
colonialism, 8, 152, 192–93, 221, 266n15
Communication Corner, 137, 219–20
"The Conditions of Listening" (Burghart),
29, 257n31
confessional television programs, 166
corpothetic seeing, 102–3
counterpublics, 173, 200, 267n12
coup of 2005 (Magh 19 *gate*), 7–9, 156, 248

Dahal, Dev Raj, 32
Dangol, Chirmei, 77–78

darśan (seeing/being seen by a higher being): Hindu practices of, 93, 101–5, 109–10; political role of, 92, 93, 115–22, 249, 264n21, 264–65nn31–33

Davis, Richard, 101

Dear Kalyan: Mero Kathā, Mero Gīt (Gautum), 169–70

death rituals, 75–79, 84, 119, 261nn38–39

dekhā-dekh (see one another), 93

Deleuze, Gilles, 97

democracy movement, 1–5; black cloths as symbols in, 8, 9*fig.*, 157; civil society and, 8–9, 120; FM radio and, 38, 124, 127; ideology of transparency of, 28, 31–35, 38, 124, 228–29, 258nn36–37; political voice (*āwāj uṭhāune*) of, 9–10; provocative silence and, 29, 257nn32–33; terminology of, 36. *See also* Peoples Movements (*jana āndolan*)

Derrida, Jacques, 13; on face-to-face interaction, 18, 21; on speech and writing, 180, 181

Des Chene, Mary, 82

Devkota, Laxmi Prasad, 178–79

diaspora (as term), 222

diaspora community, 39–40, 215–41, 269n1; as affective public, 216, 218; construction of Nepali identity in, 222–23, 225, 270nn9–11; corruption and danger facing, 223–24; dual citizenship movement of, 270n3; economic goals of, 224; educational pursuits of, 221, 224n6; FM radio and, 216–20, 222–23; as Gurkha soldiers, 8, 187, 221; interpellation through technology of, 217–20; labor migration of, 5–6, 7, 221–25, 258n35, 270n3, 270n7; material properties of voices of, 218, 227–30; *Mero Kathā, Mero Gīt* and, 184–85, 214; remittance money from, 5–6, 7, 41, 215–16, 217*fig.*, 218, 220, 237–38. See also *Rumpum Connection* program

diasporic imaginary, 229–30, 270n15

Dibya Upadesh (Shah), 80

Dipendra, Prince: allegations of massacre against, 6, 242, 247, 272n11; Probe Commission investigation of, 250–53

directness. *See* immediacy; presence

displaced persons, 114

Dixit, Kamal, 133

Dixit, Kanak Mani, 34

double-voiced discourse, 191–92, 198–99

Douglas, Susan, 144

dowry property, 261n43

dukha (suffering) discourses, 39; *bikās* and, 211–13; on *Mero Kathā, Mero Gīt*, 161–63, 171, 172, 178, 187–88, 212–13; patrilineal authority in, 209–11; of widows, 192–200

economy of Nepal, 11; contemporary work demands of, 114–15; foreign aid in, 5, 40–41, 79–80, 261nn41–42; liberalization of, 6, 10, 30–31, 262n52; privately earned money (*niji*) in, 57–58; remittance money in, 5–6, 7, 41, 215–16, 217*fig.*, 218, 220, 237–38; World Bank report on, 33. *See also* neoliberalism

education, 60, 221, 224n6, 268n22

Engels, Fredrick, 50, 259n14

English language use, 143–45

Equal Access Nepal (EAN), 182–83

ethical listening, 173

ethnic nationalism, 9, 23–24, 111, 267n9. *See also* nationalism

ethnography, 256n20; identity considerations in, 23–24; role of media (mediation) in, 16–23

face. *See* seeing face

Facebook, 141

face-to-face interaction, 18, 21, 93; of FM radio listener clubs, 139–40; of Mother's Day, 113–15; romantic love and, 103–4. *See also* seeing face

faciality, 97–98

family relations: *bolāune* (summoning) practices in, 36–37, 45, 47, 49, 51, 54, 85, 261n35; brother-sister love in, 67–74; in feminist theory, 47–48; *icchā patra* (document of wish) in, 46–47, 77; kin pronouns in, 145, 147, 269n40; love and property in, 48–55, 83–86; mourning practices in, 75–79, 261nn38–39; movement between homes in, 63–67, 73–75, 79–83; patrilineal kinship patterns in,

Mero Kathā, Mero Gīt (continued)
165–66, 178, 266n2, 267n15; as contemporary moral community, 164–65, 193–202, 205–7; criticism of, 178–79; diaspora connections of, 184–85, 214; *dukha* discourses of, 161–63, 171, 172, 178, 187–89, 212–13; effects of listening to, 207–11; Kalyan Gautum's editorial decisions in, 165, 204–7, 210–11; Kalyan Gautum's voice on, 164, 165–66, 167, 181, 212, 266n3; language use in, 147, 171; Laxmi Devi Joshi's story on, 189, 192–200; letters and letter writers of, 162*fig.*, 165, 170–71, 178, 199, 266n3, 266n8, 268n27; narratives of progress in, 189–92, 196–97, 269nn33–35; realness and truth of stories on, 163, 165, 202–5, 231, 252, 266n2, 268n31; smoothness and harmony of, 200–207, 213–14; social goals of, 169–70, 175, 177–78, 183–85, 198–200; sponsors of, 175; voiced writing of, 39, 164, 173, 179–81, 185–92, 212. *See also* Gautum, Kalyan
metalanguage, 3–4, 152, 234, 246. *See also* figure of the voice; semiotics
metapragmatics, 22
middle class: *angsa* reform movement and in, 59–60, 73–74; FM radio listening and, 129–30, 138–39; *ijjat* (honor and prestige) in, 96; imagined community of, 141–48; telephones of, 152–53. *See also* class
migration, 222. *See also* diaspora community; labor migration
monarchy, 253; dissolution of, 9, 36, 120, 248; photographs of, 92, 93, 115–21, 264n21, 264–65nn31–33; sharing of *darśan* by, 92, 115–21, 249, 264n21. *See also* Birendra, King; Gyanendra, King
moral community, 187–88, 193–202, 205–7
Morris, Rosalind, 116–17, 118, 233
Mother's Day (*āmāko mukh herne din*), 88*fig.*, 105–15; distance and absence in, 113–15, 122; at Mātātirtha pond, 88*fig.*, 107–11, 263n19
"Mourning and Melancholia" (Freud), 263n19

mourning practices, 75–79, 84, 119, 261nn38–39
Mrazek, Rudolf, 132
mukhā-mukh (face-to-face), 93
mukh herne (seeing face). *See* seeing face
Mukunda Indira (Sama), 81, 82, 267n16
Muna Ghar Pariwar program, 129
Munā-Madan (Devkota), 81, 178–79
music programming, 39, 134–35, 148, 163, 187, 266n11
My Best Friend (Kantipur FM), 140

Nandy, Ashish, 103
Narayanhiti palace massacre, 6–7, 36, 40, 118–19, 242–49, 271n1; allegations following, 6, 242, 246–47, 250–53, 272n11; mediation of, 250–53; Probe Commission investigation of, 250–53, 271n9; public speech following, 245–46, 271nn1–2
nationalism: in anti-Indian critique, 79–81, 261n42; in associations of home, 81–83; in construction of diasporic identities, 222, 225, 227, 270nn9–11; in ethnic movements, 9, 23–24, 111, 267n9; evocations of sexuality in, 80–81; in opposition to property reform, 81–83; Panchāyat regime's Hindu-centered program of, 28, 56–57, 80, 111, 115, 134, 271n7
neoliberalism, 6, 31, 219, 262n52; *bikās* (development) industry of, 30, 112, 175–77, 181–85, 189–92; commodification of communication in, 126, 135–36; evolutionary view of the future in, 189–92; intimate FM radio voice of, 128, 265n2; self-reflexive development of the individual in, 10, 166, 175–77, 183–84, 189; social hegemonies of, 170; subjectivity of the individual in, 38, 39, 166, 173. *See also* mediation
Nepal: Bhutanese refugees in, 114; calendar of, 232; citizenship requirements of, 209–11, 270n3; dissolution of the monarchy in, 9, 36, 120, 248; historical genealogy of, 247–53; Kathmandu Valley of, 24, 255n3, 256n23; labor migration policies of, 223–25, 270n3;

legal code of, 56, 258n6, 259n20; Madeshi federalist movement of, 44, 258n3; Maoist civil war in, 6, 35, 36, 157, 176, 258n2, 258n36, 260n28; multiparty democracy of, 3, 4, 119, 124, 134; nationalist movements in, 9, 23–24, 56–57, 79–83; official language of, 256n23; official religions of, 56, 259n21; outlaw of *sati* in, 192–93; political instability in, 239–41; as pure version of India, 24, 80–81, 256n24; symbol of the village in, 187. *See also* diaspora community; economy of Nepal; Kathmandu; nationalism

Nepal Television, 135

Newar society, 24

Nietzsche, Friedrich, 112, 263n8, 269n34

"Nietzsche, Genealogy, History" (Foucault), 112

nongovernmental organizations (NGOs), 5, 35, 261nn41–42; *bikās* work of, 181–85; English language use of, 143–44; FM radio sponsorship by, 135–36, 142, 265n4, 266n10; property reform movement and, 79–80

nonliberal subjectivity, 37, 48–55, 85–86, 259n15

Onta, Pratyoush, 81, 116, 134, 135, 139

Oprah program, 166, 204

Özyürek, Esra, 26

Panchāyat regime, 8, 28, 251; constitution of, 134; dissolution of multiparty rule under, 134; legal reforms of, 56, 258n6, 259n20; media censorship under, 28–29, 156, 266n18; Narayanhiti palace massacre and, 6–7, 36, 40, 118–19, 242–49; nationalist program of, 28, 56–57, 80, 111, 115, 134, 271n7; photographic images of the monarch in, 109–10, 115, 117–18; Radio Nepal of, 128–35. *See also* Birendra, King; Gyanendra, King

Panther Hotline, 166

Parajuli, Shekhar, 132

Peoples Movements (*jana āndolan*), 1–4, 6, 9; anti-Indian sentiment and, 80; banning of holidays in, 109, 111; black cloths

as symbols in, 8, 9*fig.*, 157; curfew of 1990 and, 3; expansion of the press and, 30, 124, 127, 130, 136–39, 257n34; FM radio and, 124–30, 135–36, 158; ideology of voice and transparency in, 28, 31–36, 38, 92, 124, 258nn36–37; legal reforms following, 36–37; multiparty system allowed by, 3, 6, 119, 124; public speech in, 29–30. *See also* second People's Movement (2006)

phatic speech, 39–40, 219, 233–39

photography and film: Benjamin on "optical unconscious" of, 263n15, 264n31; portraits of the monarchy and, 92, 109–10, 115–21, 264n21, 264–65nn31–33; seeing face and, 92, 98, 103, 115–23

Phulbari programs, 134–35

Pigg, Stacy, 189

Pinney, Christopher, 94, 102–3, 115

Pokhara FM, 157

political voice (*āwāj uṭhāune*), 9–10, 239–40; availability of radios and, 128; expansion of the press and, 136–39; ideology of transparency and, 28, 31–35, 38, 124, 250–53, 258nn36–37; listening and, 29, 120–21, 257n31; melodic tones and, 11; Narayanhiti palace massacre and, 244–45; power over radio and, 132–35, 156–59; in the property reform movement, 45–47, 54–55, 83–86, 258n7, 262n49, 262nn54–55; of royal photographs, 92, 93, 115–21, 122, 264n21, 264–65nn31–33. *See also* censorship; FM radio; raising voice

Povinelli, Elizabeth, 53, 257n25

prajātantra (democracy), 36, 245

presence: of *āmāko mukh herne din* (day to look at mother's face), 113–15; Derrida on face-to-face interaction and, 18, 21; in Hindu *darśan* practices, 93, 100–105, 109–10; of the mediated diaspora, 216–20, 222–23, 230–33; realness of FM radio and, 18–21, 29–30, 38, 148–56, 159–60, 252; in seeing face (*mukh herne*) practices, 37, 51, 90–91, 93–96, 121–22; technological phatic speech and, 233–39; transparency and, 28, 31–35, 38, 228–33, 258nn36–37

Press and Publication Act 2019 of 1962, 134
Prithvi Narayan Shah, 80, 117, 271n5
Probe Commission, 250–53, 271n9
pronoun usage, 145, 147, 269n40
property reform movement, 12, 31, 36–37,
    42–86, 248; agency and, 45, 46, 61–62,
    83–86; brother-sister love in, 67–74;
    challenges of feminist analysis by,
    47–48; class contexts of, 43–44, 58–62,
    67, 73–74, 260nn23–25; constitutional
    challenges by, 46, 75; familial relations
    and sentiment in, 45, 47–55, 63–67,
    83–86; gender contexts of, 43, 60–62,
    67, 260n27; Hindu patrimony and,
    53–54, 85; international donors to,
    79–80, 261nn41–42, 262n49; marriage
    and, 48–54, 57–58, 83–86, 187, 195–99;
    nationalist arguments and, 79–83;
    notions of home in, 63–67, 73–75,
    79–83; opposition to, 69–72, 79–83,
    258n7; raising voice in, 44–47, 54–55,
    83–86, 258n7, 262n49, 262nn54–55;
    reform bill of, 44, 46, 84, 258n5,
    262n50; traditional inheritance and,
    46–47, 56–57; will system and, 62. See
    also angsa relations
pseudonyms, xv
public intimacy, 25–28, 38, 257n25; affective
    publics and, 26, 163–73, 193, 200–214,
    257n25; fiction of equality in, 27; FM
    radio and, 25–28, 104, 125, 140, 148–56;
    mourning practices and, 75–79, 119,
    248–49, 261nn38–39; Narayanhiti
    palace massacre and, 242–49; stranger
    intimacy and, 25–26, 123, 140–41,
    167–68, 257n27; temporality of, 218–19.
    See also Mero Kathā, Mero Gīt program
public spheres: affective forms of, 26, 163–
    73, 193, 200–214, 257n25; counterpublic
    forms of, 173, 200, 267n12; intimate
    forms of, 168–69, 172, 182, 202; political
    voice in, 30–35, 167, 171, 200–201,
    258n36; rationalized forms of, 167,
    171–73, 212–13, 266n5, 267n8

radio. See FM radio; Radio Nepal
Radio Fields (Bessire and Fisher), 125
Radio Nepal, 128–37, 151; educational

programing on, 268n22; Gitī Kathā
    program on, 163; Narayanhiti palace
    massacre and, 242–44; news broadcasts
    on, 140, 149, 158; opposition to FM
    radio and, 143; political control of,
    134–35, 156; scripted announcers of,
    148–49, 152, 155
Raeper, William, 28
raising voice (āwāj uṭhāune), 4–5, 9–14,
    30–35, 122; affect and, 164; FM radio
    and, 126–30; personal agency and, 45,
    46, 61–62, 84–85; union of conscious-
    ness and voice in, 27. See also political
    voice; property reform movement
Rajagopal, Arvind, 101, 232
Raktakunda (Aviral), 272n11
Ramayana (TV serial), 101, 159
Ram Dev Baba, 40
Rana, Devayani, 242, 247, 252–53
Rana, Indira, 59, 74–77, 83, 84, 261n39
Rana oligarchy, 8, 177, 255n7, 256n23; con-
    sumption of seeing in, 116, 265n32;
    isolation of Kathmandu by, 156–57,
    266n19; laws of inheritance under, 56;
    outlaw of sati by, 192–93; overthrow of,
    80; power over radio of, 132–33; Singha
    Durbar palace of, 131–32
recognition, 12, 257n25. See also darśan;
    seeing face
refugees, 114
remittance economy, 5–6, 7, 41, 215–18, 220,
    237–38
reported speech, 198–99
Rimal, Prabhat, 157
ritual encounters: of āmāko mukh herne
    din, 88fig., 105–15; of bolāune, 71–72; of
    darśan, 93, 101–5, 109–10; of seeing face
    (mukh herne), 12, 17, 37, 51, 92–93,
    96–98, 105–7
romantic love, 247, 259n14; exchange of
    glances in, 103–4, 186, 268n27; in letters
    to Mero Kathā, Mero Gīt, 185–87; in
    love letters, 39, 186, 268n27; property
    relations and, 49–55, 83–86
royal photographs, 92, 93, 115–21, 264n21,
    264–65nn31–33
Rumpum Connection program, 39–40,
    216–20, 224–27, 239–41; diasporic

imaginary of, 229–30, 270n15; domestic listening to, 225–27; goals of, 225; host of, 224–25, 238–39; live production of, 230–33; sponsor of, 217, 270n2; technological phatic speech of, 39, 219, 233–39; temporal challenges of, 232–33. *See also* diaspora community

Rutherford, Danilyn, 237

Sagarmatha FM, 137
Sama, Bal Krishna, 81, 82
Sanders, Todd, 250
Sangroula, Khagendra, 79, 260n31, 271n10
satellite TV, 135
Sāthi Sanga Man Kā Kurā program, 129, 170, 182–83, 268n21
sati (widow self-immolation), 192–93
second People's Movement (2006), 4, 9, 248; curfew protests in 2006 of, 34; dissolution of the monarchy and, 9, 36, 248; FM radio in, 38, 128, 158; political voice (*āwāj uṭhāune*) of, 9–10, 34–36; secularized state after, 58
seeing face (*mukh herne*), 37, 51, 87–123; on *āmāko mukh herne din*, 105–15, 121; in colloquial usage, 88–90, 93, 263nn4–6; conflation with voice of, 93–96; interpellation of social and political subjectivity in, 93, 217; mediating practices (film, photos) of, 92, 98, 103, 115–23; moral censure and, 90, 96, 98–100; political role of, 92, 93, 115–21; ritual practices of, 12, 17, 37, 89, 96–98, 105–7; romantic glances and, 103–4, 186, 268n27; semiotic ideology of, 90–96, 105, 115, 120–23, 152; tactile connections of, 100–105, 121–22, 186
self-reflexive self, 27, 35–40; discourse of, 31, 140, 205; interior consciousness of, 28, 39, 128–29, 164, 257n26; neoliberal development of, 10, 166, 175–77, 183–84, 189. *See also* subjectivity
semiotic ideology, 37, 90–96, 105, 115, 120–23, 151–52
semiotics, 21–22, 150; indexical signs of, 145–46, 150–51, 202, 228; media ideology and, 151–52
sevā (service), 114–15, 174–75, 268n22

Shah, Kundan, 188
Shrestha, Basu, 120, 158
Shrestha, Madan Das, 163
Shrestha, Yosodha, 262n49
Shukla, Sandhya, 221–22
Shumshere, Chandra, 131–32, 192–93
siblings. See *angsa* relations; brother-sister love; family relations
simultaneity. *See* immediacy
Singh, Ganesh Man, 32
Singh, Silu, 49–50, 59, 83, 84
Singha Durbar palace, 1–2, 40, 130, 131–32, 136
Singin' in the Rain, 15
smoothness and harmony, 200–201, 206–7, 213–14
sonic voice, 218, 240–41. *See also* material properties of voice
speech about voice. *See* figure of the voice
Spivak, Gyatri, 33, 268n18
state documentation, 13
Sterne, Jonathan, 14, 94, 101, 149, 151, 263n11
Stoler, Ann, 49, 251–52
stranger intimacy, 25–26, 123, 140–41, 167–68, 257n27. *See also* public intimacy
structures of feeling, 214
subaltern studies, 33
subjecthood, 35–40
subjectivity, 5, 11–14, 239–41, 255n10; in face-to-face encounters, 18–19; of FM radio's realness and immediacy, 18–21, 29–30, 38, 122–23, 148–56, 159–60, 222–23, 230–33, 252; interpellation of, 12–13, 16, 69–73, 217–18, 256nn11–13; intersubjectivity (need for another) in, 91; language of rights in, 48–49, 85–86; marked and unmarked positions of, 171–72, 210–11, 267n9; material properties of voice and, 14–16, 73, 148–51, 164, 165–66, 171–73, 181, 212; neoliberal forms of, 10, 38, 39, 166, 170, 173; nonliberal forms of, 37, 48–55, 85–86, 259n15; self-reflective self and, 27, 31, 35–40; state documentation of, 13, 256n13; struggle between reason and sentiment in, 28, 39, 128–29, 164, 257n26. *See also* voice

summoning practices. See *bolāune swar*, 255n1

tactile seeing, 37, 100–105, 121–22, 186
Tagore, Rabindranath, 82
Tamil Nadu, 103
Taussig, Michael, 101
Taylor, Jessica, 15
technological phatic speech, 39–40, 219, 233–39
technologies of voice, 5, 7, 11, 38, 41; anterior space in, 19–20; censorship of, 6–8, 28–29, 127, 136–37, 220; colonization of the public by the private and, 38; definition of, 7; diasporic community and, 215–41, 269n1; expansion of, 30–31, 124, 127, 130, 136–39; extensions of body parts into, 149–51, 155; first radios and, 132–33, 144; indexical relationships in, 145–46, 150–51, 202; Internet as, 163, 238, 270n3; interpellation through, 217–20; mediation of, 17–23, 121–23; mediatization and, 126; phatic speech in, 39–40, 219, 233–39; power dynamics of, 132–35; public intimacy and, 25–28, 104, 125, 140, 148–56; realness and immediacy through, 18–21, 29–30, 38, 122–23, 148–56, 159–60, 222–23, 230–33, 252; telephone as, 12, 38, 39–40, 122, 152–56; television as, 135; transparency and trust in, 28, 31–35, 38, 124, 228–29, 230–33, 258nn36–37; unmarked public persona in, 171–72. *See also* FM radio; mediation; voice
Tedlock, Dennis, 22
telegraph, 152, 266n15
telephone, 38, 39–40, 122, 152–56; bluff calling practices on, 153–55, 266n15; common greetings on, 153; for communication abroad, 12, 216–20, 240–41; expansion of, 152–53. See also *Rumpum Connection* program
television, 135, 166
temporality. *See* immediacy
Thapa, Manika, 62
Thapa, Surya Bahadur, 8
Thapaliya, Shanta, 59
theory of mediation. *See* mediation

Thompson, Julia, 75
tihār holiday, 73
transliteration, xv
transparency, 28, 31–35, 258nn36–37; in culture of trust, 32–33; of diasporic voices, 228–33; as political goal, 228–29, 244–53, 250–53; realness of FM radio voices and, 38, 124, 230–33, 252. *See also* immediacy
Transparency International Nepal (TIN), 31–32
Trawick, Margaret, 103
Tsing, Anna, 213–14
the Tundikhel, 1, 40

Uma (radio host), 230–31
UNESCO, 136
UNICEF, 142, 182–83, 265n4, 268n21
unmarked public persona, 171–72
U.S. Agency for International Development, 79, 142, 266n10

vangsa (genealogy), 66–67, 87–89, 260n31; meanings of, 88, 262n3; seeing face (*mukh herne*) and, 89–91, 96–98, 121–23
Verdery, Katherine, 48–49
Vidali-Spitulnik, Debra, 172
village life, 187
Vishnu, 109–10, 263n21
vision/visuality, 94, 101, 263n11. *See also* seeing face
voice, 1–16; Bakhtin's semiotic analysis of, 21–22; censorship and, 6–8, 28–29, 127, 136–37, 220; conflation with face of, 93–96; cultural constructs of, 16, 20–23, 124–25; double-voiced discourse and, 191–92; inner voice of voiced writing and, 191; of liberal subjects, 45–46; link with political agency of, 33–35; material properties of, 14–16, 73, 148–51, 164, 165–66, 171–73, 181, 212; Nepali words for, 4, 33–34, 255nn1–2; semiotic ideology of, 20–21, 90–93, 105, 115, 120–23, 152; as sign of personhood, 4–5; subjectivities of, 5, 11–14, 27; traditional hailing practices of brothers and, 45, 85–86. *See also* figure of the voice; intimate voice; political voice; technologies of voice

voiced writing, 14; as double-voiced discourse, 191–92; intertextuality of, 187–88; of *Mero Kathā, Mero Gīt* letters, 164, 173, 179–81, 212; narratives of progress in, 189–91, 196–97, 269nn33–35; as site of mediation, 266n3

Voices journal, 33

Voices of the Poor report (World Bank), 33

Voloshinov, Valentin, 91

Warner, Michael, 25; on counterpublics, 267n12; on the intimate public sphere, 171, 172, 200; on self-reflexive discourse, 31, 140, 205

Weidman, Amanda, 15, 128, 172–73

Weiner, Annette, 67, 72

West, Harry, 250

White, Hayden, 269n35

widowhood, 192–200

Widow Remarriage Act of 1856, 192

Wildenbruch, Ernst von, 149–50

Williams, Raymond, 214

Winfrey, Oprah, 166, 204

women: *āmāko mukh herne din* and, 88*fig.*, 105–15; association of *dukha* with, 188, 192–200; education of, 60; labor migration and, 270n18; marked positions of, 210–11; middle-class respectability and, 61–62, 260n29; mourning practices of, 75–79, 261nn38–39; movement between homes by, 63–67, 73–75, 79–83; property inheritance reforms for, 42–86; raising of one's voice by, 45, 46, 83–86; visits to the family home (*bolāune*) of, 36–37, 45, 47, 49, 54, 68–74, 85, 261n35

World Bank, 33

Yanagisako, Sylvia, 51–52

Yang, Mayfair Mei-hui, 218

Z-Net Asia, 5, 255n5

South Asia Across the Disciplines is a series devoted to publishing first books across a wide range of South Asian studies, including art, history, philology or textual studies, philosophy, religion, and the interpretive social sciences. Series authors all share the goal of opening up new archives and suggesting new methods and approaches, while demonstrating that South Asian scholarship can be at once deep in expertise and broad in appeal.

Receptacle of the Sacred: Illustrated Manuscripts and the Buddhist Book Cult in South Asia by Jinah Kim (California)

Cut-Pieces: Celluloid Obscenity and Popular Cinema in Bangladesh by Lotte Hoek (Columbia)

From Text to Tradition: The Naisadhīyacarita *and Literary Community in South Asia* by Deven M. Patel (Columbia)

Democracy against Development: Lower Caste Politics and Political Modernity in Postcolonial India by Jeffrey Witsoe (Chicago)

Into the Twilight of Sanskrit Poetry: The Sena Salon of Bengal and Beyond, by Jesse Ross Knutson (California)

Voicing Subjects: Public Intimacy and Mediation in Kathmandu by Laura Kunreuther (California)

Writing Resistance: The Rhetorical Imagination of Hindi Dalit Literature by Laura R. Brueck (Columbia)

Wombs in Labor: Transnational Commercial Surrogacy in India by Amrita Pande (Columbia)